Books by Theodore Weiss

POETRY

THE WORLD BEFORE US: POEMS, 1950–1970 (1970)
THE LAST DAY AND THE FIRST (1968)
THE MEDIUM (1965)
GUNSIGHT (1962)
OUTLANDERS (1960)
THE CATCH (1951)

CRITICAL

THE BREATH OF CLOWNS AND KINGS (1971)

EDITOR

SELECTIONS FROM THE NOTEBOOKS OF GERARD MANLEY HOPKINS
(1945)

THE BREATH OF
CLOWNS AND KINGS

THE BREATH
OF
CLOWNS AND KINGS

*Shakespeare's Early Comedies
and Histories*

———◇———

THEODORE WEISS

Atheneum   New York   1971

Copyright © 1971 by Theodore Weiss

All rights reserved
Library of Congress catalog number 70-124958
Published simultaneously in Canada by McClelland and Stewart Ltd

Printed in the United States of America by
The Murray Printing Company, Forge Village, Massachusetts
Bound by H. Wolff, New York
First American Edition

DEDICATION

Inevitably this study has had innumerable only begetters, a roster no doubt longer than the book itself. From the humblest beginning of a first course in Shakespeare to the most exciting with Mark Van Doren, I recognized the communal occasion that Shakespeare is. During twenty years of teaching at Bard College my own students acted as major catalysts to my thinking about him. And through the kind and enthusiastic offices of Dr. Kolodney and Galen Williams I was able to offer two sets of lectures on Shakespeare's plays at the New York YM-YWHA. These lectures obliged me to push on to commitments and articulations I might otherwise still be shying away from. Then, when the going became most perplexed, my good friend William Humphrey provided most helpful, generously responsive intelligence. And I have been most fortunate in my editors, Ian Parsons, whose painstaking reading of the manuscript came close at times to collaboration, and Harry Ford, whose patient confidence in the work gave me the kind of support I often needed. Behind all these has stood my wife. Severe when necessary, underscoring my doubts, but also enhancing my pleasures and sense of exploit, she has overseen the script and kept the peace indispensable to the play's continuation.

CONTENTS

THE BREATH OF
CLOWNS AND KINGS

Introduction

'AND still,' I hear a chorus of voices, mine not the least among them, say, 'another book on Shakespeare!' Did it happen or did I merely dream that recently I read an advertisement in a semi-literary magazine, 'The best book on Shakespeare of the month'? (Or was it 'of the moment'?) Yet why be surprised? We know how prolific, not to say profligate, nature is, hurling thousands upon thousands of a species forth that one of its members survive. Similarly it seems to demand of us a never-ending stream of collateral creations. Not even Shakespeare was satisfied with one play. Then how should we be with one or ten or ten thousand books about him. This is the price he must pay – we with him – for being so fertile, the seed that spawns a multitude of seeds, become forests upon forests and then jungles tropical in their thriving. For a long time I dreamed of writing a book that would dissolve most of the books about him. How get to his work unless the countless creepers and barnacles be stripped away? But now – not, I must admit, out of greater charity or tolerance, not even for my own book – I realize how wrong I was. Were such an act possible who in his right mind would perform it, want to say the last word, stop all thinking, new as well as old, mad as well as judicious, on Shakespeare? In short, who would kill Shakespeare himself, the endlessly lively, changing world of his work?

But what about all these scholars, critics, play-directors – lovers, lunatics, poets? Airs were what the Elizabethans called their songs. In each of the comedies considered here the lovely air that Shakespeare composed, passing over the bed of violets that are the play's characters, extracts from them their most fragrant expression. It is to our amused profit to regard his latterday zany offspring, critics and producers alike, with some of his geniality. His plays, creations that create, multiply their own rare versions of *Pyramus and Thisbe*. We in our response to the originals patch up the new cast, those plays' latest, astonishing production. We might cite the recent stellar performance of Jan Kott; his Bottom-up rendition of *A Midsummer Night's Dream*, say, truly proves – far past Kott's intention – Shakespeare 'our contemporary'. Shakespeare's boobies, we remember, blundering and all, often save the day when their supposed superiors abominably fail. Thus the critical courtiers in several of the early comedies miss the pleasure and point of the rustic playlets they observe as they miss the real worth of their fellow comics. Shall we not with Bottom read the plays like actors who would with full animation and conviction play all the parts?

More seriously, we are the plays' latest experience, the changed circumstances in which they must live. Such work, whatever shore it lands on, is bound to be adaptable, bound, for what it encounters, to grow ever more lively, ever more itself, to surprise itself with brand-new facets. Furthermore, we apparently must have precise weather reports, not so much of the plays as of ourselves, the race at the present moment, measured against the blessed norm, the seasoned reality, that Shakespeare established. And from recent reports considerable new illumination is available. The best literary minds of the past century, particularly some of its poets, striving to understand Shakespeare and thus inspired to exceed themselves, have arrived at most valuable awarenesses.

Certainly legitimate are the scholarly protests against modern criticism's frequent failure to take into account Shakespeare's times, the importance to him of its pervasive ideas, the conditions and influence of his day's theater, and the conditions of his playwriting itself. But however helterskelter that writing and then the productions may have been, who, treating the work seriously, can resist the feeling of integrity, the figure in the carpet which Shakespeare, bent, with the creator's good sense, on the speedy weaving alone, spread behind him? The temptation is of course to find a pattern too soon, one too simple, too tidy. Then Shakespeare may elude us more than ever. Also, appealing though this perception of a pattern may be, we had better guard ourselves against stressing his development to the depreciation of the early work. We must resist the heady impulse to read hind-foremost, to use later plays against early, to assume that the early were straining, usually incapably, to become the latter. Youthful they were and they should be enjoyed as such, enjoyed—as their worthies and boobies enjoy their own antics—for the display of Shakespeare's wit, frequently for its own exuberant sake.

Our knowing the speed with which Shakespeare wrote the plays might persuade us to take for granted a natural if not unconscious facility in him (and to think we have discovered the explanation out of such intensity of concentration for the repetitions and echoes as well). Such supposition amounts to a tribute on our part, but a fairly superficial one, to the almost god-given character of the work. Anyone who examines it thoroughly must come away with an awareness not only, obviously, of what mastery went into its making, but of what prodigious capacity for learning and most of all, immense though his plunderings of others were, from himself and his practice. Ben Jonson sensibly warned, 'Our Poet must beware, that his Studie be not only to learn of himself; for hee that shall affect to doe that, confesseth his ever having a Foole to his master.' Yet as we, risks and all, can learn most from Shakespeare, the great poet but one of the greatest artists also, so he did from himself. Who else was there as gifted to learn as much from? And if we ponder the fool as master, aside from citing Falstaff or Feste or Lear's example, we can say that the fool in us is sometimes the deepest, truest part, most worth listening to and humbly honoring. Shakespeare's learning was accompanied naturally enough by an amazing economy. At times he seems the most limited major writer we have. Yet, one might propose, his supremacy derives from that very limitedness, from ringing countless changes on a few basic themes, situations, devices. Picasso said of himself, 'Actually, you work with few colors. But they seem like a lot more when each one is in the right place.' Each play, its own fulfilment, was also a seed-bed for others; and Shakespeare was the gardener to transplant and rearrange. Perhaps, therefore, one of the most astonishing and delightful aspects of his art is watching him at work from play to play, doing over and doing differently, thereby shedding new light in all directions, on work done as on work to come.

It should not be surprising then that I favor the enlightenment, scattered through notes and letters or embodied in their work, of practicing writers like Coleridge, Keats, Yeats, Eliot, Auden. In the following chapters, though at times I disagree with their conclusions, find them most germinally wrong, it is the kind of creative concentration they have brought to bear on Shakespeare that I draw on. By their engagement with their own art, making fierce raids on his work, they achieved a sense of it that only a professional highwayman, as Shakespeare certainly was before them, can enjoy. Coleridge's contribution is almost too large, and perhaps too well absorbed, to be reviewed here. Keats' notion of the negative capability alone, tossed off though it was in a letter, increasingly attracts us as a major observation on creativity. And we are indebted to him for many other obiter scripta.

But it is—admittedly in part for their proximity to us—the relationship of a Yeats, an Eliot, an Auden to Shakespeare that is most interesting. In comments and in moments of his poems (see 'Lapis Lazuli') Yeats made it clear that Shakespeare was one of his rock realities. Eliot, on the other hand, carried on a much more complicated relation. Quick though he was to remark the fluidity, the spontaneity, of Shakespeare's plays, with that side of him which inclined to tradition and convention, this freedom, as it intrigued, troubled him. He protested the ambiguity of the plays, the ready way in which they encourage, rather rely on, the actor's—for that matter also the critic's—interpretation. Eliot could adduce *Everyman* as prime evidence of precise literary realization against Shakespeare's openness. And with his hunger for doctrine, his unease before the negative capability, Eliot was also troubled by Shakespeare's reliance on intellectual odds and ends, his throwing such scraps together into what somehow, amazingly, became (several times Eliot felt obliged to question if not deny it) unified, overwhelming works.

Here, I would suggest, Eliot did better than he knew. His critical, intensely conscious mind may have gravitated to the conventional and the traditional; but his occupation as a poet, particularly in his early major works and again in the late *Four Quartets*, instinctively inclined him to the epical daring of the plays. Pound for all kinds of reasons, some personal, some adventitious, boggled at Shakespeare. Perhaps with Eliot he recognized the absurdity, the neck-breaking dangers, of imitating Shakespeare. In a very early poem not published till 1965 he can say to Shakespeare, 'Is there twist o' man or woman/Too well-hidden for thy reach?' And

> *Diadems and broken roses,*
> *Wind and Tritons loud at horn,*
> *Sack-stains half thy screed discloses,*
> *The other half doth hold the morn.*

And, relevant indeed for one so given: 'Some comfort 'tis to catch Will Shaxpeer stealing.' In any case, with Yeats and Pound in their most ambitious work, Eliot did help us to enjoy again the rousing freedoms, the saltancies through time and space, the startling juxtapositions of materials and of feelings that at first sight often seem discrepant if not irreconcilable but that Shakespeare took for granted. Also, past the audacity of technique and all that it implies, these poets, in their large, profound look at reality, tutored by their age in its extremity, encouraged us to regard unblinkingly the violence, the outrageousness Shakespeare recognized more and more as at the taproot of nature.

In several basic ways we are, therefore, better able to come at Shakespeare's plays, I believe, than audiences and readers some generations earlier. The very things that Eliot the critic demurred at and in demurring described, so made available, we, for his achievements in poetry and for the turmoil of our age, ever more admire and respond to: the sudden, the improvisatory, the incongruous. For his time and its theater but most of all by his genius Shakespeare was supremely capable of these. Recent critics have nominated him a contemporary of Beckett, Ionesco, and others in the theater of the absurd. No doubt Shakespeare can be made to include them, if as poor relatives. But to try to confine him to the narrowness of such theater is to neglect other and major parts of his accomplishment and to deprive us of what we may now need most. Practiced in violence, accustomed to outrage, we probably approach the Elizabethans again in their capacity for cruelty, madness, savagery. But we painfully lack, not to mention sweetness and tenderness, the grandeur and conviction, even in savagery, the buoyancy which usually ventilates Shakespeare's plays. The Romantics and the Victorians did appreciate the splendid and the numinous in Shakespeare, but more than not too simply and solemnly for our tastes. Our suspicion, however, out of sophistication and a grim awareness of reality that we feel the nineteenth century deficient in, concentrated on too hard, makes us liable to naiveté also, one equally partial and costly to our comprehending not only Shakespeare but ourselves. We are, Eliot rightly maintained, one of the few ages to attempt the totally materialistic experiment. No great period in the past ignored the sacramental, failed to respect the something else, the unknown; certainly not so successfully. And some of us, not satisfied to live in that shrunken vision alone, would visit it on that past.

Whatever devotions of scholarship or loving identification we may undertake, we cannot deny that with time's passage a work loses much. Gone is the very furniture of the world the work, deriving from, presents. And, more subtly, far more seriously, the all-pervasive (thus more invisible than not) thought and feeling of that world. But if the work possesses the resiliency that Shakespeare's does, equal to any weather for the extremes of weather it commandeers, in later times it is likely to preserve some fundamental strength and meaning and simultaneously to uncover new qualities in itself. As Ben Jonson said of Virgil's poetry, it is 'so rammed with life/It can but gather strength of life with being. . . .' To enjoy both aspects, the work's essential nature and our contribution to it, might well constitute our chief objective.

The following essays would indicate some of Shakespeare's buoyancy and grandeur, the wisdom of his sympathy, but no less his clear-eyed command of things as they are, and would probe into their creative sources. Generally Shakespeare addressed himself to the particular, the experienced. Santayana in an early essay, 'The Absence of Religion in Shakespeare', begins by admitting that in his plays 'we recognize the truest portrait and best memorial of man.' But then in anticipation of Eliot he goes on, 'Shakespeare, however, is remarkable among the greater poets for being without a philosophy and without a religion.' That is, Shakespeare does not provide us with 'wholeness', 'a certain totality in our views', 'some system'. Santayana does ascribe this lack to conditions beyond Shakespeare—namely the English Renaissance:

> *Shakespeare himself, had it not been for the time and place in which he lived, when religion and imagination blocked rather than helped each other, would perhaps have allowed more of a cosmic background to appear behind his crowded scenes.*

Santayana does not seem to want to admit how felicitously Shakespeare's time and place suited him, freed his unique genius to its unequalled expression, its ardent receptivity to man's most agonized as to his gayest experience or to the realizing of that 'truest portrait.'

A little earlier Santayana had said:

> *Those who think it wise or possible to refrain from searching for general principles, and are satisfied with the successive empirical appearance of things, without any faith in their rational continuity or completeness, may well see in Shakespeare their natural prophet.*

However accurate Santayana may be, it is true that Shakespeare shares with our age's major poets their fidelity to observation and fact, to things as they are. We have William Carlos Williams' 'no ideas but in things' (not, as some of his disciples seem to think, no ideas, only things) and from Yeats' last letter, written not long before his death:

> *When I try to put all into a phrase I say 'Man can embody truth but he cannot know it.' I must embody it in the completion of my life. The abstract is not life and everywhere drags out its contradictions. You can refute Hegel but not the Saint or the Song of Sixpence.*

Yeats, far more than most of his fellow writers, looked to saints and visions. But he was with his contemporaries in acknowledging saints and visions in the flesh only. Modern poets, beyond Eliot's deliberate resorting to Christianity, may long for the faith, the totality, Santayana refers to. But though they admit there's more in heaven and earth else why be a poet, they will not lie before their senses, will not, however strong their intimations of 'something else', see ghosts and gods until they see them. Our world, one could say, in nature and in man's nature, is haunted enough.

That other world man lives in, his language, for its endless past vibrant and developing in it still, is similarly haunted. Originating in man, it partakes of his very life, his breath, and of the life of those before him. Yet it also has some mysterious kinship with and dependence on the world outside. It is therefore simultaneously the instrument of his liveliest, if not most complete, mating with the past and with that outside world. Concomitant with our poets' concentration on the world and man's place in it has been their concentration on words as they relate to and affect that world. Almost equally they have concentrated on words – often their private if not secret lives – for their own sake. Some real part of Shakespeare's preoccupation, I will try to show, past the patent one of words with words, was with the community of words and things, and of words and deeds, thoughts, feelings. Steadily he pushed himself, for drama via poetry was his business, to a sharper penetration of one with the other. It was on behalf of that world of things, deeds, feelings – and not because he questioned it – that he stressed the uses of language. If his words are to be believed, he demanded of himself that his language take on ever larger amounts of what lies in, between, and behind things and the world. For him at first words, caught up in their own glittering sound, were often self-absorbed. But increasingly they found radiance and power through their absorption in and of the world.

My title confesses a fundamental interest in the ways in which, since words and mostly speech are what these plays are made of, language operates in them. For my discussion I have frankly first of all selected plays that most attract me; since they have said the most to me I feel I have more worth saying about them than about some of their contemporaries. In addition, they soon began to become a company in my mind, a group with a family likeness amenable to my closest examination. I shall not summarize my book's argument here. It needs, I hope, its local occasions to be adequately said. But the book does set out to do several things: to spread out as much of the feast of the plays themselves as it can; to study the growth and change of the plays' language, the matter of words and deeds or poetry and drama, and the nature of language itself, in theater as in living; and to say something about comedy and history, those amazing, collateral developments in Shakespeare's work.

These two worlds of history and comedy, the one public and factual, the other domestic and private, Shakespeare first explored separately. But in climax, with his talents in both matured, he brought them together and showed how one influences and helps to realize the other; in fact, out of their mating they make a third, new thing. For a time at least in solemnity (the word we must remember originally had gaiety, festivity, in it) man as a whole, rich being is restored. Holiday or play and the daily, no longer at odds, become, as in a golden age or Eden, one again. Implicit therefore in this work is a theory of play and of the play or art, its place in living. Shakespeare well knew how shortlived a play and then its influence are. But he also knew how incomplete life, and especially the most serious, hard-pressed life, is without play. I could almost characterize the plot of this book as the career and the importance developing out of it of play, the intrinsic significance of it in the attempt to recover some basic quality of ideal life, life altogether lived in whatever one does.

At the same time Shakespeare presents not only the light and the power but the shadows and the weakness in this language of comedy and history. His clowns, beyond being participants in the comic action, are illuminators, often witty commentators on that action; simultaneously many of them are fools, birds tangled up in their own gaudy feathers. And his kings, in the breath that is their words, produce peace and delight or music; but when that breath is blinded or poisoned they produce dissension and chaos or tempest that ravages and threatens to destroy the garden. For since he should be the chief gardener, keeping and disseminating this music that is peace, a king, forgetting or abusing his function, is the worst breeder and spreader of tempest. Furthermore, once that tempest is loose, he can rarely restore it to music. But, wonderful to say, these plays are by their art tempest made into music, and the greater the tempest the more magnificent the music. Such poetic drama alone, releasing tempest, can possess it too.

In My Beginning Is My End

The Comedy of Errors and *Love's Labour's Lost*

SHAKESPEARE was born full-blown out of his own head no more than anyone else. And this is perhaps the first sign of his genius: knowing when to be born; but had he appeared in another time that might have been the time to choose. Nonetheless, his age must impress us. For it was already bewilderingly rich in amusements, artistic and otherwise, as it was a world, England about to become a great power, in the dawn of its self-discovery. Beyond his own gifts Shakespeare had countless resources to draw on: greenly pagan folk entertainments, classical and semi-historical materials, the flourishing, diverse theater of his fellow playwrights. These already by their venturesomeness had developed a medium that, as Eliot said, seemed able to digest anything or at least to accommodate, often it is true in fairly raw if not startling form, most antithetical and incongruous matters. It was apparently, at least in some part, this very jostling incongruity that made many of the plays popular. To cite one example alone, Peele's *The Old Wives Tale* with its bizarre, anything-goes, almost surrealistic effects well illustrates the time's pleasure in hurlyburly. In such writers with no hesitancy all places and ages, all histories, all knowledges natural, supernatural, and spectacular were subject to assessment and, as extraordinary things were asked of them, to contemporizing.

England's efflorescence encouraged such confidence. A little island with the whole world lying open for it to pillage and enjoy, in itself it provided a magnificent model. Altogether responsive to it, its writers were no less mettlesome than its far-ranging sailors and explorers that undertook, often with scant provisions beyond appetite and courage, awesome journeys into *terra incognita*, ransacked the luscious new world, and took on lustily much more powerful nations. Like its practice in the world at large, this buccaneer spirit plunged into poetry, relevantly enough into that genre that sponsors action–drama. The playwrights' records, the dazzling trophies snatched up, of realms known and unknown, continue to astonish and delight us.

9

Into such a rowdy context our first two plays fit most agreeably. Though, like the facts of his own person, the chronology of Shakespeare's drama has never been settled, generally *The Comedy of Errors* is assumed to be his first solo work. Generally too it is adjudged the most meager and obvious member in the canon. Certainly it is spare in the kind of poetry, insight, characterization, imaginative expansiveness we identify with Shakespeare. Yet in its own way, for the manner of play it is, it has its special distinction and instant professionality. Nor, for all its sealed-in success as a farce, is it as cut off from the great future as many critics seem to think. It is hard to resist the image of the young Shakespeare, recently a schoolmaster, fresh from the country, with poems, immense ambition, and possibly a rough draft of *The Comedy of Errors* in his poke. Having been involved in collaborations, as he sought about for a subject of his own, one he could with his present experience confidently treat, what more likely material than a play he had worked with before leaving home and perhaps, in teaching and in schoolboy performing, knew intimately.

Plautus was a very popular staple of the time's schoolteaching, as he was for its playwriting. And Plautus is much in *The Comedy of Errors*. But it is chiefly his one play, the *Menaechmi*, free of deliberate deceit and deception, with no plotters or exploiters, with everyone a victim, and with its errors the product completely of chance; the gentlest of Plautus, so perhaps Shakespeare selected it. Of course Shakespeare's play is no simple translation. On the contrary, in Shakespeare's fashion it is Plautus improved, modernized and compounded, if not commented on and criticized. The changes, the refining and softening of the characters, would suggest the latter. So, for instance, the parasite is gone, the prostitute is almost touching. And romance, not to say pathos, relative to Aegeon's and his family's career, is altogether foreign to Plautus. As always, Shakespeare polished what he plundered, astonished it with a wealth he discovered in it far past its own expectations. Thus to double the amusement and the confusion from which that amusement derives—there seems to have been no limit to Shakespeare's confidence in the resourcefulness of fate, chance, and his audience's credulity!—he doubled the set of twins and elaborated the plot. If farce sacrifices character to plot, let us have twice as many sacrifices. But let the economy of the plot require prodigality in its performing: two roles with four actors to play them!

And though the play proceeds in a brisk-paced, thoroughly self-possessed, old-style, farcical way, the settings, the occasions, and the personae, translated from Latin to contemporary Englishmen, must inevitably remind us of Shakespeare's England if not his middle-class home-town. It was apparently simple enough to transport a busy, Plautine, Mediterranean seaport town to the coast of England. Beyond references to the sea and the world at large, it is a small world, full of the bustle and business Shakespeare must have known; even with weather it is the trade winds that matter and that all bend to. But whether we credit Shakespeare with the play's leanness as a mark of his superb instinct for the rights and limitations of the form employed, or whether we attribute that leanness—and his wisdom therefore in starting with so popular and so handy a form—to talents not yet developed, the play normally hews to its original mark, winds up like a perfect top and equally perfectly unwinds again. Never, in a sense, will Shakespeare be in better shape. The play works so well by its honoring the interests and concerns of the middle-class world it treats, its people with a few exceptions alike in interests as in appearance as two guilders. Business, money, things, and pleasures out of things as they relate to money are an omnipresent consideration, the climate of the play, the motive power and shaper of the plot. Appropriately the lives of the characters turn on these. Its victims, almost its puppets, they exist mainly to satisfy the plot. Our chief pleasure consists of watching them being hauled and mauled about, and the variety of ways discovered to do so, that the maximum of profit be wrung out of them. In this respect the characters are not much more than exploitable commodities.

In fact, a grimness out of such considerations so grips the play from the outset that in its materials and larger plot it is hard to believe it a comedy. The play is framed by the aged, long-parted, long-suffering parents of the twin Antipholi. Time, chance, adversity, money, and this play separate—as they will eventually unite—them all. As it opens we learn in the most somber accents that Aegeon the father for want of money is about to die. Perhaps one is too modern and too little Elizabethan, more responsive to the situation than one is supposed to be since it is a conventional matter of romance. Yet in this pathetic introduction, in the way in which fate or chance has steadily dogged him and his, poor Aegeon hardly looks like a comic character. Nor does his predicament seem the stuff of careless, carefree farce. Thus the play begins with a sentence of death and a desire to die. Law which should make society and men's living together possible and agreeable is here harsh, ruthless, even deadly, based on money, hostility, and war. All, even the Duke, are bound by this Draconic law, as though it were fate or necessity itself. What intensifies the pathos is that love and its anguish, though necessarily muted here, are already at the center of Shakespeare's work; this family has long been seeking, however terrible the hazards and obstacles, to reunite.

Aegeon, looking for his sons, has landed on enemy territory. He begins:

> *Proceed, Solinus, to procure my fall,*
> *And by the doom of death end woes and all.*

Who would think this, possibly his first couplet, Shakespeare! He seems to be at his oldest, flattest, because mainly derivative, as a beginning young writer is likely to be. The laboriousness of this first scene's verse may be ascribable to Shakespeare's inexperience or, would we be more kind, to his sense of farce and especially to the framing of the play by romantic elements that, ultra-realistic in plot and action, must be fairly unreal in their verse, in this way distanced and subdued. Already, aside from the hardships and deprivations Aegeon has endured, he suggests a view of life that must be called melancholy. Late in the play his wife the Abbess defines 'moody and dull melancholy' (here the consequences of 'the venom clamours of a jealous woman') as

> *Kinsman to grim and comfortless despair,*
> *And at her heels a huge infectious troop*
> *Of pale distemperatures and foes to life.*

But then, she admits,

> *In food, in sport, and life-preserving rest*
> *To be disturbed, would mad or man or beast.*

Her husband for his profound, protracted disturbing deserves his mood. When at the Duke's urging he tells his sad story, recounts the storm and the shipwreck that separated him and one son from his wife and the other, or the first 'error' as it means wandering, he says of the death which seemed imminent, '. . . myself would gladly have embraced. . . .' The background of the play then is the violence of nature in its wanton playfulness, expressed in storm as it sunders men. The opening of the play amounts to the violence of society expressed in war and an iron law that, as it separates men, also threatens to kill. The substance of the play will be the violence or at least the tumult of individual man immersed in his own storm of confusion. The havoc at large, the great winds, blow into the most domestic scenes and occasions. One might wonder how man, so embattled, survives at all—not to say thrives and realizes himself. Yet the same forces, we shall see, natural and/or human (we will not talk of supernatural ones), that scatter him somehow at the end gather him together again.

For all the above, the play has sometimes been judged callous, in the nature of a farce, chiefly occupied with contriving ways of torturing its victims. But at least we do not become involved, except for a few scattered, brief moments, in the agony of internal suffering. If the joke, the farce, is to work as joke, the characters as individuals must be minimized. Also, the Elizabethans apparently, like the characters, especially the Dromios, enjoyed a wry humor at their own expense, shared in the practical joke, the absurdity; still not as personal as we, they participated with vigor in the spectacle, the vitality, of their own roles wherever they might take them.

At the same time the melancholy of the opening continues. In the second scene Aegeon's son, also seeking his kin, echoes his father's pessimism. The merchant who has befriended him, leaving, says, 'Sir, I commend you to your own content.' Alone, Antipholus moodily muses:

> *He that commends me to mine own content*
> *Commends me to the thing I cannot get.*
> *I to the world am like a drop of water*
> *That in the ocean seeks another drop,*
> *Who, falling there to find his fellow forth,*
> *Unseen, inquisitive, confounds himself.*
> *So I, to find a mother and a brother,*
> *In quest of them, unhappier, lose myself.*

We may attribute such gloom to his hardships and long frustration and to the apparent hopelessness of his quest. But the sentiments of loneliness and despair washing through his words, the sense already of identity lost, seem to me to go deeper than that. Here, losing himself to find others, he has definitely not found himself; 'confounds' with its original meaning of 'dashed by waves' makes that failure clear. We know what commonplace this image of man as a mere drop of water in a tempestuous, sea-wild world has been for many writers. It may be relevant to quote Pascal's famous variation on it:

> *Man is but a reed, the most feeble thing in nature; but he is a thinking*
> *reed. The entire universe need not arm itself to crush him. A vapor, a*

drop of water suffices to kill him. But if the universe were to crush him, man would still be more noble than that which killed him, because he knows that he dies and the advantage which the universe has over him; the universe knows nothing of this.

At this juncture Antipholus derives little satisfaction from his superior knowledge. It is his insignificance and his futility alone which impress him. Yet love, we shall see, enabling him to find such another fellow-drop, will make him eager to plunge back into, if not embrace, the sea. Meantime, however, he is not ignorant of the possibility of greater confusion and loss. In the play's first 'error', confronted by Dromio of Ephesus, whom Antipholus of course mistakes for his own Dromio, and concluding that this Dromio has lost or been cheated of all the money he entrusted to his own Dromio, Antipholus observes:

> *They say this town is full of cozenage,*
> *As nimble jugglers that deceive the eye,*
> *Dark-working sorcerers that change the mind,*
> *Soul-killing witches that deform the body,*
> *Disguiséd cheaters, prating mountebanks,*
> *And many such-like liberties of sin.*

This town, like any other, is amply prepared to account for all its confusions and misfortunes. But Antipholus is so wary of such difficulty that he decides, 'If it prove so, I will be gone the sooner.' He prefers, it appears, the sea with all its uncertainties, its storms and potential shipwrecks, to the land and the busy town with its preying creatures.

The whole matter of the tempest and the shipwreck behind the play is a fascinating one, especially as we look ahead to later plays. The tempest here is a natural if not inevitable donée to an islander of a sea-going, mercantile nation; using it to get his play going, Shakespeare hardly seemed aware of its potential poetic reverberations. Nor, one must admit, for a self-respecting, well-behaved farce should he have sounded them had he been aware. Yet, though tempest and shipwreck may be part of the property of an island kingdom and though it is in the interest of farce to mute their effect on feeling, in Aegeon and his son some of the poignancy-to-be out of these images already stirs.

Similarly the grief, the sense of profound separation and loss, of Adriana, the wife of Antipholus of Ephesus, who thinks herself abandoned, amounts to an emotion far past farce. Although at home, she feels as cut off and lost, since only in relationships are we 'found', as the wandering Antipholus of Syracuse. One may dismiss her as a fairly conventional scold, a shrew expert as she should be in this play in complaint and tirade. But Shakespeare could not resist sympathy for her pain, could not resist at least the full expression of it. In such moments, as they strike against farce's customary grain, one might be tempted to see a breaking through, an almost involuntary criticism of, farce, its inadequacies for the human condition and for human expression. Certainly we know how common such criticism of the forms he used was with Shakespeare, how much the criticism became an intrinsic part of the form, an enlargement of it. Usually, however, it is the comic mocking the serious and the noble, especially when they become excessive, pretentious, hypocritical. Here in the first play the rare opposite occurs. But since the comic is this play's prevailing mode, such opposite is to be expected. Thus Adriana replies to her gentle, unwed sister who urges 'patience':

> *They can be meek that have no other cause.*
> *A wretched soul, bruised with adversity,*
> *We bid be quiet, when we hear it cry;*
> *But were we burdened with like weight of pain,*
> *As much or more we should ourselves complain. . . .*

A little later she says of her husband,

> *His company must do his minions grace,*
> *Whilst I at home starve for a merry look. . . .*
> *Since that my beauty cannot please his eye,*
> *I'll weep what's left away, and weeping die.*

Is this not more than merely the shrill screed of a shrew? Or, even more tellingly, her later words to Antipholus of Syracuse whom she mistakes for her husband:

> *Ay, ay, Antipholus, look strange and frown,*
> *Some other mistress hath thy sweet aspects.*
> *I am not Adriana nor thy wife.*
> *The time was once when thou unurged wouldst vow*
> *That never words were music to thine ear,*
> *That never object pleasing in thine eye,*
> *That never touch well welcome to thy hand,*
> *That never meat sweet-savoured in thy taste,*
> *Unless I spake, or looked, or touched, or carved to thee.*

How comes it now, my husband, O how comes it,
That thou art then estrangéd from thyself?
Thyself I call it, being strange to me,
That, undividable, incorporate,
Am better than thy dear self's better part.
Ah, do not tear away thyself from me!

Here, aside from the touching sense of loss of identity, unlike those identity-losses out of accident composing the farcical bulk of this play, we recognize a person much in love and more poignantly since it is love presumed to be denied: 'I am not Adriana nor thy wife.' This observation, mistaken though it also is, is worlds away from Dromio's bewildered 'I am not Dromio'. And as it is with love, especially love's pangs, her language, lifting, outreaches the play's customary language, becomes lyrical, the music of an inner life. Continuing, she mounts to one of the few ecstatic utterances of the play, now affirmatively strong:

For know, my love, as easy mayst thou fall
A drop of water in the breaking gulf
And take unmingled thence that drop again,
Without addition or diminishing,
As take from me thyself, and not me too.

This water-drop, deepening, thickens into fiercest blood.

How dearly would it touch thee to the quick
Shouldst thou but hear I were licentious,
And that this body, consecrate to thee,
By ruffian lust should be contaminate!
Wouldst thou not spit at me and spurn at me,
And hurl the name of husband in my face,
And tear the stained skin off my harlot-brow,
And from my false hand cut the wedding-ring
And break it with a deep-divorcing vow?
I know thou canst; and therefore see thou do it.
I am possessed with an adulterate blot;
My blood is mingled with the crime of lust;
For if we two be one and thou play false,
I do digest the poison of thy flesh,
Being strumpeted by thy contagion.
Keep then fair league and truce with thy true bed.

I have quoted this whole, long speech because it is so long, complex and sustained, in tone and concern so much out of key with most of the play. And though, like most of the comic situations in the play, it grows out of a mistake and is addressed to a mistake, I am hard put to regard Adriana's words as in any sense comic or, in their length and at the same time surefooted, swiftly growing intensity, apposite to the play. Whatever emphasis one puts on her last lines–this is already the ambiguity of tone of the major plays, the mixed feelings that deep feeling subsumes–she in being lost takes on the full onus of her husband's supposed vice and, as a loving, dutiful wife, the whole contamination.

Here, interestingly and relevantly enough, she echoes the sentiments and the basic image, even to its words, of Antipholus of Syracuse, who hears his words amazingly in her mouth, and at the same time approximates something of the ironic fierceness of Donne in a poem, say, like 'The Flea'. It is striking that as she is most possessed by passion her lines become most possessed, intricate, passionately thoughtful, as 'metaphysical' as any poet's. Also, if Antipholus speaks of himself as 'a drop of water' it is to stress his puniness and helplessness, rightfully so out of his wrenching experience of the sea. Adriana, however, applies it in reverse. What distresses Antipholus even as it anguishes also delights her: she, her drop, does not want to be and cannot be separated from that other drop, her husband. Thus she goes on to a capping use of it as the drop becomes lust-contaminated blood. Confused Antipholus of Syracuse must be to find himself in this situation, but how further baffling to hear his own image returned to him if mirror-like in reverse. Already some part of that poetic power built out of echoes is stirring here.

But later, and in a few verses, Adriana's passion increasingly will top the above. She has just given her tongue, but 'not my heart', full vent and described her husband as totally ugly. Promptly, however, the will of her heart insists on asserting itself:

> *Ah, but I think him better than I say,*
> *And yet would herein others' eyes were worse.*
> *Far from her nest the lapwing cries away.*
> *My heart prays for him, though my tongue do curse.*

There are those who would object to such stressing of these lines. Concerned with the play's status as farce, they would consider sympathy not only gratuitous but a violating of the play itself; Luciana's admonishment of her sister, the former blonde to the other's brunette, a darker nature, and the much harsher rebuke of her mother-in-law the Abbess at the end should not only warn us against sympathy but expose Adriana for the risible scold she is. We must recognize some truth in this. Yet what law or convention is there that can prohibit feeling when it comes? And as far as Luciana is concerned, is she not too passively gentle, too mildly sweet and lyrical, to serve as serious critic of her sister or, for that matter, to be in this play? Is she not by her very nature a violation of its nature as a farce? Such moments of feeling do not capsize this light, swiftly skimming skiff or swerve it off its well-plotted course, but certainly they load it with cargo richer than it is accustomed to, and intimate what feeling, only a few degrees stronger, might do.

And so it is with the rest of the play. Other grimness, or at least the potentiality of it, occurs in what is the major substance of the play, the confusions. A touch more and irreparable blows, maims, deaths must follow. One need simply notice her husband's violence against Adriana as he calls her 'dissembling harlot. . . . false in all' and threatens 'with these nails I'll pluck out those false eyes, . . .' However, the one moment of real violence, the abuse by Antipholus of Ephesus and his Dromio of scrawny Pinch the conjurer, is not shown but wittily, happily described (so were, of course, the hardships the Aegeon family endured before the play). As I suggested earlier, the family's 'natural' sufferings before the play would seem more than enough. Now they must go through more and at man's hands, mostly their own kin. This, however, is the last leg of their journey, the final purgatory or purging before reconciliation. Thrust out of a stormy sea by chance and its magic onto an island, an island that seems bewitched it is true, they are plunged into further turmoil, made to lose themselves – their names and so their persons – before they finally recover themselves, their identities, and each other. Through their confusion the law, moved by the same force which in the end reunites them, is also finally lightened and relaxed.

What is it then that, beyond its happy ending, wins this play the title of comedy and farce? Obviously the gags and slapstick that pervade it, particularly as they pertain to the two forever-put-upon Dromios, the choplogic that often serves for dialogue, especially among the Dromios and their masters, the absurdity of the confusions and, with the exception of Luciana, the Abbess, and those moments of Adriana we have commented on, the total submergence of the characters in the confusions. Fortunately the verbal exchanges tend to be brief and brisk, punctuated by well-administered blows. Blows most appropriate, the Elizabethans must surely have felt, for menials like these; what else should one named Dromio receive? Shakespeare delights—and we with him—in seeing how near he can come to the breaking of heads as to its opposite, the breaking (as he blows it up more and more) of the bubble of absurdity, the errors and coincidences, without an actual collapse. Nonetheless, these exchanges, however much they may have amused Shakespeare's contemporaries, often become tedious in their mechanical wit, dry elaboration, and local reference. But here already Shakespeare begins to exploit one of his comedy's major resources of delight—rowdy, earthy name-calling. So Antipholus of Ephesus, a fairly choleric sort, exhibits his talent:

> *Along with them*
> *They brought one Pinch, a hungry, lean-faced villain,*
> *A mere anatomy, a mountebank,*
> *A threadbare juggler and a fortune-teller,*
> *A needy, hollow-eyed, sharp-looking wretch,*
> *A living dead man.*

Gusto, we see, at various points leaps into the language itself as it does through the situations. The servants and the masters, in appearance a kind of pun, are heavily, if happily, punned in the riming of their names. Beyond names and appearance, but because of them, they are of themselves and with their scenes in the nature of a pun. For as each twin appears he, like his scene, is taken to be one thing and is quite another; thus the actions they are involved in, presumably leading in one direction, flout expectation by usually leading in the opposite. And words or rather their names, since they produce almost instantaneous but unpredictable if not perverse consequences, may be considered as close to deeds as words come.

One other obvious main provision of amusement is the earthy low humor, the wit of the Dromios when it breaks loose from its laboriousness. Dromio of Syracuse, recoiling from a woman mistakenly after him, says:

> *Marry, sir, she's the kitchen wench and all grease; and I know not what use to put her to but to make a lamp of her and run from her by her own light. I warrant, her rags and the tallow in them will burn a Poland winter. If she lives till doomsday, she'll burn a week longer than the whole world.*

Who, including Bottom and Falstaff (or Cleopatra for that matter), can light up more radiantly than that? But a different light this, and rather differently used, from the light of love his master had discovered in Luciana just a moment ago. And not much later this light will again be seen by Dromio in another light when the courtesan appears:

> *Nay, she is worse* [*than the devil*], *she is the devil's dam, and here she comes in the habit of a light wench; and thereof comes that the wenches say, 'God damn me'; that's as much to say, God make me a light wench. It is written, they appear to men like angels of light; light is an effect of fire, and fire will burn; ergo, light wenches will burn. Come not near her.*

One of Shakespeare's first poetic wealths to come bubblingly alive was this exploitation of his day's colloquial world expressed in extravagant, yet realistically racy prose. But the above kitchen talk is not all of it. Dromio's sails puffed out with their own gusto, he goes on to describe the kitchen wench's complexion:

> *Swart, like my shoe, but her face nothing like so clean kept: for why, she sweats; a man may go over shoes in the grime of it.*

And now that he's boarded her we must have all of her. This domestic humor promptly extends itself, even as with its Poland winter and Noah's flood, to take in her whole body and the world with it. We are given a naming of the parts, a cataloguing and a detailed study in human geography, remindful, if downward rather than upward moving, of a Donne's 'Loves Progress'. Is it not apt that at its most domestic moment the play should be altogether abroad, its larger setting and the setting of the times being employed to describe the play's most internal situation?

Along with this low, delicious humor as well as its slapstick goes the constant insistence by the befuddled cast that they must be beset by goblins, witches, the supernatural. But clearly for such a play no magic is needed – nor may it be – beyond the cast's own prompt superstitiousness and confusion, and whatever power might waft over it from the framing romance, nature's mysterious, chance-ridden influence. Magic's very obvious absence intensifies the ludicrousness of the situations. The more so with magic insisted on. For characters immersed in materialism, money, business, time, and the commonplace pursuit of their own pleasures, the Duke's assertion that they have all 'drunk of Circe's cup' may not be too far from the mark. They have mixed most potent illusion with their daily sack. The senses alone relied on become their own mad seduction and confusion. Money, concentrated on, and things—actually an obsession with numbers and/or abstraction—are likely to reduce people themselves to objects, and so make their confusion with one another fairly easy. (At the same time, as I have suggested, whatever the cast's interests, we have nothing like Latinate lust and greed here.)

Of course there is magic enough in the well-aimed shipwreck as in the wonder of two sets of identical twins. But this is the magic of 'chance', of the play's form as it celebrates and enshrines chance, farce's strong, imperious convention and its hold on the audience while it magically flouts expectations of reason and normalcy. Yet the characters insist ever more that they are being bewitched, 'transformed'. Dromio of Syracuse, amiably confusing Christian and pagan worlds, cries out,

> *O for my beads! I cross me for a sinner.*
> *This is the fairy land. O spite of spites!*
> *We talk with goblins, owls, and sprites.*
> *If we obey them not, this will ensue:*
> *They'll suck our breath, or pinch us black and blue.*

And a moment later his master in an aside mutters,

> *Am I in earth, in heaven, or in hell?*
> *Sleeping or waking? mad or well advised?*
> *Known unto these, and to myself disguised?*
> *I'll say as they say, and perséver so,*
> *And in this mist at all adventures go.*

In this commonsensical world the cry of madness is everywhere, hurled at everyone. Shakespeare's brilliant manipulation of 'chance', jostling them as it does, provides the madness and amply justifies the cry. Only the Dromios, however, resoundingly make it when they are assured that they are indeed transformed and into the asses they are. But here the term is flat metaphor. Not till later, when he needs it and his drama can sustain it, in an atmosphere truly compact of witchery, will Shakespeare, appreciating his own cue, materialize such a metamorphosis. *The Comedy of Errors* enjoys no magically releasing wood. Nor, for the kind of play it is, should it have one. On the contrary. The town itself, however, once the self-engendering errors begin, that is, the plot's masterly guarantee of chance and just right coincidence, is wood —not to say maze—enough. It may lack country elves and goblins, moonlit spells. But it possesses superabundantly, in the minds of its inhabitants for all their townish bustle and materialism, the necessary, fertile ground of superstition, enriched by sea tales and tales of other lands and times. A world that believes in magic and witchcraft, it is ready to find them everywhere.

One other source of witchcraft, and a potential embarrassment to the play as a farce even though it deepens it, a flickering instance of magic, the sovereign magic to be, is the brief amatory interlude between Luciana and Antipholus of Syracuse. Here begins one of the most persistent themes of the comedies, love as the great school, the enlightenment of a young man by a beautiful young woman. This is, since internal and natural, the true magic or witchery, the only source of transformation. It naturally produces the play's largest eruption into lyrical poetry, a positive one beside the plaintively lyrical outburst of Adriana: love as a promoter of feeling, of coming alive, or the great discoverer in all its confusingness of man's best nature and being. Antipholus says,

> *Teach me, dear creature, how to think and speak;*
> *Lay open to my earthy-gross conceit,*
> *Smothered in errors, feeble, shallow, weak,*
> *The folded meaning of your words' deceit. . . .*
> *Are you a god? Would you create me new?*
> *Transform me, then, and to your power I'll yield.*

Though he is more thoroughly plunged into error than ever, he instinctively knows that she or love can alone free him to the truth. And like any good young Englishman, once touched by passion he is instantly ready and ready to give all; for recognizing good fortune come his way, he leaps ahead with all delighted might to seize it by its lovely golden forelock. Luciana, whatever siren-like confusion her words may throw him into, is the one and the only one to bring him with the speed of a word and a touch home to himself.

He draws on his sea imagery again:

> *O, train me not, sweet mermaid, with thy note,*
> *To drown me in thy sister's flood of tears.*
> *Sing, siren, for thyself, and I will dote;*
> *Spread o'er the silver waves thy golden hairs,*
> *And as a bed I'll take them and there lie,*
> *And in that glorious supposition think*
> *He gains by death that hath such means to die.*

For its formal pattern, and the riming that Luciana appropriately as 'teacher' sets going, this scene soon becomes a poetic duet meet to lovers; so too it moves from alternate line riming to clinching couplets at the end, couplets in which each speaker is assigned one echoing verse. And surely Antipholus' image above is a lovely one, all the more striking for its rarity in this play, gaining magic among its many mono-syllables from its one, many-syllabled, abstract word, 'supposition', that still draws on its original concrete force. Much as Adriana, bewail-ing her fate, has made of water-drops falling in the gulf, we can appreci-ate the 'flood of tears' and, at the same time, Antipholus' reluctance, for his sufferings in the briny flood, to dive into it once more. It is, he now sees, a flood indeed that he is after, but of an order very different from the stormy woe he had been immersed in, one lolling him rather like a floating bed.

His image, as it emphasizes silver and gold, gains and means, partici-pates in the play's monetary atmosphere; but simultaneously the image goes beyond the play's world as it becomes a work of art, a painting, for its golden hairs spread over the silver waves, a bed buoyed by the waves it lulls. And like a work of art it goes even further, in that for all this gold and silver it is a gain by yielding oneself. So the image is made lovelier by its happy-poignant note of death by drowning (still attuned to his earlier image of being 'confounded'), death called on to score the extremity of his rapture. Already here we have love and/or death as a consummation with perhaps some overtones of the seventeenth century's notion of the sexual act as a little death. For the beauty of Luciana and the promise it holds out, the sea, hitherto his image of con-fusion, suddenly becomes delectable to him, a bliss to drown in. But we know he hardly means to die. On the contrary, he now has found a reason to live, and he intends to do so exuberantly, even to yielding himself, his life, to her loveliness. Thus, for this fragrant bath after his fiercer one, he will be purged of his error, his wandering as well as his mistakenly gloomy outlook; and of course he will promptly be re-united with his family. At the same time since this is a comedy, even in his rapture, already lightened by the image of the siren and by words like 'dote', 'glorious supposition', and 'think', which admit this is all a sweet exaggeration, a conscious submitting to beauty's charms, banter is not completely forsaken. He can conclude his little rhapsody with 'Let Love, being light, be drowned if she sink!'

Also since this is farce and Shakespeare, he—as he will usually do here-after in his multiple awareness of reality as well as for the fruitfulness of this awareness for drama—quickly comes down hard on this bit of extravagant poetry, ballasts it as he qualifies and rounds it out with his next scene, no less about men and women together and the transforming power of love, but love now at its earthiest, its seamiest, out of the English town and country life he knew so well and out of a realistic world of harbors, marketplaces, domestic business. Dromio of Syracuse, echoing Antipholus' very word, also admits that he is 'claimed'. But the claim for Antipholus was heavenly, a pure delight. Here it is being possessed in a most oozy, sticky way. At once we move from the open sea and heaven into the kitchen sink of love, from its spiritual to its most gross. The shimmering waves have turned to oil and grease! Accordingly, the human transformation, ennobling before, is now belittling. Convinced that the wench is a 'diviner' who would bewitch him, transform him into 'a curtal dog', all Dromio can think to do, as Antipholus of Syracuse would leap to his fate, is flee from his. In the comic mode, as well as comically, to live is to live up to whatever role we happen to be cast into. A lover leaps, a dog runs, an ass brays, and fulfilment and ripeness is all. Chance, the mother of comedy, if not of our lives, by our mettlesomeness, our ability to go with it, is made choice.

This love episode and the parodying of it may be considered the one principal link between *The Comedy of Errors* and our next play, *Love's Labour's Lost*. Errors, however, might also be said to connect them. But in the former they are usually external; in the latter, as with Adriana alone, they are usually errors of judgement, follies on the part of the lords. In fact, the plays are so different, so antipodal in occasion, structure, content, that one is tempted to say their very difference at once proclaims the youthful genius of Shakespeare. Only he in this early exercising of his gifts could have written both, and one soon after the other. Having given himself handsomely to farce with its preoccupation with situation and plot and having at once proved his mastery of it, it is as though he now deliberately decided to do without plot and to essay the opposite, a play in its way as popular, if with a different audience, as farce, one compact entirely of words. If *The Comedy of Errors* is predominantly busy acts and gags and routine exchanges also close to burlesque gestures, *Love's Labour's Lost* (its title in its thickly alliterative sound as in its meaning clearly indicates what we are in for) is almost purely language. Language with little let or hindrance, given its head, but brilliantly differentiated, brilliantly measured to characters and meticulously calculated in effect. This is a

joyous promenade through a zoo exhibiting a host of particolored creatures at their particolored best. If *The Comedy of Errors* fundamentally derives from Plautus and in fact out-Plautuses Plautus, *Love's Labour's Lost* is one of the two plays (*A Midsummer Night's Dream* is the other) which Shakespeare invents most of out of the resources of his own wits and observation, and out of the wordy revels common to the court.

Coleridge, knowing that poetic genius in its first awakenings tends to respond to the wonders and seductivenesses of language itself, was convinced that *Love's Labour's Lost* must be Shakespeare's first play. I understand that conviction, especially for a writer as word-obsessed as Shakespeare, and would normally agree with it, but I cannot share it here. Aside from *Love's Labour's Lost's* extraordinary exploitation of current courtly fashions in speech and manner, reflecting considerable intimacy with that court, an easy knowledge not likely to one newly arrived in London, the astonishing gamut of idioms displayed, at their most flourishing and most accurate, hardly bespeaks an absolute tyro. Not even Shakespeare. Also, the skill with which Shakespeare negotiates in comic counterpoint courtly floridity and village verbosity seems much too professional for a beginner. One can go through this play and, character by character, nicely catalog the prevailing modes of logomania. Shakespeare seems to have immortalized them all. For as he scoffs at them, exposes them in their ripest absurdity, he obviously delights in them, embalms these glorious May-flies and butterflies in the noblest, transparent amber, their own volubility.

No doubt as this play is the nearest we come to something made completely of words, it shares some of the faults, the excesses, it sports. No one knew better than Shakespeare the pleasure of speech for its own sake, the brave, sunlit lilt of language, listening to itself, inspired by itself, to the point at which the world and its occasions are, rather than texts, that language's happy pretext. This play's characters drink deeply of themselves as of each other; for they, brimful, are at least as surprised by their intoxicating liquor as anyone else. And shall we doubt that Shakespeare could be no less relishingly surprised? Thus we can be grateful, as he should have been (though his complaints in the sonnets about popularity and the vulgar theater, its contaminations, and his longing for loftier approval would seem to say the reverse), that, apart from his profound good sense, he was obliged by fortune to work in the theater, obliged to push his furiously verbal gifts in the direction of action, effective dramatic action, and immediate, condensed speech. Otherwise who knows what early overwhelming Mallarmé or super Dylan Thomas, not to say English Gongora, we might have had! This play may well have been the crossroad of decision: something like the strenuous drama of this dilemma, it is not hard to suspect, is being played out here.

Shakespeare and his age believed in style and styles, in figurative speech, in rhetoric; ritual and formality would make such belief inevitable. The age also believed in suiting the style to the occasion, though evidence seems to indicate that the time's speech was much happier at public than at private events. In this play however style not only tends to outrun, if not overrun, occasion, but is the occasion: far more clothes and cosmetics than body, with clothes altogether the man. Still these are faults of exuberance, of youth, a people luxuriating in the springtime wealth of their own powers. We have here a nation's gay flamboyancy and the self-confidence such uncurbed flamboyancy admits. It is as though English itself, discovering what complex, various glory it could be, were kicking up its frisky, bright-beribboned heels. In whom better than in Shakespeare. Though the sense of power, of energy, is most impressive, at this point English is happy to be, not do, to perform little more than its own exciting self. Accordingly, it basks in its own health and geniality. And though words so used, wrapped up in themselves to the oblivion of the world from which they derive, may be folly finally, in themselves they have, whatever exposure they may be put to, in loveliness as in persuasiveness a charm hardly to be summarily or simply dismissed. How shall a people be known but by the richness of the language they invent? Where else shall they live or the uniqueness of their lives be enshrined? Or what else can so fully express their exuberance, their new-found self-delight? Is not this sense of surplus, of spiritual capital past use, in itself ingratiating? A god made this world and all in it by naming it and them. Now let us be gods through names beyond this world or at least searching, vigorous names that surprise this world anew.

But more than a difference in stress on plot or language, the world *Love's Labour's Lost* presents, as well as represents, is a very different one from that of *The Comedy of Errors*. In both plays at the outset a lord is in charge. But in *The Comedy of Errors* his will is promptly by-passed as he passes out of sight, and the play moves at once to another stratum of society, the concerns and confusions of the middle class. In *Love's Labour's Lost*, however, as in later romantic comedies, as the play opens with a lord setting out the law, so it is about and for him and his, chiefly his follies and confusions. Given such a world, from the start the language lifts, is much more courtly and self-conscious. Yet the delicious, open-mouthed presence of Costard, Armado, and the rest, echoing the lords in a clownish key as in mockery, soon tells us that the lords and their language are closer to the buffoons and bumpkins whom they consider their entertainment than they know. Thus a new level of amusement and reality sets in. The courtly emphasis encourages another dimension of awareness to appear. Early, in whole scenes and in the juxtaposing of scenes no less than in individual speeches, Shakespeare learned brilliantly to make household terms and elegant (Latinized, etc.) words cohabit in mutually enriching harmony. Of course, as we have seen, this already started, if briefly, in Antipholus of Syracuse's extravagant avowal of love for Luciana beside his Dromio's earthy words on the kitchen wench.

The play opens with the King of Navarre's decision to turn his little court into a monastic academe, a serious decision on the surface, for who would deplore sobriety and contemplation. Elegant too, especially beside the opening speeches of *The Comedy of Errors*, are Navarre's first very formal words with their measured Shakespearean sonnet-like sentiments.

> *Let fame, that all hunt after in their lives,*
> *Live registered upon our brazen tombs,*
> *And then grace us in the disgrace of death;*
> *When, spite of cormorant devouring Time,*
> *Th' endeavour of this present breath may buy*
> *That honour which shall bate his scythe's keen edge,*
> *And make us heirs of all eternity.*

One may well wonder what extraordinary exploit he and his lords are about to undertake.

> *Therefore, brave conquerors—for so you are,*
> *That war against your own affections*
> *And the huge army of the world's desires—*
> *Our late edict shall strongly stand in force,*
> *Navarre shall be the wonder of the world.*
> *Our court shall be a little Academe,*
> *Still and contemplative in living art.*

Extraordinary exploit indeed! Not the desire of wisdom and purity itself actuates these lords but open pride and self-interest, a hunger for 'fame' and 'honour' or reputation. Such is the hunt, the war, this King would be launched upon, an arbitrary suppression of living in behalf of a mistaken, half-baked ideal. It is interesting to compare this harsh new law, a mere boyish if not childish fancy, with the law prevailing in *The Comedy of Errors* and its town of Ephesus, an outgrowth of actual, bitter events. As the Duke of Ephesus says,

> *The enmity and discord which of late*
> *Sprung from the rancorous outrage of your Duke*
> *To merchants, our well-dealing countrymen,*
> *Who wanting guilders to redeem their lives,*
> *Have sealed his rigorous statutes with their bloods,*
> *Excludes all pity from our threatening looks.*

Here the law is a matter of business and money, but they too are artificial and enemies of feeling. And in both cases self-interest has produced the laws: a barren, destructive self-interest at that.

As Berowne promptly informs Navarre and the other compliant lords, their decision, in its notion that it can or should flout nature and basic instinct—they are not monks or scholars—is a foolish, self-deceiving one. Is it not most palpable folly for a young king to think that for three years he can convert his realm into an academy or a monastery, ignore his role as a ruler and, most fatuous of all, turn off his own and his lords' physical nature? Actually, though of course he does not call it or recognize it as such, Navarre in good Shakespearean lordly style out of his largess—he is rich enough, and so free, to afford it—and no doubt out of boredom, means to put on a play, the most extravagant, most ludicrous of all, that of wealth imitating poverty and abstemiousness. But perhaps, as we shall see in later, more seriously developed plays, that is all that excessive affluence and satiety can come to. In Berowne's words:

> *Why, all delights are vain; but that most vain,*
> *Which, with pain purchased, doth inherit pain:*
> *As, painfully to pore upon a book*
> *   To seek the light of truth, while truth the while*
> *Doth falsely blind the eyesight of his look:*
> *   Light, seeking light, doth light of light beguile;*
> *So, ere you find where light in darkness lies,*
> *Your light grows dark by losing of your eyes.*
> *Study me how to please the eye indeed,*
> *   By fixing it upon a fairer eye;*

Who dazzling so, that eye shall be his heed,
And give him light that it was blinded by.
Study is like the heaven's glorious sun,
That will not be deep-searched with saucy looks.
Small have continual plodders ever won,
Save base authority from others' books.
These earthly godfathers of heaven's lights,
that give a name to every fixéd star,
Have no more profit of their shining nights
Than those that walk and wot not what they are.

Of course it is amusing to hear him so passionately bookish in his attack on books, to observe his playfulness as he plays with words and riotously alliterates with the best and worst of them. What but books could have prompted a line so self-blindingly bright as 'Light, seeking light, doth light of light beguile'? Even Navarre, whom Berowne is rightly preaching to, can say, 'how well he's read, to reason against reading!' But anti-intellectualism has usually found its most ardent champions among intellectuals. Who else is better able to appreciate intellectualism's weaknesses and dangers? Yet even as we never notice and reprehend sins and excesses so clearly as our own expressed in others, so we may yearn—as Shakespeare would seem to have done—with one sane part of us for a reformation in ourselves and still resist it with the rest of us by the power of habit. Nonetheless, it is amusing that Berowne should not only be so much like the others but, in the very times when out of good sense he urges them to be different, more like them than they are. However, one must not—after all this is a comedy—take his words too seriously, even though he speaks prophetically when he signs the paper and vows to be as foolish as the others:

Necessity will make us all forsworn
Three thousand times within this three years' space;
For every man with his affects is born,
Not by might mastered, but by special grace.

Nor when, in the prevailing spirit of the romantic comedies, he famously, almost fulsomely, lauds women as the true academes:

But love, first learnéd in a lady's eyes,
Lives not alone immuréd in the brain,
But with the motion of all elements
Courses as swift as thought in every power,

And gives to every power a double power
Above their functions and their offices.
It adds a precious seeing to the eye:
A lover's eyes will gaze an eagle blind.
A lover's ear will hear the lowest sound,
When the suspicious head of theft is stopped.
Love's feeling is more soft and sensible
Than are the tender horns of cockled snails.
Love's tongue proves dainty Bacchus gross in taste.
For valour, is not Love a Hercules,
Still climbing trees in the Hesperides?
Subtle as Sphinx, as sweet and musical
As bright Apollo's lute, strung with his hair.
And when Love speaks, the voice of all the gods
Make heaven drowsy with the harmony.
Never durst poet touch a pen to write
Until his ink were tempered with Love's sighs.
O then his lines would ravish savage ears
And plant in tyrants mild humility.
From women's eyes this doctrine I derive:
They sparkle still the right Promethean fire;
They are the books, the arts, the academes,
That show, contain and nourish all the world,
Else none at all in aught proves excellent.

And thereupon he passes into a veritable froth of language as he whirls round and round repeated words. In short, cut in style and swagger at least of the same glossy cloth, his words are meant to be no less exaggerated than the conduct proposed by his fellow lords.

As with his time, the debate of books versus nature or experience occupied Shakespeare from start to finish. This play, especially crammed with bookishness, carries on the debate. Books, it would seem, were for Shakespeare, almost as much as for Dante, say, or Milton, an experience, in their way as rich, deep, and meaningful as any other. In *The Taming of the Shrew* the wise Tranio urges his impetuous young master, bent on the study of virtue and philosophy, not to be 'so devote to Aristotle's checks,/As Ovid be an outcast quite abjured'. Experience, yes, but experience as we are expertly helped to it by a book, Ovid. Whatever ladies dark and light Shakespeare may have been beholden to, we do know what a writer like Ovid meant to him, almost Virgil to his Dante, most of all for Ovid's setting forth the transforming power of love. Yet since that power initially emanates from women, experience or nature must enjoy priority over books. And books are to be respected in their acknowledging women's primacy of power.

In *Love's Labour's Lost* this power figures from the start. With the vows exacted of all—appositely the play's first 'action' amounts to words—those vows are broken by the arrival, as though cued by Berowne's prediction, of the French ladies, come on serious business for the princess' father. Much needs to be made of this court's being, as it represents England and the times, a lady's world—one thinks of Elizabeth for whom this play may have been written and put on—of forms and manners that can quickly degenerate into mannerisms. Courtly love, promoted a good while ago by women, enshrined woman and love of her as the center of its code. The conflict between ethics of the medieval Christian variety and love and nature—that is, love and nature as providing a sounder ethics, has been well established. The practical, ethical doctrine of education through love was formulated in many works. In Shakespeare's view of ladies here and in his romantic comedies generally, stimulators that they are to love, they are also deep, true, sane educators, corrective—so this play will demonstrate—of the extravagances their lovers would gladly give themselves to. That is, they exact a fundamental change in their lovers' natures, a seriousness of the order which Navarre in the beginning mistakenly thought he was requiring of himself and his lords. Shakespeare's women are worldly and advocates of style and manners and ritual, but worldly in behalf of the human and the sensible as against the out-of-this-world fatuity of the young lords. Thus they will be put through the paces of experience, will be taught by a woman's flashing eye and piercing, accurate tongue to give over their idleness and to find for the stirrings of power in them, till now unemployed except in fruitless persiflage, objects and exploits worthy enough to focus, shape, and deepen that power. They will learn that, at the bottom of their program for an academy, lay, not the purity they assumed, but pride, a desire to indulge their wit for its own self-loving sake.

Yet their next steps are no less folly-ridden than their first. Now, just as they were smitten with the dream of contemplation and austerity, of fame and wisdom, they are easily and equally smitten with the notion of love, new roles to play, new gaudy words to say. Their objectives have changed, not their basic awareness or their natures.

They are still seeking occasions that will enable them to exhibit themselves. In a series of neat, quick performances the ladies, understanding their frolicsome, unemployed, youthful, would-be lovers too well, expose them to their own superficiality and confusion by confusing them further: persons so little realized can hardly tell from one situation to another who they are.

In the mistaken disguises, if here deliberately assumed, and in many of the verbal exchanges, we are not too far from the atmosphere of *The Comedy of Errors*. Nor in the exchanges between the clowns and between the clowns and the lords. But those of *Love's Labour's Lost*, befitting the play, know greater resiliency as well as complexity. One thinks of Costard's aptness when he is being exposed by Navarre, reading Armado's letter about Costard.

> Navarre: '. . . *There did I see that low-spirited swain, that base minnow of thy mirth*,' –
> Costard: *Me?*
> King [reads]: '*that unlettered small-knowing soul*,' –
> Costard: *Me?*
> King [reads]: '*that shallow vassel*,' –
> Costard: *Still me?*
> King [reads]: '*which, as I remember, hight Costard*,' –
> Costard: *O, me!*

and so on, later amusingly echoed by the exposed lords with their 'Ah, me!' Still the talk, for the kind of word-hypnosis that sets in, now and then clots and becomes mechanical like the quibbles in *The Comedy of Errors*, now not relieved, as in *The Comedy of Errors*, by slapstick and physical actions. Nonetheless, in appreciable superiority the spells, the 'bewitchment', and their unraveling are here in the hands, not of accident or fate (or of Shakespeare's manipulation of plot), but of the wily ladies.

Finally, stripped to the vanity they have been serving and obliged to acknowledge it, the lords come humbly to the ladies for their sentences and, hopefully, for love. But the ladies do not trust them yet, and the lords' cruel raillery at the clowns in their playlet might well indicate to the ladies, who abstain from that baiting, how little changed their lords fundamentally are. They must be shaken loose from their bad habits, be extricated from the hothouse atmosphere of their court, which encourages their license and supports them in a sense of callous superiority, and for a considerable spell be exposed to the world and its hardships—a true trial compared with the many playful ones of the play. If their avowed loves survive such trial and if they are properly chastened, the women will honor their suits. Something of the order of courtly love continues.

Meantime, in themselves as in their echoing of the lords, the boobies that decorate the play beguile us. The lords regard them as gay interruptions to their boredom, puffy plumes to tickle their wits further. It is the butterfly calling the fuzzy caterpillar worm. Though similarly enchanted by their words, their wits, their attitudes, the lords little realize how much they share their boobies' absurdity, their frequent confusion of the word with the thing to the point at which the thing disappears and the word is the thing and the only thing. Shakespeare knew that to some degree, like all creatures, we must bask in the ambience of our beings; we do live on and in our bodies, minds, breath. But he also knew—and this was one of the main things he was trying to show—that our worth appears when our ambience crosses with, deepens and enlarges the ambiences of others, in turn enlarged itself. Not to do so, to be insulated in oneself beyond any appeal, to be contracted to one's own bright eyes alone, is to be a comic figure or, more seriously and on a larger scale, a tragic one. But such enlargement, Shakespeare knew, for such a play, with such word-stuffed personages, is too much to ask. Thus for the play's duration he gives them their giddy, plumed heads. And wherever one turns one collides with idiot mastery.

The play's cream, of course, flagellated to huge gobs of glistening butter, is Monsieur Mouth himself, 'the refinéd traveller of Spain', Don Armado,

> That hath a mint of phrases in his brain:
> One who the music of his own vain tongue
> Doth ravish like enchanting harmony.

For one so tuned in on himself the music of the spheres must be supernumerous. And then we have perfect curdy Holofernes, the gist and pith of pedantry. In fact, one might think that villagers and yokels like Holofernes and Sir Nathaniel and Costard have little place in a court, even in its bosky, outlying preserve of a park. But the scene of this play is Babel enough to suck into its center, as into the special contagious ward of a jammed-up asylum, anyone suffering from some form of logomania. And Shakespeare wisely cannot resist their presence, their English, little-town bustle that will always be fresh in him. Why should he not immortalize, far beyond his skimpy first sketch of Pinch, some curate or curates in general, some schoolmaster or masters of a type who may have been not too long ago colleagues of his. Furthermore, Holofernes and the admiring Nathaniel are delectable witnesses of the havoc of books Berowne warned against. These two exult in their total infection, exult in it as though it were in all its poxery a conspicuous mark of very special genius. Maybe, had the lords persisted in their folly, they would have become as wise! When Holofernes berates Dull for his ignorance, Nathaniel shrewdly explains:

> *Sir, he hath never fed of the dainties that are bred in a book; he hath not eat paper, as it were; he hath not drunk ink. His intellect is not replenished; he is only an animal, only sensible in the duller parts.*

Books it is, and only it would seem as they are thoroughly, literally digested, that turn us from animals to men. These two, even as they go off to a parasitical feast, by obvious implication no less than by the way they speak, appear to have fed on nothing else. The world exists for them—is real for them only as it is—to be converted, for all its riches, into the greater riches of books. They are, in a droll sense, what the lords at the outset wished and decided to be—pure word-men, students everlasting, if not books talking. And such may well be Holofernes' and Nathaniel's function in the play: to show, in love's accurate perspective, now that love has taken over, what study and 'learning,' pursued for its own silly sake, really comes to. In any case, they are such learning's last, moldy champions and models. (With Costard, however, it is the amusing reverse: 'remuneration' and 'guerdon' are to be valued, to be found sweet, as they translate into their real value and are real things.)

In Holofernes' first speech—appropriately he and Nathaniel do not appear until late in the play, Act IV, scene II—we soon see that he has more words than things. So he teaches! He is the victim or, more kindly, the product nonpareil of his method. Talking about the deer the princess killed, he says:

> *The deer was, as you know,* sanguis, *in blood; ripe as the pomewater, who now hangeth like a jewel in the ear of* caelo, *the sky, the welkin, the heaven; and anon falleth like a crab on the face of* terra, *the soil, the land, the earth.*

If you can use four words why use one? And in this thicket let the poor deer, meaning or the thing itself, look after itself.

Properly these characters speak prose. Poetry is something for them to remark and to discuss or to pull themselves together for on special occasions. After one such effusion Holofernes says modestly enough about himself:

This is a gift that I have, simple, simple; a foolish extravagant spirit, full of forms, figures, shapes, objects, ideas, apprehensions, motions, revolutions: these are begot in the ventricle of memory, nourished in the womb of pia mater, and delivered upon the mellowing of occasion. But the gift is good in those in whom it is acute, and I am thankful for it.

And agreeing with him in the accuracy of his adjectives, we too must be thankful. Thus, amusingly enough, when Holofernes criticizes both Nathaniel's reading of Berowne's sonnet and the sonnet—a poem most relevantly emphasizing love as knowledge, the only book, etc.—with the authority and pride of the expert he says:

You find not the apostrophas, and so miss the accent: let me super-viȝe the canȝonet. Here are only numbers ratified; but, for the elegancy, facility, and golden cadence of poesy, caret. Ovidius Naso was the man: and why, indeed, Naso, but for smelling out the odoriferous flowers of fancy, the jerks of invention.

Amusing in that Holofernes should choose so well; for indeed Ovid, the poet of love and of the changes love can produce, was the man for Shakespeare, with an influence on him in language and ideas yet to be weighed. Amusing in that Shakespeare should have Holofernes take Ovid by the nose. And amusing, as well as most apt for this play, in that Holofernes, feeling words and images so deeply, should speak of smelling them out. For him as for other absorbed characters (see Bottom) nothing like a divided sensibility exists; thoughts and images are to be smelt as flowers are to be instantly thought and worded. Most amusing and important of all, our pedant via Ovid urges inspiration. For '*Imitari* is nothing: so doth the hound his master, the ape his keeper, the tired horse his rider.'

In the Fifth Act, when we meet this crew again, we hear them discussing Don Armado. Like the mottled slug resenting the emperor moth, Holofernes says disparagingly of him:

Novi hominem tanquam te: *his humour is lofty, his discourse peremptory, his tongue filed, his eye ambitious, his gait majestical, and his general behaviour vain, ridiculous, and thrasonical. He is too picked, too spruce, too affected, too odd, as it were, too peregrinate, as I may call it.*

(The academic's all-service, all-certifying 'as it were' occurs again, re-inforced by the flourish of 'as I may call it'.) Nathaniel, taken by 'peregrinate'–he says, 'A most singular and choice epithet'–fails to recognize it as criticism and 'draws out his table-book' to hoard this gem for its own sake. Then, reaching the climax of his depreciation of Don Armado, Holofernes exhibits himself at his sublime best:

He draweth out the thread of his verbosity finer than the staple of his argument. I abhor such fanatical phantasimes, such insociable and point-devise companions; such rackers of orthography, as to speak dout, fine, when he should say doubt; det, when he should pronounce debt,–d, e, b, t, not d, e, t: he clepeth a calf, cauf; half, hauf; neighbour vocatur *nebour; neigh* [we inevitably and soon get to the ass in such characters!] *abbreviated ne. This is abhominable–which he would call abbominable: it insinuateth me of insanie:* ne intelligis, domine? *to make frantic, lunatic.*

Holofernes, having long labored in his profession, is its sparkling prize, the teacher stuck in the poor, deep rut of reiteration and pro-liferation of example. But who else beyond Shakespeare could present staleness and, by stressing it as staleness, find its dewy freshness; out of pedantics press the sweetest wine!

Now that Holofernes has so succinctly described Don Armado, it is proper that at last these two besplattered, splattering inkbloods meet. The play saunters to its climax of a sunny afternoon in the triumph of their encounter, spiced further by the asides and comments of Moth and Costard, and the agreement to collaborate in a playlet, 'the Nine Worthies', a piece like jester's bells capping all the palaver of *Love's Labour's Lost*. In Armado's words,

Sir, it is the King's most sweet pleasure and affection to congratulate the Princess at her pavilion in the posteriors of this day, which the rude multitude call the afternoon.

Then, in a speech only he can manage, pretending to dismiss the very thing he splendidly emphasizes, Armado requests their assistance:

Sir, the King is a noble gentleman, and my familiar, I do assure ye, very good friend: for what is inward between us, let it pass. I do be-

seech thee, remember thy courtesy; I beseech thee, apparel thy head: and among other important and most serious designs, and of great import indeed too, but let that pass; for I must tell thee it will please his Grace, by the world, sometime to lean upon my poor shoulder, and with his royal finger, thus, dally with my excrement, with my mustachio; but, sweet heart, let that pass. By the world, I recount no fable: some certain special honours it pleaseth his greatness to impart to Armado, a soldier, a man of travel, that hath seen the world; but let it pass. The very all of all is,—but, sweet heart, I do implore secrecy,—that the King would have me present the Princess, sweet chuck, with some delightful ostentation, or show, or pageant, or antique, or firework. Now, understanding that the curate and your sweet self are good at such eruptions and sudden breaking out of mirth, as it were, I have acquainted you withal, to the end to crave your assistance.

Enchanted by such a spate—not to say eruption—of gentility, importance, finesse, and no doubt flattered to be asked to collaborate in such a noble function, Holofernes instantly changes his mind about Armado and agrees. The Nine Worthies will end the comedy as the four worthies, the lords, opened it and as their last little silly play as Muscovites will immediately precede the playlet. Navarre says, 'Berowne, they will shame us. Let them not approach.' But for the foolish failure of the lords' Russian skit Berowne sensibly retorts: 'We are shameproof, my lord, and 'tis some policy/To have one show worse than the King's and his company.' Of course The Nine Worthies will be as interrupted, now by the lords, as were the lords in their performance by the ladies.

But some of the geniality which runs through the play concentrates here, first in the princess' words:

> *Nay, my good lord, let me o'errule you now.*
> *That sport best pleases that doth least know how:*
> *Where zeal strives to content, and the contents*
> *Dies in the zeal of that which it presents.*
> *Their form confounded makes most form in mirth,*
> *When great things labouring perish in their birth.*

Or *Love's Labour's Lost*. Then the clowns, baited, rise nobly to their own defense and prove that they have, at least at present, more manliness and touching sentiment than their masters. So Costard's words in Sir Nathaniel's behalf:

> *There, an't shall please you; a foolish mild man; an honest man, look you, and soon dashed. He is a marvellous good neighbour, faith, and a very good bowler.*

Or Holofernes' rejoinder to the lords' ragging of him: 'This is not generous, not gentle, not humble.' Or, best of all, Don Armado's defense of Hector, the worthy he is playing: 'The sweet war-man is dead and rotten; sweet chucks, beat not the bones of the buried. When he breathed, he was a man.' They, and they necessarily should, share Shakespeare's respect for the slightest, the lowliest as well as for the lofty; the least cricket serves and, serving, deserves to be heard—especially as Shakespeare can hear it. One thinks of Dull the good, silent, clod constable, who also in his own way has earth sense and his unique inspired moment. This moment is made possible by his fortunately misunderstanding 'talent' for 'talon', when he responds to a bit of Holofernes' choice nonsense, applauded by Sir Nathaniel as evidence of 'a rare talent', and says, 'If a talent be a claw, look how he claws him with a talent.' So too, though a lowly country clown, Costard, with his own native wits about him, responds valiantly to Moth's reaction to the first meeting of the worthies: 'They have been at a great feast of languages, and stolen the scraps,' with

> *O, they have lived long on the alms-basket of words. I marvel thy master hath not eaten thee for a word; for thou art not so long by the head as* honorificabilitudinitatibus: *thou art easier swallowed than a flap-dragon.*

A little later, altogether taken with Moth, Costard says,

> *An I had but one penny in the world, thou shouldst have it to buy gingerbread: hold, there is the very remuneration I had of thy master, thou halfpenny purse of wit, thou pigeon-egg of discretion. O, an the heavens were so pleased that thou wert but my bastard, what a joyful father wouldst thou make me! Go to; thou hast it ad dunghill, at the finger's ends, as they say.*

Here for a change Holofernes' learning is, by its Ovidian nasality, most pungent-pert: 'O, I smell false Latin; dunghill for *unguem*.' And, whatever their self-engrossment, their blindness for their own dazzling rushfires and *ignes fatui*, these zanies are capable—perhaps more than the lords—of respecting one another in their unique gifts. With that extra fillip into awareness that Shakespeare readily discovers in his characters they listen and say in delighted astonishment: 'So I'm not the only one; he's a fine-feathered bird too!' Even their condescension is qualified. Holofernes, considering Costard's half-witticism, says: 'A good lustre of conceit in a turf of earth, fire enough for a flint, pearl enough for a swine. 'Tis pretty; it is well.'

The ladies, seeming to appreciate this in them, must appreciate a similar quality, at least potentially, in their suitors. For they do agree to treat their suits seriously if they obey the conditions laid down, this as the playlet falters for the threat of a duel between Costard and Don Armado, and as the main play quickly breaks down thereafter with the messenger's announcement, reality's abrupt interrupting, of the death of the princess' father which, he says, makes him 'heavy in the tongue'. Here we have the first expression of a theme common to Shakespeare's work: the will of a father, living or dead, casting a shadow over the young ones, threatening to thrust reality in its most sobering sense upon them. In these terms and in this atmosphere the women sentence their men. The princess, gently and decorously saying farewell, 'If over-boldly we have borne ourselves/In the converse of breath: your gentleness/Was guilty of it', repeats, 'A heavy heart bears not a nimble tongue.' Berowne underscores this with 'Honest plain words best pierce the ear of grief'. (But then he is promptly off to prove again what the princess replies, that their 'courtship, pleasant jest and courtesy' seemed but 'As bombast and as lining to the time'.)

The other three lords sent for a year 'with speed/To some forlorn and naked hermitage,/Remote from all the pleasure of the world', a real academe or monastery and not the bogus one they began with, Rosaline plainly tells Berowne, in some ways by his very knowledge the worst offender of all:

> *You must be purgéd too, your sins are racked,*
> *You are attaint with faults and perjury.*
> *Therefore if you my favour mean to get,*
> *A twelvemonth shall you spend, and never rest,*
> *But seek the weary beds of people sick.*

And in what seems a revision of this which was never deleted, for his being

> *a man replete with mocks,*
> *Full of comparisons and wounding flouts,*

> *Which you on all estates will execute*
> *That lie within the mercy of your wit,*

she repeats,

> *To weed this wormwood from your fruitful brain,*
> *And therewithal to win me, if you please,*
> *Without the which I am not to be won,*
> *You shall this twelvemonth term from day to day*
> *Visit the speechless sick, and still converse*
> *With groaning wretches; and your task shall be,*
> *With all the fierce endeavour of your wit*
> *To enforce the painéd impotent to smile.*

She recognizes his gifts, his 'fruitful brain'. But it is infested with the wormwood of wit, and this he must weed out. He must find, as she had said earlier mistakenly of him, 'the limit of becoming mirth' and stay inside it, the words so 'apt and gracious', at least as she had remembered him, 'That agéd ears play truant at his tales,/And younger hearings are quite ravishéd.' He must find in him the charity, the fellow-feeling, already remarked above in the zanies, must find, as he himself put it, the 'honest plain words' that 'best pierce the ear of grief'. Berowne is understandably overwhelmed. Only later, when the tragedies' worlds indeed become hospital-like, will some of their characters do what Berowne recoils at:

> *To move wild laughter in the throat of death?*
> *It cannot be, it is impossible.*
> *Mirth cannot move a soul in agony.*

Mirth and agony in combination will emerge in Shakespeare's tragedies as they represent, among other things, a truly metaphysical sense that the whole of man must be called on to give more than partial voice to his role in the universe: all his faculties are hardly enough, separately and together, to express his predicament, his wonder, his mystery and the world's. Rosaline replies,

> *Why, that's the way to choke a gibing spirit,*
> *Whose influence is begot of that loose grace*
> *Which shallow laughing hearers give to fools.*
> *A jest's prosperity lies in the ear*
> *Of him that hears it, never in the tongue*
> *Of him that makes it. Then, if sickly ears,*

Deafed with the clamours of their own dear groans,
Will hear you idle scorns, continue then,
And I will have you and that fault withal;
But if they will not, throw away that spirit,
And I shall find you empty of that fault,
Right joyful of your reformation.

Thus we have gone from the would-be academe at the outset, in all its artificiality and fake rules of abstemiousness, to the rigors of the world embodied in a hospital at the end. Women, as Berowne warned, will indeed educate their men, but perhaps more earnestly than even he realized. The comedy is over, and Berowne agrees, 'I'll jest a twelve-month in an hospital.'

Earlier he had acknowledged the frivolity of his tongue-jigging and had renounced it:

O, never will I trust to speeches penned,
Nor to the motion of a schoolboy's tongue;
Nor never come in vizard to my friend;
Nor woo in rhyme, like a blind harper's song!
Taffeta phrases, silken terms precise,
Three-piled hyperboles, spruce affectation,
Figures pedantical; these summer-flies
Have blown me full of maggot ostentation.
I do forswear them, and I here protest,
By this white glove,—how white the hand, God knows!—
Henceforth my wooing mind shall be expressed
In russet yeas, and honest kersey noes.

At once he had proceeded to practice his renunciation:

And, to begin, wench [a good russet term],—so God help me, la!—
My love to thee is sound, sans crack or flaw.

How much this speech is highfalutin still, with its three-piled hyperboles denying hyperbole and its maggot ostentation deriding maggot ostentation, we need not remark. But Rosaline crisply warns, 'Sans sans, I pray you.' It is hard not to find this somewhat glancing by Shakespeare at himself; he is, at least as much as Berowne, aware of the lure such language is, how easily and endlessly he can unravel it. He is different from his lords and savory louts only in that he encompasses them all. His mighty language gathers itself in voluminous folds, if most adroitly in a play so made as to require such folds. This language has to discover the situation that will stretch it, try it—a hospital perhaps?—past even its seemingly all-accommodating resources, extend it to the rending point and beyond when O's and silences will be Shakespeare's most triumphant speech and poetry. But to the end, it must be admitted, he has with his apologizing Berowne 'a trick/Of the old rage'. And though Shakespeare tries to the end, and does slough much of it, he can at best 'leave it by degrees', and never entirely.

This then, we can say, is the first play in which Shakespeare has his many-storied, thickly-frosted cake and with us eats it too. For what it amounts to is performance and simultaneously criticism in the very pleasure of that performance. A world but a world contained, enriched by a steadily present, steadily enjoying, steadily highlighting overview. If *The Comedy of Errors* offers only a few moments critical of the form it normally and gayly cleaves to, this play criticizes while it encourages and delights in the lingoes it is made of. But, beyond the two plays' meeting in a like energy, an overflowing vivacity, for the one in the superb jugglings of its plot or its crackling action, for the other in the superb juggling of its words, we might point out a similarity in their criticisms, criticisms stemming from their antipodal natures. Business world and daily world that *The Comedy of Errors* is, or a matter primarily of contrivance and manipulation, at moments it is threatened by that which it tends to ignore; feeling (and/or lyrical poetry) threatens to break loose in it. In *Love's Labour's Lost* the situation is reversed. Its aristocrat's world is mostly an atmosphere of leisure, holiday, mannered language, affectation, and its villagers and country folk, as against the busyness of the efficient townspeople of Ephesus, also have a leisure, a country pace, to indulge and to elaborate their own lingo in. But the real world, not to say that of the daily, life and death, finally breaks in and breaks up that atmosphere. As the prosaic, the commonplace, is hardly enough, so is its opposite insufficient engaged in alone. Though in their tidy bed and in the clement season they may make a most appealing sight, men, alas, are not florid birds, butterflies, flowers. But a comedy at least—and perhaps similarly moments of leisure in a court—if only for its scant and measured time-and-space, can allow its characters, and so us, some emergence, some such self-luxuriating. A play, as its name suggests, is a place and/or occasion to indulge play, excess, folly even—a clearing in which man may for a time—here specified—exercise his powers for their own sweet sake, free of routine and the more burdensome requirements of living. But the play does so only for a time and, finally, to indicate the inadequacy of such indulgence.

Appropriately since this play—after having given the opposite more than its due—sings the praises of plainness and the natural, it ends in two of Shakespeare's most accomplished, 'natural' songs. They should help to clear the air of the litter of vocables, the glut of three-piled hyperboles. Thus the songs are made of words that point directly to things, things and people harmoniously in their proper, established places, stability in vitality. Yet here too, since they are still only—and wholly—words, the overtones and undertones are hardly simple. First of all, they do constitute art. Second, these russet yeas and honest kersey noes are not that honest. For all their earth-boundness they admit the troubles and deceitfulness in the rustic or so-called natural world as well. Shakespeare, as ever, does not provide a simple, one-dimensional answer. Kersey and russet, like the plainest, most naked speech, can disguise as much as any other cloth. We have only to look ahead to Petruchio in his 'plain' treatment of Kate or to Iago with his 'plainness', his rough 'honesty'. Nature at its loveliest—it is Spring that reverberates with threats, not Winter—by that loveliness and its fertility contains potential trouble and pain for man. As Berowne recognizes early in the play, 'For every man with his affects is born,/ Not by might mastered, but by special grace.' And if natural impulse produces, as it is favored by, festivity, it also releases—not to say requires—folly, the fool in us all. At the same time it is necessary to invite, to admit, the fool in each one of us. Not to do so may amount to being the greatest fool of all. Thus the play, exposing the fool in the noble best of us, by exposing cathartically puts us in touch with our true natures and proposes humility and so some wisdom. We, superiors for a time, godlings in the gallery, scoffing at these fools below, see that we, but for the special grace of God, go similarly. And the play, releasing and then trying its lords, by example should do the same to us. But whether we would be foolishly withstanding nature, like the lords in the beginning, or whether we yield to it, like the lords at the end, folly seems (so the songs imply) to be the consequence. Not nature and the natural alone, and not wit or wisdom alone, nor both together can assure man of his fulfilment.

No Stoics Nor No Stocks
The Taming of the Shrew

WHEREVER *The Taming of the Shrew* may fall in the canon of Shakespeare's plays, its relationship to *The Comedy of Errors* is plain. Early and with *The Comedy of Errors* apprenticeship work, it is the one other play we are usually willing to regard as a full-fledged farce. The situations from the start and the plot itself seem to be put on mainly to provoke rowdy laughter. The first scene of the Induction, opening in an 'alehouse on a heath', is a guarantee that we are about to witness a frolic. Much more certainly than the lugubrious opening of *The Comedy of Errors*, told out in creaky narrative verse. The cheerful, drunken gusto of *The Taming of the Shrew*'s first words should also alert us to the fact that, however brief the time between the two plays, Shakespeare has forged ahead. Whether it be the 'fees' the Hostess has requested of Sly for his many drinks, suggested by his initial 'I'll pheeze you, in faith,' or, to her 'A pair of stocks, you rogue!', his answer:

> *Y'are a baggage. The Slys are no rogues. Look in the Chronicles.*
> *We came in with Richard Conqueror. Therefore paucas pallabris, let*
> *the world slide. Sessa!*

we know at once that we are in most promising company, an atmosphere for its spicy assurance not too many moons from our great nights in the Boar's Head in Eastcheap.

That there is stuff, rich household stuff, in Sly, the first real, inimitable character anticipating Bottom and Falstaff, his high-strutting, unbuttoned, full-voiced lingo makes amply clear. A lowly man he may be, but a man he is. The earlier Dromios, quicker, more mischievous, in some ways relate to him. But by their twinhood, as by their purpose in *The Comedy of Errors*, they must be content to share a man between them. Armado, Holofernes, Sir Nathaniel, and Costard in their individual ripeness prepare for Sly even more. Yet though their moments spotlight and encourage them, gulls and geese that most of them are,

44

to preen in their unique complement of feathers, no one of them is so fully exercised, so focused on. Costard assures us of Sir Nathaniel's manhood in its endearing characteristics. But only Sly spreads out his manhood in word and deed before us. So too, the others being incidental factors to their play's plot, his function is more striking. They close *Love's Labour's Lost* with their playlet; Sly and his scenes, no less a playlet and more for being 'real', open and are the incentive to *The Taming of the Shrew*, set its tone and intention as well. Later Shakespearean comics in their very bumblesomeness will now and then save the day; Sly helps to make the play's gay day-to-be possible. Of course he and his scenes are fundamentally a prologue, meant to set off the larger play. Nonetheless, if we allow him and his scenes to linger in the imagination, we find an amazing amount secreted in them, among other things a grand apology for art and theater.

But open or close, he shares with most of these comics a thoroughgoing self-respect. Thus his words above reveal that he knows of the chronicles, of the importance of record and fame and, whatever his adaptation of his hero's name, of his own respectable, certain place in such record. This is gilding, rather than guilt, by association. So too his scrap of Latin, 'few words' indeed, is proof immediate of his credentials. As is the courtly gesture of 'let the world slide. Sessa!' No lord, not even Falstaff, will feel freer of, more superior to, society and its onerous duties; not the one who, also letting the world slide, is about to put Sly through his paces. Obviously Sly is already royal-ripe for the role which will soon be thrust upon him! So too, though his later comments would seem to deny such knowledge, his next words, 'Go by, Jeronimy. Go to thy cold bed, and warm thee', suggest a man expansive in the theater's way. But he may, as with his Latin, have done no more than appropriate these words by thievery or absorb them by contagion. The original, out of the very popular contemporary play *The Spanish Tragedy*, is Hieronimo's talking to himself when the King resents his interruption: 'Hieronimo beware; go by, go by.' Sly, it would seem, is continuing the royal atmosphere he has already established. Then to the Hostess' threat of the 'thirdborough' whom she bustles off to get, Sly with the lofty disdain of Falstaff, scoffing: 'Third, or fourth, or fifth borough, I'll answer him by law. I'll not budge an inch, boy. [In his imagining he apparently already has a page.] Let him come, and kindly', curling up on his bench, falls asleep, ready to be played on like Bottom and Falstaff in their waking scenes. This opening snatch, with the tang of the times malty in Sly's mouth, promises us a breeziness, a strong sweet wind, that the talk of storms and ship-wreck in *The Comedy of Errors* scarcely approaches.

Now a lord enters, fresh from hunting. His—in its own way like Sly's—is a man's voice at once: free, quick, full of authority and the stamp of a distinctive person. After his brisk, capable speeches on his dogs, most appealing in their concreteness, their naming of names, their placing of places, 'at the hedge-corner, in the coldest fault', and the professional argument on the dogs' qualities, a sharp poetry of its kind, as apt for its purpose as the ale-warmed prose of Sly for his, the lord turns to find a perfect prey in Sly. Steeped in himself, yet be-fuddled also, what likelier game. The lords of *Love's Labour's Lost* had their self-stuffed boobies to entertain them and to put on plays, but hardly with the spontaneity of this lord. Not less on the scent than his dogs, at once he proceeds to 'practice' on Sly. Sizing up the situation like a good playmaker and a god in the wings, one of the first of Shake-speare's long, illustrious line of directors, the lord plots out his joke:

> *What think you, if he were conveyed to bed,*
> *Wrapped in sweet clothes, rings put upon his fingers,*
> *A most delicious banquet by his bed,*
> *And brave att.ndants near him when he wakes,*
> *Would not the beggar then forget himself?*

All of us at times dream of ourselves as changelings, with parents patently not our own and with a fortune much below our royal worth: dream of a waking that will enable us to enjoy, via recollecting, the drabness or the nightmare of what we have slept. (Of course, the reverse is harder, the state of the tragedies: waking from a 'dream' of greatness, of nobility, taken for granted, to a state as frail and folly-ridden, as mortal, as all other men's.) In the lord's words we already have another basic difference from *The Comedy of Errors*. The con-fusions there, Antipholus of Syracuse's wonder whether he is not either bewitched or in fact someone else, were fortuitous. Now Shake-speare's art, having already rehearsed something of this in the ladies' dealings with Navarre and his lords, leaps forward in subtlety, excite-ment, relevancy. Though Sly has been stumbled on, what is to happen to him is no accident. The lord is in charge and puts Sly on to see how amusingly Sly will respond. Shakespeare's preoccupation with identity ('Would not the beggar then forget himself?')—his profound awareness of the importance of roles, clothes, place—gathers momentum.

The lord's instructions follow, masterly in their stage directions, in

their adroit handling of physical properties, as deft as will be Petruchio's very specific treatment of Kate. The language is not poetry as
we normally know it in Shakespeare; it is not endlessly expansive in
meaning and power. But it does make clear that, had he cared to,
Shakespeare might very well have taken this straight road, invested
himself in the idiom of the comedy of manners. Surefooted and
effective in its masculinity, his language is redolent of the best domestic,
'real' poetry of, say, Jonson's plays.

> *Carry him gently to my fairest chamber*
> *And hang it round with all my wanton pictures.*
> *Balm his foul head in warm distilléd waters*
> *And burn sweet wood to make the lodging sweet.*
> *Procure me music ready when he wakes,*
> *To make a dulcet and a heavenly sound; . . .*
> *Let one attend him with a silver basin*
> *Full of rose-water and bestrewed with flowers;*
> *Another bear the ewer, the third a diaper,*
> *And say, 'Will't please your lordship cool your hands?'*

The lord, already the creative character at work, has such attractive
powers and powers of expression as 'Procure me music' and music
'ready' when Sly wakes. A lord, with Sly's sense of himself, free at
least for a time to let the world go by in play, he plays with a small
part of it. Out of art, that of the theater, by casting Sly in another role
and thereby uprooting him from his customary setting (what Petruchio
will be at pains to do with Kate), the lord means, at least for a while,
the duration of the play, to 'transform' Sly, to convince him that till
now he has been demeaningly mad.

At the same time the lord, borrowing Sly's last word before sleep,
requests:

> *. . . do it kindly, gentle sirs.*
> *It will be pastime passing excellent*
> *If it be husbanded with modesty.*

He does not mean, in the way of later plays, to try the whole strength
of his butt, to use cruelty on him. This is, farce and all, a comedy, a
pastime. In fact, for a time Sly's status will be much enhanced. The
cruelty may be in the waking, in restoring him to his previous 'true'
state. But this restoring the play will spare, most kindly, him and us.
In comedy, for the most part, such jostling is, except for self-insulated

creatures like Shylock and Malvolio and consummations like Armado, Holofernes, and Bottom, freeing. And since it is comedy the jostling is tempered at the crucial moment. Thus the young lords in *Love's Labour's Lost*, put on by their ladies, or the young lovers in *A Midsummer Night's Dream*, paced bewilderingly by Puck, the moon and its enchanted wood, and most of all, by their own new, antic feelings, are freed and finally reassured.

The whole of *The Taming of the Shrew*, I would say, notwithstanding its shows of violence on Petruchio's part, is fundamentally conducted with 'kindness'. Of course tactics with kindness in view may radically differ. Thus if the rough, low tinker is briefly cast on balmy days, the stiff, arrogant Kate will be thrown briefly into an alien, stormy world. Medicine is usually a bitter pill dipped in honey. For Kate it must be tart, if not bitter, on the surface and to begin with, but sweet and wholesome inside. In fact it will turn out sweet because it is bitter. In any case a cure, a lasting benefit to the patient, is intended; as it is not, one may say, for Sly. Kate is to be jostled out of her life-long 'disguise' to her real self whereas Sly is unceremoniously–that is, with great, immediate ceremony!–bustled out of his real role into a fake one. Like Kate, but much more wryly in the midst of the comedy he makes possible, he shows how much our loved, highly-touted selves depend on their environment, clothes, and what people think of us. He, sensibly it is true and quickly, accepts what Antipholus of Syracuse is mostly baffled by. Both, however, it should be remarked, like good, native Englishmen, once a likely woman is presented to them, handsomely rise to the occasion and embrace their good fortune.

So the magic of the play begins, the magic of free playfulness, of details crackling out of life intimately observed, joyously entered into and released. Now, most opportunely, an accident occurs: a company of players arrives. At once the lord recruits them to serve his jest; but again, knowing too well the excess common to players (see Hamlet), he urges modesty and care: 'for I tell you, sirs,/If you should smile, he grows impatient.' The lord then instructs a servant on what demeanor he expects of his page, who is to disguise himself as Sly's lady; whatever its exaggerations, here we have the code of a noble lady that Petruchio will teach and exact of Kate. In fact, we already hear words, 'duty' and the rest, that the educated Kate will repeat in her long speech at the end.

At once, with Scene II, the gulling of Sly is put on. His first natural waking cry is 'For God's sake, a pot of small ale.' Overwhelmed by courtesies, Sly rises to his drunken dignity and rightful person, the name he is:

I am Christophero Sly. Call not me 'honour' nor 'lordship.' I ne'er drank sack in my life; and if you give me any conserves, give me conserves of beef. Ne'er ask me what raiment I'll wear, for I have no more doublets than backs, no more stockings than legs, nor no more shoes than feet;

and then, his vigor kindling to the truth of his life,

nay, sometime more feet than shoes, or such shoes at my toes look through the overleather.

His ground-sense of experience, of a body heartily lived in, comes to the fore as proof positive of his identity. To the insistence that he is 'infuséd with so foul a spirit', he wisely says, 'What, would you make me mad?' And he seems as confused by the fear of madness as anyone in *The Comedy of Errors*. Nor, no longer a doughty 'I am', he questions, 'Am not I Christopher Sly' (we recall Dromio's bewildered 'I am not Dromio.') and promptly, proudly reels off his credentials (we recognized at the outset that, tinker though he may be, he has as much pride of birth as the next man):

. . . old Sly's son of Burton-heath, by birth a pedlar, by education a card-maker, by transmutation a bear-herd, and now by present profession a tinker? Ask Marian Hacket, the fat ale-wife of Wincot, if she know me not. If she say I am not fourteen pence on the score for sheer ale, score me up for the lyingest knave in Christendom. What! I am not bestraught.

What better establishes a man than his debts—and his debtors—for the appetite he most delights in. At this point the servants and the lord really go to work on Sly with seductive appeals to his senses. The lord says:

O noble lord, bethink thee of thy birth,
Call home thy ancient thoughts from banishment,
And banish hence these abject lowly dreams.
Look how thy servants do attend on thee,
Each in his office ready at thy beck.
Wilt thou have music? Hark! Apollo plays,
                                          [Music.]
And twenty cagéd nightingales do sing.
Or wilt thou sleep? We'll have thee to a couch

Softer and sweeter than the lustful bed
On purpose trimmed up for Semiramis.
Say thou wilt walk; we will bestrew the ground.
Or wilt thou ride? Thy horses shall be trapped,
their harness studded all with gold and pearl.
Dost thou love hawking? Thou hast hawks will soar
Above the morning lark. Or wilt thou hunt?
Thy hounds shall make the welkin answer them,
And fetch shrill echoes from the hollow earth.

Once more we and Sly are favored with well-furnished, massy, Jonsonian lines, from 'On purpose trimmed up for Semiramis' (Sly surely has no notion who Semiramis is, but in this context, with the richness of sounds her name releases, he must respond to its suggestiveness) to the last two verses that continue the hounds and their baying from the first scene. These hounds, perhaps because the description of them is a prospect rather than something seen and heard, begin to sound more like what the hounds in *A Midsummer Night's Dream* will be able 'singingly' to do.

The servants, inspired by these words, imaginatively reproductive of the real world, plying Sly with his next 'lesson', chime in with brilliant descriptions of paintings, the 'wanton pictures' the lord earlier bade them hang round 'my fairest chamber'. This is poetry, but of the hard-surfaced, enameled variety: pastoral settings, but heightened and transformed through human art and, beyond that, by the presence in them of gods and goddesses as well as mythical human beings. Pictures lifted and touched up, one might say, from the poetic world of *Venus and Adonis* as from Ovid. More, since they are paintings imaginative in themselves and a good deal more so by being translated into words, they move past the Jonsonian and the splendidly denotative to a suggestiveness that is the felicitous beginning of one major aspect of Shakespeare's poetry at its best. Already here the mere reports of paintings come breathingly alive. We see

Adonis painted by a running brook,
And Cytherea all in sedges hid,
Which seem to move and wanton with her breath,
Even as the waving sedges play with wind.

For their artfulness these lines, deceptively simple, are leagues away from the pictures closing *Love's Labour's Lost*. Cytherea is 'seen', all the more tantalizingly since 'all hid' by the sedges which, excited, are moved by her as they hide her, while at the same time they, waving, moved by it similarly, play with the wind. The combination or blending of the natural and the sophisticated (thus the carefully placed 'seem'), their interplay, so like the interplay of the natural and the artfully godly in the picture, is most skilful.

Or:

> *We'll show thee Io as she was a maid,*
> *And how she was beguiléd and surprised,*
> *As lively painted as the deed was done.*

This is indeed a motion—not to say a moving—picture, a sequence: first Io the maid and then the episode involving the loss of her maidenhood. Yet the 'And' opening the second verse suggests the simultaneity of art, like that of the great grandfather of such pictorial accomplishment, Homer's version of Achilles' shield. 'Lively', past its meaning of realistically, seems to imply that the passion in artistic work, whatever its own terms, should approach the passion, the seizure, the inspiration of a god, of living itself.

> *Or Daphne roaming through a thorny wood,*
> *Scratching her legs that one shall swear she bleeds,*
> *And at that sight shall sad Apollo weep,*
> *So workmanly the blood and tears are drawn.*

Pun that 'drawn' suggests, these verses via their pictures, drawing on Ovid and emphasizing the photographically and lovingly dwelt-on real, recommend a concentration in art commensurate with the concentration in life. These pictures represent moments of transformation, Ovidian moments, meant to speed the transforming of Sly in his particular moment. At the same time they are, as the participles propose, *happening*, going on (and on) before our eyes. The participle quality of 'painting' is here being underscored. Even Apollo, normally the god of light, in very ruthless pursuit is moved to tears (for his light is brought to bear upon 'that sight' which he has caused)—the future tense, 'shall . . . weep', tells us that, not only shall he (must he) weep when he sees that sight but over and over again since he, looking, like us is caught in it—in the picture of which he is a painted part. This is art moved by the realism of its art. Thus Sly—and Kate after—for the vividness, if simulated, of his surroundings, a setting 'false' or made up no less than a painting's, will soon be convinced of their actuality.

Accordingly, like the creatures of *Metamorphoses* above, Sly will for a time be 'transformed', but not through grief and suffering, through play; similarly we, the audience, are for a time transported out of our normal selves and absorbed into the play, its characters, given new life and more of our own by being afforded other lives. This is the beginning of Shakespeare's awareness–increasingly his work will draw on it–of the magical, transforming, redemptive power of art and music. After an exhibition of such convincing art there is nothing for it but to assume that Sly has been 'changed'. The lord says, 'Thou art a lord and nothing but a lord,' the final, overwhelming proof being: 'Thou hast a lady far more beautiful/Than any woman in this waning age.' Then the lord and his servant promptly move in on Sly by making Apollo's weeping personal to Sly, or by putting Sly in a sad, most verisimilitudinous 'picture' of his own: his most beautiful lady weeping over him for his pathetic, 'changed' condition.

Sly is indeed 'moved', from 'I am' and the next 'Am I not?' to (also appropriately moved now–for the 'change' has truly taken–from speaking tinker prose to speaking poetry, blank verse, a basic assumption of nobility)

> *Am I a lord? And have I such a lady?*
> *Or do I dream? Or have I dreamed till now?*

The fundamental confusion is on him. But at once he goes to work testing his condition in the only Slyesque, reliable way he knows: he appeals to the senses he has always staunchly lived by:

> *I do not sleep. I see, I hear, I speak.*
> *I smell sweet savours, and I feel soft things.*

They are, especially as they involve abandoning a hard, lowly life for a soft, lofty one, confirmation enough for him. His conversion is complete.

> *Upon my life I am a lord indeed,*
> *And not a tinker nor Christophero Sly.*

In all his amiable adaptability, knowing the folly of time wasted, he instantly commands, 'Well, bring our lady hither to our sight', the royal plural pronoun resting on him as lightly as his previous small Latin, his sweet new clothes and the appurtenances of the lordly bedchamber. In grand style, if recalling his first 'real' words, he concludes: And once again, a pot o' the smallest ale.' At the same time it is a far cry from that first waking plea, from his customary *'small* ale' to the superlative, refined, so noble 'small*est* ale' or what he in his new role has come to. The second servant, flushed no doubt by their success with Sly, intrepidly raises the seven years Sly was supposedly under his loathsome spell to 'These fifteen years you have been in a dream,/ Or when you waked, so waked as if you slept.' Sly, with full talent for the amazing, but with an oath most fitting as he remembers the delicacy of his present role, retorts: 'These fifteen years! By my fay, a goodly nap.'

Sly's wife, a boy playing a page playing a lady, enters. It is time for action and its final capping. Expressing his will over her, Sly whispers to the lord, 'What must I call her?' To the lord's 'Madame', Sly, unchangeably Sly, asks, 'Al'ce madam, or Joan madam?', a translating of the word to his world as 'Richard Conqueror' was. The lord assures Sly it is 'Madam and nothing else. So lords call ladies,' and Sly's genius for learning responds with 'Madam wife'. At his lady page's protestations over his fifteen-year nap, 'Ay, and the time seems thirty unto me,/Being all this time abandoned from your bed.' Sly nobly, gravely (and most sensibly, one should note) rises to the situation: ''Tis much. Servants, leave me and her alone./Madam, undress you, and come now to bed.'

Reluctantly persuaded – so reluctantly apparently that he slips back, the strain being what it is, into prose – to postpone such exertions lest his malady recur, he hears of the players 'come to play a pleasant comedy'. Theater as therapy is urged (though this play does stress the yoking of madness, or at least the madcap, and merriment):

> For so your doctors hold it very meet,
> Seeing too much sadness hath congealed your blood,
> And melancholy is the nurse of frenzy;
> Therefore they thought it good you hear a play
> And frame your mind to mirth and merriment,
> Which bars a thousand harms and lengthens life.

Sly agrees, 'Marry, I will, let them play it.' But he now betrays his ignorance of such entertainment and knows only one of its primitive sources, 'Is not a comonty a Christmas gambold or a tumbling-trick?' To the pages, 'No, my good lord, it is more pleasing stuff', Sly, perhaps still aroused, still hopeful, exclaims: 'What, household stuff?' Informed that it is 'a kind of history' instead, mere story, he submits: 'Well, we'll see't. Come, madam wife, sit by my side and let the world slip.

We shall ne'er be younger.' This last, with fifteen years already squandered, most wistfully. But his attitude, whatever his recent transformation, has not changed much from his first 'let the world slide'.

The play proper at last begins. Framed as it is, it amounts to a kind of moving 'picture' to join to the earlier, purely verbal ones, and is the lesson to cap all the others. At once we learn that the young Lucentio, as he reminds his able servant, Tranio, is on the eager scent of learning, a hunter too. Thus he has come to 'fruitful Lombardy,/The pleasant garden of great Italy', already something of an enchanted and enchanting wood, particularly 'fair Padua, nursery of arts', to find what he wants:

> *Virtue and that part of philosophy*
> *Will I apply that treats of happiness*
> *By virtue specially to be achieved.*

Passionately he feels this. He dreams it, his next words show, a great adventure, a drinking with his whole body and being. One thinks of Antipholus of Syracuse with his weariness after having been in the deep. Only a lovely young woman and love can renew his capacity, his enthusiasm, for the sea of experience. For Lucentio the process will be reversed. He says,

> *. . . for I have Pisa left*
> *And am to Padua come, as he that leaves*
> *A shallow plash to plunge him in the deep,*
> *And with satiety seeks to quench his thirst.*

Tranio, a Jonson-like servant, shrewder than his master, applauds this desire; nonetheless, he cautions his master against excessive austerity, against the mistake Navarre and his lords make. Let us not be philosopher-kings too soon or, rather, let us be philosophers as we are kings.

> *Let's be no stoics nor no stocks, I pray,*
> *Or so devote to Aristotle's checks*
> *As Ovid be an outcast quite abjured.*

This is a farce; but for the experience of *Love's Labour's Lost* behind it it has, with its involvement in art—pictures, theater, learning, books—complicated and enriched itself far beyond *The Comedy of Errors*. Like Berowne before, Tranio uses a book, Ovid, to rebuke excessive bookishness. Or, rather, Aristotle, yes, but Ovid also, and both applied: learning by doing. As suggested by the earlier paintings, the use of art *in* living is being urged as an intrinsic part of learning. Experience, the greatest teacher, is being stressed. Experience in the way that it has been put to work on Sly—yet there it is play (art), a charming con-fusion—and in the way that it will be practiced on Kate by Petruchio. Love of books is one thing, and a good thing; but at least as good and important as a book is the book of living itself, a lesson several of Shakespeare's young gallants must learn at the very moment they turn ascetically to study. Tranio prescribes:

> *Balk logic with acquaintance that you have,*
> *And practise rhetoric in your common talk;*
> *Music and poesy use to quicken you.*

(So they have been used, and most effectively, on Sly.)

> *The mathematics and the metaphysics*
> *Fall to them as you find your stomach serves you.*

And he concludes in lines that might have provided any good pro-gressive college with its motto:

> *No profit grows where is no pleasure ta'en.*
> *In brief, sir, study what you most affect.*

Berowne, we recall, preached a similarly optimistic, natural course of study.

This first lesson from the prudent Tranio, for the Paduans who now appear and unwittingly perform a little 'show' for the visitors, immedi-ately 'takes.' The show consists mainly of a putting on of the two sisters in their basic difference. Except for Kate, since this which we are watching is a 'play,' Lucentio, Bianca, and the rest are not much more, not much more differentiated, than the characters in *The Comedy of Errors*; nor, like those, for the purpose of such comedy need they be. As Lucentio hears of and then hears the headstrong Kate, bent at once on establishing her distemper, her sister Bianca by contrast instantly wins him:

> *But in the other's silence do I see*
> *Maid's mild behaviour and sobriety.*
> *Peace Tranio!*

He bids silence that, for three stresses of his unfinished verse at least, he may uninterruptedly, raptly admire. Tranio, knowing and pleased with what spell is occurring, says: 'Well said, master. Mum! and gaze your fill.' For all the remonstrances of Bianca's suitors, father Baptista will not let her marry till her older sister is taken off his hands. Alone, the suitors, complaining, impress us with Kate's shrewery. She must be so sung up, so made a champion of, for the oncoming battle royal. Tranio, when the suitors leave, observing his master's state, cleverly midwives his feeling:

> *I pray, sir, tell me, is it possible*
> *That love should of a sudden take such hold?*

Lucentio, eager to be borne out, admits:

> *O Tranio, till I found it to be true,*
> *I never thought it possible or likely.*
> *But see, while idly I stood looking on,*
> *I found the effect of love in idleness, . . .*

('Love in idleness' we shall soon see materialized into a most potent flower in *A Midsummer Night's Dream*.) So plays, pictures, merely feasting the eyes or 'experiencing' can move and overwhelm us. Lucentio must have Bianca. Accordingly, though he will never find a moment during the play for the studies he first ardently desired, he is already well enrolled in love's college, under the tutelage of Professor Cupid. Padua was indeed the right place for him to come to. And soon, again in the best interests of progressive education, in his disguise as schoolmaster, by undertaking 'the teaching of the maid', by giving her private conferences, he will learn what great efficacy books do have when plied in life itself. Especially when the study is one that the student most affects. Playing a part is also part of learning (and living); before he can even establish himself as he is, Lucentio must disguise himself to gain the end he most desires, must play a schoolmaster in Padua. Thus a play within the play within the play begins.

As they leave we abruptly return to Sly and 'reality'. The first servant says, 'My lord, you nod; you do not mind the play.' Sly tries to equal the occasion: 'Yes, by Saint Anne, do I. A good matter, surely;' but the boredom he cannot deny breaks out, 'Comes there any more of it?' To the page's 'My lord, 'tis but begun', even as Sly pretends, ''Tis a very excellent piece of work, madame lady', the truth of his feelings erupts, 'Would 'twere done!' And once Scene II begins, Sly no doubt does fall asleep and is out of the play as he is out of character. He has played his part, done what he could for us, so he is over; with his intelligence or lack of it this play is *not* for him. Also, he and his scenes are swept away, absorbed by the always more 'real' bustle of the major play.

Yet, as though in self-criticism and in fear that all the audience may follow Sly's example, Shakespeare, taking advantage of the overheated Italian tone and climate of his play, resorts to the biggest, noisiest character in his bag: he has Petruchio leap on the stage with a resounding knock, knock, rapping us all soundly awake. After such business, in its choplogic slapstick like *The Comedy of Errors* but also apt in establishing at once Petruchio's fiery spirit, Hortensio, his friend, greeting him, asks, 'And tell me now, sweet friend, what happy gale/Blows you to Padua here from old Verona?' The lustiness we have already witnessed in Sly and the lord culminates in Petruchio with his

> *Such wind as scatters young men through the world,*
> *To seek their fortunes farther than at home,*
> *Where small experience grows.*

Like Lucentio and many other Shakespearean young bloods, Petruchio is of the adventurousness of his time, also a hunter of experience and, more openly than some, of fortune. Fresh apparently from the wars as the lord was from hunting, like him Petruchio is after further 'entertainment', a likely prey in the shape of a wife. (Much later he will be teased with the inevitable pun: ''Tis thought your deer does hold you at bay.') Petruchio puts it bluntly enough:

> *And I have thrust myself into this maze,*
> *Haply to wive and thrive as best I may.*
> *Crowns in my purse I have, and goods at home,*
> *And so am come abroad to see the world.*

At the same time we see that his search, by reason of his pursed crowns and his freeing goods at home, is not a desperate one; on the contrary. One of enthusiasm (like Lucentio's), how different it is from the search, and the mood attendant on that search, of Aegeon and his son. This Elizabethan vigor alone gives the play an exuberance, a convincingness, seldom attained in *The Comedy of Errors* and keeps the play going, fairly common subplot and all, at a great, gusty pace.

Hearing of the shrewish Kate, rich and much available, Petruchio is instantly for her and in his own extravagant style. He makes no bones about his wanting wealth:

> *. . . if thou know*
> *One rich enough to be Petruchio's wife,*
> *As wealth is burden of my wooing dance,*
> *Be she as foul as was Florentius' love,*

(an ugly old woman who, it is pertinent to remember here, once
Florentius marries her, turns into a fair lady)

> *As old as Sibyl, and as curst and shrewd*
> *As Socrates' Xanthippe, or a worse,*
> *She moves me not, or not removes, at least,*
> *Affection's edge in me, were she as rough*
> *As are the swelling Adriatic seas.*

And when he learns of Kate's gold he says,

> *Tell me her father's name and 'tis enough,*
> *For I will board her, though she chide as loud*
> *As thunder when the clouds in autumn crack.*

We are ready for the stormy fray. This is love *before* sight! For the
impetuous Petruchio the mere fore-shadow of Kate, her impressive
reputation, is more than enough (in addition of course to her wealth).

Sure of his own powers, he knows she is a mettlesome mate perfect
for him. When he is asked, 'But will you woo this wild-cat?' Petruchio
replies:

> *Why came I hither but to that intent?*
> *Think you a little din can daunt mine ears?*
> *Have I not in my time heard lions roar?*
> *Have I not heard the sea, puffed up with winds,*
> *Rage like an angry boar chaféd with sweat?*
> *Have I not heard great ordinance in the field,*
> *And heaven's artillery thunder in the skies?*
> *Have I not in a pitchéd battle heard*
> *Loud 'larums, neighing steeds, and trumpets' clang?*
> *And do you tell me of a woman's tongue,*
> *That gives not half so great a blow to hear*
> *As will a chestnut in a farmer's fire?*
> *Tush, tush! Fear boys with bugs.*

Swaggerer that he may seem, a kind of roaring boy (he translates all
experience into terms of sound, noise), Petruchio will soon amply
prove himself. Having been to the wars and at sea, he finds it time now
to try the most civil of conflicts, the merry war of love, the invigorating
tussle it deserves to be only when it engages doughty, happily matched
opponents of the type presented here. The above speech is a delight in
its liveliness, and in the way this liveliness sweeps on from 'a little din'

through the beasts at their most aroused, the more tempestuous sea, to man at his most brawling, then quickly (and deliberately absurdly by contrast) to 'a woman's tongue', much less fearful than a chestnut crackling in a farmer's fire, actually a cosy domestic moment (see the songs ending *Love's Labour's Lost*) like that of tales told at the hearth about hobgoblins able to scare little boys. But such is the backdrop against which this play, for all its domesticity, is cast and best seen, and much more effectively than the described storm and shipwreck of *The Comedy of Errors*. Because of his much greater experience, Petruchio's words, as they prepare us for his success, help also to justify the prudence Kate will come to in the end.

Act II, Scene I, echoing Petruchio's treatment of his servant Grumio, though there in fun and here in seriousness, shows Kate bullying her sister and shows how much, therefore, Kate needs and deserves the treatment Petruchio will soon be meting out to her. She says, rightly singling out the quality that first delighted Lucentio as it does all Bianca's suitors, 'Her silence flouts me, and I'll be revenged.' Kate, we shall discover, has more reasons than we know to resent that silence and its resolute contents. She recognizes Bianca's success and the source of that success, but knowing it makes her, in envy and rancor, rail and be shrewish the more. And surely some touch of pity is drawn from us, as with Adriana in *The Comedy of Errors*, when Kate says to her father:

> She is your treasure, she must have a husband;
> I must dance barefoot on her wedding day
> And for your love to her lead apes in hell.

Then, though roughly, piteously:

> Talk not to me. I will go sit and weep
> Till I can find occasion of revenge.

By the play's end Petruchio will provide her with such occasion, if not for revenge then at least for self-justification and the exposure of Bianca; that her silence and modesty are not entirely what they seem and that the loud ones are not necessarily worse than the quiet ones.

At this low point Petruchio appropriately appears, asking for Kate the 'fair and virtuous'. Taking the tack he will pursue with her, loud laudation of 'her beauty and her wit,/Her affability and bashful modesty', he pushes on—for he accurately says of himself, 'I would fain be doing'—to the wooing. Baptista pointing out the obstacles,

Petruchio reassures him and describes the potent homeopathic treatment he means to submit Kate to:

Why, that is nothing; for I tell you, father,
I am as peremptory as she proud-minded;
And where two raging fires meet together,
They do consume the thing that feeds their fury.
Though little fire grows great with little wind,
Yet extreme gusts will blow out fire and all:
So I to her and so she yields to me,
For I am rough and woo not like a babe.

Yet even as he assumes victory, an impressive mark of Kate's prowess appears in Hortensio, his head broken by the lute she crowned him with. Petruchio, hearing of Kate's impatience and tart outburst, admiring her as one of his ilk, desires her the more and cries out:

Now, by the world, it is a lusty wench.
I love her ten times more than e'er I did.
O, how I long to have some chat with her!

Alone while he awaits Kate (judiciously enough he has her sent for rather than go to her), he tells us what course of opposites he means to take with her to disarm her and to shake her loose from her encrusted, cursed condition. He knows what a love-lorn woman and, most of all, a shrew yearns to hear, needs to if she is to 'save face' and so be able to shed her shrewishness. These are the only 'charms' potent against the spells that have bewitched her into a scold.

. . . I will attend her here,
And woo her with some spirit when she comes.
Say that she rail; why then I'll tell her plain
She sings as sweetly as a nightingale.
Say that she frown; I'll say she looks as clear
As morning roses newly washed with dew.

(Nightingales and roses, such able devices were used successfully on Sly.)

On her entering he attacks, with an overwhelming speech of praise, no courtly lover better, cunningly rich in reiteration of her name, that part of us we all love best to hear, abruptly ending in his asking her to be his wife. The swift, biting exchange that follows proves how splendidly matched they are. Of a superb, improvisatory-seeming sprightliness, they know little limit to the ranging and the high-spirited raging of their tongues. Both master word-catchers and -snatchers, they are neck and neck in speeding wherever their words and puns may take them. But again Petruchio showers her with flattery, something she has never had and has been bitterly long waiting for. For a moment even she is beguiled enough to ask, 'Where did you study all this good speech?' Once more, however, his courtly lover talk is peppered with badinage and bawdiness, relishsome in its tangy utterance. Then he tells her firmly enough:

> *And, will you, nill you, I will marry you.*
> *Now, Kate, I am a husband for your turn.*
> *For by this light, whereby I see thy beauty,*

(as in his flattery earlier he shows his understanding by appealing to her on the side on which she feels most neglected and so is most vulnerable to, her beauty)

> *Thy beauty, that doth make me like thee well,*

(he too, it is clear, is 'forced' to love)

> *Thou must be married to no man but me;*
> *For I am he am born to tame you Kate,*
> *And bring you from a wild Kate to a Kate*
> *Conformable as other household Kates.*

He will in fact, by insisting on the delicacy she fundamentally is and longs to be recognized as, produce or at least release that delicacy. The power of words, of saying so, their ability to effect basic changes, will have few happier examples. With this match arranged, the suitors can press on to their prize, Bianca.

Act III, Scene I, shows learning applied. Gremio, employing Lucentio to win Bianca for him, had urged Lucentio to use only 'All books of love'. Sensibly using Ovid, his *Epistolae*, to instruct Bianca and to achieve the goal he desires, Lucentio courts her by way of Latin, a practice bound to make his student extremely interested in learning the lesson: when did language, especially a foreign, long dead one, ever translate more movingly, winningly! She proves how well she can learn by translating the passage back to him with the caution befitting a student, but with the promise and independence right in a gifted, earnest learner. The same device tried on her by Hortensio via music does not affect her nearly so much; as Tranio said, 'No profit grows

where is no pleasure ta'en.' Affecting (liking) makes us most available
to learning.

The next scene is wedding time, but with no Petruchio in sight. A
servant tells us of his coming and, to whet our appetites, of his get-up,
this in wonderfully local details, the 'russet yeas and honest kersey
noes' Berowne promised to do his wooing in; what in truth, though
with delicate asides for her, Petruchio is doing with Kate. All the daily,
earthy objects in the play not only ensure the well-ballasted atmosphere
of comedy, but of reality—a kind of hodgepodge collage; art with real
things in it, enjoyed as they are left in their own skin: jerkins, old
breeches, boots that have been candle-cases, an old mothy saddle,
stirrups, cruppers, pack-thread, beef, pots, chestnuts, mustard, all
needed to furnish and feed the play's vitality.

Petruchio finally arrives, and to Baptista's remonstrances at his
appearance, Petruchio, even as he is here 'disguised', and in russet and
kersey and 'playing', speaks up for plainness and the truth:

> *To me she's married, not unto my clothes.*
> *Could I repair what she will wear in me,*
> *As I can change these poor accoutrements,*
> *'Twere well for Kate and better for myself.*

Yet by such 'poor accoutrements' he does mean to 'repair' what he will
wear in her. Tranio, anticipating the much improved 'Though this be
madness, yet there is method in 't', says, 'He hath some meaning in his
mad attire.' Off they go to the wedding which, through Petruchio's
roughhouse conduct in church, is better told than seen, and is again a
wanton picture 'described'. Putting on a circus in a church may be
highly amusing, but in more ways than one it is dangerous. In Gremio's
words,

> *Tut, she's a lamb, a dove, a fool to him!*
> *I'll tell you, Sir Lucentio: when the priest*
> *Should ask if Katherine should be his wife,*
> *'Ay, by gogs-wouns,' quoth he, and swore so loud,*
> *That, all amazed, the priest let fall the book,*
> *And as he stooped again to take it up,*
> *This mad-brained bridegroom took him such a cuff,*
> *That down fell priest and book, and book and priest,*
> *'Now take them up,' quoth he, 'if any list.'*

And what did Kate in all this?

Trembled and shook; for why he stamped and swore,
As if the vicar meant to cozen him.
But after many ceremonies done,
He calls for wine. 'A health!' quoth he, as if
He had been aboard, carousing to his mates
After a storm, quaffed off the muscadel,
And threw the sops all in the sexton's face,
Having no other reason
But that his beard grew thin and hungerly
And seemed to ask him sops as he was drinking.
This done, he took the bride about the neck
And kissed her lips with such a clamorous smack
That at the parting all the church did echo.
And I, seeing this, came thence for very shame;
And after me, I know, the rout is coming.

A merry rout it is. Not satisfied or finished yet, Petruchio, acting more the groom with a wild filly than a bridegroom, allows Kate no loitering, no moment's peace to recover from the wedding, but plucks her, wisely, out of her accustomed environment (like Sly), and makes her entirely dependent on him. Her dependence he declares in his baldest speech:

Carouse full measure to her maidenhead,
Be mad and merry, or go hang yourselves.
But for my bonny Kate, she must with me.
Nay, look not big, nor stamp, nor stare, nor fret;
I will be master of what is mine own.
She is my goods, my chattels; she is my house,
My household stuff [see Sly's meaning], my field, my barn,
My horse, my ox, my ass, my anything.

Whatever she is, she is certainly much to him if not—for all these commonplace terms—all. Promptly then he takes the antic pose of the courtly lover and knight, her heroic defender; he draws his sword to shield her.

Fear not, sweet wench, they shall not touch thee, Kate.
I'll buckler thee against a million.

Off they go, these 'quiet ones'. Grumio says, 'Went they not quickly, I should die with laughing.'

And we speed ahead to Petruchio's country house to greet them.

Grumio, waiting for us, regales us most vividly with what he's been through on the trip home. He is cold, beaten, and worn. Again, the more outrageous part of the tale is told rather than seen. Grumio is at his savory best in the speech in which he, refusing to tell, teases Curtis by telling all:

> *Tell thou the tale. But hadst thou not crossed me, thou shouldst have heard how her horse fell and she under her horse; thou shouldst have heard in how miry a place, how she was bemoiled, how he left her with the horse upon her, how he beat me because her horse stumbled, how she waded through the dirt to pluck him off me, how he swore, how she prayed, that never prayed before, how I cried, how the horses ran away, how her bridle was burst, how I lost my crupper, with many things of worthy memory, which now shall die in oblivion and thou return unexperienced to thy grave.*

'Worthy memories' and their recording, Sly also knew, make our lives; 'experience' is what a man must have to say he has lived. In this rousing speech the praises of experience, however rough and trying it may have been, in the after-savoring at least, are once more being sung. And again, for all the turmoil reported, in the way that it is reported a good inland English winter scene this is, cosy as *Love's Labour's Lost's* concluding winter song, one to warm ourselves at.

Petruchio and Kate enter, with Petruchio in a perfect uproar. All bearishness, for his treatment of Kate is intensifying, he lashes out on all sides, belaboring his servants with words, epithets, blows. While he strikes out however, he interjects with sweetest words: 'Sit down, Kate, and welcome', and 'Nay, good sweet Kate, be merry.' Finally, even she expostulates with him, 'Patience, I pray you; 'twas a fault unwilling.' But on he goes, letting her neither eat—the meat is burnt, not good enough for her and bad for both of them 'Since, of ourselves, ourselves are choleric. . . .'—nor sleep. In Peter's words, 'He kills her in her own humour.' And according to Curtis:

> *In her chamber, making a sermon of continency to her;*
> *And rails, and swears, and rates, that she, poor soul,*
> *Knows not which way to stand, to look, to speak,*
> *And sits as one new-risen from a dream.*

She is not far from the condition of the duped Sly. Petruchio's scene-ending soliloquy confirms the above:

My falcon now is sharp and passing empty,
And till she stoop, she must not be full-gorged,
For then she never looks upon her lure.

As in the hunt, sometimes in the affairs of men and women methods of 'training' must be severe, not to say seemingly ruthless: too much is at stake for faltering softness or sentimentality. Summarizing his bed-and-board set-to with her, he says:

Ay, and amid this hurly I intend
That all is done in reverent care of her;
And in conclusion she shall watch all night.
And if she chance to nod, I'll rail and brawl,
And with the clamour keep her still awake.
This is a way to kill a wife with kindness,
And thus I'll curb her mad and headstrong humour.

Not that he is altogether in love with his stringent measures. Thus he concludes,

He that knows better how to tame a shrew,
Now let him speak. 'Tis charity to show.

In Scene II, eavesdropping with Tranio and Hortensio, we find Lucentio and Bianca well along in love; their lessons are perfectly learned since they have, opportunely and practically as Tranio first urged, Ovid's 'Art to Love' in hand. Hortensio in disgust at 'this proud disdainful haggard', a phrase and thought he arrives at, it is true, in part because wily Tranio has just cued him with 'Fie on her! See how beastly she doth court him!' (Petruchio, we recall, a scene ago had called Kate 'my haggard'), trots off to marry a wealthy widow who has long loved him: 'Kindness in women, not their beauteous looks,/ Shall win my love; . . .' A side of Bianca, till now not suspected by her suitors, has begun to show. In any case, the day is won by Lucentio, who needs only to perform the last trick, the spiriting up of a 'father' to approve the dowry and the wedding. Patly an old pedant appears and, for a lie (borrowed it would seem from *The Comedy of Errors*' opening), is easily persuaded to don the role.

With the next scene Kate's education is completed. Petruchio so far succeeds as to get Kate to 'thank him'. Then in perhaps his gayest, most extravagant moment he, having in practice as in words made much of the folly of clothes, the little truth that is in them, has a field day with the tailor. Such a full-blown moment for its bringing to a climax one of the play's major themes, this matter of clothes and their importance—whether it be the royal robes of Sly or Petruchio in his outlandish marriage-rig or this present occasion focusing on Kate and her vanity—is justified. Especially since it is also the climax of Kate's education. At the same time Petruchio's invective, his effervescent name-calling, controlled in all its seeming impulsiveness, achieves something of the tang of genius. Of the offered cap Petruchio says,

> *Why, this was moulded on a porringer,*
> *A velvet dish. Fie, fie! 'tis lewd and filthy.*
> *Why, 'tis a cockle or a walnut-shell,*
> *A knack, a toy, a trick, a baby's cap.*
> *Away with it! Come, let me have a bigger.*

Kate flares up, 'I'll have no bigger. This doth fit the time,/And gentle-women wear such caps as these.' A happy opening for Petruchio, he has her: 'When you are gentle, you shall have one too,/And not till then.' The gown is similarly disposed of. Finally, the tailor himself needles out of Petruchio his rarest performance, a royal dressing-down:

> *O monstrous arrogance! Thou liest, thou thread, thou thimble,*
> *Thou yard, three-quarters, half-yard, quarter, nail!*
> *Thou flea, thou nit, thou winter-cricket thou!*
> *Braved in mine own house with a skein of thread?*
> *Away, thou rag, thou quantity, thou remnant,*
> *Or I shall so be-mete thee with thy yard,*
> *As thou shalt think on prating whilst thou livest!*

It is somehow right that Petruchio's extravagance should find its most felicitously outrageous limits in belittling (in its emphasis by opposites a little like Sly's lofty 'pot o' the smallest ale') and be cosy and homely when it is most belittling with its '*winter*-cricket' as though being a summer-cricket were not little enough! In an aside Petruchio sees to it of course that the tailor is paid and used 'kindly'. Once more he praises ‚the real thing':

> *Well, come, my Kate; we will unto your father's*
> *Even in these honest mean habiliments.*
> *Our purses shall be proud, our garments poor;*
> *For 'tis the mind that makes the body rich.*
> *And as the sun breaks through the darkest clouds,*
> *So honour peereth in the meanest habit.*

> *What, is the jay more precious than the lark,*
> *Because his feathers are more beautiful?*
> *Or is the adder better than the eel,*
> *Because his painted skin contents the eye?*

Such 'honesty' is what he is after teaching Kate. Not 'beauteous looks', as Hortensio said, but 'kindness in women' is what a man finally desires, the decent truth—not its outer, 'painted' concealments—of her nature. In their last 'crossing' Petruchio says, 'Let's see, I think 'tis now some seven o'clock,/And well we may come there by dinner-time.' Kate, still preferring her own senses and mind, still clinging to her own version of the 'truth', contradicts him: 'I dare assure you, sir, 'tis almost two,/And 'twill be supper-time ere you come there.' Her continued 'daring' must be broken. To Petruchio's

> *It shall be seven ere I go to horse.*
> *Look, what I speak, or do, or think to do,*
> *You are still crossing it. Sirs, let 't alone.*
> *I will not go today; and ere I do,*
> *It shall be what o'clock I say it is.*

Hortensio, amused and more accurate than he knows, almost cuing Petruchio, as the scene after the next will show, says, 'Why, so this gallant will command the sun.' Promptly in Scene V, on the road, though the sun is shining, Petruchio insists it is the moon. When Kate maintains it is the sun, he says,

> *Now, by my mother's son, and that's myself,*
> *It shall be moon, or star, or what I list,*
> *Or ere I journey to your father's house.*

At last Kate learns:

> *Forward, I pray, since we have come so far,*
> *And be it moon, or sun, or what you please.*
> *And if you please to call it a rush-candle,*
> *Henceforth I vow it shall be so for me.*

She realizes it must be as with the comic spirit itself: 'what you please.' At once, testing her, Petruchio, on her agreeing that it is the moon, declares it the sun. Promptly she:

> *Then, God be blessed, it is the blessed sun.*
> *But sun it is not, when you say it is not,*
> *And the moon changes even as your mind.*

In her last verse we see that, though she finally recognizes that she must be acquiescent to his will, she is by no means broken by or to this moon-man, this seemingly lunatic lover; her wit is still hers, still piercing-sharp and this time equal in understanding and amusement, if not thereby superior, to the occasion. Good woman that she is, she now knows what she must do to get what she wants. At the same time, most capably in this human scene that concerns him, Petruchio in imagination is as much master of the elements as Prospero will in practice be!

Having won, Petruchio is determined to try his success further, in the most difficult circumstance: the human one. Kate passes with flying colors. Vincentio, Lucentio's real father, turns up and meets them; and at Petruchio's suggesting that the old man is a lovely maid, Kate immediately responds in a like larking vein. She has altogether learned the essential lesson that Petruchio is after, that of comedy and of this play itself. Petruchio has helped her to discover how to act, that is, how to be an 'actor' and so herself. She now knows how to play, how, by not taking herself too seriously and so being submerged in herself, to be free of her own fiercely limited rigors and her self-concern. Only so, in the ability to play many parts, including no less that of carefree fool, can she be even partially relieved of the burden of one small ego and simultaneously earn and enjoy it. Petruchio has taught her how to transform violence, the product of her frustration, into useful strength and pleasure, best of all gaiety. At last she has become a proper, light-footed, lovely partner in the dance Petruchio leads to the music of the solidly rooted, earthly sphere; at his abrupt reversal she too neatly, delicately turns and admits the old man an old man. Things as they are can indeed become things as they are if they are not too simply taken for granted but first submitted to the test of wit and gaiety, so confirmed.

Sly and Kate as they are tested by wit and gaiety, so confirmed, involve the testing of a major issue of the play, the nature of education. Is education a matter of learning from, of trimming oneself to, others, an imposition, as with Sly, of their wills and characters on us (also the will and character of the past and/or convention); or is it a matter of learning oneself, a galvanizing, a realizing of that self as, for all the seeming imposition on her of Petruchio's will, it is with Kate? Of course at certain moments, possibly those closest to the ideal, may it not be that both are happening simultaneously? With Petruchio's intelligent if insistent will, informed by experience, imposed on Kate, she uncovers her own will, the will that till now had been trammeled in wilfulness: the individual and living tradition are splendidly serving each other. Sly, we can say, is 'played' with and briefly 'changed', but only externally and for mere, sheer fun (we have no need to know how soberly the fun will leave him). Kate, at the outset at least seemingly not too much more than a puppet or player *in* the play, put on, an essential part of the fun, is also plucked out of her habitual world and self, but for serious reasons and, we are to assume, in permanent change. Sly of the 'real' scene is, by his state and his nature, mere practical joke; Kate of the 'play', and through practical joking, is earnest and fundamentally cured. (Or is that perhaps Shakespeare's final irony–that such cure, such permanent change, is likely only in a play and that in real life we, like Sly, change only while the play is going on?)

In any case, through Sly and Petruchio and Kate we see how far this play and Shakespeare's art have advanced. First there is the obvious accomplishment in character of these three; then we gladly recognize the superiority of this play's language, even if it is in many instances not much more than a refinement of the words as blows, as actions, in *The Comedy of Errors*. But it is, above all, a matter of character and language together. For the characters through their language consti-tute the first in Shakespeare to engage us fully as individuals; here we have the emergence of a voice, a way of speaking, that is one man's and one woman's only. Naturally for its engrossment in language *Love's Labour's Lost* took a very considerable stride in this direction. Who can forget those quintessentials of themselves, Armado, Holo-fernes, and the rest? Yet small beside Sly and Petruchio and Kate, they are mainly set pieces, exhibited briefly like vaudeville skits to regale us with their wares.

But, probably most important of all in terms of development, Adriana's shrewishness, slight and unexamined in her play, has become the primary issue of *The Taming of the Shrew*. That is to say, one problem, providing dramatic intent and intensity, unifies the play. Thus the manipulation of character and the absurdity of situation which amounted to almost the whole of *The Comedy of Errors* are now elevated and exploited beyond themselves, if only for the fact that one character, Petruchio, is deliberately, artfully cultiva-ting the confusion–and manipulating Kate–to cure deeper, more serious confusion. Of course the princess and her ladies of *Love's Labour's Lost*, in their skilful treatment of the 'shrewish' lords, to bring them to their senses and their proper roles, anticipate some measure of Petruchio's therapy. But how much lighter handed and less serious their treatment is (thus at their play's end they are hardly satisfied that a complete cure has been affected). Petruchio has done for Kate what the ladies hope a year in a hermitage and a hospital will do for their lords. That is, in the play Petruchio has been able to provide the reality, if in play, that the ladies can only point to outside their play. At the same time, though Kate's problem, central to its play, may seem much more troubling than Adriana's or the skittish-headedness of the lords of *Love's Labour's Lost*, as it has grown in seriousness so has the gusto it inspires. This counterweight in its buoyancy, the madcap serenity pervading the play, quickly makes us grateful for Kate's shrewishness: that it should be the capable provoker of such ready, robust wit and high jinks in Petruchio. We are grateful also for Shakespeare's economy, the consequence of that wit's antics beyond their own amusement—to wit, that Kate, still mettlesome, is now able to use her energies, a thoroughbred no longer wantonly wild, able to ride.

Here we see how brilliantly Shakespeare has understood the resources of farce, has exploited it to its ultimate fulfilment. For *The Taming of the Shrew* is of a different order from *The Comedy of Errors* in that the former is a farce far more openly and deeply serving romance and more serious matters; the farcical elements, enjoyable for themselves alone, are needed to transform Kate and to abet the relationship of Petruchio and Kate even as that relationship makes the Lucentio-Bianca romance possible. Our knowing this sweetens the play, provides its overall serenity, and ensures the play against any callousness. In fact its blows, since they grow out of and are executed for thoughtful, careful love, ask to be, the more seemingly truculent they are, construed as tenderness and solicitude. Such is the economy of *The Taming of the Shrew* that the romp which the shrewishness provokes is the one thing that can solve that shrewishness. The greater the romp the quicker, the surer, the solution.

However casually, not to say accidentally, the shrew may have occurred to Shakespeare as a likely source of conflict and comic drama (Lot's wife of the guild plays must still have been popular in Shakespeare's day), she, one is tempted to think, is Shakespeare's first seriously displaced person, the first character in his work to feel out of joint with her life, to find no satisfaction for herself in her society, to possess far more energy than her role or her society permits expression of. She is dramatically more promising surely, for being at home and for being at odds, therefore, with herself and her kin, than those like Aegeon and Antipholus of Syracuse, who in the main are physically displaced and at odds with their kin through external errors. This shrew's spirit, curdling, strikes out at all people as obstacles, blames them for her internal confusion. Potentially great vitality and joy, thwarted, turns into poison. Of course the shrew's sphere, of resentment and influence as of complaint, is a limited one; naturally so, for her limited power as a woman, restricted normally to the domestic world and comedy. Yet, we shall soon see, from this displaced being Shakespeare will move on to other, more ambitious, more serious 'shrews' and malcontents.

Strikingly enough, *The Taming of the Shrew*, even though shrewishness seems its crucial issue, has nothing like Adriana's laments, apart from that one moment in which Kate cries out for revenge. *The Taming of the Shrew* is then, one might say, a purer comedy, a more consistent, realized one. However, the perturbation in Adriana, in Antipholus of Syracuse and Aegeon, their lyrical outcry of grief and loss may suggest, by very discrepancy from the rest of the play, a reaching out to a realm beyond that of *The Taming of the Shrew*. If *The Comedy of Errors* seems to teeter by the side of a stormy sea and the storms that war and money produce, *The Taming of the Shrew*, for all its talk of gales and seas, is far and snugly inland, especially once the English winter takes over. There is a wholeness, a singleness, in *The Taming of the Shrew* rarely met with in the more ambitious comedies.

In addition, whatever moments of low, domestic vivacity *The Comedy of Errors* may contain, the liveliness of *The Taming of the Shrew*, with its timely, local things and occasions plucked out of English soil and air and pressed onto the page, achieves an immediate timelessness, a moment of immortality. One cannot forget Dromio's superb, cosy Poland winter, but it is a flourish of speech, a metaphor, which has been translated and enacted in English terms in *The Taming of the Shrew*. So, too, the domestic objects in *The Taming of the Shrew* are more consonant with this kind of streamlined comedy than the sumptuous poetic arias that crop up in the later more romantic, magic-swept comedies. (The paintings I have stressed in this play, deliberate and more precisely framed by function, in their classical contents [a little like the artfully exploited quotations from Ovid] might be thought to anticipate those later arias, inserts also to set off the larger, more natural context.)

Finally, just as the merry war has been won, by both peppery lovers since both have been conquered, so has the battle of farce. Having dealt with it in most masterly fashion here, Shakespeare will not, judiciously enough, engage it again. How prudent this supposedly most prodigal artist can be! Yet we may look forward to one persistence of the farcical in the plays to come—for at his best Shakespeare is not so foolish as to waste or fail to use material he has been successful with in the past—and can say of the most ambitious plays that some godly—if not diabolical—farceur, never seen or heard but profoundly felt, seems to be in charge of all events. And, however cleverly or passionately or nobly the main character may turn, for such turning that farceur reigns the more.

Meantime this play, for Petruchio's success with Kate, is ready to be wound up. The last act exposes the various disguises, and the romance of Lucentio and Bianca is sealed. In the final scene the most important exposure is arrived at, this since the 'raging war is done'. It is banqueting time, time for general revelry and loose talk. Petruchio, however, is still much himself: 'Nothing but sit and sit, and eat and eat!' He needs, no less than ever, to be doing, especially while there are those who still think he is to be beshrewed by Kate. Tranio's hunting taunt, ''Tis thought your deer does hold you at a bay', gives Petruchio an opportunity to demonstrate his success by putting on his last little clinching play: a wager and proof as to which of the three wives is 'the veriest shrew of all'. His confidence in Kate, as in his skill at teaching her, and his love for her are reflected in his

> Twenty crowns!
> I'll venture so much of my hawk or hound,
> But twenty times so much upon my wife.

We see that, though he formerly lumped her in with his possessions, 'My horse, my ox, my ass, my anything,' at the very moment of marrying, and later called her 'my haggard', and though like a good, hardheaded Elizabethan he does put a specific, relative value on her, it far surpasses that of his other highly esteemed belongings. Also his love, by its vigor and depth, seems to surpass that of the other two husbands. As we might expect, their wives refuse to come. But at Petruchio's summons Kate instantly appears, 'What is your will, sir, that you send for me?' And Petruchio in triumph caps his triumph with

> Go fetch them hither. If they deny to come,
> Swinge me them soundly forth unto their husbands.
> Away, I say, and bring them hither straight.

Kate, the tamed taming, the taught teaching, hauls in the other two 'As prisoners to her womanly persuasion'. Baptista, awed, adds twenty thousand crowns: 'Another dowry to another daughter,/For she is changed as she had never been.' Bianca, on the other hand, the supposedly wholly silent, wholly modest one, hearing that Lucentio has lost a hundred crowns through her disobedience, tartly says, 'The more fool you, for laying on my duty.' Bianca, it would seem, picking her mate when he thought he was picking and working hard to win her, has simply bided her time. At this Petruchio charges Kate to instruct the women in a long, closing speech, requiring kindness of wives and obedience. As vigorous as ever, Kate still berates her sister:

> *A woman moved is like a fountain troubled,*
> *Muddy, ill-seeming, thick, bereft of beauty.*
> *And while it is so, none so dry or thirsty*
> *Will deign to sip or touch one drop of it.*

But a woman kind and gentle is, we have seen, a wholly refreshing sea a man would plunge his entire being in.

Then Kate reaches the substance of her message:

> *Thy husband is thy lord, thy life, thy keeper,*
> *Thy head, thy sovereign; one that cares for thee,*
> *And for thy maintenance commits his body*
> *To painful labour both by sea and land,*
> *To watch the night in storm, the day in cold,*
> *Whilst thou liest warm at home, secure and safe;*
> *And craves no other tribute at thy hands*
> *But love, fair looks, and true obedience,*
> *Too little payment for so great a debt.*
> *Such duty as the subject owes the prince,*
> *Even such a woman oweth to her husband; . . .*
> *Come, come you froward and unable worms!*
> *My mind hath been as big as one of yours,*
> *My heart as great, my reason haply more,*
> *To bandy word for word and frown for frown;*
> *But now I see our lances are but straws,*
> *Our strength as weak, our weakness past compare,*
> *That seeming to be most which we indeed least are.*
> *Then vail your stomachs, for it is not boot,*
> *And place your hands below your husband's foot.*

Modern commentators, some of the best, are embarrassed by this out-spoken doctrine of male superiority. By one ingenious apology or another they try to explain it away; it cannot be a basic sentiment of the sweet, gentle, modern Shakespeare. Yet, forgetting his robustious time and the robustious nature of the play, its hearty, rollicksome, farcical nature, they also blink other occasions of similar attitude. In *The Comedy of Errors*, we recall, the patient Luciana urges like sub-mission on the shrewish Adriana; and near the play's end Aemelia, wife to Aegeon, mother to the Antipholuses, and an abbess, roundly rebukes Adriana for her misbegotten conduct. Adriana is, we are led to assume, moved; but how much more, how much more effectively (the chief point of *The Taming of the Shrew*), Kate is we see by the fact that she, thoroughly groomed and bridled, not only absorbs this wisdom but exerts it in brisk admonishment of others. Portia too, not too many plays away, in the noble wisdom she is born to, and so does not have to learn, demurely says of herself to Bassanio:

> *Happy in this, she is not yet so old*
> *But she may learn. Happier than this,*
> *She is not bred so dull but she can learn.*
> *Happiest of all is that her gentle spirit*
> *Commits itself to yours to be directed,*
> *As from her lord, her governor, her king.*
> *Myself and what is mine to you and yours*
> *Is now converted.*

So Musical a Discord

A Midsummer Night's Dream

HAVING wandered into a nighttime forest where everything, suddenly encountered, looms large–the bushes bristly; sprites in their sparkling atmosphere; the little creatures resonant among their grasses; those grasses and flowers themselves, singled out by the studious, cool moon–we are standing on hallowed ground. Druidically sacred, it is the sphere of midsummer, of moonlight, and of magical dreams. And we, once that wood's enchantment begins, are–spells, mirages, shades and all–at home in it, like shimmering midges in their hourlong shaft of sunlight. Pausing once by a field eye-deep in thickest moonlight, frightening almost for its loveliness, I felt the overpowering presence of another realm, an element in which unknown laws, strange customs, life intense as a humming bird's prevail. Was not this fieldful of dewy silver such life briefly visible? *A Midsummer Night's Dream* plots and proclaims that realm. As in Bottom's almanac, this airy, luminous forest, waiting only for the magic casement to be flung open, is always to be found here.

After the splendid apprenticeship spent on plays like *The Comedy of Errors, Love's Labour's Lost* and *The Taming of the Shrew*, Shakespeare was ready for the consummation that is *A Midsummer Night's Dream*. Had he written nothing more or better after it, he would still be one of the chief luminaries of English literature. Not one of the towering oaks that compose the tragedies, *A Midsummer Night's Dream* lives, a perfect little parterre, far below them. Or perhaps it would be better to say that we have entered the wood but only the first, light-ringed zone of it, not the swart, snarled mid-region waiting ahead. Here in terms of the form Shakespeare had now evolved, the language he had achieved, his powers were in equipoise and, at the same time, everywhere at their most copious.

Having recently enjoyed popular success with his narrative poems, both out of Ovidian stories, compact of verbal pictures and arias, in *A Midsummer Night's Dream* he expresses to the full his capacity for the lyrical. We need hardly remark how resilient the lyrical had become for him. Here it is at its climax, underscoring and becoming action or the dramatic. The range and the ease throughout the play, the fresh, diverse delight, seem to know no limit. Now whether it be a Duke and his Lady with their noble blank verse, heightened by the mythical; the King and Queen of the fairies with theirs, also noble blank verse, but of a supernatural as well as a 'natural' quality; the young lovers, properly in riming couplets; the rustics, at least as properly in prose and in their later, deliciously absurd 'theatrical' verse with its clamorous alliteration and mechanical rimes; or nature itself by way of the local fairies in gossamer songs and dance—Shakespeare with equal authority finds their own true voice and the power to sweep them up rapturously, harmoniously together.

But what is it that Shakespeare has learned from his earlier plays for this one? Becomingly before a royal wedding, *A Midsummer Night's Dream* opens with the prospect of revelry. But at once, like *The Comedy of Errors*, it encounters a potential harshness: the rigors of the law and society, old father Egeus' insistence that his daughter Hermia marry the man of his choice and Theseus' verdict that she either comply with her father's wishes or choose between dying and a nunnery. This preliminary threat, little as it is meant to distress and little as it does, plunges the two sets of lovers into the enchanted wood and, accordingly, into a suspension for a time of law and order or into a series of confusions in their own way like those of *The Comedy of Errors*. Quite rightly, like the confused in that earlier play, the lovers are little discriminated: see their youth, their inexperience, the impetuous if fitful character of their appetites and passions; by such the confusions are made even more natural. Of course Theseus' sentence is milder and much more readily dissolved in dewy moonlight and gaiety, and in the generous atmosphere of love (for all its dangers), than the ponderous law of *The Comedy of Errors*. Furthermore, in its initial need for entertainment *A Midsummer Night's Dream* follows *Love's Labour's Lost*. However, for the idle lords of Navarre that entertainment is to be a sober school, meant to banish love and the appetites; for the eminently practical and impatient Theseus it is merriment to while away the time before his marriage, a reluctant choice for him at best. Also the two plays end with a little awkward 'real' play, one in 'the posterior of the day', the other after 'the vaward of the day'. But again what a difference. The Pyramus and Thisbe play is ordered from the start; moreover, it is, in its goatish key—sheepish might be more accurate—almost a little concluding satyr play, perfectly attuned to the play at large. Nonetheless, we shall see, its putting on and reception does resemble that of the playlet in *Love's Labour's Lost*.

But what, past extended professional competence, makes *A Midsummer Night's Dream* more dimensional, more compelling? Perhaps the matter of magic and witchery deserves first consideration. The characters of *The Comedy of Errors* increasingly bemoan their conviction that they must be bewitched. Yet from the start we know by their conventional—not to say ordinary—natures, as by the workaday world they occupy, that they are not and cannot be. We recognize the confusions befalling them for the crass accidents and coincidences they are. And in *Love's Labour's Lost*, whatever bewitchment there may be, it is little more than the spell, a shallow one at that, of the lords' own youthful powers, the charm—for the others as for the lords—of their own words and wit. This self-hypnosis must be broken by reality and a counter-magic, love; as Kate in *The Taming of the Shrew* must be wakened out of her spell, her wretched nightmare, by a rudely shaking kiss from Petruchio. In *A Midsummer Night's Dream*, however, the spell is real enough and quite unabashed, with its mystery and magic clearly embodied in the season and the place, in the moon and the potion, as well as in the busy, certain presences of the fairies. In all these, and especially in the stirred and disturbed spirits of the lovers. And we find the magic even more convincing in that, unlike *The Comedy of Errors'* crew, these lovers are so sunken in their spell that they never fully realize it, never cry out 'Witchcraft!'

For this is a magical moment, that time of year when nature and the natural in man, drawing most closely together, rise potently to the surface, as it is that time of life in the young lovers. Whatever temporary turmoil may ensue, life and nature's forces are identified with men here in a way the opposite of what happens in tragedy. The play's opening occasion, festivity prior to a royal wedding, invites at once this sense of magical stirrings, exultancy (troubling though it may be also), fecundity. Navarre of *Love's Labour's Lost*, to observe his initial vow, has to camp the French ladies outside his court in an adjoining field. Thus he and his lords have to deal with them 'in the field'—that is, seemingly against their wills they are drawn out, via a kind of civil war, into nature and their own natures. In *A Midsummer Night's Dream*, however, since the time of going a-Maying, a bringing of nature into the town, we quickly and deliberately enter a special wood where the necessary 'changes' can be experienced. The wood waits nearby, steeped in moonlight, to accommodate this conjunction of nature and man.

Moreover, by formal edict, a new brief 'law', Theseus proclaims merriment and release. He bids his master of revels:

> *Awake the pert and nimble spirit of mirth;*
> *Turn melancholy forth to funeral.*
> *The pale companion is not for our pomp.*

Promptly, as though in happy obedience, the moon begins to weave its spell. For everywhere it is the moon that supervises, though it be the moon as seen and responded to by the characters according to their natures. *A Midsummer Night's Dream* is, beside *The Comedy of Errors* and *Love's Labour's Lost*, open, fluid, all grace; superbly subject to the 'changes' the moon sponsors. Thought of against the raucous comedy of Kate's 'sponsor', dragging her through many moony changes, this grace, even as it deepens our pleasure in *The Taming of the Shrew*, impresses us the more with *A Midsummer Night's Dream*. Shakespeare has here hit upon a medium, a natural yet magical ambience, that makes all kin.

Theseus, Duke that he is, begins the play. Immediately we see what kind of nobleman we are to deal with here; a man truly, felt as a person, he is altogether different from the faceless, lifeless Solinus, Duke of Ephesus, or the fairly anonymous King of Navarre, and an extension of *The Taming of the Shrew's* lord as of its up-and-doing Petruchio. Theseus chafes at delay; a leader and man of affairs, he is all for the business of life. A daylight man, he resents the moon, finds it no more than an obstacle:

> *O, methinks, how slow*
> *This old moon wanes! She lingers my desires*
> *Like to a stepdame or a dowager*
> *Long withering out a young man's revenue.*

It is amusing and right that he should translate the moon into terms of money, inheritance, activity. Hippolyta, on the other hand, recommends patience and more poetically stresses night over day. When Theseus speaks of 'four happy days' that will 'bring in/Another moon', she retorts, 'Four days will quickly steep themselves in night,/Four nights will quickly dream away the time, . . .' The play will be just such a precipitous dream. But then, true to her life as an Amazon warrior, she concludes,

And then the moon, like to a silver bow
New-bent in heaven, shall behold the night
Of our solemnities.

At this point Theseus declares for merriments and assures Hippolyta
that though he wooed her with his sword he will wed her 'in another
key,/With pomp, with triumph, and with revelling.' They have just
come from a war in which, fighting the Amazons, Theseus took Hippolyta, their queen, prisoner; a likely background for love!

But now, with youth and mirth proclaimed, the old stern law in the
shape of age, or Egeus, intrudes. Cross-note that he is, he demands
justice. He claims—and here we have the first assertion of witchcraft in
the play and of love as such a witchcraft—that Lysander has 'bewitched
the bosom of my child'. What are his spells, his charms?

Thou hast by moonlight at her window sung,
With feigning voice, verses of feigning love,
And stolen the impression of her fantasy
With bracelets of thy hair, rings, gawds, conceits,
Knacks, trifles, nosegays, sweetmeats, messengers
Of strong prevailment in unhardened youth.

Old though he is, Egeus has not forgotten the vulnerability of youth or
the ways in which it works and, trifling as they may now be to him,
the potency of its properties. But he cannot believe in his daughter's
love for Lysander as something real, above and beyond mere 'love-
tokens' interchanged. Nor in Lysander's love for her, with his *'feigning*
voice' *'feigning* love'. Perhaps Egeus is too old to believe in love itself
as more than feigning. Theseus, despite his festive lover's mood,
cannot ignore his basic role as ruler; thus his verdict. Again we encounter his indifference, if not hostility, to the moon. For him it is not
magic and delight, but a denial of life:

You can endure the livery of a nun,
For aye to be in shady cloister mewed,
To live a barren sister all your life,
Chanting faint hymns to the cold fruitless moon.
Thrice-blessèd they that master so their blood
To undergo such maiden pilgrimage;
But earthlier happy is the rose distilled,
Than that which, withering on the virgin thorn,
Grows, lives, and dies in single blessedness.

It is obvious from the movement of his image from 'thrice-blesséd' (with whatever praise he musters for those 'that master so their blood') to 'single blessedness' (surely between them 'double blessedness' is being implied and encouraged), from the happy 'rose distilled' to that 'withering on the virgin thorn', where the sympathies of this would-be married man must lie. A seize-the-day man, 'withering', we saw in his first dowager image for the moon, is one thing he cannot abide.

Against this troubled backdrop Lysander admits: 'The course of true love never did run smooth, . . .' And in words either reminiscent of or preparatory to *Romeo and Juliet* (we do not know which play came first: if *A Midsummer Night's Dream*, Shakespeare is by it prompting himself to the writing of *Romeo and Juliet*; if *Romeo and Juliet*, *A Midsummer Night's Dream* is in part a comic version, an amiable parody, of *Romeo and Juliet*), Lysander speaks of 'war, death, or sickness' laying 'siege' to love,

> *Making it momentany as a sound,*
> *Swift as a shadow, short as any dream,*
> *Brief as the lightning in the collied night,*
> *That, in a spleen, unfolds both heaven and earth,*
> *And ere a man hath power to say 'Behold!'*
> *The jaws of darkness do devour it up.*
> *So quick bright things come to confusion.*

For a young lover at the inception of his career, pretty grim words. One might have expected such prescience from a Romeo, say, or a Troilus. But these are words, merely told, never seen or, beyond the brevity of this play's dream and the shadow-quick shifts of love it prompts, never experienced here. It is as though Lysander had just come from witnessing a performance of *Romeo and Juliet*. These young lovers are quick bright things quickly to come to confusion as they scheme to escape by way of night and the wood to Lysander's aunt, amusingly enough of Theseus' description, 'a dowager/Of great revenue.' However, the darkness that closes down on them, whatever its threatening aspects, will at most be brier-prickly, not ravenous jaws; and it will nip at them in amusement, as though to say an ignis fatuus can, after all, lead one aright even as it leads him astray. So off they go to the summer wood which they need hardly have had a strong excuse to plunge into.

Yet when the lovers complete their plan, on Helena's entrance we learn that the two girls at least have had through their love some actual foretaste of the greater confusion ahead. Hermia confesses:

> *Before the time I did Lysander see,*
> *Seemed Athens as a paradise to me.*
> *O, then, what graces in my love do dwell*
> *That he hath turned a heaven unto a hell!*

Strong language this, especially since she does have Lysander's love. However, since her father forbids this love, Athens, the place in which that forbidding is borne out, must become a hell of frustration to the heaven it was before her seeing Lysander. Also we learn what, ironically enough, happens to paradise when love enters it. Helena is even more experienced since she has, with Demetrius' love for Hermia and his consequent disdain for her, suffered all the pangs of thwarted love; she has already attained some deeper understanding, that which this play will emphatically prove: 'Things base and vile, holding no quantity,/Love can transpose to form and dignity.' We might be impressed, if not awed, by love's so mighty power, its 'graces'. But Helena soon makes clear that this capacity of love is based on fancy and folly, not reason or understanding:

> *Love looks not with the eyes, but with the mind,*
> *And therefore is winged Cupid painted blind.*
> *Nor hath Love's mind of any judgment taste;*
> *Wings, and no eyes, figure unheedy haste.*
> *And therefore is Love said to be a child,*
> *Because in choice he is so oft beguiled.*

Yet she also knows how much exteriors alone determine youthful, headlong love; thus Demetrius 'errs, doting on Hermia's eyes'. 'For ere Demetrius looked on Hermia's eyne,/He hailed down oaths that he was only mine, . . .' She herself, she admits, is similarly smitten. So much so that she decides to betray her dear friend Hermia by telling Demetrius of Hermia's flight if only to have his sight and possible thanks. Love is patently more potent than any other related impulse— unless, as we shall see, it be hate. Already then these young people are the servants of their desires. Hermia and Lysander are about to engage in an act of stealth which must result for its willfulness in troubled, if not broken, pleasure; for they have, whatever the provocation, broken away—their first declaration of defiant freedom—from home, parents, society, the law. They have truly gone into the dark and into the dark or chaos of their own natures, have decided to rely wholly on their naked wishes. Similarly Helena flouts friendship in hopes of bettering her love's lot.

But the pastoral note has begun. The wood nearby, just as it bespeaks Robin Hood, who made a law out of liveliness and sportiveness against life-curbing laws, bespeaks the pagan and is fragrant of the first garden. For the Englishman not many things can elicit an enthusiasm like that which he knows for his own garden. Certainly it is a persistent presence, a master metaphor in Shakespeare's work. For Elizabethan times, with their hearty endorsement of folk festivities, out of the dim, green past and identified with the changes in nature and the seasons, nature was still very present, much alive, and still to be conjured with. At the same time, this play, celebrating such a ripened moment, for we believe it was originally meant to be a royal epithalamium, may well be a gentle spoofing of the affectations of lords and ladies; one thinks of Queen Elizabeth on her royal stool milking the royal cow! In any case, though the natural is welcomed here, it is, like the wedding-to-be, the natural and the physical finally sealed or contained, if not restrained, and consummated in the social and Christian rites of marriage.

Nonetheless, for the play's duration it is moonlight, much more than Theseus or the community, that prevails. The changes and choices, the merry confusions of *A Midsummer Night's Dream*, unlike those of *The Comedy of Errors* and more elegantly than those of *The Taming of the Shrew*, are subject to nature and/or the moon, the planet most neighborly to the earth. These changes may seem ominous, but we realize almost from the outset that they are full of benignity and a guarantee of good fortune. The moon naturally mingles with the central theme of love and its absurdities, a world seen in an ambiguous, mercurial light. The lovers, 'lunatics', are mooncalves led astray, as by their own unpredictable impulses, by a sudden whiff of moonlit fragrance; love-in-idleness, a simple of the moon, its juice dropped upon their sleeping lids, collaborates with their young, coltish senses and their even friskier dreams. The lyricism permeating the play is indeed what might be uttered by moonlight, while the wood's small folk, crickets, fairies, rustics alike, strike up a silver-shrill obbligato.

It is this pervasive wash that may make us fail to realize how diverse the elements in this play are, what a commodious world it comes to. The fluency of movement throughout helps to mute this diversity; so does the celerity of the fairies, who claim to be swifter even than the moon and equalled in speed by one thing only, thought or the poet's imagination. Theseus is more accurate than he knows: 'The poet's eye, in a fine frenzy rolling', does 'glance from heaven to earth, from earth to heaven, . . .' Merely to summarize the physical contents of *A Midsummer Night's Dream* is to be impressed with its astonishing plenitude and span. It contains, first of all, lords and ladies, headed by Theseus, one of the main mythical heroes of Greece and king of Athens, and Hippolyta, Queen of the Amazons (of course, like Richard Conqueror by Sly, both have, via Ovid, Plutarch and, most of all, Chaucer, been thoroughly naturalized and domesticated). Then it presents the commoners, the young lovers. Surrounding these are the fairies, also a various lot, from King Oberon and Queen Titania out of fabulous India (the only 'gods' in this 'Greek' play!), more exotic than Theseus and Hippolyta, summoned like rainbow-plumed birds by the jubilant occasion, to the English garden variety of fairy. For us these latter are 'real' since they are almost all we know of fairies, all the fairies we know; or at least, since Shakespeare is for most of us our main source of knowledge about fairies, what we assume them to be; moreover, like the potent 'love-in-idleness', to begin with they are herbs, blossoms, natural phenomena or Cobweb, Peaseblossom, Mustardseed. And Oberon like Theseus is also served by a kind of clown and lord of revels, a Philostrate, Puck, the bustling madcap mischief-maker; the most vernacular of the fairies (though naturalized among them for the first time by Shakespeare), in self-identification he gives us a series of pictures, homely yet indicative of the imaginings of country life:

> *I am that merry wanderer of the night.*
> *I jest to Oberon and make him smile .*
> *When I a fat and bean-fed horse beguile,*
> *Neighing in likeness of a filly foal.*
> *And sometime lurk I in a gossip's bowl,*
> *In very likeness of a roasted crab,*
> *And when she drinks, against her lips I bob*
> *And on her withered dewlap pour the ale.*
> *The wisest aunt, telling the saddest tale,*
> *Sometime for three-foot stool mistaketh me.*
> *Then slip I from her bum, down topples she,*
> *And 'tailor' cries, and falls into a cough,*
> *And then the whole quire hold their hips and laugh,*
> *And waxen in their mirth, and neeʒe, and swear*
> *A merrier hour was never wasted there.*

This colloquial accounting for accidents also applies to his freedom, like that of the imagination, to gird the globe; he is at once the most local and the most cosmic of the creatures here, imagination's own most mischievous factor. All these are, finally, neighbored by the English rustics (Athenians no doubt!), who are to Theseus as the little fairies are to Oberon, earthlings felicitously beside the little fairies, out of the English countryside together.

Then, as though this amazingly mixed crew, 'airy nothings' many of them, drawn from folklore and books and made very Englishly at home, were not enough, Shakespeare enlarges his scene in time and space with frequent allusions to the past and to fabulous places; he imports all kinds of exotic spices by regaling us with stately, deliberate arias, magnificent lyrical inserts. However, we first hear the fairies flitting about hummingbird-fashion:

> *Over hill, over dale,*
> *Thorough bush, thorough brier,*
> *Over park, over pale,*
> *Thorough flood, thorough fire,*
> *I do wander everywhere,*
> *Swifter than the moon's sphere.*

But these fairies are more than merely presences everywhere in nature. When we learn of the quarrel between Oberon and Titania, aptly—for this play of 'changes'—over the changeling boy she will not surrender to him, Titania speaks in formal, leisurely vein of the consequences of their quarrel: a natural perversion of nature in the chain of being. She says:

> *The nine men's morris is filled up with mud,*
> *And the quaint mazes in the wanton green*
> *For lack of tread are undistinguishable.*
> *The human mortals want their winter cheer.*
> *No night is now with hymn or carol blest.*
> *Therefore the moon, the governess of floods,*
> *Pale in her anger, washes all the air,*
> *That rheumatic diseases do abound.*
> *And thorough this distemperature we see*
> *The seasons alter: hoary-headed frosts*
> *Fall in the fresh lap of the crimson rose,*
> *And on old Hiems' thin and icy crown*

An odorous chaplet of sweet summer buds
Is, as in mockery, set.

Distemper it is that destroys or prevents, with the season's upheaval, all the normal, natural pleasures of song and dance; something that the fairies, the spirits of song and dance, usually look after. The patterns that men set up for themselves in nature, their orbits of delight, are now wiped out, like the pattern of the seasons. And here we have another version or vision of the moon. Enraged by these derangements, she releases rheumatic diseases. That enemy of dancing, rheumatism, prevails, and the seasons themselves are sexually topsy-turvied (actually not in this play), a confusion ideal as a setting for the falling in love of the fairy Queen with an ass. Think of the odorous wreath askew on his shaggy ears! But for loveliness, even reversed, for nature so beautifully subverted, these verses are surely to be relished, not to be mourned over or taken very seriously. Shakespeare in the distancing and limiting of language, for this play's dream's sake no less than for the occasion of its putting on, ensures our sense of delight; this is at most 'gallant chiding,' 'sweet thunder'. And the play itself will set all right.

Again, when Oberon requests the boy of her, Titania answers in lavish, leisurely style:

> *The fairyland buys not the child of me.*
> *His mother was a votaress of my order,*
> *And in the spicéd Indian air, by night,*
> *Full often hath she gossiped by my side,*
> *And sat with me on Neptune's yellow sands,*
> *Marking the embarkéd traders on the flood,*
> *Where we have laughed to see the sails conceive*
> *And grow big-bellied with the wanton wind,*
> *Which she with pretty and with swimming gait*
> *Following, her womb then rich with my young squire,*
> *Would imitate, and sail upon the land*
> *To fetch me trifles, and return again*
> *As from a voyage, rich with merchandise.*

This speech is, as before, playful and full of feminine wellbeing, a most amiable moving-picture: in its fertility it overflows into play, *imitation*, not to say metamorphosis, on a gayly grotesque scale.

When she leaves, Oberon resolves to punish her. Summoning Puck, he delivers himself of a most sumptuous recitative. The first words, 'Thou rememberest', makes the formal, framed quality of the speech clear:

> *Since once I sat upon a promontory*
> *And heard a mermaid on a dolphin's back*
> *Uttering such dulcet and harmonious breath*
> *That the rude sea grew civil at her song,*
> *And certain stars shot madly from their spheres*
> *To hear the sea maid's music?*

Is one amiss to find here something reminiscent of the 'paintings' in *The Taming of the Shrew?* There too it was a girl (see also the moving 'sweet mermaid' that Luciana of *The Comedy of Errors* becomes for Antipholus of Syracuse) and the golden stratagem that girl became in art (here in singing) to move man, god, nature past their nature.

First of all, as Titania had described the disheveling, for her and her husband's squabble, of nature and then described a human by the sea, a girl in her fulfillment, happily mimicking that sea and sea-business, so here Oberon, sitting somewhere on some promontory, also describes a disheveling of nature, but a confusion because it is superlative harmony! This speech is as great a paean to music and its efficacy as even Shakespeare will sing. A mermaid on a dolphin's back, gifted like Arion or Orpheus, rather than imitating the sea and its ships as the pregnant woman does, calms or, better, civilizes the rude sea with her singing. This sea, usually governed by the moon and the stars, itself the source of shipwrecks, now forgets itself, its common function, to listen to a lovely voice. Even more impressively perhaps, and further witness to the power of music, 'certain stars' ('certain' in its certain vagueness is most precise, most effective), themselves prime musicians *and* a music (who better able to appreciate music?), now listen and eagerly break out of their spheres into a sweet chaos at hearing—at desiring to hear—her song. Their shooting madly from their spheres suggests simultaneously their perfervid feeling, gone mad with pleasure, but also their disruption of order for some greater order. For a moment the universe seems fixed, as in this moment, listening to a mermaid singing. Yet in this very fixity, with the world—of the play certainly—held or focused to a pure intensity, and with the whole play summed up in this moment of transparent emergence, are we not in the midst of drama to challenge the most lively action? This is one of many moments in the play in which, as I proposed earlier, we meet the lyrical at its climax—as with the various poems in *Romeo and Juliet*—and becoming action or the dramatic.

Then we learn of 'the cold moon' and 'the chaste beams of the watery moon', usually identified through its 'imperial votaress' with Elizabeth, the virgin queen, able to 'quench' 'Cupid's fiery shaft'; but it quenches not so completely that it does not strike 'with love's wound' 'a little western flower' and turn it from 'milk-white' to purple. This turning is one of love's transformations, like the mulberry's in Ovid's Pyramus and Thisbe story, not used in this play except for this pansy, 'love-in-idleness', and, literally one might say, plucked from Ovid, one of Shakespeare's 'odoriferous flowers of fancy'. However, it is still informed with the efficacy of love's wound.

When Puck returns with the flower Oberon delivers himself of another set-piece. Here the neat couplets, framing the pastoral picture, help to make it a little lyric complete.

> *I know a bank where the wild thyme blows,*
> *Where oxlips and the nodding violet grows,*
> *Quite overcanopied with luscious woodbine,*
> *With sweet musk-roses and with eglantine.*

It is Titania's pastoral bower, her boudoir, of itself a flower-bed to accommodate 'love-in-idleness':

> *There sleeps Titania sometime of the night,*
> *Lulled in these flowers with dances and delight.*
> *And there the snake throws her enameled skin,*
> *Weed wide enough to wrap a fairy in.*

(Even the snake is beneficent, useful.) Entirely delectable, Oberon's language tends to modulate the 'hateful fantasies' he means to fill her with. She and the lovers are to be put upon like Sly in his new clothes and elegant surroundings. As though summoned by Oberon's fragrant words, those words embodied, a picture come alive, the scene immediately following, in 'another part of the wood', is plainly the bank Oberon has described. And here is Titania among her fairies, being entertained by them: 'Lulled in these flowers with dances and delight.' Her appearing so promptly in the place of Oberon's description (indeed it is practically her cue) gives credence to his description as that confirms her fairy-fabulous setting. But then, like Theseus with Athens, Oberon is in charge of his world and more. He has wise, over-seeing powers that considerably exceed Theseus'. Titania bids her fairies sing her to sleep. They sing their lovely song, a charm against 'spotted snakes with double tongue,/Thorny hedgehogs', 'Newts and blindworms', and their fellows: a charm, alas, powerless before Oberon and love-in-idleness.

The snake soon crops up again; but–for us a fairly Freudian one– only in dream or nightmare: Hermia, abandoned by Lysander and intuitively aware of it in her sleep, wakes with a cry:

> *Help me, Lysander, help me! Do thy best*
> *To pluck this crawling serpent from my breast!*
> *Aye me, for pity! What a dream was here!*
> *Lysander, look how I do quake with fear.*
> *Methought a serpent eat my heart away,*
> *And you sat smiling at his cruel prey.*

Yet threat is implicit here along with the possibility of greatest danger throughout the scenes of the lovers' confusions. And the kind of cruelty that resides potentially in lovers themselves is surely indicated, as it is by Oberon's use of love-in-idleness on Titania. Even before the wood's own magic began, when Helena and Demetrius rushed into it, he distractedly seeking Hermia and threatening to leave Helena 'to the mercy of wild beasts', Helena said to him, 'The wildest hath not such a heart as you.' But she is so abjectly in love with him that she prefers his cruelty to his absence. When he warns her, '. . . I shall do thee mischief in the wood', she gladly accepts, in words echoingly opposite to Hermia's on her father-frustrated love for Lysander: 'I'll follow thee, and make a heaven of hell,/To die upon the hand I love so well.' At once we have revealed to us what ugly possibilities, the irrational and violent, not to say the malevolent, lurk in the young lovers, a wood in themselves apart from the wood, once desire overrides reason and conscience. However, beyond Puck's donning of animal shapes to scare the rustics, not until the play's end will the ugly, the truly painful, threatening animals and frightening, 'real' circumstances be more than glanced at. Even there they will be little more than mentioned, 'pic- tured', held in abeyance as they have been for the play's duration. This 'dream' cannot afford more. Nor, celebration and lovely lark that it is, should it.

The main business of the play now begins: the triple confusions of the lovers, the rustics, Titania and Bottom, or each group a quaint, not to say fantastic, picture come alive. We shall not have more arias like Oberon's until the confusions and the dreams are over and that other music, morning's, can sound forth. As the moon lights up first one lot of its minions, then another, they are busy performing their parts. Oberon, with his designs on Titania, in passing—perhaps part of that impulse—also has designs, if more kindly ones, on the young lovers. But through Puck's mistake the design backfires. The juice may be foolproof in itself; its application is not. Marvelous we must judge this little flower that it can do so much for its recipient, enable him to (make him?) love whatever he looks upon. And yet just as, mixed with one's vision, it makes or enables its recipient to see, it also dupes him since it gets him to love what he normally, sensibly would not. It seduces him, blinds him to his own best wishes. In one little flower then is condensed the ambiguity of nature and love itself. His eyes anointed, Lysander, waking, seeing and so loving Helena, as he abandons the sleeping Hermia can say, 'Of all be hated, but the most of me!' If the wildest sea can be made civil, why cannot the civil, with the right note awakening the primitive in it, be made wild and savage? Again, as with the confusions and the blows in *The Comedy of Errors*, we know how close to disaster our lovers come were Puck who misleads them not also near to look after them. We know what fear, like babes in the woods, the girls experience and what harm the two young men would do each other. Of course we do not blame Puck alone. In his first entrance into the wood Demetrius had already said, 'Where is Lysander and fair Hermia?/The one I'll slay, the other slayeth me.'

In a sense, it is love that catapults the young couples, innocently enough, into fear or a dark wood, the dark and depth of which they had not anticipated. For it is as much the dark and depth latent within themselves—one feels that their fear will seal, even as it matures (out of very danger and the threat of grim loneliness, abandonment, and lost identity), their love. They have taken a plunge that will finally prove beneficent, but only as it is unknown and potentially full of terrors and outrages. Thus they have a first real taste, in the ruthlessness of their young, stirring natures, of the confusion always ready in life. Contraries love and fear may be; they are also interdependent. Can we not say that the lovers, having relished the first terrors of delight, know in the savor of fear a richer delight and love? For they have encountered depths in themselves they hardly suspected, that part of them released that till now had been restrained or hidden under the veneer of society and civilization, that part sympathetic with the 'unregenerate' nature of the wood or nature. For a time, free of conventions and open to the pleasures of holiday, they also learn the risks of such openness.

Beyond the lovers' own strong, tyrannical impulses Puck is the director if not puppeteer or, more kindly, number-caller in the dance the lovers perform. Shakespeare had his experience with *The Comedy of Errors*, its deft confusions, and *Love's Labour's Lost* to draw on; the expertness of the intricate, accomplished dance movements evolved through the latter. Here too it is still a Romanesque or Italianate order and symmetry that we witness. The balancings are extraordinary, but extraordinary also for seeming so easygoing, so natural. Their pattern, Italianate though it may be in its symmetry, is Englishly free in the fluidity that fills it. If *The Comedy of Errors* has its two sets of twins, dogged by Puckish 'chance', and *Love's Labour's Lost* its four lords partnered off with four French ladies who call their tune as Puck does the young lovers', in *A Midsummer Night's Dream* the royal pair is counterparted by the royal fairy pair, the whole climaxed in the coupling of Titania and Bottom and resolved in the comic coupling of Pyramus and Thisby, most comical because tragical, 'very tragical mirth'. Puck in charge of the young lovers, as well as the rustics, bids this one partner change places with the other, the other with that one, and then, in good dance fashion, back again. And the dance itself, exhilarating, asking everything of them as they daringly swing out in it, also contains them. Thus the design (of Oberon) or the dance saves them and becomes the artful design inside darkness or their dream. And if it is a dark wood, we must remember that it is also—for the moon and the season, the occasion—a sacred one. As I suggested at the outset, this is not yet the wooded midnight, the benighted wood, of the witches and their brewing. For these are youths not yet ready—nor should they be in comedy—for the ultimate implications, the deeper truth, of what they see and feel. And for the present a happy, a classical balance is maintained.

But now, since this riotous dance, the chase and flight of the lovers, is soon followed by the flight of the rustics and the chase by Puck, it is time that we turn to the real ballast, puff-ball though it may be, of the play, its ground-basic humor and its self-poking burlesque: the rustics. At once by what they are they bring the moon and the play down to earth. In *A Midsummer Night's Dream* all is, in a sense, transformed by moonlight; but moonlight itself is transformed by what it gloriously —if for a time only—alchemizes, itself the philosopher's stone. Intelligent light that the moon sheds, it seems to find itself out by the beings it studies. One is tempted to say that the moon, reflecting on the rustics in their clumsy antics, has never seen itself in such a sweet and silly light before. Certainly the rustics, though shown in the shining round, inevitably true to themselves to the end, learn nothing. The voice of the English countryside, native with the little folk of the field, nature's herbs and minerals, rough golds, they, once the moon bears down on them, are released by it with marvelous purity and undistracted resonance. We revel in this genius of loutishness distilled. Literalists of the imagination, delectable toads and newts in an imaginary garden, for them what is is; happily enough, since their minds and bodies are one, their minds and the world they know are one. Accordingly, everything is at once no sooner thought than real. For such creatures the link with everyday life cannot and must not be broken; they would be lost without it, would lose their identity. At the same time this diurnality, this everyday literalness, concentrated on so purely, achieves a poetry of its own. Lumbersome if not claybrained, with words for them hardly separable from things—for they cannot rise, or succumb, to generalizing—they live wholly in, are wholly part of, their world.

The poet, the literalist of the imagination, among them, and their leader, is of course that rose of ragweeds, that lion of locusts, Bottom. From the start his mettlesomeness, his restless and irresistible energy, is on total display. When Quince the carpenter, therefore properly in charge of the play, introduces these worthies by calling the roll of players, Bottom betrays himself in his first word, 'Ready'. And he is, even more than Sly, for anything and everything. Like Shakespeare's greatest characters—for Bottom, though on the lowest rung of the ladder, is one of the greatest—he brims over with life, his particularly Bottomesque variety of it. One character, one body, one role, is hardly enough for him. He must be playing many—if not all—parts. As far as he is concerned the world is mainly a treasury or wardrobe of wonderful possibilities for self-expression. In this respect ('Greek' that he is!) he is a kind of low Odysseus with Odysseus' reluctance to be one only, his fertility for diverse roles, his instant inventiveness as he makes up stories about himself. So too, wherever he is, whether among his cronies or the fairies or the lords, Bottom shares something of Odysseus' capacity to be at home. It is the will to live and to live multifariously.

When Bottom learns that he is to play Pyramus, not a tyrant but 'A lover that kills himself most gallant for love', he says:

That will ask some tears in the true performing of it. If I do it, let the audience look to their eyes. [He would be the last to underestimate his powers!] *I will move storms. I will condole in some measure. To the rest.*

But he can hardly stop now; having no more than thought of the role of a tyrant, he must rush on:

Yet my chief humour is for a tyrant. I could play Ercles rarely, or a part to tear a cat in, to make all split.

And at once, moved by his own words, he explodes into impromptu verses:

> '*The raging rocks*
> *And shivering shocks*
> *Shall break the locks*
> *Of prison gates.*
> *And Phibbus' car*
> *Shall shine from far*
> *And make and mar*
> *The foolish Fates.*'

Inevitably this is what happens to the sun and the moon filtered through such minds: a true Ovidian translation! So Hercules was also trimmed. As inevitably Bottom's critical comment, nothing if not objective, must follow.

This was lofty! Now name the rest of the players. This is Ercles' vein, a tyrant's vein. A lover is more condoling.

Again, when Flute is reluctant to play Thisby: 'I have a beard coming', Bottom generously, spontaneously offers: 'An I may hide my face, let me play Thisby too.' That is to say, not rather than Pyramus but also! And the idea for him is indeed the deed:

I'll speak in a monstrous little voice, 'Thisne, Thisne!' 'Ah Pyramus, my lover dear! Thy Thisby dear, and lady dear!'

Taking both parts, as he proposes to do, he has already begun their intimate dialogue. Likewise when Snug, 'slow of study', hesitates over the lion's part, Bottom valiantly springs forth:

Let me play the lion too. I will roar that I will do any man's heart good to hear me. I will roar that I will make the Duke say, 'Let him roar again, let him roar again.'

Practiced in all the human and semi-human roles, Bottom is not a man to be caught napping. Such cheerful readiness and such art are bound to prove most salubrious, bound to do any man's heart good. Nor can they be confined; so much himself, he must be more than himself to be himself. The positive or affirmative capability, he is bursting to be all things, but mainly as an enlargement and intensification of himself, the world be-Bottomed. He is like the bumpkins in *Love's Labour's Lost*–and its lords too for that matter–but more so, the climax of their line and breeding, in the profession and savoring of his own powers. In addition, glowingly insulated and intact though he may be, so abundant are his powers that he must seek out others to share them with. Athenian that he is he *is* the measure of all things. He and his cronies, 'measurers' or artisans, men of things, handy men identified with their crafts, can see the world and its beings in their own terms only; the literal is inevitable for them. But Bottom is a literalist so totally that he becomes imaginative totally. Things are there and all, but not as burdens; on the contrary. They can, known so simply, especially for one of Bottom's boundless energy, be simply and directly and joyously dealt with.

When the others, sharing their attitudes very precisely with the ladies, assure him that the ladies will be frightened by his lion roars, he promptly agrees and as promptly presses on to a happy remedy:

> *I grant you, friends, if you should fright the ladies out of their wits, they would have no more discretion but to hang us. But I will aggravate my voice so that I will roar you as gently as any sucking dove; I will roar you an 'twere any nightingale.*

The world is there–or here–to be coped with, to be used as necessary or as you will. As Bottom can and should play lion, so obviously it is in the nature of a dove, a nightingale, to find the lion in it and to utter lion in its own voice. Who could be more blissfully imperturbable, more blissfully adapted to and adapting of the world? Only Quince's well-qualified assurance,

> *You can play no part but Pyramus; for Pyramus is a sweet-faced man, a proper man as one shall see in a summer's day, a most lovely, gentlemanlike man. Therefore you must needs play Pyramus.*

contents him.

Later in Act III, when they are met to rehearse, it is bully Bottom who has all the answers to the formidable difficulties that putting on their play presents. Always they confuse art–or the play–with reality; always they are most sensitive to the swooning hyper-sensitivity of the ladies (the rustics' notion of what nobility is, particularly feminine nobility, their romantic, idealistic assumption of its ultra-refinement, is, though ludicrous, quite touching; at the same time it is even more ludicrous in that they inevitably think that the ladies' minds and feelings must be, like their own, literalist). Bottom supplies instant solution after solution to all their most prodigious dilemmas. For Pyramus' so offensive sword drawn to kill himself? A prologue, but not, as Quince would write it, in the usual ballad meter of alternate lines of six and eight syllables; rather, since Bottom can never have enough, in eight and eight. For that 'most dreadful thing', the lion, than which 'there is not a more fearful wild-fowl'? Not another prologue but, fecund as Bottom is, another device that he has ready:

> *Nay, you must name his name, and half his face must be seen through the lion's neck. And he himself must speak through, saying thus, or to the same defect, 'Ladies,' or 'Fair ladies, I would wish you,' or 'I would request you,' or 'I would entreat you, not to fear, not to tremble. My life for yours. If you think I come hither as a lion, it were pity of my life. No, I am no such thing; I am a man as other men are!' And there indeed let him name his name, and tell them plainly he is Snug the joiner.*

Bottom cannot let go, cannot – his absurd redundancies, his adjustments of would-be delicate phrasing, make clear – even in mere anticipation have enough of the stage.

And still problems haunt this play. Since Pyramus and Thisby meet by moonlight, moonlight will have to be produced on the night of performance. Bottom, inspired as ever, shouts, 'A calendar, a calendar! Look in the almanac. Find out moonshine, find out moonshine.' A delicious scene, these hayseeds, eagerly hulked over, with thick fingers fumbling through the almanac, looking for moonlight in a book. As though all they need do is open the almanac and moonlight will swell out of the pages. And so it will, so it will, as it does out of this play's pages. But are they so different from most of us with our notion that a statement, a statistic, if printed in a book must be 'a fact', a reality? At length the last, seemingly insurmountable difficulty occurs to them:

> *Then, there is another thing: we must have a wall in the great chamber; for Pyramus and Thisby, says the story, did talk through the chink of a wall.*

This challenge, like all the rest, is nothing to Bottom:

Some man or other must present wall. And let him have some plaster, or some loam, or some roughcast about him [*it is Bottom's variations and elaborations, his rich, unbeatable resourcefulness, his effervescence, rarely satisfied with one phrase, one qualification, that constitute a substantial part of his charm*]*, to signify wall. And let him hold his fingers thus, and through that cranny shall Pyramus and Thisby whisper.*

What imaginations these are, after all, that two fingers spread can compose a chink in a wall!

Now, as they begin their rehearsal, Puck, entering, though one of the more delicate fairies had called him 'thou lob of spirits', says in amusement (and amazement too): 'What hempen homespuns have we swaggering here,/So near the cradle of the Fairy Queen?' We know we are in the presence of Shakespeare's brightest, surest magic: his ability, exploiting his age's appetite for such extraordinary juxtapositions, to deposit such yokels, most of all Master Bottom, near–harmoniously near–the Fairy Queen. We are about to witness a meeting of the most astonishing kind, and out of it the luscious fruits of the oxymoron in action. But if anyone is lovable, deserving of love in his naturalness– that is, being a natural–and in his self-fulfillment, it is Bottom; never more so than when, through Puck's kind offices, Bottom becomes literally what he is, a perfect ass. He might, for his longing earlier and in the setting of a wood, have turned quite fittingly into the lion of the little play or, when earlier Oberon envisioned what loves Titania might waken to once the juice took effect, '. . . lion, bear, or wolf, or bull,/ . . . meddling monkey or . . . busy ape.' But, no, whatever happy incongruity there may be in it, Bottom is meant to be an ass and nothing but an ass. Such is the power of this wood: it enables all to become what they essentially are. In any case, for a Bottom real change is impossible. The more 'changed' he is the more he changes into himself. Fortunately, unlike fairytale characters, changelings, and tragic figures, he is impervious to the enchanted wood and to the profound hazards it entails for one who has once seen it, and thus been alienated forever from the everyday world.

Bottom's moment of transformation, for its appropriateness to the play being rehearsed, is worth considering. Flute as Thisby has just spoken, Quince complains, '. . . all your part at once, cues and all.' Quince continues. 'Pyramus enter. Your cue is past. It is "never tire."'

Then as Flute repeats this description of Pyramus, 'O–"As true as truest horse, that yet would never tire",' Bottom, true horse, untiring indeed, gallops on with his ass's head. Here Shakespeare is reaping the ripened harvest of his earlier plays: movement from metaphor to its literal enactment, most cogently in one as literal as Bottom, and out of Shakespeare's long devotion to Ovid. Already the workaday *Comedy of Errors* in its cries of witchcraft and transformation–its conviction that the Dromios were asses–smacked of Ovid. In *Love's Labour's Lost* and *The Taming of the Shrew*, Shakespeare named, praised and urged Ovid. At last, though Ovid is not mentioned any more than magic is, he is wholly present, supervising in a sense like the moon, in a play that everywhere celebrates and dramatizes metamorphosis, particularly metamorphosis provoked by love. Shakespeare now translates what has possessed him into a triumphant as well as a comic possession. He exercises the whole gamut of metamorphosis: from a change of the most grotesquely physical kind, Bottom become an ass, to a change prompted from without, the flower-juice on Titania and the lovers' eyelids, to a change of heart and mind.

Love-in-idleness has been successfully transplanted from *The Metamorphoses* into the English countryside. The lovers–that is, the men, inconstant like Shakespeare's earlier male lovers; the girls do not change–goaded by the season, nature, and the season of their own natures, and inspired by this flower, naturally go through a series of 'changes', much like the moon's. But they do not change shape; being so much alike, they do not need to; rather they change seeing, and so feeling. Earlier, when Demetrius flees from her, Helena does directly borrow from *The Metamorphoses*, and suggests the comic use they all are being put to in its terms, by wryly reversing the expected order of things: 'Apollo flies, and Daphne holds the chase.' So she accounts for the absence of beasts in this wood, '. . . I am ugly as a bear,/For beasts that meet me run away for fear.' But it is with Bottom and Titania that the 'borrowing' is at its best. Obeying the grain of his nature like the other victims of metamorphosis, Bottom does not become a stag or a flower (unless it be the very flower of an ass) but what earlier plays predicted. Comically enough, a kind of goddess, Titania, does not, by falling in love with and pursuing a handsome mortal, sponsor the change; rather as Bottom changes does she fall in love with him. Yet susceptible as she is, with the juice on her lids, she might have fallen in love with him had he remained what he was. But the largest, most winning employment of *The Metamorphoses* occurs of course in the rustics' *Pyramus and Thisby*. This is what happens, what is bound to happen, when one of the lovely, poignant tales of Ovid passes through such minds and experiences an earth-change, rich, strange, grotesque, marvelous. And here, in comedy, it is Ovid as delight; the notion of an ever-changing world, nature's incessant creative energy, its geysering forth of countless shapes and species, especially as midwived by the moon, is celebrated—life a luscious, gliding dream.

The scenes following between Bottom and Titania are quite symbolical of this play—all for love: the real, the daily, the crude and earthy wedded to the poetic and the magical, one loving and needing the other, or the lofty and the delicate by way of russet and kersey. However incongruously this match may strike us, it is much more than a yoking of opposites by violence. Rather, in all its absurdity it incarnates Coleridge's definition of great poetry. To wed Bottom—rock-bottom reality or earthiness—to Titania—ethereality itself—by love, by moonlight and the essence of a magical flower, this is what great poetry is made of in its ability to discover the compatibility, the unity, the community of all things. For all its absurdity this match is endearing and idyllic, the momentary conjunction of earth and moon in a twilit music, that of poetry. But it is in the nature of Bottom to make such meeting and mating possible. He alone of the mortals—probably for the good, stout ass in him—has direct traffic with the fairies and probably because he alone—though to begin with he would flee the woods—sees nothing outlandish in them, accepts them for what they are and as they are. For they, whatever their difference, are in the wood with him and, since he 'sees' them, they indubitably are. The others, frightened by Puck, disguised as the only animals met in this wood, 'Sometime a horse I'll be, sometime a hound,/A hog, a headless bear, sometimes a fire', scatter hither and yon. (Puck, knowing these rustics and following the vein of his earlier song about his mischief-making among the villagers, becomes realistic animals to chase them. Apparently in his own shape he would not have scared them. But, since they are set off by Bottom as an ass, Puck is simply following suit. And at the end he is what he indeed is: fire or *ignis fatuus*.)

Bottom, standing his ground, singing to keep his courage up as only a true ass can sing, like a very nightingale, wakens Titania. He, the humor of the piece, being in the dark and in the dream with the others (all of us are in this ark together), helps to mitigate the fearfulness of the dark, to lighten it. So his own song, a singing in the dark ('I see their knavery. This is to make an ass of me, to fright me, if they could.

. . . I will sing, that they shall hear I am not afraid'), does for him. Weaver that he is, he may not furnish the clue leading out of this maze, but he proves equal to living in and enjoying it. The goddess and the fairies are for him. Perhaps when we are most the fool, the ass perfect and unassuaged, we come closest to the gods! And he sings a sweet little earthy song, of the *Love's Labour's Lost* variety. Full of common birds and mainly details about them, it is reassuring; but Bottom even comforts himself, drolly enough, with the cuckoo, as though to say, cuckoldry, since it is so common, is a human, realistic, if not natural anchor! Titania, as Bottom had predicted Theseus would do for his roaring, exclaims,

I pray thee, gentle mortal, sing again.
Mine ear is much enamoured of thy note;
So is mine eye enthrallèd to thy shape.

This is indeed the reverse of the mermaid enchanting the sea! But if a mermaid could charm a rude sea, why not a beast, an ass, enthrall a delicate Fairy Queen? If the king of the gods, Zeus, could in his passion assume the shape of a bull or a swan to win a mortal woman, why not a mortal, especially such a mortal, irresistible as a goose or an ass to a fairy goddess? The magical flower-juice opens its victim's eyes to the truth, the loveliness in all things rightly or at least poetically looked upon. Titania is smitten. Meantime, Bottom carries on as confidently as ever. And he has knowingness enough to utter more than asinine wisdom:

Methinks, mistress, you should have little reason for that. And yet,
to say the truth, reason and love keep little company together nowa-
days.

Talk of 'reason', by the way, often turns up in this play, as often as not where it least applies. Lysander, his eyelids bathed and therefore the victim of unreason, makes much of 'reason', and thinks deludedly that now 'Reason becomes the marshal to my will, . . .' Theseus, consider-ing himself the spokesman of commonsense, will of course sing the praises of 'cool reason'.

When Bottom meets his attendants he knows them at once, knows how to greet them, and lordly—like Sly in *The Taming of the Shrew*, how to employ them. For they are naturals all, at last together dewy cheek by hairy jowl. Whatever dream this may be, through his work-man's past he is in touch with his 'servants' and 'subjects', a feelingful, even tender relationship. Thus his dream is full of the actual, the directly lived and vividly encountered. In a sense he never takes the dream as anything but actual. He has heard so much all his life, in fairy and folk tales, of fairies that they are, understandably enough, hardly a surprise to him. In the next scene Bottom has moved from his first meeting's courtesy to a masterly, kind ordering about of these sprites. An ass, steeped in the luscious ways of meadows and nature, would well appreciate the conditions Bottom finds himself in. But what is most wonderful amid all this moony fantasy is Bottom's earthy details, his good, knowing sense and touch of drollery if not comedy, yet his delicacy and solicitude as well. Bidding 'Mounsieur Cobweb' bring him a 'honey-bag', he urges him to be careful: '. . . and, good moun-sieur, have a care the honey-bag break not. I would be loath to have you overflown with a honey-bag, signior.' For all his healthy egotism, and perhaps because of it, Bottom has a deep respect for the private life, the inner drama, of whatever he meets, a respect and a sense of fellow-ship or fellow-feeling. And he is, amusingly and touchingly enough, at his most human and intimate as an ass. The earth in him speaks out in kindness to other earthlings. Like Sly's notion of theater, Bottom's taste in music comes to 'I have a reasonable good ear in music. Let's have the tong and the bones.' His ear is indeed reasonable and good—that is, for an ass. Similarly, when Titania asks him what he would eat, he replies,

Truly, a peck of provender. I could munch your good dry oats. Methinks I have a great desire to a bottle of hay. Good hay, sweet hay, hath no fellow.

The sociable, not to say sweetly civil, nature of Bottom, ass and all, comes splendidly to the fore in that last sentence.

Then with all of them, the lovers and Titania and Bottom, as though sharing one dream, asleep side by side, the sleep, the spells, wait to be broken. Titania is properly released first. Thereupon, in the early dawn of the last day before the marriage, Theseus, Hippolyta, and his train appear. Theseus is of course to be identified with dawn, order, and pursuits that, though they be savage, are profitable, prepared, and 'civilized', like war and the hunt. The woods are to be entered for spoils and the sport thereof, not for their own pleasure and certainly not for self-pursuit. And the hunt, like war, would admit violence and death. To establish the time and the mood, it is the bustling promise of the hunt we are involved in. Brisk, capable man that he is, in the midst of this busyness Theseus delivers himself of a lovely piece of practical music, as compatible with him as Oberon's speeches were with him. Though it ushers in the day and daytime living, while Oberon's ushered in the business of the night, one waking the lovers, the other setting them to dreaming, in its way Theseus' speech is no less lyrical and lucidly self-realizing.

> *Go, one of you, find out the forester,*
> *For now our observation is performed,*
> *And since we have the vaward of the day,*
> *My love shall hear the music of my hounds.*
> *Uncouple in the western valley, let them go.*
> *Despatch, I say, and find the forester.*
> *We will, fair Queen, up to the mountain's top*
> *And mark the musical confusion*
> *Of hounds and echo in conjunction.*

An overseeing, overhearing mountain-top is right for such a lordly pair. And it is reminiscent of Oberon's 'promontory' which was also a place for marvelous music, if of a mermaid and a dolphin affecting the sea and certain stars rather than of hounds rousing a valley with their baying. Theseus' and Hippolyta's words echo with ample, waking music, present and omnipresent sound. Hippolyta proves herself, in the reality of her presentation of her mythical past, apt mate for Theseus:

> *I was with Hercules and Cadmus once*
> *When in a wood of Crete they bayed the bear*
> *With hounds of Sparta. Never did I hear*
> *Such gallant chiding; for, besides the groves,*
> *The skies, the fountains, every region near*
> *Seemed all one mutual cry. I never heard*
> *So musical a discord, such sweet thunder.*

Clearly Theseus' hounds are hunting creatures, and we might expect them at last to track down the often mentioned beasts of this wood. Has their master, huntsman extraordinary, not even caught his love Hippolyta? Yet he and his hounds also defer to the spell of this play. Thus the hounds are let loose to do what this play is up to, the making of music, and to join, in Hippolyta's verses, the lovely dogs of legend. So loosened, they hunt the play's only true prey, the lovers and the rustics. And the play's only wild beasts, those in the lovers' minds and spirits, are routed or at least put to sleep by day and waking.

Surely the speeches of both Theseus and Hippolyta, lovely arias, are reminiscent of Oberon's, with music and its influence their common center. One is also put in mind of Shakespeare's *Venus and Adonis* and of Venus' importuning of Adonis as she finds his a 'mermaid's voice', and speaks of its 'Melodious discord, heavenly tune harsh-sounding,/ Ear's deep-sweet music, and heart's deep-sore wounding.' But here since Theseus and Hippolyta are mortals, if royal ones and mythical, much occupied with the business of living, it is not a mermaid but their much loved, familiar hounds which are responsible for the music. One might, if out of the grotesquery of Titania and Bottom's scene, discover resemblance in Titania's delight in Bottom's neighish song. An ass or a hound, heard sympathetically, would be their own versions of very nightingale. In any case, how could anyone do better with hounds? And not only does all nature, as for Oberon's mermaid, seem to listen but to respond. Like the rude sea grown *civil*, this sound is *chiding* that is *gallant;* more, a baying that unites, makes a musical discord, all one mutual cry, as though the sea, being its natural self, should not only be civil but make all around it so.

Theseus in the following words brings these hounds and their music even closer:

> *My hounds are bred out of the Spartan kind,*
> *So flewed, so sanded, and their heads are hung*
> *With ears that sweep away the morning dew;*
> *Crook-kneed, and dewlapped like Thessalian bulls;*
> *Slow in pursuit, but matched in mouth like bells,*
> *Each under each. A cry more tunable*
> *Was never holloed to, nor cheered with horn,*
> *In Crete, in Sparta, nor in Thessaly.*

His hounds are best seen in their absence, best presented through vivid description. In Shakespeare's work, especially in the earlier plays, there are verses which engender many distinguished descendants. One moment, adequate and attractive in its place, like the lord's description of his dogs in *The Taming of the Shrew*, amounts to a sketch or stage directions in lovely descriptive poetry for the scene and action of related material in a later play. This way Shakespeare's work is interrelated; a line, possibly rather modest in itself, points to greatness gathering in the near or far distance, an echo as of a host soon to be down on us with thundering grace. What impresses here is what poetry these very real hounds, out of their very reality, evoke from the seemingly matter-of-fact Theseus, a beginning no doubt of that triumph of practicality become poetry, Hal or Henry V. How daringly, as if on the swing of their cry, Theseus sweeps from their ears and the morning dew to Thessalian bulls (can one deny the outrageous lovely pun of 'dewlapped'?) and then, the sound itself welling out, to the reverberatory 'matched in mouth like bells,/Each under each', with its splendid leveling off of rime from 'bulls' to 'bells', still ringing as it fades out in 'tunable'. Also, those hounds, ugly as they are, 'so flewed, so sanded', with heads and ears so low-slung they mingle with the morning dew, are lovely too, close fellows of Bottom just a dulcet bray and a dew-bedabbled ear away. For that matter, what is this play itself but many voices 'matched in mouth like bells,/Each under each.'

The lovers, caught between the imprints, waning fast, of dream and the impact of the horns' music, wake—the true end of the hunt; with them found, it is called off. Hunting, it would seem, beyond one human for another, is not for this play, this drama of a dream. A great rubbing of eyes and minds ensues. Their dream was so absorbing that they cannot remember it. It has consumed itself. Demetrius says, 'These things seem small and undistinguishable,/Like far-off mountains turnéd into clouds.' An Ovidian image, it belongs to a genre of imagery very popular with Shakespeare for suggesting the mercuriality of life, of even the seemingly most substantial, lasting things. The lovers, much puzzled, leave, and Bottom wakes, as he should, ever ready: 'When my cue comes, call me, and I will answer', then utters the true moral of the play, 'I have had a dream past the wit of man to say what dream it was.' Any critic prods this dream, this 'most rare vision', Shakespeare gives us full warning, at his own risk. Bottom underlines the amazement with an easy confusion of the senses befitting him:

> The eye of man hath not heard, the ear of man hath not seen, man's hand is not able to taste, his tongue to conceive, nor his heart to report, what my dream was.

Something has transpired so extraordinary that man's powers, the senses and the heart together, even in extraordinary exertions, cannot hope to deal with it. There is, therefore, nothing left but to eke out the last profit from this dream:

> I will get Peter Quince to write a ballad of this dream. It shall be called Bottom's Dream, because it hath no bottom, and I will sing it

in the latter end of the play, before the Duke. Peradventure, to make it
the more gracious, I shall sing it at her death.

Even he, it seems, cannot resist the pun on his name; he must have
heard it somewhere and recently! The eternal ham, never done, finding
opportunities to exhibit himself and committing art in placing and
timing to make the most of himself, he must enable us to witness this
play from a Bottom point of view. The ballad, apparently, will emphasize the unfathomability of the dream.

At last in Act V, Scene I, we have the official version of what
happened: Theseus utters what is perhaps—for mistaken reasons I
suggest—the most famous single speech in the play. It is noble,
splendidly poetic, yet patronizing and sceptical. At Hippolyta's ''Tis
strange, my Theseus, that these lovers speak of', he shrugs their
dreams off: 'More strange than true. I never may believe/These antique
fables, nor these fairy toys.' This is especially amusing coming from a
figure, a mighty mythical hero, out of antique fable, and from the
play's ruler, responsible in a basic sense for the freeing of the dreams as
for the presence of Titania and Oberon. He explains:

> *Lovers and madmen have such seething brains,*
> *Such shaping fantasies that apprehend*
> *More than cooling reason ever comprehends.*

Reasonable man that he is, he does not realize how accurate his observation may be. Bottom, who knows 'Man is but an ass if he go about to
expound this dream . . . a patched fool', also knows it can be dealt with
—as it is in this whole play—in poetry only; thus the ballad he looks
forward to. Theseus is no doubt speaking out of very considerable
experience. But he is not praising these seething brains and fantasies;
on the contrary. 'The lunatic, the lover, and the poet/Are of imagination all compact.' By their Plato-like lumping of lunatic, lover and poet
together, these lines should make clear what contempt Theseus feels
for such fantasies. We might wonder that he, an ardent lover, should
be so belittling of the lover. But himself well over the romantic, moony
parts of first love, a mature—not to say veteran—lover, he must mean
the young, addled, out-of-this-world lover, the one in love with love
and not with a particular woman, the capricious lover he long ago was
when he too threaded his way through love's labyrinth. Thus now,
whatever his impatience before his desire for marriage and loving, he
has curbed that impatience out of decency and for a decent round of
revelry. He continues:

> *One sees more devils than vast Hell can hold,*
> *That is the madman. The lover, all as frantic,*
> *Sees Helen's beauty in a brow of Egypt.*

(Or, one might say, Adonis handsome in a pair of shaggy ears!)

> *The poet's eye, in a fine frenzy rolling,*
> *Doth glance from heaven to earth, from earth to heaven;*
> *And as imagination bodies forth*
> *The forms of things unknown, the poet's pen*
> *Turns them to shapes and gives to airy nothing*
> *A local habitation and a name.*

Such giving, since it is, after all, to airy nothings, is not exactly something to applaud.

> *Such tricks hath strong imagination*
> *That, if it would but apprehend some joy,*
> *It comprehends some bringer of that joy;*
> *Or in the night, imagining some fear,*
> *How easy is a bush supposed a bear!*

Attractive though these lines are in themselves, one can see the derision intended out of this eminently pragmatical Athenian's superiority as he finds a common frenzy in all three, a sad failure to see things as they are. For him the tricks of a strong imagination are tantamount to the will-o'-the-wisp that a man follows to his own dismay.

But Hippolyta, more sympathetic to the moon to begin with, is not so easily convinced. She says,

> *But all the story of the night told over,*
> *And all their minds transfigured so together,*
> *More witnesseth than fancy's images,*
> *And grows to something of great constancy,*
> *But, howsoever, strange and admirable.*

So many could not have been transported together, could not have shared a mere 'dream' that was nonsense, pure fantasy. Theseus, however, is too knowing, too arrogant to admit the possibility of any truth in the night's story. This dismissal is a kind of capping irony, a little like the superior Puck's mistake when he who scoffs at those foolish mortals is also taken in by appearances, through the eye—no one is fool- or ocular-proof—and applies the love-juice to the wrong lids.

Ruler that Theseus is, he refuses to know and to believe what strange things have gone on behind his capable back.

Here the Apollonian, embodied in Theseus, the ultra-confident day-man, since this is comedy, is still disdainful of the dark—mere shadows, hallucinations, folly. The nobleman of good sense, reason, stability, action, Theseus is, like Berowne before him, able to pierce foolishness. But, unlike Berowne, he does not see his participation in it. Shake-speare knew it a matter of scale as he knew the Theseus in Bottom and, perhaps more importantly, the Bottom in Theseus, as well as touches of both in us all; Bottom sees only what he sees; Theseus refuses to see what he does not care to. In its world the beetle is a glittering monarch, proud as the lion or the sun. In the chain of being for all its hierarchy every link is important and in itself, in its own terms, in its own place paramount, with its strength and meaning running through the others as their lives, dependent on it, run through it.

Of course it is amusing to think of what Theseus came to outside this Elizabethan setting. King of Athens, he was one of the more fabulous Greek heroes whose business it was to spread light and reason and to clear out chaos and the monstrous beasts. Yet, as I mentioned earlier, in the midst of his most heroic deeds of light he, led by Titania through the moonlit night, knew all the irrational changes of love. When Oberon would reply to Titania's charges that he has been in love with Hippolyta, he says of Theseus

> *Didst thou not lead him through the glimmering night*
> *From Perigenia, whom he ravished?*
> *And make him with fair Aegle break his faith,*
> *With Ariadne and Antiopa?*

Nonetheless, Theseus is no more aware of enchantment than those just come from it and, apparently, much more opposed to it. Thus a bit later, just before the rustics' playlet, he dismisses Ovid as old stuff (no metamorphosis for solid Theseus) and says of 'The battle with the Centaurs, to be sung/By an Athenian eunuch to the harp', 'We'll none of that. That have I told my love,/In glory of my kinsman Hercules.' In the Ovidian tale Theseus and Hercules fought off the centaurs. And Theseus talks of them in passing as though centaurs, those half men, half horse (and even more relevantly, supposedly conceived in cloud), were, like the minotaur or ass Bottom, normal and daily. But those centaurs, honored guests at a wedding, had interrupted it with attempted rape; we'll have no further interruption of weddings here! Similarly Theseus shrugs off the rending of Orpheus, the great magical musician, as 'an old device'. Theseus, like most of the rest in the play, believing in his eyes and ears alone and his consequent notion of reality, belongs to those who say, when the mysterious occurs, it's happened (that is, it could happen) and so it's natural, not magical, not mysterious at all.

But we must not forget that Theseus is, for comedy's sake, the sanity required; his common sense has become scepticism to keep the play from floating off gossamer-fashion in the moonlight. And then, good, wise ruler that he is, even as he belittles dreams and fantasies he decides to hear the homespun play and defends the crew's intentions in the way we heard royalty do in earlier plays:

> *I will hear that play;*
> *For never anything can be amiss,*
> *When simpleness and duty tender it.*

When Hippolyta demurs, he says,

> *The kinder we, to give them thanks for nothing.*
> *Our sport shall be to take what they mistake;*
> *And what poor duty cannot do, noble respect*
> *Takes it in might, not merit.*
> *Where I have come, great clerks have purposéd*
> *To greet me with premeditated welcomes,*
> *Where I have seen them shiver and look pale,*
> *Make periods in the midst of sentences,*

(such periods *will* appear in the playlet, but out of ignorance not fear: Theseus is sorely mistaken if he expects these players, at least cocky Bottom, to shiver and look pale.)

> *Throttle their practiced accent in their fears,*
> *And, in conclusion, dumbly have broke off,*
> *Not paying me a welcome. Trust me, sweet,*
> *Out of this silence yet I picked a welcome,*
> *And in the modesty of fearful duty*
> *I read as much as from the rattling tongue*
> *Of saucy and audacious eloquence.*
> *Love, therefore, and tongue-tied simplicity*
> *In least speak most, to my capacity.*

Sponsoring the 'observation' with its lovely, 'natural' freedom, Theseus must also guard against its excesses, its becoming serious and more than its moment, holiday threatening to overwhelm the daily. Shakespeare, we have already seen, was always moving from artifice to art, as he was from description and the lyrical to action, was always leaning toward the plain, the 'classical'; yet always he was detained, so ingrained was its habit in him, by the complex, the suggestive.

Nonetheless, Theseus, despite his belief in plainness over eloquence, mocks the playlet in its performance as much as anyone else. This playlet is the triumph of the play and the triumph of misunderstanding of love and language: what *might* have happened to the lovers for a parental obstacle in this play (as it does happen in *Romeo and Juliet*). Having provided us with spectacle in the wood, 'real' love and passion that proved ludicrous, as ludicrous in its way as what we are about to witness, the lovers now watch with us the comic spectacle, an absurdity they nowise, despite the patent resemblance, connect with their own. Shakespeare is enjoying a buoyantly playful take-off of his own art, the art of acting, staging, and the rest in his day. The confusion of imagination and reality is complete (in the way Theseus said it often is) as is, for instance, the confusion of words, meaning, senses. Bottom in his great consistency of character, not only adjusts language to his own idiocy, but even his senses and the world to cocksure malapropery.

Yet preposterous though he and the playlet are, they are not so remote from Ovid's version or the heart of the play as they might at first sound. When Bottom first addresses the wall 'O wall, O sweet and lovely wall', and thanks it as a 'courteous wall' (should we not remember the 'civil' sea?) for helping him to see his love but then cries out, for the unseen Thisby, 'O wicked wall, through whom I see no bliss!/ Cursed be thy stones for thus deceiving me!' absurd as this may be in its fits and starts, if we look at Golding's Ovid we find the same thing in reverse: '"O spiteful wall," said they, "why dost thou part us lovers thus?"' And then in less than three lines '"And yet thou shalt not find us churls; we think ourselves in debt/For the same piece of courtesy, in vouching safe to let our sayings to our friendly ears thus freely come and go."' Like the rude sea properly approached, the wall (or anything) can grow civil or courteous. How much humor is implicit in Ovid may be hard to say, but certainly we can enjoy its gentle tone in Shakespeare's version of the tragedy. Again, the duet of love between Pyramus and Thisby, making a delectable shambles of former great, frustrated lovers, twits the romantic even as the duet celebrates it.

Finally, the double death surely owes something to Golding's Ovid: his Pyramus, assuming Thisby devoured, after

> . . . *he had bewept and kissed the garment which he knew,*
> *'Receive thou my blood too,' quoth he, and therewithal he drew*
> *His sword, the which among his guts he thrust, and by and by*
> *Did draw it from the bleeding wound, beginning for to die,*
> *And cast himself upon his back. The blood did spin on high*
> *As when a conduit pipe is cracked, the water bursting out*
> *Doth shoot itself a great way off and pierce the air about.*

This garment kissing, this gut thrusting, this by and by, this beginning for to die, this casting himself upon his back, and especially the spinning, shooting blood as out of a conduit, are they so far from Pyramus and Thisby's deaths here by moonlight in an ecstasy of absurdity? Apart from Golding, Bottom, who need learn from no one, must inevitably be a long day's dying, one of the most lively on record, to be bettered only by the fatter, sprightlier 'resurrection' of Falstaff.

With the playlet and so the play over, only bed is left; and Puck. He suddenly, in a kind of epilogue, introduces the real world: that of darkness, violence, death; strange after the stage lion of the playlet or the verbal beasts, and little more, of the lovers in the wood:

> *Now the hungry lion roars,*
> *And the wolf behowls the moon,*
> *Whilst the heavy plowman snores,*
> *All with weary task fordone.*
> *Now the wasted brands do glow,*
> *Whilst the screech owl, screeching loud,*
> *Puts the wretch that lies in woe*
> *In remembrance of a shroud.*
> *Now it is the time of night*
> *That the graves, all gaping wide,*
> *Every one lets forth his sprite,*
> *In the churchway paths to glide.*

But, having mentioned these, he promptly disposes of all, at least for this play and its people (and those for whom the play was put on), with 'Not a mouse/Shall disturb this hallowed house'. Only once before did similar words occur, spoken also by Puck in Act III, Scene II, when he warned Oberon of oncoming day:

My fairy lord, this must be done with haste,
For night's swift dragons cut the clouds full fast,
And yonder shines Aurora's harbinger,
At whose approach, ghosts, wandering here and there,
Troop home to churchyards. Damnèd spirits all,
That in crossways and floods have burial,
Already to their wormy beds are gone.
For fear lest day should look their shames upon,
They willfully themselves exile from light
And must for aye consort with black-browed night.

But Oberon assured him that he and the other fairies were 'spirits of another sort', at home in morning and daytime. Yet it is true that they work best at night by moonlight. Thus in the end Oberon and Titania bless all the newly married beds and 'consecrate' them with a remarkable holy water, 'field-dew' or nature in its fertility and beneficence. Then to conclude, Puck swears us into the dream:

If we shadows have offended,
Think but this, and all is mended,
That you have but slumbered here
While these visions did appear,
And this weak and idle theme,
No more yielding but a dream, . . .

These are 'airy nothings', 'shadows', after all; but, past being fairies, airy nothings like all characters in plays and, in this world of chance and change, all creatures.

As Theseus put it a little earlier, when defending the playlet and its cast against Hippolyta's 'this is the silliest stuff that ever I heard', 'The best in this kind are but shadows, and the worst are no worse if imagination amend them.' His imagination is not so meager after all; nor, as it seemed, altogether limited to the reasonable, the practical. Some good part of his attitude no doubt is ascribable to his understanding as a ruler, his royal courtesy to his subjects. When Hippolyta retorts, 'It must be your imagination, then, and not theirs', he gives the answer that most brilliantly applies to this play, with its gigantic sympathies: 'If we imagine no worse of them than they of themselves, they may pass for excellent men.' And they may, they may, Bottom and his crew and all the rest. Only at the playlet's end, when lion offers an epilogue or a Bergomask dance, does Theseus call it quits and a night:

'No epilogue, I pray you; for your play needs no excuse. Never excuse, for when the players are all dead, there need none to be blamed.' To conclude the human part of the play formally, he then delivers himself of the following verses:

> *The iron tongue of midnight hath told twelve.*
> *Lovers, to bed: 'tis almost fairy time.*
> *I fear we shall outsleep the coming morn*
> *As much as we this night have overwatched.*
> *This palpable-gross play hath well beguiled*
> *The heavy gait of night.*

Fairy time it is. Puck and the other fairies enter for their share of the watching and to close the play as they bless and consecrate it. And finally Puck begs the audience to be as gentle with this play as Theseus was with that of the homespuns:

> *So, good night unto you all.*
> *Give me your hands, if we be friends,*
> *And Robin shall restore amends.*

In Money and in Love

The Merchant of Venice

IN *A Midsummer Night's Dream* we found ourselves in a wood charmingly moonlit for most audiences. But sometimes that wood is read so darkly that it is almost construed to be an offshoot of Dante's. Then it seems to invite unrule, if not misrule, anarchy, blatant animality. Modern critics, bred on cold war and black comedy, may discover a ravenous bear in every bush and a serpent coiling behind the gentlest smile. But what such response amounts to is that we, trying to appropriate Shakespeare and his plays to our world, are sounding ourselves rather than them. To some degree, it is true, we cannot help reading Shakespeare backwards, not only from us, but from the darkest work he later came to. Nonetheless, we may maintain, in striving to read *A Midsummer Night's Dream* in its own light, that, whatever threats and darknesses it affords, it does so chiefly to spell the changes of the moon. The play's magic is responsible in the first place through its delicious energy for those threats. One touch of that magic and the threats of nightmare, the confusions, no matter how ensnarling, dissolve and into a golden fanfare, an enrichment of revelry.

The Merchant of Venice, however, is a different story. Not far behind it lay Shakespeare's sorties into historical tragedy and into the tragical history of *Romeo and Juliet*. And despite the elegance and wealth, the 'gentleness', of *The Merchant of Venice*, in it a real measure of the hungry lion that Puck mentions at the end of his play does roar, and the wolf does behowl the moon. Moreover, that measure of savage animality is oppressively translated into its most troubling manifestation: the human become ferocious. In truth one is hard put not to conclude that here Shakespeare decided to see how much freight, grimmer than ever, he could compel comedy to carry. Certainly comedy is not used to being so strenuously tried.

This trying depends on the increased presence of the 'real' world. In *A Midsummer Night's Dream* the real world is briefly under the spell of a beneficent if somewhat wayward fairy rule. In *Romeo and*

Juliet the romantic, moonlit circle of love is framed and then destroyed by the real world; for Romeo and Juliet are two against that world, crushed once they attempt, beyond the circle of each other's arms, to cope with it. But in *The Merchant of Venice* Shakespeare, by what he has learned from this recent work, puts those two worlds for the first time in side-by-side competition and collision. The lovers of this play are much more directly in the real world; and they deal with it by no magic other than their own wits, humanity, and the maturity required of them. At the same time, through their wealth and high status, through the availability to them of an inspirational, moon-struck realm like Belmont, they do enjoy perquisites not at the disposal of most of us. Nor are they so innocent or so profoundly, awingly, foolish as to think themselves superior to the real, able by their intrinsic greatness to dispense with means or, for that matter, the world we live in. Yet, we shall see, at crucial moments Antonio and Portia out of selfless love and with whole hearts offer to do so. These two worlds, Venice and Belmont, in necessary, ominous confrontation, determine the drama and the expanding seriousness of the play.

But we should take our bearings from the play's own setting. First of all, it is called *The Merchant of Venice*. And though one understands how easily this title may be assumed to mean Shylock—already in 1598 the play appeared in the Stationers' Register as 'a booke of the Marchaunt of Venyce, or otherwise called the Jewe of Venyce'—we should recognize that for Shakespeare the merchant and true center of the play is not Shylock but Antonio. The name Shylock, transliteration of the Hebrew 'shalach', in the King James version of the Bible translated 'cormorant', indicated at once to anyone who knew the word what repugnance he was expected to feel toward Shylock. It is a rich, accomplished gentleman, Antonio, living at the heart of the most prosperous mercantile society of the time, with whom we are concerned. For aspirant London, Venice provided a model of wealth, power, culture, sophistication. Indeed it was one of the chief goals of a young English worthy undertaking his Grand Tour. In the play, Venice is in all its panache and glory. Like London it is mainly a sea city. A port built on many islands, it is open to the world and dependent for its wealth and well-being almost entirely on the sea, never on what it makes, only on what it does, on trade and business.

Surely it is not too far-fetched at this point to be reminded of *The Comedy of Errors*, laid in the little sea-port of Ephesus, with that play's emphasis on trade and the life-and-death dependence on money. The

Duke of Ephesus, invoking the irrevocable laws of his realm, says at
the outset in sentence on the foreign merchant Aegon:

> *The enmity and discord which of late*
> *Sprung from the rancorous outrage of your Duke*
> *To merchants, our well-dealing countrymen,*
> *Who, wanting guilders to redeem their lives,*
> *Have sealed his rigorous statutes with their bloods,*
> *Excludes all pity from our threat'ning looks.*

Like the world of *The Comedy of Errors*, only more so, that of *The
Merchant of Venice*, since it involves many peoples and nations brought
together primarily by business, must rely for peace and order, not on
fellow-feeling and sympathy, the bond that exists between the true-
blooded Venetians themselves, but on the law, rigorously observed.
And since Venice is much more important than Ephesus, so much more
essential and difficult must the maintaining of order be. At the same
time, in the Venetians presented we are dealing with beings of a cast
far superior to the Ephesians. For these Venetians are sophisticates,
aristocratically banded together in love and mutuality. Furthermore,
the challenge, the ominous legal problem, at the opening of *The
Comedy of Errors*, concerning a foreigner, is promptly forgotten and
not resumed till nearly the end of the play. In *The Merchant of Venice*,
on the other hand, an important citizen's collision with the law because
of the representations of a foreigner, Shylock, with that citizen's life
at stake, is the play's principal occupation. Rowdiness, apposite to a
farce and to fairly commonplace characters, prevails in *The Comedy of
Errors*; the law a side issue, that rowdiness batters its way through to
understanding and resolution. But in *The Merchant of Venice* love and
understanding, practiced by the noble Venetians and Belmontese, a
love and an understanding particularly evoked by the threat to Antonio,
save the day.

Like *A Midsummer Night's Dream*, however, *The Merchant of
Venice* is at present liable to being viewed with a jaundiced eye. Not
only may there be little sympathy for Shylock but for his opponents as
well. All may be adjudged contaminated by money, interested in each
other mainly as useable or profitable objects. Under such a view the
play is almost pushed into the company of the dark or problem
comedies, *Measure for Measure* and *Troilus and Cressida*, say, or a
world everywhere soured and corroded. Yet might we not consider it
a shame to increase what we already have—and amply—when it means

losing something else, a rare accomplishment, in times like ours rarer than ever, with its seriously questioned yet finally adequate equilibrium?

Comedy though it is, *The Merchant of Venice* opens with–a major chord it turns out–Antonio's expression of a melancholy uncommon to his bustling, gay world of Venice, a melancholy which Theseus at his play's opening expelled to funerals, and which was often crucial later on in Shakespeare's work, Is it completely amiss to suggest that Antonio may be the first tremor of what will become that earthquake Hamlet? Until then, all the young gentlemen–with the temporary exception of Antipholus of Syracuse and the gloom-cast, tragedy-bound Romeo–are for this life and its performances; they believe in it as they belong to it. This melancholy hardly seems fitting to a well-furnished, widely befriended and beloved merchant-gentleman like Antonio. Yet he says,

> *In sooth, I know not why I am so sad;*
> *It wearies me; you say it wearies you;*
> *But how I caught it, found it, or came by it,*
> *What stuff 'tis made of, whereof it is born,*
> *I am to learn;*
> *And such a want-wit sadness makes of me*
> *That I have much ado to know myself.*

(It is amusing to have Antonio admit what T. S. Eliot accused the later Hamlet and, even more severely, Shakespeare of–not knowing the melancholy's source. And not knowing it so that Antonio is no longer sure of the all-important who-I-am.)

Antonio's admission is especially striking against the backdrop of the plays we have examined. Comedy notwithstanding, melancholy, we realize, has been with us from the start. But in a very practical, if not simple, way. Already Aegeon and his Syracusan son were melancholy, and for reasons that seemed on the whole clear and convincing enough; circumstances had estranged them from their loved ones, their worlds, therefore from themselves. Also, more comically in view of the kind of confusions besetting him, Dromio of Syracuse wondered who he was. Sly too, plucked out of his usual world and dropped into an altogether new one, soon questioned his identity. Only one character so far–beyond the sketch of Adriana in *The Comedy of Errors*–at home and with her own, was painfully dislocated: Kate who, till Petruchio freed her, for confusion of personality was confined to a hateful, always more alienating role. Certainly the confusions, rich and unseating though they may have been, of *A Midsummer Night's Dream* were—if not to the young lovers and the rustics to us—amply accounted for. But unlike all these, Antonio happily, securely it would seem, occupies the center of his world and the bosom of his dearest friends. Nevertheless, that Antonio's mood, his presentiment, is justified and that he is truly 'to learn' we know. One might propose that a whiff of the future's destructive winds, not to say the stink of mortality, always but a breath away, has already reached him. The significant hiatus after 'I am to learn', the three pregnant if empty feet, silent perhaps so that he may listen to the murmur of the distant gathering storm, it will be the business of this play to fill.

Antonio's two friends, typical Venetian dandies, fairly anonymous, no less similar and echoing than their names, promptly, obligingly explain him to himself. At once by their words and manners, the very flower of their world, we see what kind of world this Venice is; their speeches constitute the air it lives in. Dramatically alone, described in the words and gestures of its citizens, does Venice emerge for us. Elegant young worthies, with a bit of the breeze of Petruchio in them and easily lost among Romeo's companions or, for that matter, the King of Navarre's carefree lords, these are also free by their station to encourage and to indulge their wits and their moods. But how much more eloquent they are than most of their predecessors. Happy highfalutins, they are set sweepingly asail on their self-inspiring breaths. By Venice's sophisticated culture, one they feel fully deserving of, no less than by Shakespeare's ripening art, these have a surpassing grace, a kind of luxury powerfully coiled upon itself.

That luxury is evident at once in Salarino's first words:

> *Your mind is tossing on the ocean,*
> *There where your argosies with portly sail,*
> *Like signiors and rich burghers on the flood,*
> *Or, as it were, the pageants of the sea,*
> *Do overpeer the petty traffickers,*
> *That curtsy to them, do them reverence,*
> *As they fly by them with their woven wings.*

His 'as it were' (we might remember Holofernes and Nathaniel) is a courtly little flourish, the lavishment of a mind at ease, able to enjoy as it cultivates itself. But Antonio tells him that he is wrong. Antonio, there is no doubt, is one to be extremely sensitive to what he does. And

having put himself out so far at sea, he might well feel the reverbera-
tion of events shooting back over those distant lines. However, unlike
Shylock, say, he is not one to live principally, let alone exclusively, in
and through his business. (Yet, we shall learn from his later observation on poverty in old age, some root truth does exist in what Salarino
says. And does before the uncertainty, the frailty, that all their wealth,
gaiety and gallantry, not to say high-spiritedness, are based on.)

Salarino's lovely words are worth examining for themselves and for
what they have to do with the whole play. He sees Antonio's argosies
as gentlemen (or Antonio himself), signiors and rich burghers, splendid
spectacles and performances, that, when the lesser ships in their larger
motion on the waves curtsy—or, naturalistically, bob—to them,
properly for their loftier height look over the smaller, overlook them
and at the same time lord it over them: 'overpeer'. In this one word we
have a neat knotting of several dimensions of experience: in those
ships' very physical demeanor their spiritual superiority is established.
Superiors that they are, they almost exact worship. Well these little
boats might 'do them reverence', for the argosies angelically 'fly by
them with their woven wings'. Wealth here becomes so buoyant that
it flies and in its grace achieves the one touch of 'religion' in this scene.
Thus in his first verses Salarino is warning Antonio of the truth—to
wit, that these ships are treading water, and the bigger ones because
of their weight and size, their larger exposure to storm, their greater
appeal to pirates, most dangerously. But simultaneously to mollify
Antonio he swaddles all in most lightsome, wind-and-water-confident
language. This is the fine-blowing comic spirit, the poetic power, that
prevails in this often shaken play.

At once his near double, Salanio, echoes Salarino. And Salarino, as
though never stopped, or taking impetus from Salanio's slighter
words, makes his own breath and his imagination the inspiration of
Antonio's distress no less than of the world's hurlyburly:

> *My wind, cooling my broth,*
> *Would blow me to an ague when I thought*
> *What harm a wind too great at sea might do.*
> *I should not see the sandy hour-glass run*
> *But I should think of shallows and of flats,*
> *And see my wealthy Andrew docked in sand,*
> *Vailing her high-top lower than her ribs*
> *To kiss her burial. Should I go to church*

And see the holy edifice of stone
And not bethink me straight of dangerous rocks
Which, touching but my gentle vessel's side,
Would scatter all her spices on the stream,
Enrobe the roaring waters with my silks,
And, in a word, but even now worth this,
And now worth nothing?

The sequence of his thought is fascinating. Even at life-giving dinner, when he prepares to eat, that which makes his broth drinkable blows up into an ague, the human counterpart of tempest. We see what storms lurk in the very breath we live by. The hour-glass, measuring our time, our life, runs into shallows and flats, runs out into ruin and death. And, most paradoxical climax of all, the church which ought to symbolize the spiritual life and salvation, since it is the Rock by which we live, should he go to it would immediately—it is clearly the 'stone' of that edifice and not the 'holy' that impresses him—remind him of natural rocks to wreck his gentle ship (that gentle vessel's side obviously suggests the frail body housing us) and to waste his wealth. This wealth, we notice, consists not of necessities but, like his verses, of spices and silks. Yet in his describing the dangers and enacting their consequences, though he comes—most aptly with the power of the word to his succinct yet parenthetical 'in a word'—to 'nothing' (those investing everything in this life can hardly expect something after), how magnificently he sets out by way of the music of his poetry to dispel those dangers, or at least to contain them. In short, he and Salanio are at the start trying to do for Antonio what the Fifth Act will attempt to do for the entire play. For a moment ('in a word)' Salarino has succeeded in enrobing the roaring waters with his verbal silks. But we know how much Antonio's gentle side will soon be threatened by a swiftly oncoming, dagger-sharp rock. The problem will be how to enwrap the elemental and the elements, here a Shylock of bare gabardine, in the silks of music. Or at least silks will have to prove their superiority over gabardine.

Meantime we appreciate that these are men of the world, with the riches of the church itself drawn on by them to adorn this world. Of course the church, in its original, stark intention—is this church Saint Mark's?—would be a rock to scatter such finery. But these are not men to play, whatever boredom wealth and leisure might produce, at the King of Navarre's school of night and poverty. And art too, like religion, rich though Venice may have been in magnificent monuments of both, is, beyond language and manners, given short shrift. Aside from the likelihood, however, that Shakespeare never saw Venice, one who has can say of it, its plenteous art treasures and churches notwithstanding, that it is itself a shimmering mirage; in fact it amounts to a stage in the shifting clouds, witnessed at best in its exuberance and its evanescence, filled like its canals with floating, changing figures. (It is perhaps pertinent to remember that in itself Venice, the waters incessantly lapping at it, is almost like a great, preciously cargoed ship in that little by little it is sinking into the sea: this too, too solid world is indeed melting.) But among Venice's instant, living pictures, beyond the play's verbal images and gayly plumed characters, what are paintings, statues, works of art? Rather, like Theseus, chafing at delays, these Venetians are all for living and action, for the here and now. Much more than Theseus, however, they value play for its own sake, value the conversion of living into it. Their masque, for instance, will be undertaken not to dispose of time before a marriage but in part to act as a setting for an elopement and marriage, themselves felicitous ingredients in the festivities. Though like Theseus they know of churches and nunneries and may acknowledge their thrice blessedness, like him they much prefer the 'earthlier happy'. No less a noble spirit than Portia, virtuous though she is, chafes at her cloister-like confinement and yearns to be freed into love, marriage, and living.

We shall soon recognize, however, that the Venetians' worldliness, their concern with the world and its furnishings, is fundamentally different from Shylock's. Different too in depth and style from that of the earlier comic figures. And this difference is at once perceptible in their expression and most consummately realized there. Their speech is more transparent, much easier, roomier, more gracefully available, with little slapstick or chop-logic. The verse no longer resembles a machine that, running itself on an iron track, almost becomes in its elaborateness engrossed in itself. In addition this verse is, by its time, place, and occasion, far from the earlier, massive, piled-up adjectives and nouns, marshalled like an army with its battering rams, appropriate for the histories, especially those built rough-hewn stone upon stone. By contrast these Venetian speeches, one with their element, are all fluency. Picture-laden, they have developed from the lovely verbal-pictured arias of Oberon, Titania (we might compare for amusement Salarino's 'rich burghers on the flood' with Titania's reversed image, her pregnant 'vot'ress' imitating 'the embarkéd traders on the flood'), and Theseus. But more than that, these Venetian speeches, mirroring the world from which they derive, through their lyrical power also do superb dramatic work. In fact, they might move one to say that, like the gallant ships gliding in the wind, they inspire—at least seem to—the very buoyant breezes they ride.

Antonio assures the pair that, since his wealth is fortunately not entrusted to one ship or place, concern for his merchandise cannot be responsible for his sadness. They naturally then assume that he must be in love, second, it would seem, if a close second, to wealth and often connected with melancholy. To his denial Salanio replies:

> Then let us say you are sad
> Because you are not merry; and 'twere as easy
> For you to laugh and leap and say you are merry
> Because you are not sad. Now, by two-headed Janus,
> Nature hath framed strange fellows in her time:
> Some that will evermore peep through their eyes
> And laugh like parrots at a bagpiper,
> And other of such vinegar aspect
> That they'll not show their teeth in way of smile,
> Though Nestor swear the jest be laughable.

The bagpipe and the vinegar aspect, it is clear, anticipate Shylock. The reversibility of joy and grief, though tossed off casually here, as casually as the suggested shift of moods, Shakespeare well appreciates and will increasingly explore. ('Two-headed Janus' might remind us of Socrates' notion at the end of The Symposium of the oneness of comedy and tragedy, two sides of one coin. It also seems worth mentioning that, though these gentlemen are officially Christian, they spice their talk with foreign condiments; most of their allusions, a reflection no doubt of their Renaissance cultivation, are Greek and Roman, almost never Christian. Is it that they take their Christianity for granted? Or is it that there is no ostentation, no conspicuous ornamentation, in flourishing one's own? In any case, in their worldliness at least, in their devotion to earthly living as to friendship, these Venetians might be considered thoroughly pagan.)

Now, at the entrance of 'better company', particularly the young nobleman Bassanio, some notches above the rest, the pair, like petty traffickers, curtsying, withdraw. Gratiano, seeing Antonio's sad demeanor, though soon after dismissed as a chatterbox by Bassanio and Antonio, penetratingly warns the latter, 'You have too much respect upon the world./They lose it that do buy it with much care.' Antonio's reply, intending to deny the charge, in its very denial admits it (if in fact one accents 'buy' and 'respect upon the world', Gratiano's words much more accurately apply to Shylock); for already in his premonition Antonio is aware of life's brevity and unreality and the grief underscoring it:

> *I hold the world but as the world, Gratiano,*
> *A stage where every man must play a part,*
> *And mine a sad one.*

Gratiano, in Mercutio style or that of the Falstaff-to-be, happily accepts the theater image:

> *Let me play the fool!*
> *With mirth and laughter let old wrinkles come,*
> *And let my liver rather heat with wine*
> *Than my heart cool with mortifying groans.*

More than a mere 'seize the day' or 'gather ye rosebuds while ye may', this is a wisdom aware that, in the inevitability, not to say the economy, of wrinkles, the same face and flesh are used by sorrow and by mirth, that as we use ourselves so are we used. (I am reminded of a passage in Isak Dinesen's *Shadows on the Grass*. She has recognized that the ancient African women, her friends, are humoring her in her doctoring of them.

> *After a minute or two I could not help laughing. And as, scrutinizing my face, they caught the change in it, they joined me. One after another all faces round me lightened up and broke in laughter. In the faces of toothless old women a hundred delicate wrinkles screwed up cheeks and chin into a baroque, beaming mask—and they were no longer scars left by the warfare of life, but the traces of many laughters. The merriment ran along the terrace and spread to the edge of it like ripples on water. There are few things in life as sweet as this suddenly rising, clear tide of African laughter surrounding one.*)

Gratiano seems to be a bit of that sweet old England, that leaven at the center of life and living, that Shakespeare never altogether lets go. An answer to the Aesop fable of the cricket and the grasshopper, in Gratiano we have the summer fool of joy against the all-year wintry grimness and begrudgingness of a Shylock.

Why should a man, whose blood is warm within,
Sit like his grandsire cut in alabaster,
Sleep when he wakes, and creep into the jaundice
By being peevish?

On Gratiano's leaving, we learn one chief source of Antonio's melancholy, a source he is perhaps too fastidious to admit to others: his awareness of Bassanio's sworn intention to undertake a 'secret pilgrimage' to a lady. Bassanio, to justify the pilgrimage, emphasizes his prodigality and his great debts, particularly to Antonio: 'To you, Antonio, I owe the most, in money and in love. . . .' This coupling of money and love is important and necessary to remember against the later Shylockian 'My daughter! O my ducats!' for their difference as for their similarity. Owing Antonio so much, Bassanio speaks of his plan to recoup all. Antonio says,

I pray you, good Bassanio, let me know it;
And if it stand, as you yourself still do,
Within the eye of honour, be assured,
My purse, my person, my extremest means,
Lie all unlocked to your occasions.

In his even closer coupling of 'My purse, my person', Antonio's unhesitating beneficence reveals itself at once. Bassanio's plot is simple: the normal and noble sport of young English blades, to go rich-wife hunting. That is, to go after Portia in Belmont, 'a lady richly left' who once from her eyes—and this may be his true end, concealed under the glitter of gold and his reluctance to confess, especially to Antonio, that he is prompted to this expedition primarily by love—did give him 'fair speechless messages'. For her worthiness, in her person no less than in her purse, Belmont like Venice is a magnetic spot:

. . . the four winds blow in from every coast
Renownéd suitors. And her sunny locks
Hang on her temples like a golden fleece,
Which makes her seat of Belmont Colchos' strond,
And many Jasons come in quest of her.

The ancient pedigree of such fortune-hunting gives it dignified status. But though Portia is, happily for English taste (and, I suppose, for Italian too), a blonde and though the image is an arduous attempt to unify wealth and beauty, wealth and the genuine or the naturally living,

I find this image, its paganism and all, a difficult, uncomfortable one. Later, rising to the test of the caskets, Bassanio in a related image will deride mere show and dead 'ornament':

> So are those crispéd snaky golden locks,
> Which makes such wanton gambols with the wind
> Upon supposéd fairness, often known
> To be the dowry of a second head,
> The skull that bred them in the sepulchre.

One wonders what he would say were one to judge inherited wealth so. But for him, Portia's wealth is no less her rightful own than the hair that grows on her head. And perhaps the discomfort I feel here is mine alone, that of one much later on in the debasing of gold or wealth which time has gradually produced.

Adventurer that he is, no doubt one part of his charm, Bassanio is ready to dare all on this suit:

> O my Antonio, had I but the means
> To hold a rival place with one of them [the suitors],
> I have a mind presages me such thrift
> That I should questionless be fortunate!

Proceeding on hunches, he responds, like his earlier kin in Shakespearean comedy, to the eyes' intelligence; he trusts his instincts, reliable indications of things to come. He and his aristocratic kind are ones to risk all, to step out—no other exhilaration like it—into the open, the unknown; for they have fundamental belief in themselves, the world, and the powers-that-be behind it. It is an affirmativeness, like Odysseus' or an English Renaissance gentleman's, that such daring requires. At once, though Antonio has no present moneys (his words seem to gainsay what he insisted on to his first two friends: 'Thou know'st that all my fortunes are at sea;/Neither have I money nor commodity/ To raise a present sum'), he agrees in a rather portentous metaphor to exercise his credit, 'That shall be racked, even to the uttermost,' to furnish Bassanio forth to Portia.

Here I cannot resist referring to comments on this situation, comments involving a sentiment fairly common for some time. In the words of a recent critic:

> The relationship between Antonio and Bassanio . . . suddenly
> blossoms under his touch into a lightly-sketched but subtle relation-

ship between a rich, gifted and melancholy homosexual and a brisk,
shallow adventurer with a handsome profile. Ths play begins with
Antonio's sadness . . . there is no mystery about it; he loves Bas-
sanio and must shortly lose him to a woman.

Such critics with their bold, practical directness, cutting through all
nonsense, suffer nothing of Eliot's self-confusing complexity: they see
at once, and say as promptly, what is wrong. One can be much impressed by such penetration, especially since nothing in the play—can
we ignore the promptitude with which Antonio abets Bassanio's
fortune-hunting?—supports the charge. Of course there are always the
sonnets to draw on, but they do lie somewhat outside this play. Might
it not be enough to regard Antonio's feelings as actuated by a deep
sense of loss and, from this one dear instance, a best friend about to go
off on a crucial mission, a sense of the loss underlying all life? And are
not such critics simply relieving themselves of the burden and the
mystery by resorting to a Freudian formula? But think what a delight-
fully modern play it would be were homosexuality gayly, bravely, not
to say brazenly asserted. Could we not then better understand Shylock's frustration, envy, rancor before such love? And would we not
have further reason to rejoice at our acuity in recalling that from the
Middle Ages onward a moneylender was especially reprehended for
putting money to an 'unnatural act of generation', and that consequently in the *Inferno* Dante lumped usurers in the same circle of hell
with the sexual perverts? Homosexuality prospered in Shakespeare's
day, and it is a great reassurance to be able to ascribe motives, especially basic ones, to characters. Also, ours is too knowing an age to be
taken in by mere affection between two members of the same sex.
But if the critic believes what he says, should he not at least admire
Antonio and congratulate him on his instantaneous, noble self-sacri-
ficing? And in his mood, for its constancy if not pervasiveness, may
one not suspect a little more than sadness at the loss of a lover or the
very mystery that our critic dismissed? Shakespeare, we might say, is
not yet concerned to explore that condition in which the mood of a
central character exceeds every available circumstance adducible to
explain it; he is not yet ready to propose that man may be of a complexity, profundity, mystery in his nature larger than any motive, than any
accountability: an actor at least as much as he is a reactor. And man's
wonder and prime distinctiveness may lie in this, in the fact that, more
than adequate though the conditions around him appear to be to

justify his feelings, something else in him eludes or surpasses those conditions. Lost love may seem to many sufficient explanation for Antonio's mood. Yet this explanation, shedding its simple light upon him, also casts a hard-to-fathom shadow around and behind him.

Having just heard Portia's praises sung, in Scene II we turn to her and her very different world of Belmont. Relevantly enough, the scene parallels the first. Sharing top nobility (though Bassanio is closer in class to her), and therefore, we may assume, similar feelings and sensitivity, with Antonio, she begins: 'By my troth, Nerissa, my little body is aweary of this great world.' She even shares Antonio's word 'aweary'. Cloistered till now, she might be expected to utter the reverse sentiments, ones of frustration and resentment at her confinement. Yet she has known the grief of her father's death, and the winds have blown the world, in the variegated shapes of suitors, to Belmont. She, one small creature that she is, is at the mercy of that great, wide world or whatever portion of it the sea may toss up on her shore. Thus the Prince of Morocco says,

> *Why, that's the lady. All the world desires her.*
> *From the four corners of the earth they come*
> *To kiss this shrine, this mortal-breathing saint.*
> *The Hyrcanian deserts and the vasty wilds*
> *Of wide Arabia are as throughfares now*
> *For princes to come view fair Portia.*
> *The watery kingdom, whose ambitious head*
> *Spits in the face of heaven, is no bar*
> *To stop the foreign spirits, but they come,*
> *As o'er a brook, to see fair Portia.*

This speech means to stress Portia's loveliness and delicacy, her powerful allure for the precious, noble merchandise she is, yet merchandise withal. She may be a shrine, a 'mortal-breathing saint'. But we know, and she does too, that the pilgrimage the princes make to her is not primarily a religious one. The 'foreign spirits', with 'the Hyrcanian deserts and the vasty wilds' upon them, are bearing down on Belmont and Portia out of more than merely a devout wish to 'see' and to be worshipful before her. Nerissa, a little like Salanio on the interchangeability of sadness and merriment, pertly replies to her mistress' complaint of weariness:

> *You would be, sweet madam, if your miseries were in the same*
> *abundance as your good fortunes are; and yet, for aught I see,*

they are as sick that surfeit with too much as they that starve with nothing.

It is, she says, the familiar problem of superabundance, of being burdened and bored by too much. After it what? Yet under this abundance—its silks and spices—the body, for the rich no less than for the poor, moves on in its ruthless, impersonal force at its own pace, to the strictly enforced laws of mortality.

In the conversation that follows Portia, for all her youth and inexperience, is given ample, necessary opportunity to display her native wit and wisdom. (Juliet, similarly cloistered, anticipates her.) One chief possible source of Portia's weariness appears: she chafes at her 'bondage', her need to submit to the world's way. Lovely and different from Venice though Belmont may be, Portia is also under law, restrained by the will of others, here the last rigorous will of her dead father.

O me, the word 'choose'! I may neither choose who I would nor refuse who I dislike; so is the will of a living daughter curbed by the will of a dead father. Is it not hard, Nerissa, that I cannot choose one, nor refuse none?

Again we encounter a situation that Shakespeare enjoyed employing: a daughter restrained by a father's will. Hermia in *A Midsummer Night's Dream* fled and finally prevailed over her father's will, though the law supported him. Juliet ignored her father's testy will and died in so doing. Here, interestingly, Portia yields to a dead father. His will is no less hard upon her than Shylock's on Jessica, who escapes only by disobeying him whereas Portia will be freed and made happy by obeying hers. But she does know how difficult it is to submit, how much the blood or passion flouts reason and the laws:

I can easier teach twenty what were good to be done, than to be one of the twenty to follow mine own teaching. The brain may devise laws for the blood, but a hot temper leaps o'er a cold decree.

Nerissa assures her, and we have no reason to question Nerissa's words: 'Your father was ever virtuous, and holy men at their death have good inspirations', something that can scarcely be said about Shylock (or, for that matter, old Capulet). Then, to establish her superiority, essential for the important role she is to play, Portia is given further opportunity to exhibit her wit and shrewdness in her leisurely, penetrating portraits of her suitors. These by character, manner, country are all clearly unsuited for her. Only Bassanio, suddenly mentioned at the end of the scene and in anticipation, 'was the best deserving a fair lady'.

In the next scene, returning to Venice and 'a public place', we meet the last principal figure, the one needed to make Bassanio's plan possible and, for dramatic purposes, to threaten all as well. Shylock opens the scene, and aptly enough the first clinking words in his mouth are of money. His curt, hoarded phrases—he makes a few do in economical repetition as much work as possible—expose him at once. His tight-lipped (for he will open no bag wider than he must), pebbly-hard, efficient prose is superb against the mellifluency of the Venetians and Portia. To compare the happy swell of Salarino's verse with Shylock's

> *But ships are but boards, sailors but men. There be land-rats and*
> *water-rats, land-thieves and water-thieves—I mean pirates. And*
> *then there is the peril of waters, winds, and rocks.*

is to know at once what worlds apart Shylock and the Venetians are. Could there be a more triumphant reduction of Salarino's eloquence than 'the peril of waters, winds, and rocks'? Ships, two scenes ago angelic creatures, are now 'but boards'. And sailors 'but men'. That phrase, 'but men', makes forever clear Shylock's opinion of his fellows. Beyond the deep-bitten malice and the joy in that malice as he rasps out his contempt for the world, his is a voice that yields nothing; it admits, in man no more than in nature, no possibility past brute matter and the ruthless elements. It is the rasp of a world made up mainly of obdurate things, objects grinding upon each other. This play, like earlier ones, will call for 'plain' speech; expression setting out to be an accurate, trustworthy reflection of reality will be fundamental here too. But nothing like Shylock's speech, this bringing all things down to earth and nothing but earth, will be meant; no such stripping and beggaring of the world through language to drabbest dead stuff so that one can lock it up in airless dark to be sure of it, altogether to subdue it. Nonetheless, we cannot deny that, in addition to his own character, Shylock's words do reflect the physical base of Venice or the world.

The matter of the play's so-called anti-Semitism should not detain us long. I do not doubt, and I have already suggested it, that Shakespeare meant us to despise Shylock for what he is. I shall not attempt to invoke the nature of Shakespeare's world, its difference from ours in matters of experience and prejudice. All that I do feel obliged to say is that this is one individual who, happening to be a Jew, is, more importantly, a most meager man, a wretch no more and no less than others in Shakespeare who happen to be, as they are individual men, Irish, Welsh, French, Italian, English. One can judge the play an indictment of all Jews, and grossly anti-Semitic, if one cares to. Certainly in an age like ours, with our humanitarianism and simultaneously the monstrous persecution and destruction of the Jews, it is difficult not to. But the play, in my understanding of it, involves no such indictment. What it does say is: see what happens to a man altogether committed, with a passion wellnigh religious, to materialism; how it has destroyed him even as it would through him destroy others. That the play opposes usury, the love of money for its own sake, and the use of it to control others, is obvious. But what is also obvious to me is Shylock's luxuriating in his obsessional hatred. That he is caught in the vicious net of his time and place we know well enough, but that he makes the most of that net, lives a reactor to it and nothing else, with little inner life, selfhood, dignity, we also must know. He has learned nothing but the most niggardly greed from his world or his experience. Nor have books, the Old Testament, say, served him any better; nothing of the splendor and nobility of the prophets or Job touches him. Thus he means to better his world in the very thing he says he despises it for.

When Bassanio invites him to dine with him and Antonio, Shylock's answer underlines his contempt for them, his prejudice. And his first aside when Antonio appears makes his loathsomeness more than plain:

> How like a fawning publican he looks!
> I hate him for he is a Christian;
> But more for that in low simplicity
> He lends out money gratis and brings down
> The rate of usance here with us in Venice.
> If I can catch him once upon the hip,
> I will feed fat the ancient grudge I bear him.
> He hates our sacred nation, and he rails,
> Even there where merchants most do congregate,
> On me, my bargains, and my well-won thrift,
> Which he calls interest. Cursèd be my tribe
> If I forgive him!

That Antonio is a Christian is reason enough to hate him. But far more important—beside it, the Christianity might be forgiven—is Antonio's 'low simplicity', his foolishness; the true source of Shylock's hatred is that Antonio lends out money gratis and thereby hurts Shylock's business. In short, Shylock does not object so much to the system he is obliged to live in as to an interfering with it, an attempt at lightening its severity. For Shylock—his phrase, 'low simplicity', while it reflects his contempt for Antonio also reflects his pride in his awareness of, his good sense in accepting, making the best of, the 'true state' of things— it is a simple world, one to eat or to be eaten in. Though he will not eat with Antonio, he is eager to 'feed fat the ancient grudge I bear him'. The eventual pound of flesh, though he bluffly and with a pretense of amusement denies it (he insists the bond is no more than 'a merry sport', 'this merry bond'), is indeed merry sport for him—revenge, his chief pleasure after profit:

> A pound of man's flesh taken from a man
> Is not so estimable, profitable neither,
> As flesh of muttons, beefs, or goats.

Again his contempt for man even on the most naturalistic terms and in his reducing man to those terms is evident. (Similarly for Shylock sheep and cows, though worth more than man, are not creatures but their use alone.) We can almost catch him, knife whetted, gloating over the pound of flesh, his most relished dish. That, once had, so Shylock believes, will fully and finally expose Antonio, show how little there is to his supposed superiority.

In their exchange, after Shylock has offered his Old Testament story of Jacob and Laban, and of Jacob's victory during 'the work of generation' between Laban's rams and ewes as an instance of 'thrift' which is a 'blessing', Antonio, having remarked,

> This was a venture, sir that Jacob served for;
> A thing not in his power to bring to pass,
> But swayed and fashioned by the hand of Heaven.

sardonically asks: 'Was this inserted to make interest good?/Or is your gold and silver ewes and rams?' To which Shylock simply, amusingly replies, 'I cannot tell. I make it breed as fast.' Thereupon, in an aside to Bassanio, Antonio delivers a central truth of the play, one that Bassanio, we shall see, immediately takes to heart and will have in mind later with the caskets:

> *Mark you this, Bassanio,*
> *The devil can cite Scripture for his purpose.*
> *An evil soul producing holy witness*
> *Is like a villain with a smiling cheek,*
> *A goodly apple rotten at the heart.*
> *O, what a goodly outside falsehood hath!*

Then to Shylock's remonstrances Antonio says,

> *If thou wilt lend this money, lend it not*
> *As to thy friends; for when did friendship take*
> *A breed of barren metal of his friend?*

Yet though he knows Shylock well enough, in his eagerness to help Bassanio, and in overconfidence perhaps, Antonio accepts Shylock's terms and even seems ready to expect the best, a change, in him. When Shylock leaves, Antonio can generously say: 'Hie thee, gentle Jew./ The Hebrew will turn Christian; he grows kind.' But Bassanio, recalling Antonio's recent observation, says: 'I like not fair terms and a villain's mind.'

With the Second Act, now that the bond has been agreed to, its counterpart in Belmont can and should begin: the choosing of the caskets. The first to try them, though he will fail since he fails to follow his own words, is a likely antithesis to Shylock. The Prince of Morocco and a tawny Moor, he makes us feel his nobility:

> *Mislike me not for my complexion,*
> *The shadowed livery of the burnished sun,*
> *To whom I am a neighbour and near bred.*

His urging resembles Antonio's observation on 'A goodly apple': judge a man not by his appearance but by the use he makes of himself. So too, in words relating oddly to what's to come, the Prince proposes that they

> *Bring me the fairest creature northward born,*
> *Where Phoebus' fire scarce thaws the icicles,*
> *And let us make incision for your love,*
> *To prove whose blood is reddest, his or mine.*

Portia's reply, echoing Bassanio's—and Antonio's—sentiments in the previous scene, in its good sense prepares us for her later role: 'In terms of choice I am not solely led/By nice direction of a maiden's eyes.'

Then in short, swift scenes, speeding up the business of the play, we learn through the clown Launcelot, a servant of Shylock, and through Jessica how oppressive Shylock is, how in his rigors tedious. There is nothing for it but that both must flee from him. Thus Jessica says to Launcelot:

> *I am sorry thou wilt leave my father so:*
> *Our house is hell, and thou, a merry devil,*
> *Didst rob it of some taste of tediousness.*

Launcelot going off to serve Bassanio, she elopes in the garb of a page with one of the Christian gentlemen, to act as his torchbearer in the masque preparing. Portia later, disguised as a man and a lawyer, will be Bassanio's torchbearer, bringing light to bear against Shylock in her court play ('So shines a good deed in a naughty world'). Now Shylock's own daughter will relieve him of a good share of his wealth. Salanio, when he learns that torchbearers have not yet been hired, expertly says of the masque: "'Tis vile unless it may be quaintly ordered,/And better in my mind not undertook.' Jessica in her youth, beauty, love, but disguised, will help to light up the festivities, see to it that they are 'quaintly' or elegantly ordered and not 'vile'. (A little later Shylock will call 'vile' what for a Salanio safeguards against the vile, the fife or music.)

A literalist who cannot afford imagination, with no room, time or mind for play, fantasy, self-relieving disguises, Shylock would rightly lock up all against the masque. By his nature he must loathe the carefreeness of a masque or play, the surplus of high spirits, wellbeing's overflow: life with no use or purpose other than its own exercise and delight. For him this signifies prodigality, painful waste. Accordingly, with good premonitional sense he identifies the masque-to-be with misfortune for himself. How does he know that 'There is some ill abrewing towards my rest'? '. . . I did dream of moneybags to-night' – moneybags, his only concern, his only sensitivity. Out of harmony with the rest, responsive only to the reassuring chime of coins, he hates music, makes its instruments repulsive in his superb description of them. Bidding Jessica lock up, he says:

> *and when you hear the drum*
> *And the vile squealing of the wry-necked fife,*
> *Clamber not you up to the casements then,*
> *Nor thrust your head into the public street*
> *To gaze on Christian fools with varnished faces,*
> *But stop my house's ears, I mean my casements;*

> Let not the sound of shallow foppery enter
> My sober house.

It is a habit with him, little that he can stomach anything beyond things as things, to need to translate what few images he uses immediately on use. Earlier he told us that by 'land-thieves and water-thieves – I mean pirates'; here for 'my house's ears' he must at once explain: 'I mean my casements.' Shylock's literalism might remind us of Bottom and his crew and at the same time impress us with the ease with which the comic can become the sober and worse. Shylock may be no more self-absorbed and sealed-in than other characters we have met in the comedies. But they are amusing whereas he is severe, repressive, ominous. They delight – and delight us – in their folly; he oppresses, with his folly threatening those around him. Yet finally for this folly, his self-engrossing myopia, he is no less a clown than the others, in fact the principal clown of his play.

Meantime, the business of Belmont proceeds. The golden and the silver caskets are exposed in the folly of choosing them, precisely like Shylock's mistaken, foolish choice.

> '*All that glisters is not gold;*
> *Often have you heard that told.*
> *Many a man his life hath sold*
> *But my outside to behold.*
> *Gilded tombs do worms infold.*'

Then, promptly, as though for this exposure, we learn through Salarino and Salanio in Scene VIII of Shylock's transport at the loss of his daughter and his ducats (for his almost exclusive choice of the latter he loses both):

> *I never heard a passion so confused,*
> *So strange, outrageous, and so variable,*
> *As the dog Jew did utter in the streets:*
> *'My daughter! O my ducats! O my daughter!*
> *Fled with a Christian! O my Christian ducats!*
> *Justice! the law! my ducats and my daughter!*
> *A sealèd bag, two sealèd bags of ducats,*
> *Of double ducats, stolen from me by my daughter!*
> *And jewels, two stones, two rich and precious stones,*
> *Stolen by my daughter! Justice! Find the girl!*
> *She hath the stones upon her, and the ducats!*'

Confused, strange, and variable indeed. We might linger with profit over his 'O my Christian ducats!'; might enjoy the strange and confused, yet revealing (through the artful 'confusion') movement, starting with 'My daughter!' and ending with 'the ducats!', ringing all the changes on those two words; might enjoy the movement—an orderly mounting of feeling if not the order of reason—from 'my ducats and my daughter!' to 'A sealéd bag' to 'two sealéd bags' to 'Of double ducats', climaxing in the poignant 'Stolen by my daughter!' Surely Shylock's obsessive concentration, his miserly insistence on detailed, reiterated recollection, a clutching of his words that they nearly seem to be their objects, is no less ludicrous than it is painful.

Salanio rightly warns, 'Let good Antonio look he keep his day,/Or he shall pay for this.' Shylock's hatred for Antonio now knows no bounds. Then, in contrast with Shylock's turmoil and wretchedness before his double loss, we hear of Antonio's conduct before a similar loss. Salarino says of him:

> *A kinder gentleman treads not the earth.*
> *I saw Bassanio and Antonio part.*
> *Bassanio told him he would make some speed*
> *Of his return. He answered, 'Do not so;*
> *Slubber not business for my sake, Bassanio,*
> *But stay the very riping of the time;*
> *And for the Jew's bond which he hath of me,*
> *Let it not enter in your mind of love.*
> *Be merry, and employ your chiefest thoughts*
> *To courtship and such fair ostents of love*
> *As shall conveniently become you there.'*
> *And even there, his eye being big with tears,*
> *Turning his face, he put his hand behind him,*
> *And with affection wondrous sensible*
> *He wrung Bassanio's hand; and so they parted.*

When Shylock meets these two he proves resoundingly the accuracy of their words. His most famous speech, the one usually tapped for sympathy, must be repeated. At Salarino's saying to him, 'Why, I am sure, if he forfeit, thou wilt not take his flesh. What's that good for?' Shylock replies:

> *To bait fish withal. If it will feed nothing else, it will feed my revenge.*
> *He hath disgraced me, and hindered me half a million; laughed at*

my losses, mocked at my gains, scorned my nation, thwarted my bargains, cooled my friends, heated mine enemies. And what's his reason? I am a Jew. Hath not a Jew eyes? Hath not a Jew hands, organs, dimensions, senses, affections, passions; fed with the same food, hurt with the same weapons, subject to the same diseases, healed by the same means, warmed and cooled by the same winter and summer, as a Christian is? If you prick us, do we not bleed? If you tickle us, do we not laugh? And if you wrong us, shall we not revenge? If we are like you in the rest, we will resemble you in that. If a Jew wrong a Christian, what is his humility? Revenge. If a Christian wrong a Jew, what should his sufferance be by Christian example? Why, revenge. The villainy you teach me, I will execute, and it shall go hard but I will better the instruction.

'Villainy' he sees it. Yet he will not change it or leave it. No, all he can do, hard though it will be, he admits sardonically, is try to better or exceed it. That he is like other men in his physical furnishings is obvious enough. But this fact, I would say, stresses his differences and failure all the more. He employs his furnishings for purely physical and reductive purposes; the tug of the drossy earth rather than the inspiration of the heavens is primary in him. He is, in a sense, the reverse of an Antonio, not to mention later figures stripped of position and wealth: the more Shylock has the less he is; the less they have the more they become.

When Tubal reports his news to Shylock, his passions are at their most 'confused'; here joy and misery nakedly commingle. His savagery and his pathetic, huge egotism come to the fore:

A diamond gone, cost me two thousand ducats in Frankfort! The curse never fell upon our nation till now: I never felt it till now.

We see again how much he lives and feels only in his purse, how much his is a nature suppressed except as it explodes in rage or rancor. He has no sympathy for anyone beyond himself: the curse never fell on his nation till now because, he admits, *he* never felt it till now. And his odious self-pity no less than his universal malice asserts itself:

. . . and no satisfaction, no revenge; nor no ill luck stirring but what lights o' my shoulders, no sighs but o' my breathing, no tears but o' my shedding.

Certainly he is to be pitied for his total self-absorption. And certainly we tend to sympathize with the underdog even if he happens to be a dog; the show of passionate feeling, though it be snarling, wretched, outrageous, destructive feeling, impresses us. Shylock's speech does give us the naked, beating pulse of a person caught, locked up, in his voice, or the very shape of feeling which is that person. And feeling for many of us, hating, resenting, raging, nearly choking on one's own spleen, is enough, if not virtually a sign of its opposite: goodness, manliness, self-possession. We discover a kind of charisma in the certitude of a position fully realized in its one dimensionality, not complicated or embarrassed by qualifyings or other awarenesses. At the same time something distresses here like the howlings of a tortured beast, the beast that Shylock has Ovidianly become in succumbing to the vices of greed and hatred. For all his involvement, his clutching and being clutched by objects, he is almost being ripped apart; as though in these things that he has identified himself with, some of his own dearest flesh were being torn from him.

But what clearer revelation of Shylock's character do we need than this:

I would my daughter were dead at my foot, and the jewels in her ear! Would she were hearsed at my foot, and the ducats in her coffin!

One can hear, echoed in these words, the even more ominous harshness of Lady Capulet when she reports to her husband Juliet's refusal to marry Paris: 'I would the fool were married to her grave!' Beyond Shylock's grating anguish, his wish is in fact the apogee of his miser's dream: the one living person he has cared about and his wealth, the two dearest parts of him, buried away forever for safe keeping, banked in that perfect vault, the grave! How exactly opposite his desire is to Portia's, and certainly to Bassanio's, as she speaks to Bassanio when he is about to choose a casket: 'Away then! I am locked in one of them./ If you do love me, you will find me out.' Love, the better part of us in action, is enlivening and enlarging, not a fettering in breathless dark. Still there is some striking resemblance between Shylock's vision of his daughter in a coffin with his jewels and ducats and Portia's portrait in the lead casket. Juliet, we recall, is released from the tomb and death only in art: her play and a golden statue. But Bassanio, in the way of good art, will let Portia out; thus he says, she is more than any picture or thing in a box (see Browning's 'My Last Duchess'). Such is the oppressive danger of wealth; when one collects it, and lovely objects also, people themselves are liable to seem collectable.

Finally, Shylock's outcry over the ring Leah gave him, tossed away by Jessica for a monkey (the play ends with rings dealt with lightly but humanly and lovingly), is, I suggest, overvalued in that he says he would not have given the ring for 'a wilderness of monkeys'. Even if we do not accent the 'wilderness', are we being hardhearted to propose that he is doing little more than using the initial figure and simply multiplying it? Thus, concluding with talk of Antonio and his misfortunes, Shylock says: 'I will have the heart of him, if he forfeit; for, were he out of Venice, I can make what merchandise I will.' Late that it is, we might understand his unmitigable hatred for Antonio and what he has come to represent in Shylock's mind. But his resentment continues to derive at least as much as ever from Antonio's being the only obstacle to his profits. Murder is plainly what he intends. His departing words, 'Go, go, Tubal, and meet me at our synagogue. Go, good Tubal; at our synagogue, Tubal', tell us what we already realize too well: that for him, like Antonio's friends when they refer to the church, his official place of worship is physical alone, a place to do business in, a money-changer's best meeting ground. But a basic difference obtains here also. Unlike the church for those Venetians, the synagogue hardly serves to fillip Shylock's imagination to a gliding out upon the high seas of poetry.

With Shylock's confused cries still echoing, and his preference in caskets plain enough, we move to Belmont and its crucial scene: Bassanio's choosing of the casket. To clear his head, and the air also, of polluting snarls like Shylock's, and to set up the conditions of harmony inherent in music that she desires, Portia orders a song. Meantime, she prays that Bassanio may free her from the casket, and so from her present confining life. Her handsome verses on music, foiling this climactic moment, bear repeating for themselves and for contrasting the condition of these characters with Shylock's.

> *Let music sound while he doth make his choice;*
> *Then, if he lose, he makes a swan-like end,*
> *Fading in music. That the comparison*
> *May stand more proper, my eye shall be the stream*
> *And watery death-bed for him. He may win;*
> *And what is music then? The music is*
> *Even as the flourish when true subjects bow*
> *To a new-crowned monarch. Such it is*
> *As are those dulcet sounds in break of day*

That creep into the dreaming bridegroom's ear
And summon him to marriage.

Portia's streaming eye recalls the similar image in *The Comedy of Errors* when Antipholus of Syracuse begs Luciana, 'O, train me not, sweet mermaid, with thy note,/ To drown me in thy sister's flood of tears.' One instance this is of the argosy of such images in Shakespeare's plays. But Portia, beyond this image, is bent on suggesting the multiple use of music; and her description culminates, naturally enough for her, in thoughts of marriage, preceded by the image of herself a 'true subject' to Bassanio, her hoped-for, 'new-crowned monarch'.

Then, to add a last flourish to her words, she resorts, not to Christian sentiments or figures, but, in tune with the rest of the play, to a Greek scene. In its extremity it far surpasses the present moment, yet it is apt for the urgency of her emotion. In her words Bassanio now goes:

> *With no less presence, but with much more love,*
> *Than young Alcides when he did redeem*
> *The virgin tribute paid by howling Troy*
> *To the sea monster.*

Alcides or Hercules rescued Hesione from a sea-monster, not for love but for a pair of horses. Thus Portia can truly say that Bassanio acts 'with much more love'. At the same time we should remember that Bassanio is undergoing his trial for a fortune also, and that for the Greeks, like the Old Testament Jews, gifts, the good things of this world, especially superior live-stock, were never underestimated. Portia's image may seem melodramatic. Yet with not only her own fortune and future at stake but soon, we learn, Antonio's too, the relevancy of this act of 'redeeming virgin tribute' from a 'sea monster' is not hard to appreciate. Her sense of the importance of the occasion has moved her to find a lofty, ancient parallel, and in her very intensity to put that parallel on as a little play with herself at its center. Thus, playing the part of Hesione, 'I stand for sacrifice', she concludes by assuring Bassanio, 'Go, Hercules!/Live thou, I live.'

The song, while Bassanio ponders the caskets, urges inwardness rather than shallow 'fancy' or light love which, the moment it is 'engendered in the eyes,/With gazing fed . . . dies/In the cradle where it lies.' In short, the song recommends the deep, contemplative mood that music itself inspires. And Bassanio, perhaps at first surprisingly, responds to it so. Golden spirits are not to be taken in by massy, inert, 'barren' gold. Nor, whatever his earlier talk of the 'fair speechless messages' received from Portia's eyes, by mere show. Contemplativeness seems to overtake Bassanio completely. He plunges into a little pre-Hamlet essay on appearance and reality. We might say that he is discovering the truth—the poet's way—in expressing it. Thus he canvasses all instances of deception, from law to religion, to valor, to beauty. In fact, though longer at it, his realization is not so far from that of the man he dismissed as a blatherskite near the play's opening, Gratiano with his:

> *There are a sort of men whose visages*
> *Do cream and mantle like a standing pond,*
> *And do a wilful stillness entertain,*
> *With purpose to be dressed in an opinion*
> *Of wisdom, gravity, profound conceit,*
> *As who should say, 'I am Sir Oracle,*
> *And when I ope my lips let no dog bark!'*
> *O my Antonio, I do know of these,*
> *That therefore only are reputed wise*
> *For saying nothing; when, I am very sure,*
> *If they should speak, would almost damn those ears*
> *Which, hearing them, would call their brothers fools.*

Since it is love no less than wealth that Bassanio is after in the person of Portia, and since this trial is the one chance he has of attaining both, it is interesting that his essay should climax itself in the longest, fiercest attack on bogus and bought beauty:

> *Look on beauty,*
> *And you shall see 'tis purchased by the weight;*
> *Which therein works a miracle in nature,*
> *Making them lightest that wear most of it.*

Here, in a passage I quoted earlier, having deprecated wigs, he generalizes:

> *Thus ornament is but the guiléd shore*
> *To a most dangerous sea; the beauteous scarf*
> *Veiling an Indian beauty; in a word,*
> *The seeming truth which cunning times put on*
> *To entrap the wisest.*

In conclusion, convinced by his own words, he chooses:

> *Therefore, thou gaudy gold,*
> *Hard food for Midas, I will none of thee;*
> *Nor none of thee, thou pale and common drudge*
> *'Tween man and man. But thou, thou meagre lead,*
> *Which rather threatenest than dost promise aught,*
> *Thy plainness moves me more than eloquence;*
> *And here choose I. Joy be the consequence!*

But what are we to make of Bassanio? For his prodigality, his patent fortune-hunting, he has offended many. How is he finally different from Shylock? A daring young man, he is, in tune with Shakespeare's outlook and the age's, out to experience the world no less than to possess it. An aristocrat by whom a fortune is naturally needed, he shares Antonio's lighthanded if not cavalier attitude toward wealth. Bassanio has always been a venturer, a taker of chances, out for living and a good living at that. The motto on the lead casket, 'Who chooseth me must give and hazard all he hath', would prove the only adequate challenge for this all-or-nothing young lover. But these Venetians are generally men at large. Though Antonio's wealth is much at sea in precarious ships, he does not worry about it. One might say that on the contrary their far-off, breezy investments bring home to these Venetians some happy measure of their amplitude. Shylock, on the other hand, intensely aware of the very real dangers of seafaring trade, would make his wealth grow by burying it (that talent it is death to hide) or by wresting it from other men's hides. No doubt he desires gold and precious objects in the first place for their tangible sense of power. But he has confused them with their purpose, fallen into a kind of idolatry. He lusts after them for their own sake. Bassanio, confronted by the caskets, already educated by his lighthearted life, his friendship with Antonio, and most of all his love for Portia, knows he must not put his basic trust in things. Such is the transforming power of love. Or, rather than transforming, love in this play is maturing and real-izing; it releases the best in man. Love does this, and the catalytic agent Shylock, who, challenging the others, summons their most abundant humanity. Most telling are Bassanio's last words to the lead casket, especially since they come from a man who is all elegance: 'Thy plain-ness moves me more than eloquence.' Such sentiments, met with frequently in Shakespeare, we remember in the speeches of the princess in *Love's Labour's Lost* and of Theseus before the loutish players. This matter of plainness, so crucial to Shakespeare and this play, will soon be occupying us further.

Portia in an aside now does give way to confusion, but unlike Shylock's of a sweetest kind:

> *How all the other passions fleet to air,*
> *As doubtful thoughts, and rash-embraced despair,*
> *And shuddering fear, and green-eyed jealousy!*
> *O love, be moderate; allay thy ecstasy;*
> *In measure rein thy joy; scant this excess!*
> *I feel too much thy blessing; make it less,*
> *For fear I surfeit.*

Here she seems to be elaborating Nerissa's first words to her: '. . . they are as sick that surfeit with too much as they that starve with nothing.' Opening the casket, Bassanio utters lines at first most strange. Finding Portia's portrait in it, he studies it; and while the real Portia stands impatiently by, he regales us with a little treatise on art and its magic, reminiscent of the pictures, the efficacious art, that Christopher Sly was transformed by:

> *Fair Portia's counterfeit! What demigod*
> *Hath come so near creation? Move these eyes?*
> *Or whether, riding on the balls of mine,*
> *Seem they in motion? Here are severed lips,*
> *Parted with sugar breath; so sweet a bar*
> *Should sunder such sweet friends. Here in her hairs*
> *The painter plays the spider, and hath woven*
> *A golden mesh t' entrap the hearts of men*
> *Faster than gnats in cobwebs: but her eyes—*
> *How could he see to do them? Having made one,*
> *Methinks it should have power to steal both his*
> *And leave itself unfurnished.*

There are great paintings, great works of art, in this play after all, in Belmont if not—at least not directly mentioned—in Venice. But these words are hardly the plainness Bassanio has been praising or at any rate normal notions of plainness. Does he not seem to be back where he was before taking the test? Surely his words remind us of his very recent condemnatory ones on 'those crispéd snaky golden locks', but with the hair in this painting even more a copy, an imitation, than the wig; at least the wig was actual hair. And his 'The painter plays the spider, and hath woven/A golden mesh t' entrap the hearts of men/ Faster than gnats in cobwebs' might appear an extremely odd description of the artist, his art, and the consequences of this beauty, so cunningly contrived. Especially when we remember that Bassanio used the same 'entrap' in denouncing 'ornament': 'The seeming truth which cunning times put on/To entrap the wisest.' Have we not returned to the world of his early description of Portia's 'sunny locks' that 'Hang on her temples like a golden fleece'?

Not satisfied, he goes on to express a young lover's awe at the power of a lovely woman's eyes (at second hand!), something we might have thought he had left behind. But, aside from Bassanio's need to rise to the occasion, to find a gallant compliment for the painting and so for the loveliness, Portia herself, inspiring it, perhaps the substance of the speech lies in what Bassanio implies rather than says: the extraordinary, objective, selfless power of art. For these eyes, potent though they are, do not blind or overwhelm the artist; rather, he sees by them and by his art to paint them. Art is lovely, far lovelier than wigs or cosmetics in that it is faithful to the beauty it has seen and at the same time to itself, the art that makes the devotional act of reproduction or, more accurately, recreation possible. Of course behind all this enthusiasm shines the greater enthusiasm for the thing itself, 'creation' or Portia whom this 'demigod/Hath come so near.' The artist in Bassanio cannot forever deny the man; instead this art helps him turn with deeper appreciation to the real.

> *Yet look, how far*
> *The substance of my praise doth wrong this shadow*
> *In underprizing it, so far this shadow*
> *Doth limp behind the substance.*

Not art—if doted on, also a kind of idol-worship or idolatry—not gold—or golden fleeces—can for Bassanio, unlike Shylock, begin to rival reality and the living.

Heeding the stage directions of the scroll, Bassanio, at last turning to Portia herself, kisses her: 'Fair lady, by your leave;/I come by note, to give and to receive.' Key words these, the sweetest human exchange, or what the Venetians, with Shylock their opposite, are bountiful in. At this point, having survived the test and its strain, Bassanio yields to the delicious bewilderment of his joy. And Portia, in a lovely, humble speech—'You see me, Lord Bassanio, where I stand, /Such as I am'— —wishes:

> *. . . for you*
> *I would be trebled twenty times myself,*
> *A thousand times more fair, ten thousand times*
>   *more rich;*
> *That only to stand high in your account,*
> *I might in virtues, beauties, livings, friends,*
> *Exceed account.*

How much Portia's sentiments, her 'I *would* be', draw additional strength from these sentiments reversed in Shylock's nearby to-do over his 'two thousand ducats' with his 'I *would* my daughter were dead at my foot . . .! *Would* she were hearsed at my foot, and the ducats in her coffin!' must be clear. We notice that 'livings' or riches figure prominently in Portia's wish, no less prominently than the other gifts or possessions. But this accounting, like Antonio's, is one of bounty, of bestowing all one has on a beloved other.

Describing herself as 'an unlessoned girl, unschooled, unpractised' before the wisdom of Bassanio's choice, she, with the other wise women we have already met in Shakespeare, submits herself and all she has to him. She has found her place and role:

> *Happiest of all is that her gentle spirit*
> *Commits itself to yours to be directed*
> *As from her lord, her governor, her king.*

She is right to submit to him. For if she and her picture have moved him to true feeling and awareness, he alone moves–emancipates–her, till now not much more than a picture and a curtained one at that. Fortunately her father's will and hers know perfect agreement in Bassanio. But we need not be troubled by her submissiveness; her conduct in the rest of the play will prove how little she is 'unlessoned', how much her wise father's daughter, and how little merely Bassanio's possession. A captive, released by love like a genie, she will work for Bassanio; a girl, she will prove to be a most capable, mature woman. In fact Portia is the proof very positive of what Kate at the end of *The Taming of the Shrew* says a dutiful wife can and should come to.

Then to seal the whole, Portia symbolizes her property and herself in a ring she gives to Bassanio:

> *Which when you part from, lose, or give away,*
> *Let it presage the ruin of your love*
> *And be my vantage to exclaim on you.*

She yields to him, but he too has obligations, expressed in worldly, physical acts and things. Bassanio, overjoyed, finds words to say what he says cannot be said, tops her earlier speech on her joy and his own with a confusion surpassing hers:

> *Madam, you have bereft me of all words,*
> *Only my blood speaks to you in my veins;*
> *And there is such confusion in my powers,*
> *As, after some oration fairly spoke*
> *By a belovéd prince, there doth appear*
> *Among the buzzing, pleaséd multitude;*
> *Where every something, being blent together,*
> *Turns to a wild of nothing, save of joy*
> *Expressed and not expressed.*

In this access of joy and its consequent thoughtlessness he vows: 'But when this ring/Parts from this finger, then parts life from hence.'

Promptly then, at the moment when he by his choice and kiss turns to the real Portia, the real world of Venice breaks in on them with the news of Antonio's disaster. Joy at its extreme collides with extreme grief. Salerio says of Shylock,

> *Never did I know*
> *A creature that did bear the shape of man*
> *So keen and greedy to confound a man.*
> *He plies the Duke at morning and at night,*
> *And doth impeach the freedom of the state,*
> *If they deny him justice.*

Shylock's own daughter confirms this:

> *When I was with him I have heard him swear*
> *To Tubal and to Chus, his countrymen,*
> *That he would rather have Antonio's flesh*
> *Than twenty times the value of the sum*
> *That he did owe him.*

Aside from whetting our appetite for the mighty struggle to come, these ominous words offset Bassanio's description to Portia of Antonio:

> *The dearest friend to me, the kindest man,*
> *The best-conditioned and unwearied spirit*
> *In doing courtesies, and one in whom*

The ancient Roman honour more appears
Than any that draws breath in Italy.

Both Shylock and Antonio are 'unwearied' in diametrical causes. But Antonio, we recall, beyond doing courtesies, was altogether wearied. It is worth remarking that Bassanio, in harmony with the play's tone, singles out for praise Antonio's ancient Roman—not Christian—honor, right no doubt for an 'Italian' in a Renaissance play. Portia of course equals the occasion and in good Antonio style offers her wealth to redeem Antonio.

The next quick scene in Venice, to confirm in action what we have just heard, presents Shylock and Antonio together. It opens with Shylock's 'Jailer, look to him. Tell me not of mercy./This is the fool that lent out money gratis!' Or the fault in Antonio that rankles in Shylock above all else. To Antonio's attempts at talking to him, all that Shylock in terrible, reiterative fixity, the stony obsessiveness that he is given to, can say is:

I'll have my bond. Speak not against my bond.
I have sworn an oath that I will have my bond.
Thou call'dst me dog before thou hadst a cause;
But, since I am a dog, beware my fangs.

On his leaving, to Salarino's 'It is the most impenetrable cur/That ever kept with men', Antonio perceptively replies:

Let him alone.
I'll follow him no more with bootless prayers.
He seeks my life; his reason well I know.
I oft delivered from his forfeitures
Many that have at times made moan to me;
Therefore he hates me.

And with practical sense of the state's welfare he points out,

The Duke cannot deny the course of law.
For the commodity that strangers have
With us in Venice, if it be denied,
Will much impeach the justice of the state, . . .

Scene IV, briefly back in Belmont, serves to reinforce our good opinion of Portia and Antonio. Lorenzo tells Portia:

Madam, although I speak it in your presence,
You have a noble and a true conceit

Of god-like amity, which appears most strongly
In bearing thus the absence of your lord.
But if you knew to whom you show this honour,
How true a gentleman you send relief,
How dear a lover of my lord your husband,
I know you would be prouder of the work
Than customary bounty can enforce you.

Lorenzo's witnessing word is a most worthy one; for, we shall soon see, he is a man of sense, representative of the play's golden mean, and the one to blend Christian and Jew in happy marriage. Portia nobly responds:

I never did repent for doing good,
Nor shall not now: for in companions
That do converse and waste the time together,
Whose souls do bear an equal yoke of love,
There must be needs a like proportion
Of lineaments, of manners, and of spirit;
Which makes me think that this Antonio,
Being the bosom lover of my lord,
Must needs be like my lord. If it be so,
How little is the cost I have bestowed
In purchasing the semblance of my soul
From out the state of hellish misery!
This comes too near the praise of myself,
Therefore no more of it.

Aside from its courtly conceit, its high courtesy, her speech does stress the important bond, the harmony of 'lineaments, of manners, and of spirit', which these Venetians and Belmontese share.

When she goes off with Nerissa to prepare their disguises for the trial, we turn in the next short scene to a strange if interesting and important intermediary exchange, first between Launcelot and Jessica, then between Launcelot and Lorenzo. Whatever plausible pause is needed here, the scene has some meaty matter for this play in general. Launcelot and Jessica banter each other. In an outlandish sea image he assures Jessica that, however they regard her past, she must be damned.

Truly then I fear you are damned both by father and mother; thus when I shun Scylla, your father, I fall into Charybdis, your mother. Well, you are gone both ways.

With this further drawing on pagan lore it is particularly relevant that
Launcelot should call Shylock a most perilous rock. Jessica counters,
'I shall be saved by my husband. He hath made me a Christian.'
Launcelot's rejoinder is, in this bustling state of Venice, not to say the
workaday world, pertinently practical:

> *Truly, the more to blame he. We were Christians enow before; e'en
> as many as could well live, one by another. This making of Chris-
> tians will raise the price of hogs. If we grow all to be pork-eaters, we
> shall not shortly have a rasher on the coals for money.*

The spirit and its freedoms notwithstanding, this is food for melancholy.

Then on Lorenzo's entering, to Launcelot's punning on 'Moor' and
'more', Lorenzo in sharp impatience exclaims:

> *How every fool can play upon the word! I think the best grace of
> wit will shortly turn into silence, and discourse grow commendable
> in none only but parrots.*

Here we have the other side of the coin of Gratiano's attack in the first
scene on 'wilful stillness'. Undeterred, Launcelot continues his 'wit-
snapping' till Lorenzo cries out:

> *Yet more quarreling with occasion! Wilt thou show the whole
> wealth of thy wit in an instant? I pray thee, understand a plain man
> in his plain meaning.*

To Launcelot's last word-juggling, in manner reminiscent of the earlier
comedies, Lorenzo says:

> *O dear discretion, how his words are suited!*
> *The fool hath planted in his memory*
> *An army of good words; and I do know*
> *A many fools, that stand in better place,*
> *Garnished like him, that for a tricksy word*
> *Defy the matter.*

For a mere fluff of foolery such semi-wits gladly sacrifice truth, the
thing itself – that is, if they know it in the first place. In short, by plainness Shakespeare does not mean the anti-poetic or the bare, dry bones
of a Shylock, but language bent on the truth which in turn supplies
language with its strength and pertinency; and also language not lost
in its own fool's dazzle.

Turning to Jessica, Lorenzo asks her for her opinion of Portia. Again her praises are most extravagantly sung, with very heaven taxed to outfit Jessica's image of her. A long time ago we heard Portia called a 'mortal-breathing saint'. After such high-flown stuff, the two briefly indulge in persiflage surprisingly much like that for which Lorenzo had just rebuked Launcelot; in fact its basic image and the punning on it are his: on food and the eating thereof. Apparently for souls that 'bear an equal yoke of love' and 'converse and waste the time together' such persiflage is not only forgivable but attractive and amusing. The surplus of good feelings, fine breeding, amiable wits, it is that which makes us noble men, exceeding the mere exigencies of living and common day: those moments of play and holiday that may appear at any time among kindred spirits.

Hard on the heels of such converse and time-wasting comes Act IV, the climax of the play, necessarily back in Venice with the clinching of court (or courtiers) and courting (or the lovers) in a most serious play-scene, a court of justice. The Duke at once builds up the rigors of Shylock's character when he says to Antonio:

> *I am sorry for thee: thou art come to answer*
> *A stony adversary, an inhuman wretch*
> *Uncapable of pity, void and empty*
> *From any dram of mercy.*

Official report that this is, we have no reason to question it. Antonio replies:

> *I have heard*
> *Your Grace hath ta'en great pains to qualify*
> *His rigorous course; but since he stands obdurate,*
> *And that no lawful means can carry me*
> *Out of his envy's reach, I do oppose*
> *My patience to his fury, and am armed*
> *To suffer, with a quietness of spirit,*
> *The very tyranny and rage of his.*

This patience and quietness of spirit, though it might be judged Christian, recalls rather Bassanio's words on Antonio's 'ancient Roman honour' and suggests Roman stoicism. The Duke still cannot believe what adamant, surpassing any flint, Shylock means to be. Refusing to explain 'Why I rather choose to have/A weight of carrion flesh than to receive/Three thousand ducats', Shylock answers with:

But say it is my humour, is it answered?
What if my house be troubled with a rat,
And I be pleased to give ten thousand ducats
To have it baned? What, are you answered yet?
Some men there are love not a gaping pig;
Some that are mad if they behold a cat;
And others, when the bagpipe sing i' the nose,
Cannot contain their urine; for affection,
Master of passion, sways it to the mood
Of what it likes or loathes. Now, for your answer:
As there is no firm reason to be rendered
Why he cannot abide a gaping pig;
Why he a harmless necessary cat;
Why he a woollen bagpipe; but of force
Must yield to such inevitable shame
As to offend, himself being offended;
So can I give no reason, nor I will not,
More than a lodgéd hate and a certain loathing
I bear Antonio, that I follow thus
A losing suit against him. Are you answered?

Answered indeed! This seemingly reasonable hatred that equates a rat, a pig, a cat, and a whining bagpipe with a man! But this hatred is an impulse; and impulses or instincts, like natural phenomena, floods, storms, volcanoes, are not to be explained or gainsaid.

Antonio rightly says:

I pray you, think you question with the Jew.
You may as well go stand upon the beach
And bid the main flood bate his usual height;
You may as well use question with the wolf
Why he hath made the ewe bleat for the lamb;
You may as well forbid the mountain pines
To wag their high tops and to make no noise
When they are fretten with the gust of heaven; . . .

Man is to be admired for his passion and his will, but chiefly if he is in charge of them in the way that he is in charge of and uses reasonably the things of the world. Given his potentialities, if man is not more than a wolf or a sea he is much less. At Bassanio's trying to hearten him, Antonio reveals the full weight of his sadness:

I am a tainted wether of the flock,
Meetest for death. The weakest kind of fruit
Drops earliest to the ground, and so let me.

It is such 'wearied' awareness of nature and its unhuman laws, and of men's participation in them, that makes Antonio understandably melancholy. Gratiano's reviling of Shylock provokes no more from Shylock than a further arrogant, almost amused assertion of his being a natural force, and of the folly, the ineffectuality, of words: 'Till thou canst rail the seal from off my bond,/Thou but offend'st thy lungs to speak so loud.'

Now, when all seems lost, Belmont, if in disguise, confronts Venice: love, feeling, wisdom grapple with law, passion, malice. Beyond the dangers of the moment, those of a woman loose in an arduous man's world, and the Elizabethan love of disguises, Belmont and Portia, for their representing music and the ideal, cannot, it seems, enter the rough world of Venice directly; they must, to be themselves and to exert their powers fully, undertake a disguise which that world will respond to, or in considerable measure meet it on its own terms, in its own language. Almost like a goddess, the heaven on earth she has been called, Portia must assume a human disguise and human means, words of persuasion and the law, to work her will. And such is the range of this world. Shylock is at one end; Antonio and Bassanio are in between, men of Venice, but with a substantial touch of Belmont in them; Portia is at the other. The Venetians donned disguises for their masque, their revelry, and for the freeing of the spirit by way of the body; she dons a disguise for this grave scene and for the freeing of body and spirit by spirit. At the same time, disguise, law and all, it is the noblest poetry Portia, the 'mortal-breathing saint', tries on Shylock. Here again we see how much Shakespeare has moved on in drama by the juxtaposition and collision of two ways of speaking, with everything that those two ways reflect: the lyrical at its most eloquent versus the prosaic pushed to the point of pure literalism.

Of course Portia urges mercy. Her famous speech, for the first time in the play drawing seriously on Christian doctrine, the loftiest parts of it, is moving. In moments of greatest crisis this doctrine is there to be called on. The 'gentle rain' which she recommends or the tempering of justice with mercy, 'an attribute to God himself', enables her to say 'That, in the course of justice, none of us/Should see salvation.' But rock that Shylock has been compared with and the 'main flood', gentle rain is hardly enough to melt or move him. And here is the crux of the play, of a grimness in the person of Shylock beyond anything in earlier comedies. How much can this society take or absorb? How much give is there in it? Has it the strength and resiliency to endure, not to say thrive, against such a basic threat? Are its noblest teachings still pertinent, not to say effective? At this late date, apparently, it requires more than a fair lady with loveliest poetry to make this 'rude sea' 'civil'. 'Certain stars' may shoot 'madly from their spheres/To hear the sea-maid's music.' But Shylock's 'certain loathing' is not so easily to be loosened from its deep-rutted orbit. In his words, 'There is not power in the tongue of man/To alter me.'

Accordingly, since she cannot transform Shylock by Orphic music, mixed with Christian sentiments, into a nobler man, Portia is obliged to show her realistic mettle, to meet him, alas, on the only terms he appreciates: eye for eye, tooth for tooth. If love fails, law must take over. With justice or the leaden, precise letter of the law that he has insisted on she balks him. When he hears that he is to lose his wealth he says pathetically enough, for we see what little else he lives by:

> *Nay, take my life and all; pardon not that.*
> *You take my house when you do take the prop*
> *That doth sustain my house; you take my life*
> *When you do take the means whereby I live.*

On the other hand, Bassanio a few moments ago, we remember (little, it is true, to Portia's liking), gladly volunteered all he has for friendship:

> *Antonio, I am married to a wife*
> *Which is as dear to me as life itself;*
> *But life itself, my wife, and all the world,*
> *Are not with me esteemed above thy life.*
> *I would lose all, ay, sacrifice them all*
> *Here to this devil, to deliver you.*

Yet we also remember Antonio's self-consoling words just preceding Bassanio's when, thinking to embrace death, Antonio said to him:

> *Grieve not that I am fall'n to this for you;*
> *For herein Fortune shows herself more kind*
> *Than is her custom. It is still her use*
> *To let the wretched man outlive his wealth,*

> *To view with hollow eye and wrinkled brow*
> *An age of poverty; from which lingering penance*
> *Of such misery doth she cut me off.*

He too, though he recognizes our folly in clinging to fortune, admits our mortal weakness, our sad reliance on means, and the consequent horrors of poverty in old age. But then with Antonio's Christian mercy Shylock's sentence is commuted: his wealth at his death is to be turned over to Lorenzo and Jessica, and he is to become a Christian. However harsh the latter may sound to modern ears, we must remember that, for this society, being a Christian could alone save a man's soul. Altogether crushed, Shylock disappears from the play.

At this point Portia, pressed by Bassanio to 'Take some remembrance of us, as a tribute,/Not as a fee', asks for his gloves and then his ring, her gift. Recoiling, Bassanio says, '. . . it is a trifle!/I will not shame myself to give you this.' At her insistence he explains his reluctance, the distinction that he and his like can make between things in themselves and their human value: 'There's more depends on this than on the value.' And he gives the ring's background. Portia anticipates her own sensible conduct when she replies:

> *That 'scuse serves many men to save their gifts.*
> *An if your wife be not a mad-woman,*
> *And know how well I have deserved the ring,*
> *She would not hold out enemy for ever,*
> *For giving it to me.*

At Antonio's urging, Bassanio finally does yield it. And the ring comes round, much like the play. Antonio gladly gave all for Bassanio to win Portia and her wealth; now Bassanio repays him by giving up for him, symbolically that is, what he himself has won. Their friendship has not only ridden out the storms but is richer, deeper, than ever because of them.

Thereupon the Fifth Act, with sweetness and light--especially a fanfare of moonlight as out of the wardrobe, the almanac, the huge casement of *A Midsummer Night's Dream*—and with magnificent music, seeks to cleanse the air again, to dispel the wranglings, the uglinesses, surrounding Shylock. We are transported out of Venice to Belmont, Portia's moon-drenched garden, to the couple, Christian and Jew, united in love and, accordingly, in elegant, lyrical 'converse'. Absorbed in a mellifluous Romeo-and-Juliet-like duet, they draw heavily on famous pagan lovers, figures of gold in literary memory, all of them interestingly enough doomed. But then one of our most effective charms is made of others' distant woe. This woe helps to gild and immortalize these others, who in turn help to move and mellow the present and, at the same time, since they are figures of romance, to make more real the present characters. Also, few pleasures delight us more than that of identifying ourselves with splendid examples of the past. 'In such a night as this' establishes the free-flowing of all times, the immortal moment of lovers, and the joining of our pair with the great company of antiquity. Now a sweet wind, not a shipwrecking one or the storm of Shylock, that frettens the mountain pines into an uproar beyond recall, is blowing. And one with the noblest aspect of this play's gentle folk, it gently kisses the trees, so gently that they make no noise. For this is a wind that can be controlled, since it lives in and is summoned forth from melodic verses or the warmed breath of lovers, finding Troilus' sighs in theirs. Love possesses some portion of Orpheus' power, if not with creatures like Shylock.

These lovely ancient pictures, almost constituting a gallery, might hang on Portia's walls. Inserts or inlays a little like Portia's casketed portrait in Bassanio's word-painting (or her own picturing of herself as Hesione and Bassanio as Hercules just before his casket-choosing), they recall again the paintings that 'transformed' Christopher Sly. 'Patens of bright gold' they are, in the motion of words quiring like an angel to this pair, looking to the sky and stars, brightest in the dark night of the past. All framed by 'in such a night', these inlays climax in recent pictures of Lorenzo and Jessica's own. But this pair's pictures are also already glossed by being past: in the memory (or this play as well as in them), the latest in the list of romantic lovers. And sharing something of their predecessors' glamor, they also share something of their underlying furtiveness. In Lorenzo's words,

> *In such a night*
> *Did Jessica steal from the wealthy Jew,*
> *And with an unthrift love did run from Venice*
> *As far as Belmont.*

The ambiguity of 'steal', especially up against 'wealthy', is clearly deliberate; so is 'unthrift' ('thrift', we recall, is a favorite word of Shylock), with both suggestive of secretiveness in the night and, as with the lovers in *A Midsummer Night's Dream*, of illicit acts. Jessica, responding with quick, gently mocking humor, steals Lorenzo's word from him:

> *In such a night*
> *Did young Lorenzo swear he loved her well,*
> *Stealing her soul with many vows of faith*
> *And ne'er a true one.*

At their duet's end Jessica says, 'I would out-night you', did not reality or matter-of-fact break in. The classical allusions themselves, idealized though they are, in their being instances of frailty, all involving 'elopement', stealth, and their disastrous consequences, do suggest human reality. They prepare us in a gradual declension for the episode of the rings, a further bringing down to earth of the play's characters. With that episode's charges and counter-charges, its earthy stressing of sex, we return to things as they are, to the world the audience itself will, at the play's end, return to. Herein lies the aptness of Gratiano's last 'realistic' words; it is also apt that he in his worldly wisdom should—and for his volubility and his belief in it—have the last word.

But it is fascinating that, before this end is reached, the play's loveliest music is entrusted to Lorenzo, who recently urged 'plainness'. The matter-of-fact that stopped Jessica does not stop him. The messenger Stephano tells them that Portia is on her way. According to him she has been at devotional exercises: 'She doth stray about/By holy crosses, . . .' Of course this announcement is simply a continuation of Portia's subterfuge when, before undertaking her disguise and her trip to Venice, she declared that, until Bassanio's return, she and Nerissa would be at a monastery, where she vowed 'to live in prayer and contemplation'. But promptly Stephano assures us that her straying about by holy crosses is no surprising departure for her. For though 'she kneels and prays' by the crosses (and 'a holy hermit' is appropriately in her company), she does so, in sweet harmony with her previous wishes, 'For happy wedlock hours'. In short, her return is not matter-of-fact.

And Lorenzo bids Stephano, '. . . bring your music forth into the air'. Then Lorenzo delivers himself of a bounty of verbal beauty, drawn out of the same wellspring as *A Midsummer Night's Dream*, but of a profounder gravity.

> *How sweet the moonlight sleeps upon this bank!*
> *Here will we sit and let the sounds of music*
> *Creep in our ears. Soft stillness and the night*

Become the touches of sweet harmony.
Sit, Jessica. Look how the floor of heaven
Is thick inlaid with patens of bright gold.
There's not the smallest orb which thou behold'st
But in his motion like an angel sings,
Still quiring to the young-eyed cherubins.
Such harmony is in immortal souls;
But whilst this muddy vesture of decay
Doth grossly close it in, we cannot hear it.
Come, ho! and wake Diana with a hymn!
With sweetest touches pierce your mistress' ear,
And draw her home with music.

Here the deepest truth of the play emerges. In this honied speech the play's principal themes converge: money, language, and love. These must be used judiciously if happiness is to be achieved. All are media of exchange, and if one of them becomes a thing in itself, rather than a means to other things – to feeling, understanding, basic sympathy – it becomes meaningless (so money, and therefore love, has done with the sealed-in, stony Shylock; and language, with a fool like Launcelot). Money for its own sake, like language, is barren; an enemy, not an enhancement or encouragement, of life. But in Lorenzo's speech we have gold as it should be: alive, fluent, come to singing in its motion, not the drossy stuff that Shylock loves. And we are out of the dark wood and in the moonlit garden of love, that moves the stars as the music of their motions moves us. Shylock, grossly closed in, can do little more than clutch his muddy vesture round him. Thus for all his turbulent intensity he is finally a comic figure, comic for his meagerness, his dingy obsessiveness, even if this is in the Shakespearean way the dingy, the meager, made impressive, resonant, and disturbing. Word-mongers, by the giddy, thick clatter, a leaden echo if they could but realize it, of their tongues, are equally muddy, equally impervious. In Lorenzo's speech Shakespeare has triumphantly wed the pagan and the Christian. The music of the spheres, an ancient Greek notion, he transforms to angels singing, quiring to the young-eyed cherubim. Immortal souls, not altogether locked in by their mortal bodies, for moments at least are permeated by this harmony. And Lorenzo, bidding the music sound to waken Diana, still asleep apparently upon the bank, to remind her of her most radiant, active self so that she brighten Portia's path, tells that hymn to draw Portia home. One might say that music, for a spirit like hers, attuned to heavenly harmony, is her home.

While the music plays, Jessica confesses: 'I am never merry when I hear sweet music.' She is acknowledging the struggle between body and spirit that music prompts: the ambiguity, neither earth nor heaven, that Antonio seems to have lived in from the start. Troubling music is; for its motion, uninterrupted by things, shakes us in our mortal home. In any case, it is a grave, even solemn mood that sweet music produces, not simple, rhapsodic joy. Lorenzo offers an explanation:

> *The reason is, your spirits are attentive.*
> *For do but note a wild and wanton herd,*
> *Or race of youthful and unhandled colts,*
> *Fetching mad bounds, bellowing and neighing loud,*
> *Which is the hot condition of their blood,*
> *If they but hear perchance a trumpet sound,*
> *Or any air of music touch their ears,*
> *You shall perceive them make a mutual stand,*
> *Their savage eyes turned to a modest gaze*
> *By the sweet power of music.*

Long ago Portia remarked, 'The brain may devise laws for the blood but a hot temper leaps o'er a cold decree.' Not laws, but music (like love and sweetest, deep reason) it is that fills us with a sense of all-fluent order or harmony, and for a time our own natures are forgotten and absorbed in the greater nature of that harmony.

Now, almost inevitably, Lorenzo turns to Shakespeare's favorite classical poet, the singer of music's capacity to transform all, Ovid; and to the mythical poet behind him, the paragon of all poets, the all-transforming Orpheus:

> *Therefore the poet*
> *Did feign that Orpheus drew trees, stones, and floods;*
> *Since nought so stockish, hard, and full of rage*
> *But music for the time doth change his nature.*
> *The man that hath no music in himself,*
> *Nor is not moved with concord of sweet sounds,*
> *Is fit for treasons, stratagems, and spoils.*
> *The motions of his spirit are dull as night,*
> *And his affections dark as Erebus.*
> *Let no such man be trusted. Mark the music.*

Feigning though Ovid may have been, music does—if only for the time of its sounding—transform the hardest nature. All, that is, except man-shaped stones like Shylock; he is no less clogged and deaf, no less fundamentally dead, than his merely mineral gold. Add rage to him, in the way it has been in this play, and what can penetrate to him? The next verses are obviously the final disposing of Shylock's nature. With no music in him he cannot be moved by music from without, and is therefore attuned to wretchedness and destruction only.

The music does its magical work; as though on its passage Portia and Nerissa enter. After discussing the light which they see burning in Portia's hall, they talk of the music itself. Portia says: 'Nothing is good, I see, without respect./Methinks it sounds much sweeter than by day'. Or 'In such a night as this.' Nerissa suggests, 'Silence bestows that virtue on it, madam.' A moment ago Lorenzo had said, 'Soft stillness and the night/Become the touches of sweet harmony.' Portia, continuing her own thought, points out:

> *The crow doth sing as sweetly as the lark*
> *When neither is attended, and I think*
> *The nightingale, if she should sing by day,*
> *When every goose is cackling, would be thought*
> *No better a musician than the wren.*
> *How many things by season seasoned are*
> *To their right praise and true perfection!*

Her good sense knows what must happen, amid a daytime crowd of cacklers, to the loveliest music; each thing needs its apposite season or conditions to be realized and appreciated. A mob of Shylocks would jeer music out of existence or at least out of hearing (see what happened to Orpheus among the screaming Maenads). But perhaps a Shylock is a nighttime setting meet enough for the rich music of this play to be heard against, as the musics of Troilus and Cressida, Thisbe, Dido, and Medea are most poignant and moving for their somber settings. Lorenzo recognizes Portia's voice. And she says with that ready, sanitative wit, able to see and mock itself at least as much as others, thereby helping to anchor and balance the scene (and the whole play): 'He knows me as the blind man knows the cuckoo,/By the bad voice.'

Bassanio, Antonio and the others now return. With blithe comments Portia makes them welcome. But instantly the matter of the rings breaks out, a quarrel, in Gratiano's words, 'About a hoop of gold, a paltry ring. . . .' Now at last gold and love are linked, with the motto, poor though it is, 'like cutler's poetry/Upon a knife', the bond between the love and the gold. But much more important, Nerissa reminds her husband, were 'your vehement oaths' and his swearing 'that it should lie with you in your grave' (a last use of Shylock's lines, here of course an expression not of hatred but of passionate, lasting love). Like glittering, snipped hair the wit flies; and we enjoy the truth concealed from the two husbands, in the way it was by the disguises which the ladies assumed to guy their lovers in *Love's Labour's Lost*. Portia, happily mischievous with her troubled husband, takes 'plain' words to Gratiano:

> *You were to blame, I must be plain with you,*
> *To part so slightly with your wife's first gift;*
> *A thing stuck on with oaths upon your finger*
> *And so riveted with faith unto your flesh.*
> *I gave my love a ring, and made him swear*
> *Never to part with it; and here he stands.*
> *I dare be sworn for him he would not leave it*
> *Nor pluck it from his finger for the wealth*
> *That the world masters.*

Promptly she learns the truth. And she and Bassanio exchange a jingling aria on his giving away the ring. At that she squeezes a final bit of wry, not to say ribald, amusement from the situation:

> *Let not that doctor e'er come near my house.*
> *Since he hath got the jewel that I loved,*
> *And that which you did swear to keep for me,*
> *I will become as liberal as you.*
> *I'll not deny him anything I have,*
> *No, not my body nor my husband's bed.*
> *Know him I shall, I am well sure of it.*

To Nerissa's insisting that she will do the same with the doctor's clerk Gratiano mutters, 'Well, do you so. Let me not take him then;/For if I do, I'll mar the young clerk's pen.'

On Antonio's intercession Portia returns the ring to Bassanio with 'by this ring, the doctor lay with me.' Then she discloses all and with it the great good news that Antonio's argosies 'Are richly come to harbour suddenly.' Antonio thanks her, 'Sweet lady, you have given me life and living.' And the play closes, with the chatterbox having the last word, a riming couplet that amounts to spirited ribaldry, started we saw by Portia: 'Well, while I live I'll fear no other thing/So sore as keeping safe Nerissa's ring.' The fertility rites of young married lovers have been at least verbally observed. This last little play of the rings, a mock sobriety and trial, Bassanio undergoes as a gentle finale to the larger trials. Once again, out of largeness of heart, he gave away what was most valuable to him and once again, in a basic sense, he proved his nobility, the wisdom he has come to. Portia, in forgiving him and giving him the ring, likewise exhibits love's resiliency, grace, resource.

Here at last the issue of love versus profit, generosity versus usefulness, or gentlemen versus merchants (also gentlemanliness in some merchants versus the pure businessman) can be directly examined. For the early Elizabethans, like the Greeks and the Old Testament Jews, goods were still good since gifts from God; in fact, since the whole world was his handiwork, made for man's tending and delight, these goods must be deemed precious, and so used, but never hoarded or worshiped. At this time, it appears, Shakespeare and his society were still young enough in spirit and in expectation to consider wealth an amiable if necessary means, one issuing, properly managed, in benevolence and splendor (Antonio, Bassanio, and Portia are similarly openhanded). Nonetheless, as I have suggested, through and beyond Shylock serious trouble seems to be stirring, perhaps the chief source of Antonio's sadness—to wit, his strong sense of mortality, the all-out price of life, the irreversibility, whatever our resources, of the limited, earthbound flesh. What music can reach, let alone transform, this? For the time being, however, Belmont, that lovely, bountiful height, closer to the heavens and the stars than most lands, Belmont, informing the main characters, has carried the day and, with its moonlit gusts of music, swept all before it.

The Anarch Supreme

Richard III

Our age, both in life and in letters, has explored to the full the potentialities of the superman; and it has reaped his catastrophic harvest. Yet the forthrightness of such a figure, in relentless pursuit of nothing but himself, persists in fascinating us. In a play like *Richard III* the self-assurance of Richard, his enthusiastic assent to his nature and his masterly employment of it, especially against the malaise and pettiness of those around him, has its own kind of persuasiveness. The diabolic qualities, the temerities and histrionics, of a Hitler, turning lie after lie into pseudo-fact, wrenching individuals and whole nations to his will, have magnificently, terribly, prepared us to appreciate Richard. He may have drowsed through the Victorian era. But Auschwitz, Hiroshima, and their proliferations have certified him; so have the widely broadcast theories of human nature struggling to equal, and thus accommodate, our age's most outrageous happenings. And Richard has awakened again, fresher, more credible than ever. In a newspaper reviewer's recent words, ours is

> a time when our 'tolerance' tends to take the form of general agreement that we are all capable of the worst crimes had we but the conditions for committing them.

Richard, we shall see, is not only wholly capable of the worst crimes but, much more impressively, capable of creating those conditions.

Richard III, following the *Henry VI* trilogy, concludes Shakespeare's first attempt at tragic history. As Shakespeare conceived it, Richard's villainy is perfect, his expression of it breathtakingly superb. After the *Henry VI* plays *Richard III* by way of this villainy involves a great leap ahead in drama as in art. For the play constitutes, via several of Shakespeare's most popular contemporaries, a new method of organizing material; drama has here advanced from mere historical sequence – a linear, chronological development – to a central figure, one eminently Renaissance-like and true to the times, responsible for what is happening. More than that he acts as focus, sounding board, someone we can identify with. Simultaneously Richard is playwright, director, chief actor, principal member of the vast audience he has captivated, and most discerning critic. Whatever the play may lack in subtlety and depth, or in delicate poetry, especially beside the often rhapsodic *Richard II* and the wonderfully resilient, diverse *Henry IV* plays, it compensates for in its unabating power, in its sudden thunderous strokes, and in the sardonic, ruthless élan of Richard.

That power starts at once in the first speech, which is of course Richard's and of course 'solus':

> *Now is the winter of our discontent*
> *Made glorious summer by this sun of York,*
> *And all the clouds that lowered upon our house*
> *In the deep bosom of the ocean buried.*
> *Now are our brows bound with victorious wreaths,*
> *Our bruiséd arms hung up for monuments,*
> *Our stern alarums changed to merry meetings,*
> *Our dreadful marches to delightful measures.*

The first word he utters is appropriately 'now', the time—and the only time—that Richard lives in and to the hilt. For all its richness the speech begins simply enough and would appear to reflect complete pleasure. Winter or war has at last been ended by Richard's brother Edward IV, the sun of York, and grim battle has yielded to balmy peace and merriment. In a series of elegantly balanced verses, parallelism apposite to and suggestive of peace, in their formality apposite also to a royal play, a reassuring prologue, Richard seems to be making the most of this happy change.

But suddenly another note sounds:

> *Grim-visaged war hath smoothed his wrinkled front,*
> *And now, instead of mounting barbéd steeds*
> *To fright the souls of fearful adversaries,*
> *He capers nimbly in a lady's chamber*
> *To the lascivious pleasing of a lute.*

War, he tells us, instead of pursuing its normal, not to say proper, business, is, in the person of his brother, capering 'nimbly in a lady's chamber'. Rather than being an awesome rider of mettlesome steeds' war itself or his brother becomes a sportive horse (the word 'caper, means a playful leap, a skip or jump, and though usually applied to a horse, behind it in derivation lurks the goat), ridden by desire. Abruptly the next line makes Richard's real feeling about this 'glorious summer' clear. With one hissing, lovely phrase, 'the lascivious pleasing of a lute', he spits out his contempt for love and music, both merely sensual to him, sybaritic, and therefore reductive of man.

His unmitigated scorn now breaks out openly, and he unfolds himself, turns to the personal, in the next long sentence:

> *But I, that am not shaped for sportive tricks,*
> *Nor made to court an amorous looking-glass;*
> *I, that am rudely stamped, and want love's majesty,*
> *To strut before a wanton ambling nymph;*
> *I, that am curtailed of this fair proportion,*
> *Cheated of feature by dissembling nature,*
> *Deformed, unfinished, sent before my time*
> *Into this breathing world, scarce half made up,*
> *And that so lamely and unfashionable*
> *That dogs bark at me as I halt by them –*
> *Why I, in this weak piping time of peace,*
> *Have no delight to pass away the time,*
> *Unless to see my shadow in the sun,*
> *And descant on mine own deformity.*

He hates his brother who has brought peace, and cast him by his sunny looks into ugly shadow.

> *And therefore, since I cannot prove a lover,*
> *To entertain these fair well-spoken days,*
> *I am determined to prove a villain,*
> *And hate the idle pleasures of these days.*

This very first soliloquy, despite its formality and initial, bland phrases, is entirely consonant with Richard's secretive nature which hides nothing of itself from itself. It is right for one who is fundamentally alone, and therefore given to talking and scheming with himself. Rarely has soliloquy been more essential or natural to its user's character. At once we are allowed to enter the privacy of a diabolical soul.

And the sympathy attendant upon such entering works. One does respond to his plight by way of the many 'I's' of this speech (like those in the parallel speech near the play's end); and more since the commas after the four major, introductory 'I's' make us stress them in pausing, and since all that follows the commas collects in concentration on those 'I's'. The speech, its powerful utterance notwithstanding, is a long complaint by one who insists, the passive 'am's' make plain, that he has been horribly put upon. Thus the last 'am' in 'am determined' has an interestingly ambiguous force: 'I resolve' certainly, but also, since I am curtailed, 'I am forced' or predetermined 'to prove a villain,/ And hate. . . .' Shall a man, proud as this one, submit to the ignominy of his deformity? If from the start he was made to look like a hideous villain he will play the part for all that it is worth.

Yet, acknowledging his misshapenness and inadequacy though Richard does, by the triviality and superficiality which his language imputes to those more handsome, more 'fashionable', he easily conveys the sense that he is their superior, and indeed superior to nature itself. Complaint his speech may be. But it is obvious that he admires his state, is wholly compatible with it, and would have no other. Already in the Third Act of *Henry VI*, Part III, Richard, gnawingly envious of Edward for his success with women, pondered what he might make of his life; only two courses seemed possible to him: gaining the crown or, since that seems unlikely, devoting himself to love. But the absurdity of this latter role sweeps over him:

> *Oh, miserable thought, and more unlikely*
> *Than to accomplish twenty golden crowns!*
> *Why, love forswore me in my mother's womb*
> *And for I should not deal in her soft laws,*
> *She did corrupt frail nature with some bribe*
> *To shrink mine arm up like a withered shrub,*
> *To make an envious mountain on my back,*
> *Where sits deformity to mock my body, . . .*

Dwelling on his deformity, he concludes:

> *Then, since this earth affords no joy to me*
> *But to command, to check, to o'bear such*
> *As are of better person than myself*
> *I'll make my heaven to dream upon the crown*
> *And, whiles I live, to account this world but Hell*
> *Until my misshaped trunk that bears this head*
> *Be round impaléd with a glorious crown.*

Absurdly limited are the options that he puts before himself. Yet we may well pity him, and not least for his understandable need to over-bear those of better person than himself.

But later, in Act V, on stabbing saintly King Henry, he admits that he has 'neither pity, love, nor fear'. 'Indeed, 'tis true that Henry told me of', namely, that the elements themselves were disturbed at Richard's unnatural birth:

> *The owl shrieked at thy birth—an evil sign.*
> *The night crow cried, aboding luckless time.*
> *Dogs howled, and hideous tempest shook down trees.*
>
> .　.　.　.　.　.　.　.
>
> *Teeth hadst thou in thy head when thou wast born,*
> *To signify thou camest to bite the world.*

And stabbing the dead Henry again and again, Richard admits, in details often straight out of Holinshed:

> *For I have often heard my mother say*
> *I came into this world with my legs forward.*
> *Had I not reason, think ye, to make haste*
> *And seek their ruin that usurped our right?*
> *The midwife wondered, and the women cried,*
> *'Oh Jesus bless us, he is born with teeth!'*
> *And so I was, which plainly signified*
> *That I should snarl and bite and play the dog.*
> *Then, since the Heavens have shaped my body so,*
> *Let Hell make crooked my mind to answer it.*

A sense of being 'ordained', of being sent from the start with a tremendous mission, is, apparently, ingrained with him, a sense—beyond the sardonic—of being intentionally endowed with teeth.

Yet he does blame the Heavens for his body. And in his first soliloquy in *Richard III* his feelings about 'frail nature' have intensified. Not only does he dismiss human beings as mere shallow creatures, but for what it has done to him he despises nature as a cheat and dissembler. He believes that he has separated himself from nature, from society, and from all spiritual complications, that in his isolation he enjoys rare freedom and is entirely his own man. Such a notion might commend him to modern man. But naturalistic though his attitude may be, and Renaissance-like in his illusion of freedom, he is still serving— and is empowered by—a very medieval hell. Despite his blunt self-knowledge he cannot see that his sense of superiority, like the body nature gave him, may derive from nature and be no more profound or realistic than the impulses of others. Nonetheless, the imperious vigor of his verse and the appeal of its biting irony, accurate in what he has chosen to describe, are hard to resist in their very calculated limiting of those poor dupes who, wasting their powers on courting an amorous looking-glass, are overwhelmed by self-love (he has no inkling of how much more overwhelming his own narcissism is that it will have to try to turn the whole world into its twisted image to use as looking-glass).

Usually, we have observed, in Shakespeare's plays when a war is over, merriment and the merry war of love begin. With full hope Edward, now king, concludes *Henry VI*, Part III:

> *And now what rests but that we spend the time*
> *With stately triumphs, mirthful comic shows,*
> *Such as befits the pleasure of the Court?*
> *Sound drums and trumpets! Farewell sour annoy!*
> *For here, I hope, begins our lasting joy.*

We know from what has preceded that Edward does indeed subsume the merry war of love in 'the pleasure of the Court'. And Richard's first words in *Richard III* have admitted as much. Therefore Richard unhesitatingly plumps for the negative of the two courses he believes available to him. In this sunny court, by proceeding to make shadows and darkness, his own element, prevail everywhere, he will prove how shallow and unreal this sun and its weather are. His contempt for peace and pastimes is out in the open. In his mind things are never to be done for themselves alone but for the profit they provide. Yet, he will amply demonstrate, his energy's pride and its pleasure in itself hardly let us think such profit-making the whole story. But how prove his villainy and his hatred but by reawakening and spreading hatred among those who might otherwise know peace and love: his own brothers first of all, Edward the King who should establish and keep peace, and Clarence who has done everything in his power to make Edward king. And how shall this catalyst of discord work? With plots, inductions, 'drunken prophecies, libels, and dreams', words all, like the lover's, and for courting also, but to produce a yielding of quite the opposite sort.

Now we understand that the 'our' of Richard's first verse says more than merely 'we, the people of England' or 'I and my royal family'; it means the crown Richard aspires to and will at any cost obtain. Thus his malice in its undefiled energy, his motives in their clarity (I am 'subtle, false and treacherous'), his bewitching, not to say corrosive, wit caper before us. But first, a hulking predatory bird, he broods gloatingly over the world; already carrion-crammed, it is to become increasingly his private hunting ground. This play is indeed his in the speed with which it responds to his 'playful' plans and inspirations. A man straining with all his might to haul the present into the future, for him the thought must be at once converted into action. Few characters are, fortunately, so headstrong, so frighteningly gifted at imposing and satisfying their wills. Furthermore, his explosive yet wily nature is not to be interrupted or distracted; and seizing on everything, he instantly makes it his own. A most spontaneous villain, a perverse creator, like the blackest magician he seems able to summon what or whom he wishes and in that summoning to perform on it. Thus while he tells us of it he is snaring his brothers with 'a prophecy, which says that G/Of Edward's heirs the murderer shall be' (a prophecy too true since G, we already realize and so Richard certainly takes it, stands for Gloucester rather than for George; no doubt Richard in his eager availability to such prophecies is spurred on to act by this one, to midwife it to its fulfilment by a subtle adaptation of it); this prophecy will fix it that 'This day shall Clarence closely be mewed up.' And Clarence, so magically cued, appears, under arrest and for mewing in the Tower.

Here, as in *Love's Labour's Lost* and *The Taming of the Shrew* and in comedies to come, a lord is putting on a play, but with what a difference! Instead of preserving peace and beguiling it with pleasantries, this Duke proposes to forward the delights of disaster, to cast his twisted shadow so strongly over the land that its sun will shine no more. Navarre also wanted to frustrate life and living, out of a foolish notion of honor and fame. In all his bumblesomeness, however, love quickly disabused him. Richard, on the other hand, is altogether ready for his part. A playmaker, he plays for keeps. Hurt in his core manhood and too deeply to recover, he must prove himself at everyone else's expense. Already, we noted, in the third part of *Henry VI* Richard made his position clear:

> *I have no brother, I am like no brother;*
> *And this word 'love,' which greybeards call divine,*
> *Be resident in men like one another,*
> *And not in me. I am myself alone.*

The theme of loneliness we met in our first play. Antipholus of Syracuse on his first appearance, and in the way of comedy, tells us:

He that commends me to mine own content
Commends me to the thing I cannot get.
I to the world am like a drop of water,
That in the ocean seeks another drop,
Who, falling there to find his fellow forth,
Unseen, inquisitive, confounds himself.
So I, to find a mother and a brother,
In quest of them, unhappy, lose myself.

Obviously the impulse of Antipholus and that of Richard are anti-thetical. We need not point out how much Antipholus is like his brother, drop unto drop. Earlier, in *Henry VI*, Part III, Richard had confessed that he too was lost, not in a vast sea but in what might seem a Dantean wood. However, he is, in his own mind, lost for very different reasons:

And I—like one lost in a thorny wood,
That rends the thorns and is rent with the thorns,
Seeking a way and straying from the way,
Not knowing how to find the open air,
But toiling desperately to find it out—
Torment myself to catch the English crown.
And from that torment I will free myself,
Or hew my way out with a bloody ax.

What most of us would consider a thorny wood he considers a clearing, or views the world in the reverse of the comic spirit that knows its 'home' in and through others.

However, we might suggest, with more than fancy alone, that Richard's struggle is also Shakespeare's. Anyone can see that Shakespeare and his gifts, often tangled, often flagging, in *Henry VI*, Part III, were instantly galvanized when Richard appeared. He winged the hand that bred him. He and he alone, it would seem, by the tremendous charge of his will, not only 'suddenly' inspired Shakespeare, put him in immediate touch with the mainsprings of his young genius, but hacked his—so Shakespeare's—way through the thorny wood, the clutter of chronical matter and the elaborate, artificial language this play had long ensnarled them in. Despite his aloneness—it does account for some of his distinction—Richard possesses the voice of true, naked, personal feeling, and singly in his play possesses a mysterious interior life. Antipholus yearns for his kin, yearns to find and to complete

himself by finding his others. Richard–such the mistake of tragedy–
thinks he has found, and completed, himself by throwing off the foolish
'soft laws' of love, by divorcing himself utterly from his own kin and
from all men. In short, Antipholus, hating and suffering his 'aloneness', has done and continues to do all he can to end it; Richard,
exulting in his, means to exert all his strength to extend it. And in so
doing he has, in a desperate sense, defined himself. But it will be a
definition that must, by its growing exclusiveness, more and more
confine, and finally crush, him.

Shakespeare's comedies usually develop out of a company, a well-lit
group that shares a common world and attitude. One person of that
group is normally its leader, almost a choreophagus. But another
character in the play, Kate the Shrew, say, Shylock or Malvolio,
representing a counter, antistrophic element, threatens the peace and
welfare, or at least the equanimity and congeniality, of the group. It
then dances more precariously around him; out of this threat, however,
while it digests, changes or rejects the shrew or dissident, it finds new
strength, pleasure, harmony. In Shakespeare's history plays, on the
other hand, especially as they develop, the dissident is more important,
more critical to the play, emphatically so since he for a time at least
attains power to become its center. For that time, calling the shrewish
tune, he makes the world around him, now often an entire nation, dance
to his will. The movement, it is true, also customarily begins with a
group and often a domestic one, a family but a royal family at that, and
its responsive, surrounding court; blood ties, generations, and all that
they mean in Greek tragedy are abundantly exploited. Already these
early historical tragedies adumbrate the crucial figure of tragedy to
come, that individual who falls completely out of step, even finally
with himself. Richard might have become such a character, but he is
too assured from the start, too rooted in his role, too simply for all his
hidden nature a public figure and himself; he knows no doubt, no
struggle, is never–most dramatically of all–at odds with himself, at
least not until near his end. It is only the outside world that opposes him.

Meeting his brother Clarence, Richard, like a good poet able to
enjoy to the full the ambiguous resources of his material, promptly
finds still another way of milking the prophecy by interpreting the G
to be 'My Lady Grey', the King's wife. She, he insists, has persuaded
the King to imprison Clarence and is, with Mistress Shore, responsible
for their danger. Women do figure in Richard's career but mainly as
enemies and pawns. Since the Queen and Mistress Shore will be chief

factors in his rise, he must quickly emphasize them. Meantime, his malign wit is at work:

> Glou. *How say you, sir? Can you deny all this?*
> Brak. *With this, my lord, myself have naught to do.*
> Glou. *Naught to do with Mistress Shore? I tell thee, fellow,*
> *He that doth naught with her, excepting one,*
> *Were best to do it secretly alone.*

And we hear him in his sardonics when Clarence is led away:

> *Go, tread the path that thou shalt ne'er return,*
> *Simple, plain Clarence! I do love thee so,*
> *That I will shortly send thy soul to heaven,*
> *If heaven will take the present at our hands.*

With Clarence gone off to the Tower, Lord Hastings, just released from it, appears. Learning from him that the King is sick and near death, Richard, never missing an opportunity for a dig, especially a potentially profitable one and one we know he means, drawing on a saint he frequently invokes, solemnly observes:

> *Now, by Saint Paul, that news is bad indeed.*
> *O, he hath kept an evil diet long,*
> *And overmuch consumed his royal person.*

Alone again, he leaps to his plot:

> *He cannot live, I hope, and must not die*
> *Till George be packed with post horse up to heaven.*
> *I'll in to urge his hatred more to Clarence,*
> *With lies well steeled with weighty arguments;*
> *And if I fail not in my deep intent,*
> *Clarence hath not another day to live.*
> *Which done, God take King Edward to His mercy,*
> *And leave the world for me to bustle in!*

It is, I think, worth noticing that the capering from the start is consonant with his impetuous, not to say unbridled, centaur-like nature; despite the allusions to other animals that persons around Richard use to describe him, Richard most frequently draws the horse into his speech. And it is natural for him to do so. He is, in fierceness as in shrewdness, a creature sealed in if not clogged – most happily it would seem, whatever rationalization it may be on his part–by his earthen hump. But because of this being sealed in he amounts to the earthly, the bestial, in man cultivated and matured, by its engrossing of all other qualities, into almost magical strength and cunning. Richard, his words make clear, hardly intends, like the fools most men are, to confuse the two worlds or to let one, heaven, influence or weaken the other; this world is more than enough for him. Totally social, materialistic nature that he is, 'bustle' is the word for him.

> For then I'll marry Warwick's youngest daughter.
> What though I killed her husband and her father?
> The readiest way to make the wench amends
> Is to become her husband and her father.

Sarcasm or not, we know Richard well enough by now to be inclined to believe that to a marked degree he believes these lines. Are not bodies bodies and interchangeable? In any case, Shakespeare is at especial pains to clarify the facts so that we can have no doubts about what follows.

Immediately now, in the most adverse conditions possible, Richard exhibits and proves himself at his audacious best. For his improvisatory powers not even corpses, apparently, can escape him. By his words and his will, so potent is he, he seems to conjure Lady Anne. She, leading a funeral procession, stops it so that she can 'obsequiously lament' her father-in-law, murdered Henry VI. She delivers herself, this being a ritualistic moment, of a very formal lament in the self-conscious, highly wrought language common to the play and to Shakespeare's early, derived style. One of the principal pleasures of this play is to hear Richard's idiosyncratic utterance hard against that style, just as it is to hear him adapting his expression to it in public when it suits his purpose. Referring to her husband, Henry's son, also killed by Richard, Anne spends the bulk of her lament cursing Richard and all attached to him, child and wife, or the wife she will become. Her lament over and the funeral about to move on, Richard steps forth; and, while Anne exclaims, 'What black magician conjures up this fiend?' (we know, as she does not yet, that Richard is his own magician), he by his forceful presence halts it. Anne says—accurately, we shall see, for herself as well—to the coffin-bearers:

> What, do you tremble? Are you all afraid?
> Alas, I blame you not, for you are mortal,
> And mortal eyes cannot endure the devil.
> Avaunt, thou dreadful minister of hell!

Thou hadst but power over his mortal body,
His soul thou canst not have, therefore be gone.

Imperturbably, responding to her words, he begins the wind-up of his spell on her: 'Sweet saint, for charity, be not so curst.' Devil though he may be, she by her opposite nature must be reminded of her role and its sweeter, truer occupations. What better appeal to a woman? Anne rails and he lets her while she describes the world and, much more so, the world to come: '. . . thou hast made the happy earth thy hell,/ Filled it with cursing cries and deep exclaims.' Magically, for Richard's presence, the corpse's wounds 'Open their congealed mouths and bleed afresh.' Sign sufficient that Richard is communicant of some appalling primitive energy. Corpses are indeed not impervious to him, let alone the living. When she finishes he pursues his course: 'Lady, you know no rules of charity,/Which renders good for bad, blessings for curses.' Versed in theology and Christian commonplaces, he means to hold his opponents and professors of Christianity to it. She answers him in the stichomythic, aphoristic parallelism frequent in this play and in the style of the times: 'Villain, thou know'st nor law of God nor man./No beast so fierce but knows some touch of pity.' Richard sardonically takes her words at face value: 'But I know none, and therefore am no beast.' Anne's 'O wonderful, when devils tell the truth!' allows him to pursue antithetically the line of flattery he has set going: 'More wonderful, when angels are so angry.' Thus, admitting he killed Henry, drawing on the old notion he is fond of: 'Let him thank me that holp to send him thither,/For he was fitter for that place than earth' (in this reference to Henry's touching failures as a king and to his purity, his longing for a religious role, Richard is not too far from the mark), Richard demonstrates at once the power of words. When she answers, 'And thou unfit for any place but hell', he, audacity itself, counters, 'Yes, one place else, if you will hear me name it.' Or, to her 'Some dungeon', 'Your bed-chamber'. She, again unaware what curse she is calling down upon herself, retorts, 'Ill rest betide the chamber where thou liest!' Richard volleys with 'So will it, madam, till I lie with you.' Stunned if not hypnotized, all she can say is 'I hope so.'

Seeing her rattled and available, Richard quickly pushes flattery to the utmost:

> *Is not the causer of the timeless deaths*
> *Of these Plantagenets, Henry and Edward,*
> *As blameful as the executioner?*

And to Anne's 'Thou wast the cause, and most accursed effect,' he rises in marvelous, most seductive accusation:

> *Your beauty was the cause of that effect –*
> *Your beauty, that did haunt me in my sleep*
> *To undertake the death of all the world*
> *So I might live one hour in your sweet bosom.*

What unparalleled, high-fantastical wooing! Truth apart, by its very total extravagance, it must be most impressive. How could he dare to say such an outrageous thing if he did not mean at least some part of it? That violence like this should be violent out of love and tenderness! Of course, despising love, Richard is free to blaspheme it to any degree. And he has confessed to everything, and to the much more that he would do, simply to use it against her. Thus he swears her in not only as the accomplice but the only true begetter of his crimes; she and she alone is the real culprit. What woman could resist a passion for her beauty so overpowering that it would, to have that beauty, gladly destroy the world; just as here, to clear a path to her, it has destroyed the two nearest to her? We already appreciate the horrible truth of what Richard is admitting; that for the beauty in the world, a beauty he in his deformity can have no part in, a beauty that, making him the uglier, haunts him in his sleep, he would indeed 'undertake the death of all the world.' But now for her the crueler, the more heinous he 'honestly' confesses to being, since this cruelty is all for her, the more attractive he threatens to become. Is there a more convincing lie than the truth once it is launched by a winsome falsehood? Though Anne continues to struggle in this 'merry war of love', she is thoroughly hooked. Her spit he uses, and her eyes, which she wishes 'basilisks to strike thee dead':

> *I would they were, that I might die at once,*
> *For now they kill me with a living death.*
> *Those eyes of thine from mine have drawn salt tears,*
> *Shamed their aspects with store of childish drops.*

By the many tear-making occasions he has till now withstood this moment supplies him with an opportunity to impress her further with what power is hers and how smitten he is. So, too, while his 'manly eyes' have never been for tears:

> *My tongue could never learn sweet smoothing words,*
> *But now thy beauty is proposed my fee,*

My proud heart sues, and prompts my tongue to speak.
Teach not thy lip such scorn, for it was made
For kissing, lady, not for such contempt.

With cunning art he dwells on the two physical foci of courtly love, the eye and the tongue, and consummately proves himself in the very role he originally scoffed at. At last, confident that he has sufficiently shaken her, he ventures his master stroke:

If thy revengeful heart cannot forgive,
Lo, here I lend thee this sharp-pointed sword,
Which if thou please to hide in this true breast
And let the soul forth that adoreth thee,
I lay it naked to the deadly stroke,
And humbly beg the death upon my knee.

'True breast', 'the soul . . . that adoreth thee', and 'humbly beg' against 'revengeful heart' and 'not forgive', how carefully he has chosen his charged words. When she offers at his breast with his sword, he, risking all, ruthlessly drives his point home:

Nay, do not pause, for I did kill King Henry,
But 'twas thy beauty that provokéd me.
Nay, now dispatch; 'twas I that stabbed young Edward,
But 'twas thy heavenly face that set me on.

With Henry and Edward his witnesses, this is too much for her; she drops the sword and he triumphs: 'Take up the sword again, or take up me.' Still at Anne's 'Arise, dissembler. Though I wish thy death,/I will not be thy executioner', he presses on, 'Then bid me kill myself, and I will do it.' To her 'I have already', he, explaining, makes it impossible for her to proceed:

That was in thy rage.
Speak it again and, even with the word,
This hand which for thy love did kill thy love
Shall for thy love kill a far truer love.
To both their deaths shalt thou be accessary.

Thoroughly subdued, all Anne can say is 'I would I knew thy heart.' He has twisted her like the ring he puts on her finger. Was there ever an abler courtly lover?

Only one possible comparison, if a far-fetched one, have we met so far. Certainly in broadness of stroke, in perversion of common sense and the facts, and in an amorousness more than verging on burlesque, this courting might be thought to resemble Petruchio's treatment of Kate. He, too, amazed and paralyzed her with protestations of love while, out of similar, seemingly passionate concern for her, he smote all around her and threatened the rest. And he changed her, too, till she obeyed echoingly his every word and whim. But with what a difference! Self-interested though Petruchio may be—after a fortune and a likely wife—he is exposing Kate to such treatment for the happiest realization of herself. If his play is farce it is farce with the best of intentions. Richard, however, is at play (both, it is true, do what they do in considerable measure out of sheer enjoyment, the joy of doing), not alone for his fortune's sake, but to gratify the shrewishness and the fiendish gifts in him, to thwart and to destroy others. In his gay abuse of them, and in his savage delight in betrayal, the element of farce does assert itself; through their feebleness and shallowness, as well as through the villainy of most of them, the betrayed little solicit our sympathy. But though Petruchio was often, in farce's fashion, seemingly feeling-less, he was so out of a fundamental regard for feeling. Richard, on the other hand, a monstrous farceur through and through, makes much of feeling for his absolute lack of it; he exploits it like everything else for purely selfish, inhuman ends.

The comedies we have till now reviewed have been mainly romances in which the chief characters are sorely buffeted by circumstances. But as it turns out they are happy victims; saddened while they seek to recover from the blows, they struggle, for all the errors, theirs as well as their surroundings', toward a love which they do finally arrive at. Those errors, one can say, make the arrival possible. *The Comedy of Errors*, *The Taming of the Shrew*, and *Love's Labour's Lost* are roughly contemporary with *Richard III*. The atmosphere of the domestic, a contained world whatever winds blow through it (its setting is often fabulous though its story or contents are local and real), prevails in these comedies. But in the histories we encounter a larger, public, war-torn world, a whole nation in travail. A little too tidily one might propose that if the early romances are bent on love and its eventual fulfilment, the histories tend to concentrate on a world hostile to and expending most of its powers against love. Richard, hating love, exerts all his extraordinary energy to destroy it. A victim also, instead of feeling grief and melancholy he is bitter and hates nature; and out of a kind of exultancy in revulsion he resolves to revenge himself on nature by way of her more favored offspring. This play is also about love then, what happens when love the humanizer, the element we need to live, is successfully denied. Consequently, though the setting of this history is fact, or the kind of fact that filtered through Holinshed and folklore, because of the demonic rages in Richard the fabulous quickly breaks out in the unfolding story, because of his rages and the magical that richly adheres to folklore 'fact'. History, it is clear, has not yet been freed from the fabulous or reduced to the reasonable, the factually explicable. In very considerable degree Richard's fascination, we shall discover, resides in this semi-mythical source expressing itself through time or the historical.

Submitting to him for the prime undertaker he is, Anne even leaves the corpse and the funeral to him! Alone, Richard cries out in delighted astonishment at his success:

> *Was ever woman in this humour wooed?*
> *Was ever woman in this humour won?*
> *I'll have her; but I'll not keep her long.*

A capping touch it is, properly Shakespearean (a resemblance can be found in the old Vice's pleasure in his skill, in his gloating over his triumphs); a comment on the rich incredibility of this scene and on Richard's power, this touch in some measure cleverly offsets our incredulity. Like the artist pondering his handiwork, Richard revels in having done more and better than he expected; with the incredibility of the scene once more sweeping over him, he realizes he is a genius:

> *What! I, that killed her husband and her father,*
> *To take her in her heart's extremest hate,*
> *With curses in her mouth, tears in her eyes,*
> *The bleeding witness of my hatred by;*
> *Having God, her conscience, and these bars against me,*
> *And I no friends to back my suit withal*
> *But the plain devil and dissembling looks,*
> *And yet to win her, all the world to nothing!*
> *Ha!*

This last line's long exclamatory silence, as he falls almost into a trance, brilliantly, broodingly expresses his awe also before the capacity of the race, particularly women, to be gulled and abused. However little he may have needed confirmation in such matters, this is a moment in which his worst, most contemptuous thoughts of mankind, and of love, might seem thoroughly verified. And what better

proof does he need of the effectiveness of stark temerity? Not satisfied
yet, he squeezes more amazement, delight and vanity out of his triumph:

> *Hath she forgot already that brave Prince,*
> *Edward, her lord, whom I, some three months since,*
> *Stabbed in my angry mood at Tewksbury?*
> *A sweeter and a lovelier gentleman,*
> *Framed in the prodigality of nature,*
> *Young, valiant, and no doubt right royal,*
> *The spacious world cannot again afford.*
> *And will she yet abase her eyes on me,*
> *That cropped the prime of this sweet Prince*
> *And made her widow to a woeful bed?*
> *On me, whose all not equals Edward's moiety?*
> *On me, that halts and am misshapen thus?*

He makes the most of the difference—what delicious incredulity he
gathers out of the repeated, accented 'me'–to make the most of his
success. However, from his dwelling on them one can believe that he
recognizes (and recognizes as a good) the virtues ripe in Edward.

At last, in a most amusing reply to his opening soliloquy, Richard
allows himself to be 'persuaded':

> *My dukedom to a beggarly denier,*
> *I do mistake my person all this while.*
> *Upon my life, she finds, although I cannot,*
> *Myself to be a marvellous proper man.*
> *I'll be at charges for a looking-glass,*
> *And entertain a score or two of tailors,*
> *To study fashions to adorn my body.*
> *Since I am crept in favour with myself,*
> *I will maintain it with some little cost.*
> *But first I'll turn yon fellow in his grave,*
> *And then return lamenting to my love.*
> *Shine out, fair sun, till I have bought a glass,*
> *That I may see my shadow as I pass.*

The sun he had shied away from he need fear no more. On the contrary.
By his skill he can brazen out his ugliness as supreme glamor. We must
not treat lightly his 'although I cannot', his refusal to lie to himself, and
the bitterness implicit in 'Since I am crept in favour with myself.' Yet
in view of the éclat with which he has wooed and won Anne, surely we

can minimize now, however much it may have initially corroded him, his sense of inadequacy, his sexual envy. This sense and his resentment of his ugliness did their work long ago; at this time, as he struts in his deformity, it is meeting and triumphing over immense, if not seemingly impossible, challenges that most delights him.

I have made so much of this scene not only for its own fascination and for the excitement of watching a great gift in the process of discovering and fulfilling itself through a most difficult assignment, but also for the fact that already by the end of this second scene we know virtually all that there is to know about Richard. After it, beyond piling up more and more of the same and achieving his announced end, the crown, he has nowhere to go. In a sense Richard did spring full-blown from his mother's tormented womb. For his being so well established by history we enjoy mainly the witnessing of his character-istics in action. Unlike Shakespeare's later creations, characters in the making, here portraiture of a more ancient, classical variety detains us; character already in full charge of its powers and completely realized. For the play is just that: a series of his acts, his foreseeable yet un-predictable virtuoso performances. This is the daring of the play and at the same time, perhaps, for us (not for the Elizabethans with their prodigious appetite for expectation gratified rather than for novelty or surprise) something of the play's monotony if not its weakness. But a prodigious act like Richard's, for the incredible risks he gladly runs, continues to astonish. And with this first mad love-scene we can understand that Richard has given more than fervent assent to his misshapenness. In fact, it seems not extravagant to infer that he has overtaken and 'improved' it; he now is a perfect portrait, if not product, of what he is internally.

Shakespeare, in his impulse to present such a character for its own absorbing sake, knew its surefire effectiveness with an audience. Shakespeare's genius, like his age's, in its ebullient youth was alert to the extreme; out for the most extravagant wherever it could be found, the age garnered adventures and aggrandizings in distant time as in far-off places. There was, in this respect, the very present spectacular practice and success of Kyd and Marlowe to encourage Shakespeare. The monolithic figure had already toweringly emerged in Marlowe's Tamburlaine and Barabas. Taking up the whole world in himself, this titan by his power and his audacity masters it, betters it at its own game. We need not remark that Shakespeare in his talent for learning was already improving Kyd's and Marlowe's best lessons by entering his character at a depth and with a complexity surpassing theirs. Through Shakespeare's giving himself to the forging of such a subtle, brute heart, we are free for a time to be that tiger wrapped in a monstrous manshape. Sucked into his unfolding, secret will, and thus in a sense implicated in it, we cannot help relishing, with him, his being's most private nature, cannot help participating in the gusto of his perform-ance. Not though we soon realize that this superman, like most, is, rather than superman, subhuman: fiendishly efficient because of one fixed idea only, he represses or lacks almost all human, pause-making attributes and concerns. It is hardly surprising, therefore, that in his all-out 'specialist' competence he can sweep virtually all before him.

Moreover, spellbinder though he is, master of naturalistic impulse and motive, Richard may strike some of us as being a little incomplete, if not slightly naive, even here. He does use human life with the prodigality of most men for wood, stone, water. The sexual is also something he regards in one way only (through his disfigurement we have seen that he has come to identify love with the body alone), mere lust, therefore utterly contemptible; of the smallest interest except as it abets his purpose. The history plays, it is true, by their public scene and reliance on the known tend, in the first examples, to be simpler than the comedies, more available, more single, if not at times nearly one dimensional. By their nature they would seem to exclude the engaging medley of materials common to Elizabethan comedy.

But again it may be a matter of concentration. Through Shake-speare's genius for amalgamating, Richard brilliantly compounds in himself choice ingredients from, he proudly tells us, the popular medieval Vice or Iniquity, the blood-and-thunder Senecan world, and the Machiavel. (Already in *Henry VI*, Part III, Richard boasts:

> *I can add colours to the chameleon,*
> *Change shapes with Proteus for advantage*
> *And set the murderous Machiavel to school.*

And in the verses just before Richard competes with other worthies:

> *I'll play the orator as well as Nestor,*
> *Deceive more slily than Ulysses could,*
> *And, like a Sinon, take another Troy)*

He also contains something of the violence and outrage of Greek tragedy and the Old Testament. But when naturalized in their English, islanded conditions, these elements seem to have gone through a considerable sea-change. Among the various possibilities, for instance, that Richard never explores are the delights of cannibalism (for a much fuller exploitation of human excess it is to his contemporary Titus Andronicus we must look). Nor does sexual experiment, as I have suggested, or the delectabilities of the torments of others, occupy him. Having denied the sexual in himself, he finds his sensuality's satisfaction by way of his mental powers, in manipulating others, his will cowing and destroying theirs, and in bloodletting.

Nevertheless, one has to admit the multiple, impressive play in him of the elements mentioned. Some real share of his distinction and dramatic appeal lies no doubt in the tension in him between these old elements and the 'historical' figure—that is, against the timeless, essential qualities in him, we experience a vivid, existential person wholly identified in and with a particular time and place, and with a series of specific events. In fact, this particular moment in history affords a perfect setting for the version of the timeless, the demonic, that Richard is. In the earlier *Henry* plays, a resonant, most fertile ground for him, his character had ample time and opportunities to develop, mature, and set; in *Richard III* he is at the peak of his powers. Thoroughly immersed in a most complicated world of plots and crime, he is 'natural' to this jungle; nourished by all its heinous conditions, he emerges from the welter a fullblown canker. Accordingly, Richard glories in his time and place and its events; this bloody world is his especial, delicious preserve; and he, its chief growth and gardener, means to keep it so. At the same time he exceeds his time and place. Altogether temporal though he is, we feel the mythical power that he is really serving. The tension that this duality produces reflects again Shakespeare's genius for making the best of whatever worlds and modes are available to him, for playing one against another in the emergent harmony of one entirely convincing personality. Richard, we can say, fills his moment, his play's moment, the way he fills his own taut skin. Like his creator he makes a virtue, a passionate joy, of the given and the necessary. However, it is his roots in a past far beyond the medieval, his kinship with Cain, and the nourishment he derives therefrom, that gives him this exultancy; and it encourages his illusion of freedom, which he mistakenly attributes to his 'aloneness,' his uniqueness.

Certainly it is his energy, as he lights vulture-like on one situation and then another, and thereby on a further realization of his nature and power, that fixes us no less than his victims. Unlike most men, by the iron resolution that grips him, Richard is never—at least not till near the end–vague, hesitant, idling, porous. His sense of hurt, of personal injustice (who does not have some of this?), soliciting our sympathy, how can we resist him in his capacity then to convert that sense, unlike most who rather sulk or yield to enervating daydreams, into most efficient action? Each occasion, large and small, is a store of powder for his fire to touch off, and thus to reveal, in a lightning flash, his true, monstrous majesty. Similar to Milton's Satan, similarly 'wronged',

> *As when a spark*
> *Lights on a heap of nitrous Powder, laid*
> *Fit for the Tun some Magazin to store*
> *Against a rumor'd War, the Smutty grain*
> *With sudden blaze diffus'd, inflames the Air:*
> *So started up in his own shape the Fiend.*

But, alas, though Richard, war's magazine that he is, exults to be so framed and revealed, dazzling others no less than himself, no angel stands by to accost him and to curb. But what an outrageous wonder this is: the dream, if completely perverted, of the artist, the imposition of a giant will on all, his subject-matter. So realized, each situation serves to spawn a host of promising others, always more precisely shaped to mirror their maker. It is a world truly molded in one's own image.

Yet, as we have proposed, far more than any of his triumphs, much though they please him, Richard relishes through them the exercise and the distinctive taste of himself. Such is the Satanic passion that ravens through the whole world for the savoring of itself. In Richard we first meet a force that appears to be elemental, evil unmixed and well nigh infinite. No wonder he is at ease. No wonder his acts seem almost pretexts for his displaying himself. And the more they are extravagant the more they become a self-fulfilling, self-multiplying joy. In his intactness he convinces us that he is above all fear, invulnerable, to and for himself alone, and imbued with a jollity, a most ingratiating reck-lessness. At least one might say of such a figure, especially against the much feebler creatures around him, that his is a life altogether lived. No less a moralist than Dante much preferred those who will to act, even if that will be in tow to gigantic evil, to the stillborn, the time-servers. But what a cost such will is to others, and to itself, *Richard III* makes irrefutably plain. Either men exercise basic good will toward each other, respect the spiritual ecology essential to their natures, or they destroy all.

The play's next scene in the King's palace also stresses love and good will or rather their flouting, their being used as with Anne for the reverse of themselves; this time the flouting occurs within the immediate royal family itself. Having tried and established himself in the first two scenes, first with a brother, then with a 'love', Richard is now ready to assert himself publicly. The King, dying, wishes to establish amity between Richard and the Queen's kin. But almost on his entrance, even while thundering forth his love, Richard ensures its opposite. And he does so in a pattern he enjoys making the most of: insistence on his honesty, his Iago-like 'plainness':

> *They do me wrong, and I will not endure it.*
> *Who are they that complain unto the King*
> *That I, forsooth, am stern and love them not?*
> *By holy Paul, they love his Grace but lightly*
> *That fill his ears with such dissentious rumours.*
> *Because I cannot flatter and speak fair,*
> *Smile in men's faces, smooth, deceive, and cog,*
> *Duck with French nods and apish courtesy,*
> *I must be held a rancorous enemy.*
> *Cannot a plain man live and think no harm*
> *But thus his simple truth must be abused*
> *By silken, sly, insinuating Jacks?*

Who can call these words merely a first draft for the supple, virile speech of later plays? They reflect Richard's common tack, stressing his ugliness, his inability to 'flatter and speak fair', thereby most ably flattering and speaking fair. We feel his imputation that those who 'speak fair', the silken Jacks, all gallant, handsome men, must be hypocrites and of the company of the lovers he scorned in his opening speech. Drab outsides, we see, and plain speakers can, no less than fancy, deceive and conceal the simple truth. Soon for Richard's contribution wrangling has the day. He says to Queen Elizabeth,

> *You may deny that you were not the mean*
> *Of my Lord Hasting's late imprisonment.*
> Riv. *She may, my lord, for—*
> Glou. *She may, Lord Rivers! Why, who knows not so?*

And at this his suddenness is off.

> *She may do more, sir than denying that.*
> *She may help you to many fair preferments,*

> *And then deny her aiding hand therein,*
> *And lay those honours on your high deserts.*
> *What may she not? She may, yea, marry, may she—*
> Riv. *What, marry, may she?*
> Glou. *What, marry, may she? Marry with a king,*
> *A bachelor, and a handsome stripling too.*
> *I wis, your grandam had a worser match.*

His own casual word, as a rime might do for a poet, has prompted him to the thought he reaches; for he lives on such passing inspirations.

Fittingly at this juncture, as though this were the atmosphere most congenial to her and as though she were cued by Queen Elizabeth's 'Small joy have I in being England's Queen', the former Queen, Margaret, appears. The play's prime railer, she is chief opposite to Richard, therefore the play's other major figure, and almost its Senecan ghost-like Fury or Revenge. Though officially banished, she has come to add her poison to the brewing witch's broth. Echoing with great curses and name-callings Richard's every word, she steps forth to burst in on the wrangling. Soon, for her potency, the rest turn on her, and she vents her splendid spleen on them all. When Richard says, 'Have done thy charm, thou hateful withered hag!' she, with the abrasive humor everywhere in this play, spins a mighty, nonstop, prophetic curse on him:

> *And leave out thee? Stay, dog, for thou shalt hear me.*
> *If Heaven have any grievous plague in store*
> *Exceeding those that I can wish upon thee,*
> *O let them keep it till thy sins be ripe,*
> *And then hurl down their indignation*
> *On thee, the troubler of the poor world's peace!*
> *The worm of conscience still begnaw thy soul!*
> *Thy friends suspect for traitors while thou livest,*
> *And take deep traitors for thy dearest friends!*
> *No sleep close up that deadly eye of thine,*
> *Unless it be while some tormenting dream*
> *Affrights thee with a Hell of ugly devils!*
> *Thou elvish-marked, abortive, rooting hog!*
> *Thou that was sealed in thy nativity*
> *The slave of nature and the son of Hell!*

Thou slander of thy mother's heavy womb!
Thou loathèd issue of thy father's loins!
Thou rag of honour! Thou detested—

At one with the time's almost Biblical belief in the actuality, if not the sacred efficacy, of words, Richard interjects 'Margaret'. She is so wrapped up in her cursing that at Richard's naming her all she can say, almost mindlessly, surely foolishly, is that she 'looked for no reply'. She bids him, 'O, let me make the period to my curse!' But Queen Elizabeth, seconding Richard's intention, assures her, 'Thus have you breathed your curse against yourself.' Nonetheless, the violent seeds of Margaret's curse have been sown, and they will bear their overwhelming crop. Margaret rounds on Queen Elizabeth passionately and accurately:

> *Poor painted Queen, vain flourish of my fortune!*
> *Why strew'st thou sugar on that bottled spider*
> *Whose deadly web ensnareth thee about?*
> *Fool, fool! thou whet'st a knife to kill thyself.*
> *The time will come that thou shalt wish for me*
> *To help thee curse that poisonous hunchbacked toad.*

Richard, happy to display his sanctimonious side, pretends pity for Margaret:

> *I cannot blame her. By God's holy Mother,*
> *She hath had too much wrong, and I repent*
> *My part thereof that I have done to her.*

He even goes so far as to say, 'God pardon them that are the cause' of Clarence's imprisonment. Then he murmurs to himself, '. . . had I cursed now, I had cursed myself.' Superior he may think himself, and indifferent to if not scornful of heaven or another world; still we are right to infer that he believes in that heaven's existence and in the strength of curses, prophecies, libels, and in the potency of words generally. Thus when he is alone and the murderers he has summoned appear, Richard, urging them to his own conduct, warns:

> *But, sirs, be sudden in the execution,*
> *Withal obdurate, do not hear him plead.*
> *For Clarence is well-spoken, and perhaps*
> *May move your hearts to pity if you mark him.*

But the first murderer, cut, his words reveal, of Richard's cloth, cocksurely dismisses the warning:

> *Tut, tut, my lord, we will not stand to prate.*
> *Talkers are no good doers. Be assured*
> *We go to use our hands and not our tongues.*

And the next scene takes us to the murderers' deed. First, however, responding nobly to the feeling for words, dreams and curses, witnessed in the previous scene, Clarence describes with the well-spoken language that Richard remarked 'the fearful dreams' and 'ugly sights' his night came to. The speech may far exceed that necessary to the play's progress. But pithy and supple it is, in a way that most of the talk in the play, other than Richard's, is not.

> *Methought that I had broken from the Tower,*
> *And was embarked to cross to Burgundy,*
> *And in my company my brother Gloucester,*
> *Who from my cabin tempted me to walk*
> *Upon the hatches. There we looked toward England,*
> *And cited up a thousand heavy times*
> *During the wars of York and Lancaster*
> *That had befall'n us. As we paced along*
> *Upon the giddy footing of the hatches,*
> *Methought that Gloucester stumbled, and in falling*
> *Struck me, that thought to stay him, overboard,*
> *Into the tumbling billows of the main.*
> *O Lord! Methought what pain it was to drown!*
> *What dreadful noise of waters in mine ears!*
> *What sights of ugly death within mine eyes!*
> *Methought I saw a thousand fearful wrecks,*
> *Ten thousand men that fishes gnawed upon,*
> *Wedges of gold, great anchors, heaps of pearl,*
> *Inestimable stones, unvalued jewels,*
> *All scattered in the bottom of the sea.*
> *Some lay in dead men's skulls, and in the holes*
> *Where eyes did once inhabit there were crept,*
> *As 'twere in scorn of eyes, reflecting gems,*
> *Which wooed the slimy bottom of the deep*
> *And mocked the dead bones that lay scattered by.*

Again we have Shakespeare's genius and his enthusiasm, if in simpler form, for mingling loveliness and death, met in Antipholus' declaration of love to Lucinia in *The Comedy of Errors*, or for mingling loveliness and ruin, anticipative of Salarino's early speech to Antonio in *The Merchant of Venice*. All three share the condition of being in the mind alone, Antipholus' deriving from desire, the others' from fear of the sea. But all three have a beauty which will culminate in *The Tempest*, where the sea-change will at last be complete. One of Shakespeare's earliest verbal pictures as drama, interestingly enough Clarence's speech, though it reports no more than a dream, has a vividness, a directness, beyond that of much of the play's dialogue even at its most savage. Inestimable and unvalued indeed are these jewels, now little more than stones, scattered over the bottom of the sea, scattered like the bones of men who yearned for them. At last total fulfilment is upon these adventurers. Their brains and their eyes have become those things which in life passionately occupied both. Again one has the sense of those adventurers becoming, as in a play that celebrates the outrages of a figure like Richard, works of art. Accordingly, set-piece though this speech may be and mainly an imaginative reconstruction, something like Juliet's rehearsal of the tomb, it is most magical. But the element of prophecy and accuracy is also here. So is that of relevancy to the ruthless, greedy careers of Clarence and his brothers. Clarence, seeing what giddy footing they are at, already senses Richard's involvement in his ruin (hence the loaded 'tempted'), but interprets it as accidental, merely stumbling. And good brother that he is, in fact–whatever his earlier crimes–one of the few decent people in this play, he is struck overboard by Richard in the act of trying to save him.

Then Clarence's memory, by its very extraordinary claims, leaps into a higher state of forcefulness–he could not die:

> *. . . and often did I strive*
> *To yield the ghost. But still the envious flood*
> *Stopped in my soul, and would not let it forth*
> *To find the empty, vast, and wandering air,*
> *But smothered it within my panting bulk,*
> *Which almost burst to belch it in the sea.*

The thing that should have killed him kept him alive. To the keeper's 'Awaked you not with this sore agony?' Clarence impresses the dream's astounding power on us with 'Oh no, my dream was lengthened after life.' Next, overwhelming though this 'physical' experience of drowning had been, began the much worse trial:

> *O, then began the tempest to my soul,*
> *Who passed, methought, the melancholy flood,*
> *With that grim ferryman which poets write of,*
> *Unto the kingdom of perpetual night.*

From the waters, the real English waters that his dream had started with, he swept straight on into the mythical Styx. There he was first greeted by his father-in-law, Warwick: 'What scourge for perjury/Can this dark monarchy afford false Clarence?'

> *Then came wandering by*
> *A shadow like an angel, with bright hair*
> *Dabbled in blood, and he shrieked out aloud,*
> *'Clarence is come, false, fleeting, perjured Clarence,*
> *That stabbed me in the field by Tewksbury.*
> *Seize on him, Furies, take him unto torment!'*
> *With that, methought, a legion of foul fiends*
> *Environed me about, and howléd in mine ears*
> *Such hideous cries that with the very noise*
> *I trembling waked, and for a season after*
> *Could not believe but that I was in Hell,*
> *Such terrible impression made the dream.*

One might, were it not so absorbing, find this speech long, distracting, and delaying in a play chiefly punctuated by quick, brief thoughts promptly leading to quick, decisive acts versus brisk if protracted harangues. Yet Clarence's words, different in their scenic clarity though they may be, have some of the potency packed into the women's static, stone-towering tirades, the potency tantamount to action in feeling-charged words. In addition, his speech, the first important instance of it, prepares us for dream and its significant place— also a matter of words and images or vision—in this play. We can echo the keeper's 'No marvel, my lord, though it affrighted you;/I promise you, I am afraid to hear you tell it.' Clarence's verbal powers have been thoroughly established. So too his following prayer:

> *O God! If my deep prayers cannot appease Thee,*
> *But Thou wilt be avenged on my misdeeds,*
> *Yet execute Thy wrath in me alone.*
> *O spare my guiltless wife and my poor children!*

establishes his goodness and his solicitude for others. His deep feeling for his family is particularly striking against the complete indifference that Richard delights in.

Then while Clarence sleeps, the murderers appear, in the play's first prose. The second murderer is already troubled by conscience. However, for the reward he anticipates he dismisses conscience when, in a kind of catechism, he describes the woe and burden it is. But first he scares himself by speaking of 'the great Judgement-Day': 'The urging of that word "judgement" hath bred a kind of remorse in me.' Thus in the broad, rasping humor appropriate to such low-life associates of Richard, he says of conscience:

> *I'll not meddle with it. It is a dangerous thing—it makes a man a coward. A man cannot steal but it accuseth him; he cannot swear but it checks him; he cannot lie with his neighbour's wife but it detects him.' 'Tis a blushing shamefast spirit that mutinies in a man's bosom; it fills one full of obstacles. It made me once restore a purse of gold that I found; it beggars any man that keeps it. It is turned out of all towns and cities for a dangerous thing, and every man that means to live well endeavours to trust to himself and to live without it.*

The comment that this little essay is on Richard and the others in the play we need not pause to emphasize. The murderers agree, a kind of mocking fulfilment of the dream, to drown Clarence in a wine-barrel. But rather than kill him in his sleep the second murderer foolishly proposes, '. . . first let's reason with him.' After a long exchange the second murderer, to stop Clarence's eloquence, distracts him, and the first, stabbing him, drowns him in the malmsey-butt. However, the second murderer does indeed repent:

> *A bloody deed, and desperately dispatched!*
> *How fain, like Pilate, would I wash my hands*
> *Of this most grievous murder!*

(His is a first fairly innocent expression for the many cleansing-wished-for, hand-washing scenes to follow. But though Pilate and therefore Christ are acknowledged here as source, in later similar moments they will generally be so by implication alone. For the addition of the sea in those moments we must turn to *Titus Andronicus* and Aaron's defense of his blackamoor baby:

> *Coal-black is better than another hue*
> *In that it scorns to bear another hue;*

For all the water in the ocean
Can never turn the swan's black legs to white,
Although she lave them hourly in the flood.)

With the murder still reverberating in our ears, in the Palace dying King Edward congratulates himself for having united the enemies, a would-be scene of love! Richard, entering, protests himself, as ever, a lover of men and of peace. But when Queen Elizabeth urges the King to free Clarence, Richard has his chance to upset all and to renew dissension by proclaiming the fact of Clarence's death. Richard, always ahead of the game, casts new suspicion on the Queen and her brothers. Remorse at his belated memory of the many heroic, loving services Clarence once performed for him racks Edward and, as Richard hoped, speeds his death. With Edward's death in all its cruciality the choral, antiphonal effect, tended by the women, grows; soon it will achieve a swollen *Dies Irae*. Next, to enlarge the scene through the multitudinous world, Shakespeare lets us feel the reverberations of the death among the people, the common citizens of London; they anticipate the worst.

Now we move to the supposed crowning of the young Prince, come to London. For the sharpness of the royal young in this play—young York in fact, and he alone, proves a verbal match for Richard—it is most prudent of Richard to clear them out of the way. Having twisted the past and the present to his purpose, and having eliminated his superiors and his peers, Richard must also look after the threatening future. After the scene in the Tower, a perfect setting for what is to follow, where the nobles await the Lord Protector Richard and his decision on the coronation's date, the plots and crimes accumulate. Richard, appearing, claims that he has long been a sleeper and apologizes for being late. Then, in tune with his suddenness, he asks the Bishop of Ely to send for some of the strawberries that Richard saw in his garden when last in Holborn. Plucked though they are out of Holinshed, these strawberries, like Brutus' instrument and book in *Julius Caesar*, are persuasively, locally 'real' and, since entirely in character, most useful. While all wait for the strawberries, Richard whispers to Buckingham, now his second, and they withdraw. It is the moment needed for the dramatic shift Richard intends. Ely returning, even as Hastings assures the rest that all is well, Richard and Buckingham re-enter and without pause Richard plays a new part:

I pray you all, tell me what they deserve
That do conspire my death with devilish plots
Of damnéd witchcraft, and that have prevailed
Upon my body with their hellish charms?

Hastings, as Richard had no doubt hoped, dooms himself out of his own mouth. For earlier he had told Catesby, when the latter was sounding him out for Richard, 'I'll have this crown of mine cut from my shoulders/Ere I will see the crown so foul misplaced' (upon the head of Richard). Richard histrionically exhibits himself: 'Look how I am bewitched; behold, mine arm/Is like a blasted sapling, withered up.' Preoccupied as he has been with his appearance, it is ironically right that he should now make more of it. He is one always to exploit what exists. Also, it is time to move on, to clear away the last opposition. Thus he puts on this scene to blame Queen Elizabeth, 'that monstrous witch' who 'Consorted with that harlot strumpet Shore,/That by their witchcraft thus have markéd me.' To Hastings' reply 'If they have done this thing, my gracious lord—', Richard, cued by Holinshed, seizing on Hastings' 'if' as an imputation of doubt, thunders:

If! Thou protector of this damnéd strumpet,
Talk'st thou to me of 'ifs'? Thou art a traitor!
Off with his head! Now, by Saint Paul I swear,
I will not dine until I see the same.

Again we see how lives depend on a word. Those luscious strawberries must not be kept waiting. Thus with one little fantastic ruse of a scene three enemies have, like flies, been flicked away. Richard's bloodiness and treachery, complete, are blatantly in the open. Aside from the almost irresistible onrush of events here, the plot deserves such repetition since—so events continue to demonstrate—Richard is the plotter nonpariel. He is ingratiating indeed for his driving, unerring sense of direction, his superb ability to make something always gleefully choice for himself out of chance. So ubiquitous is this ability that at last chance itself seems helpless, one of Richard's many victims, or at least his raw material if not his happy accomplice.

Poor Hastings, who a moment ago had said blithely and absurdly of Richard:

I think there's never a man in Christendom
Can lesser hide his love or hate than he,
For by his face straight shall you know his heart.

too late recognizes his blindness and the folly of ignoring dreams and omens:

> *Woe, woe for England! Not a whit for me,*
> *For I, too fond, might have prevented this.*
> *Stanley did dream the boar did raze his helm;*
> *But I disdained it, and did scorn to fly.*
> *Three times today my foot-cloth horse did stumble,*
> *And startled, when he looked upon the Tower,*
> *As loath to bear me to the slaughter-house.*

In its way this play is almost as rich and meaningful in dreams as a play probably written not long after it, *A Midsummer Night's Dream.* At this time Shakespeare was, it seems fair to suggest, occupied with dreams and their meaning, and he was well aware of their usefulness in drama. But such awareness goes hand in hand with his unequalled capacity for the multifariousness of language also. No one has realized better than Shakespeare the free play of the mind, the sudden surfacing of instinctual, concealed knowledge, in dreams as in words, puns and the rest. No one has realized more thoroughly that humor, especially of the joke variety, shares a basic condition with dreams, and with language poetically conceived. Unlike dreams jokes employ words; but like dreams they employ words less for ideas, the conveying of thoughts, than for conjuring up sharp, sensuous imagery, for offering hidden or latent meanings in and through the announced content. Richard, that practical joker par excellence, scoffs at dreams beyond his own very real one of the crown, a resolute dream that never lets him sleep; similarly he dismisses the world of the spirit, not to say heaven; he does so, that is, till the end when it breaks in on him also in the gripping form of dream.

But what is perhaps most striking here is the very different use Shakespeare put dreams to in comedy and tragedy. Obviously part and parcel of the worlds dreams derive from, they in turn mirror and image those worlds. In comedy dreams, though they may at first confuse, often provide no less than the mainspring of the plot and tend finally to be cleansing, expiatory; they partake of the very nature of comic art, for comedy is often a dream, a dream-recess away from harsh, oppressive, daily reality. How much the whole matter of appearance versus reality involves dreams we need not say, or how much reality is mainly served by appearance. In tragedy, on the other hand, dreams, especially when they occur to sinful people, tend to be ominous if not deadly. Of course we must remember that the setting of a play like *A Midsummer Night's Dream* is moonlit summer, a time of lightsome omen and giddy dreams; that of *Richard III*, essentially a dissension-torn world, darkest winter, at least in its prevailing mood. When this mood begins to break near the end, when in short the tragic begins to give way, the good Richmond will have reassuring, strengthening dreams.

Ready for another major performance, surely a basically comic one whatever its tragic consequences, Richard and Buckingham now appear on the Tower-walls in rusty armor, and Richard instructs Buckingham in play-acting.

> *Come, cousin, canst thou quake, and change thy colour,*
> *Murder thy breath in middle of a word,*
> *And then begin again, and stop again,*
> *As if thou wert distraught and mad with terror?*

Buckingham is most confident: 'Tut, I can counterfeit the deep tragedian. . . .' And both soon prove their thespianism by convincing the Mayor at least. As in comedy worlds are often made to seem other than they are to confuse their characters—see Christopher Sly and Kate—so Richard changes his world at will. For a perverted, mad dream he ruthlessly juggles reality. Thus to rid himself of Edward's children, Richard orders Buckingham to declare them bastards:

> *Moreover, urge his hateful luxury*
> *And bestial appetite in change of lust,*
> *Which stretched unto their servants, daughters, wives,*
> *Even where his raging eye or savage heart,*
> *Without control, listed to make his prey.*

In the past Richard had not, quite apart from his envy and resentment, stressed Edward's lustiness for nothing. For that matter not even Richard's mother is spared the violence and shame of his efforts to throw doubt on the legitimacy of Edward himself. This little invention is but an extra twist of the knife, the all but gratuitous flourish of the master artist who puts nothing above his art. The citizenry, in its good common sense, is unimpressed by this charge or by Buckingham's attempts to make Richard king. The mere thought of it and of him is enough, like a basilisk, to turn them into 'dumb statues or breathing stones,' while they 'Stared each on other, and looked deadly pale'.

Therefore Buckingham, inspired no doubt by Richard's art and by his earlier words:

> *If you thrive well, bring them to Baynard's Castle,*
> *Where you shall find me well accompanied*
> *With reverend fathers and well-learnéd bishops.*

proposes a mighty stratagem:

> *The Mayor is here at hand. Intend some fear.*
> *Be not you spoke with but by mighty suit.*
> *And look you get a prayer-book in your hand,*
> *And stand betwixt two churchmen, good my lord,*
> *For on that ground I'll build a holy descant.*
> *And be not easily won to our requests.*
> *Play the maid's part—still answer nay, and take it.*

A coy maiden's part would truly be the last, best part for Richard to play! But it is a role he need hardly be urged to. Here literally he will, as he had said,

> *. . . clothe my naked villainy*
> *With odd old ends stolen out of Holy Writ,*
> *And seem a saint when most I play the devil.*

Thus he undertakes his most profane role, following the stage direction, 'aloft, between two Bishops'. And he acts the shrinking maid indeed, insisting on his great 'poverty of spirit' and many mighty 'defects'. But Buckingham hammers away at Edward's illegitimacy; Richard must willynilly continue the rightful line. With tremendous reluctance he allows himself to be 'enforced' 'against my conscience and my soul'. Cleverly he banks this occasion for future expenditures:

> *But if black scandal or foul-faced reproach*
> *Attend the sequel of your imposition,*
> *Your mere enforcement shall acquittance me*
> *From all the impure blots and stains thereof;*
> *For God doth know, and you may partly see,*
> *How far I am from the desire of this.*

The royalty learning of Richard's enthronement, Anne recognizes how, queen now, having been pitifully, grossly weak, she has cursed herself. Furthermore, she informs us, in preparation, that, contrary to his claim, Richard is little the sleeper:

For never yet one hour in his bed
Did I enjoy the golden dew of sleep,
But with his timorous dreams was still awaked.

Apparently he is not so impervious to his crimes after all, not so free
of fears and dreams, as he would have us, and himself for that matter,
believe. The laments pile up. So do the crimes. At length even Buckingham falters before Richard's heinousness, and his request:

> *Shall I be plain? I wish the bastards dead,*
> *And I would have it suddenly performed.*
> *What sayest thou? Speak suddenly, be brief.*

'Suddenly', the word closest to his nature, it all must be. Buckingham,
hesitating, loses Richard, who in his abandon now asks his page for a
murderer. Putting it out that Anne is 'sick and like to die', Richard
decides:

> *I must be married to my brother's daughter,*
> *Or else my kingdom stands on brittle glass.*

For a moment even he scents the monstrousness of what he is engaged
in:

> *Murder her brothers, and then marry her!*
> *Uncertain way of gain!*

But in words that pave the way for Macbeth's bettering of the thought,
he concludes:

> *But I am in*
> *So far in blood that sin will pluck on sin.*
> *Tear-falling pity dwells not in this eye.*

At least for the first time he acknowledges that, though he cannot weep
pitying tears, he is caught up in a terrible course of evil; his choice of
the word 'sin', without any ironic or sneering overtones, admits an
awareness of the profound culpability of his acts that we have hardly
encountered in him before. May this not be considered the first sign of
some wavering in his till now intact villainy?

Having hacked his way to the throne, Richard gradually undergoes
a fundamental change. Certainly he is no longer 'free'; no longer can
he know the zest of a major goal, of a major, seemingly impossible
challenge which till now took him upward and upward. For at this
point he has something to fear losing. Thus with only a holding,
conservative course open to him, his detachment is over and he is

precariously one with his role, truly 'impaled' with the crown. Ironically enough, as he succeeds he becomes mortal, if not human. Having clambered to the heights over a mound of corpses, what future can be left to him but falling? For now the whole world is on the outside, as he formerly was, threatening him. Little wonder he grows more and more turmoiled, gives way more and more to fitful, confused action. He who had been all actor must become mere reactor. At the same time through his fear, something he had never known before, and through his deepening suspiciousness he succumbs to blind and desperate acts, 'sudden' in a fashion the opposite of his previous deliberate if 'sudden' course.

But as he says, it is much too late to reconsider now. And while he dismisses Buckingham, the murder of the children is done and reported with for us great, not to say excessive and unlikely, 'piteousness' by the leader of the murderers. Perhaps, for the promise of those children, this excessive report is offered in tribute to them. In any case the Elizabethans would hardly think this a moment for simple realism. Richard, about to rush off to young Elizabeth as 'a jolly thriving wooer', to beat Richmond to her, learns that the enemy is gathering against him. His old impatience asserts itself:

> *Come, I have learned that fearful commenting*
> *Is leaden servitor to dull delay.*
> *Delay leads impotent and snail-paced beggary;*
> *Then fiery expedition be my wing,*
> *Jove's Mercury, and herald for a king!*

Shakespeare is learning from—and through—this master actor that commenting is indeed leaden to drama, learning what sudden devices one must use to be effective. Leaden, that is, till Hamlet! And even he in twist and turn of speech, and in action to avoid action, will have learned much from Richard.

Then, as though to counterweigh this 'fiery expedition', the great lyric lamenting of the play breaks forth. In addition to Richard's speed, Shakespeare has discovered the splendid drama of massing the old, static style against the new. Already strikingly, against the women's heavy, stylized, anonymous speech, Richard's has been lithe, individual, crackling with his mercurial personality. He in his dispatch, all nimblest energy and free enterprise of the imagination become the deed, is, compared with the slowness, the stiffness of the rest, something of the new Renaissance megalomaniac opposed to the old, medieval order. However, we recognized earlier, the forces in him that he feels free to use—more accurately that use him—are more medieval and pre-medieval than not. Like a sentient ram he batters away at this massive, wailing wall. But this bulwark of breath, 'fearful commenting' though it may be, provides one of the few stops to his wing of fiery expedition; and it will prevail against him. Again, if his words are substantial and capable, so are theirs. Since he is all destruction these women, his hated 'nature's' prime agents by being the source of life, a life he has usually wiped out, are inevitably among his chief enemies. All their children have stood in his way. Thus their many woes focus on the womb, especially for the tomb it has become through Richard.

The women have gathered, like one mighty choral voice, to cry woe over their beloved dead. Margaret's most queenly time is now. With a magnificent 'ubi sunt' she unburdens herself. Fulfilling her prediction, the women beg her to instruct them in her perfected art, 'well-skilled in curses'. Queen Elizabeth, finally a queen and mistress of her role, to the Duchess of York's 'Why should calamity be full of words?' explains:

> *Windy attorneys to their client woes,*
> *Airy succeeders of intestate joys,*
> *Poor breathing orators of miseries,*
> *Let them have scope! Though what they will impart*
> *Help nothing else, yet do they ease the heart.*

The Duchess, responding to Elizabeth's observation, yet hoping for more, for furious words to be deeds indeed, urges:

> *If so, then be not tongue-tied. Go with me,*
> *And in the breath of bitter words let's smother*
> *My damnéd son, that thy two sweet sons smothered.*
> *The trumpet sounds; be copious in exclaims.*

This is their call to arms. Hearing them, Richard commands:

> *A flourish, trumpets! Strike alarum, drums!*
> *Let not the Heavens hear these telltale women*
> *Rail on the Lord's anointed. Strike, I say!*

He clearly fears their words and their effect on heaven. But the women curse him still, and with terrible burdens for the battle-to-be; his mother in her words to him, a last fine maternal blessing, says:

> *Therefore take with thee my most heavy curse,*
> *Which in the day of battle tire thee more*
> *Than all the complete armour that thou wear'st!*
> *My prayers on the adverse party fight,*
> *And there the little souls of Edward's children*
> *Whisper the spirits of thine enemies*
> *And promise them success and victory.*

Again we hear how weighty and real words are for these people. As are spirits and the souls of the dead. (The notion of the efficacy of children's souls, of innocence, will, we know, not be dramatized by Shakespeare until a good deal later.) The Duchess has accurately set the stage and predicted the action on it.

Yet when she leaves, Richard, in no way daunted it would seem, dares to turn to Queen Elizabeth with a request. To her retort 'I have no more sons of the royal blood/For thee to slaughter', he replies, 'You have a daughter called Elizabeth,/Virtuous and fair, royal and gracious.' She movingly responds:

> *And must she die for this? O, let her live,*
> *And I'll corrupt her manners, stain her beauty,*
> *Slander myself as false to Edward's bed,*
> *Throw over her the veil of infamy.*

But Richard, after much worse than slaughter, begs her, in a style reminiscent of his now long-ago wooing of Anne, for this daughter in marriage. An exchange follows, fulsome to us if not to the Elizabethans. But then, aside from the time's enthusiasm for such rhetoric, Shakespeare often pulls out all the stops in this play, taxing words, clanging one against another, as though he were exploring language and human lungs to their limits. When Elizabethan says, 'Yet thou didst kill my children', Richard attains what may be his greatest effrontery; in a cold rapture of temerity he offers her compensation in the shape of a marvelous paradox, one inevitably concentrated on sex and knotting together death, generation, and resurrection:

> *But in your daughter's womb I bury them,*
> *Where in that nest of spicery they will breed*
> *Selves of themselves, to your recomforture.*

Inspired by the women, as his deeds of destruction have inspired them, he applies their womb-tomb image, if fantastically, in reverse: the womb does indeed become a tomb, but in so becoming it becomes a womb again. When Elizabeth leaves he thinks—this time, we soon learn, mistakenly—that he has won her too. Now, late as it is and habituated as he is to his successes and to human weakness, his contempt is no longer marked by amazement or delight: 'Relenting fool, and shallow changing woman!' It would seem that his contempt is underscored by resentment, bitterness. Is there no one with honorable feelings? Then shifting reports of the enemy flood in; and Richard, strident in a way that he has never been before, is at his most fitful and, strangely for him, of frequently 'changing' mind.

The last act opens, fatal time that it is, on All Souls' Day, a time when the dead draw near; and well they might with the battle about to pour forth blood. Their approach may already be affecting Richard. He says:

> Give me a bowl of wine.
> I have not that alacrity of spirit,
> Nor cheer of mind, that I was wont to have.

While he sleeps, we turn to Richmond in his tent. Praying, he commends himself to God. In tune with All Souls' Day, and with all that Richard has done, ghosts appear via conscience to curse, and so burden, Richard and to comfort, and so inspirit, Richmond. Rightly, for such a moment, the scene is highly stylized and not at all realistic; the ghosts that Richard has made, in ritualistic fashion much like that of the women, their mothers and wives whom they here continue, turn from one tent to the other directly beside it. When they vanish Richard starts up, his first words prophetic with 'Give me another horse! Bind up my wounds!' For the moment shaken to the core, and well he might be by the ghosts' endless refrain of 'Despair, and die!', he utters words of a sort we have never heard from him before:

> Have mercy, Jesu! —Soft! I did but dream.
> O coward conscience, how dost thou afflict me!
> The light burns blue. It is now dead midnight.
> Cold fearful drops stand on my trembling flesh.

But perhaps we are to understand that the 'timorous dreams' Anne spoke of were not so far from this. We might, for all we have been through with Richard, be startled to hear him now appeal to Christ. Yet, we recall, at the beginning he did not deny the other world, only— so he thought—its pertinence to him. His conscience, apparently, for all that he has thought and done, is still not completely quenched. His view of it, however, in calling it 'coward' does resemble his customary attitude, just as it does his first murderer's sentiments.

These, Richard's first large waverings, his terrible energy finally exhausting itself, turning on itself, are wonderful to behold. First he tries to reassure himself. Dreams and their ghosts notwithstanding, there's no one here beyond himself (of course, he will soon have to recognize, his early wish to be alone has been fulfilled: beyond himself there's no one for him anywhere); so 'What do I fear? Myself?' Surely no less than ever 'Richard loves Richard'. Yet in the honesty he has always had with himself, he cannot deny that a murderer is here and that the murderer is he who might revenge himself upon himself. But why fear and hate himself? Because, he sees, he has committed such 'hateful deeds'. The struggle grows:

> *I am a villain—yet I lie, I am not.*
> *Fool, of thyself speak well. Fool, do not flatter.*
> *My conscience hath a thousand several tongues,*
> *And every tongue brings in a several tale,*
> *And every tale condemns me for a villain.*

Much though he might yearn to, he cannot lie to himself. His conscience, so long ignored and repressed, bursts forth in him in riptide. Briefly at least his argument is, in Yeats' term, genuine because with himself rather than with others; he has, if much too late, found— better, been found out by—his inner being. On this All Souls' Day he is at last rent open. Not nearly so impervious as he thought, words can indeed pierce and melt him. All his crimes, risen up against him, cry 'Guilty! guilty!' and he gives way to pathetic despair:

> *There is no creature loves me,*
> *And if I die, no soul shall pity me.*
> *Nay, wherefore should they, since that I myself*
> *Find in myself no pity to myself?*

It is his honesty again, plus his superb writhing here like a trapped animal, trapped within itself, that saves this speech from being fairly incredible and bathetic.

At the same time we see, in his returning to it with obsessive, hypnotic frequency, how much he is forever locked in his insulated, hardened 'self'; batter against it with all his might, he can never break through. His opening speech already made clear that Richard is one of the loneliest men to have lived, at least in literature. If at first his solitude pleased him as he chose it, pleased his mighty pride in its sense of superiority, now he is truly alone in the icy circle of his isolation, one of the supreme traitors of mankind. In the comedies, *Love's Labour's Lost*, for example, we have already met characters sealed off from others and the world by their egotism. But theirs, in that it was not harmful to others, was at least an amusing egotism. In such cases one has the feeling of superb, ultra-alive portraits, galleries of individuals framed by an impressive light emanating from their own persons, but a light primarily to illuminate them on their eccentric courses like glow-worms. Richard's is a light also, a fascinatingly hell-phosphorescent one that, cold though it be like the Tower to which it belongs, draws others to it like moths, to be instantly seared. Let us say that Richard, like Lucifer, is charismatic in the way that the destructive is, especially it would seem for modern man. Bakunin could maintain, 'The passion for destruction is a creative passion. . . .' Richard's flame lights up most plainly the clammy darkness of his intent and his hellish deeds. And finally that flame, fed on so many, bends back upon itself. In a fundamental sense Bakunin's maxim applies: whatever its trail of havoc, Richard's flame by its burning, that will eventually burn itself out, is lustrating England.

So Richard has dreamed 'a fearful dream' to balance the dreams of Clarence, Stanley, and the rest. He tells Ratcliffe, 'I fear, I fear—.' And to Ratcliff's 'Nay, good my lord, be not afraid of shadows,' he confesses at last the super-reality and the impressiveness, even to him, of the so-called other world:

> *By the Apostle Paul, shadows tonight*
> *Have struck more terror to the soul of Richard*
> *Than can the substance of ten thousand soldiers*
> *Arméd in proof, and led by shallow Richmond.*

The shadows that he, hating the sun, desired at the outset are now upon him thicker than night. It is conclusively not, as some might argue, his concern over the ensuing conflict and its outcome that is principally troubling him. But he is still himself, and because of that more ignominious than ever:

> *Come, go with me.*
> *Under our tents I'll play the eavesdropper,*
> *To hear if any mean to shrink from me.*

Thus while Richard skulks off at his lowliest, Richmond rises from sweetest sleep and dreams, full of confidence. With Richard's characteristic 'Come, bustle, bustle', the battle draws near. His final words to his troops:

> *Let not our babbling dreams affright our souls.*
> *Conscience is but a word that cowards use,*
> *Devised at first to keep the strong in awe.*
> *Our strong arms be our conscience, swords our law.*
> *March on, join bravely, let us to't pell-mell—*
> *If not to Heaven, then hand in hand to Hell.*

defiant though they are, would obviously encourage himself no less than his followers. His oration to his army, based on spitting contempt, is curt and fierce. He concludes: 'Spur your proud horses hard, and ride in blood./Amaze the welkin with your broken staves!' Once more in the extremity of action out of defiance and desperation, he is himself: against the 'a thousand several tongues' of conscience now 'A thousand hearts are great within my bosom.' And he urges 'Our ancient word of courage, fair Saint George,/Inspire us with the spleen of fiery dragons!' So much so that promptly in the next scene of battle we learn:

> *The King enacts more wonders than a man,*
> *Daring an opposite to every danger.*
> *His horse is slain, and all on foot he fights,*
> *Seeking for Richmond in the throat of death.*
> *Rescue, fair lord, or else the day is lost!*

Richard's dream has come true. We see him for the last time, shouting with more irony than he knows, for he has indeed forever—here literally as at the end it should be—lost that most potent part of himself: 'A horse! My kingdom for a horse!' He is killed by Richmond who, crowned, at once moves to peace. Civil war—'England hath long been mad, and scarred herself'—is finally over. The 'smooth-faced peace' that seemed imminent at the play's beginning, and that Richard thwarted, is at last established. But the nightmare of Richard has been a long, awesomely consistent one. And if the crimes and terrors of this time, like those of the long time before it, had to compress themselves into this single monstrous figure to be dealt with, the cost has been a nearly overwhelming one.

Now at the end, for the deep feeling that Richard has evoked in us so that we have been almost willing to connive with him, something in him persists in being fundamentally elusive. His boldness, his blunt self-publicity apart, one gropes for terms cogent enough to manage him at all. And the notion of the Dionysian, relative to tragedy, comes to mind. It would account in some large part for this play's having no subplots, for its needing to be simple because Richard in his very passionate singleness is many and all plots happening at once; even more certainly for its finding no room for clowns or fools—imagine another beside Richard's all-impatient sardonics!—because he is his own mighty jester prevailing in this bloody graveyard of a world. One might suggest that this play is a fascinating fusion of the old and the new: the Dionysian, finding its latest home, reasserts itself afresh in the imperious Renaissance will. Certainly the Dionysian is present, not to say celebrated, in Richard. A gleeful life-force, self-intoxicated and bent on expressing itself, in its flagrancy it soon breaks through the customary forms and conventions of society or morality; flouting them, it exposes their inadequacy and hypocrisy. In this sense the force is attractive, even refreshing. And so it is for its immense vitality. Having given life to Richard, Shakespeare would seem to have been breath-lessly paced—given rich, surprising life in turn—by Richard. We are, in Webster's words, our deeds' creatures. Our creations create us. In addition to Richard's speech-force—its urgency recommending the dramatic need of action, speed, and rapid change—Richard enabled Shakespeare, an actor also, to explore the skills of the consummate actor. All bustle that Richard is, he is the play's one altogether con-vincing breather among a cast chiefly shadows; chalk figures, he changes them to suit his purpose; then, to suit his purpose, he rubs them out. It is true that there is a superabundance of breath in the women that will help to blow him down; but aside from the mighty Margaret that breath by its massed nature is, we saw, as it should be, virtually anonymous. For it is a whole nation and a whole world that Richard has been violating. So tremendous are the needs of his thwarted personality.

But already, as early as in this play, early for England if not for the Continent, Shakespeare is revealing not only the appeal but the repulsiveness potential in the Renaissance will: its stupendous glamor and, no less, its often hideous consequent destructiveness. If Richard is something like the Renaissance will incarnate, he is equally, in his total, eager submission to it, evil incarnate. Whatever his lusty attrac-tiveness, we cannot deny that he treats all men, even himself finally, as mere objects. Thus his efficiency. Too late he discovers, to his amazement and confusion, that he too has feelings, is subjective and subjected, is more than will and conscious self-control. Herein lies his repulsiveness. His is a Dionysianism so passionately self-serving, so deliberate if not cold-blooded, that, corrosive rather than life-giving like the Dionysian at its best, it turns all not only to destruction but to cheapness, ignominy, pointlessness.

At the same time we must realize that in his very triumph of excess Richard is serving, unknown to himself, an end much greater than his own; in his own person and by what he does he is making it possible for the long-cankered terror of England to end. Thus *Richard III* is indeed a kind of satyr play, completing the havoc-ridden *Henry VI* trilogy, no less than the havoc first begun long ago with the killing of Richard II. Like a Dionysian satyr, rending all in his riotous path, Richard in the end—nothing else would seem to be able to satisfy his nature—must be torn to pieces, sacrificed in the way he has sacrificed others, that peace and fertility may return. But, this end notwithstanding, we cannot help remarking, sadly enough, that many of the resources usually identified with the Apollonian—not the least of these being Richard's intelligence, his rationality, his understanding of others—instantly obey his Dionysian summons; we have seen how shrewdly, calculatingly Richard uses every occasion, person, word. Therefore, we cannot be blamed, I think, for finding resemblances between Richard's nature and the terrors of our time, the manner in which the demonic has often seized on the rational for its own monstrous forwarding. We are hardly done with Richard yet.

The Breath of Kings

Richard II

IN *Richard III* Shakespeare saw how far a man committed to action can go. In his next historical tragedy he undertook Richard III's opposite, a man given over almost exclusively to words. *Richard II,* since it is Richard II's play, focuses foursquarely on language itself and also on its immense bearing on action and the world at large. I have tried to show that language in itself not less than in its impact occupies a major role in *Richard III.* But Richard III, tremendous though his delight in language may be, is primarily concerned with it as it helps to midwife actions bent on his attaining the crown. Richard II, with the crown already his, needs no actions; on the contrary. Thus one might suggest that in this early phase of his development Shakespeare explored first the resources and the consequences of action and then the resources and the consequences of language, language so self-engrossed that for a time at least it swaddled itself and the world. Such would seem to have been his course in comedy if we accept *The Comedy of Errors* and *Love's Labour's Lost* as his first work in that genre; and such, though on a much larger scale since a whole nation was affected, in the histories.

At this time the chronicle or history plays were so popular that Shakespeare had already been involved in four of them. Of the group the last, *Richard III,* had given that mode a new definition. Now Shakespeare moved back in time to the beginning of this giant cycle for the story crucial to it all of Richard II. Almost ten years may have elapsed during the writing of this cycle's eight plays. Shakespeare and his art obviously changed a great deal in that time. Still it is tempting to propose, in a whole view of them, that these plays, the tetralogy consisting of *Henry VI* in three parts and ending with *Richard III,* together with the tetralogy that *Richard II* begins and that *Henry V* concludes, constitute what we might call an English epic. And so regarded, it is the greatest epical work having to do with English history.

In *Richard II* Shakespeare struck to the core of his society. Richard II was the last of the Plantagenets, and of all the kings Shakespeare dealt with in this sequence the only wholly legitimate one. Yet for all his legitimacy his play shows him no less alien to his country than Richard III. Again, as with Richard III and happily for tragedy, the alienation is in the main character; outside events apart, the king who should establish and preserve order is the source of turmoil, if not a kind of King of Misrule. And more centrally and disturbingly than Richard III. For Richard II is beyond question entitled to the office of king; nor is his estrangement in any way traceable to his physical being, deformity that provokes, or at least is used by Richard III to excuse, his destructiveness. On the contrary, it is Richard's beauty and his easy assurance of his right to his role, plus that role itself and his mistaken interpretation of it, that help to encourage the weakness in his character and will.

The resemblances and differences between these two Richards are fascinating. Both sublime egoists, they never question their supremacy, their superiority over all others. Ingratiating themselves with others only to use them, they are essentially alone, encapsulated in their self-interest, their self-love. Richard II does have flatterers and sycophants and even a loving wife; but these matter to him only while they cater to his whims and reflect his own notion of himself. Also, both are constant actors. Here, however, the differences begin. Performance is a prime pleasure for Richard III: the acting upon others, the manipulation of them to his own will; but it is, pleasure and all, a means with the end never lost sight of. He is, therefore, something like a double man in action: being most himself when performing his opposite. For Richard II, however, who assumes the crown forever his, love of performance is such that it utterly beguiles and possesses him. He plays himself, himself the King, singly, openly, capriciously for all he is worth. Richard III, playing a part and many parts, is fully aware of his playing; Richard II, also playing a part but believing in it, does not till too late realize it is that. Richard III is attractive for his openness, his rare daring to see himself as he is, and also for the decisiveness of spirit attendant on that seeing; and for the wit, the wantonness, even the gay touch, if not abandon, of a Mercutio. Richard II, on the other hand, utterly taken in by his own act and art, knows himself not at all. Such a fundamental dissimilarity makes all the difference in their respective employments of language and in their expectations of it. Richard III promptly turns his words into deeds, whereas Richard II, for the God's breath in him, assumes that his words are deeds and better than deeds. One talks to act; the other acts, if he acts at all, to talk. Richard II's words, substitutes for deeds, would snare them into tapestried poems. He believes he must, king that he is, in himself the consummation of the race, be a preserver, one to keep things as they are, to balk action or emerging 'history' with all-entangling ceremony. Understandably, whereas Richard III finds his being in doing, Richard II wants to be, not do.

Already in *Love's Labour's Lost* we had a bored king and his courtiers, if of a minor kingdom, assume that they could dismiss daily life with its customary demands. Who else beyond a king (unless it be a modern billionaire) has the power and the means to establish such an artificial, 'free' world. For most of the play something of the purpose of the King of Navarre is carried on. He and his with their entertainers, idling, bask in their own verbose speeches and strutting gestures, peacocks of the kind Richard III despises. Only at the end, past the buffetings the ladies put them to in a sort of elegant Punch and Judy show, are the lords obliged to expose their natures and their gifts to the rigors of reality. In *A Midsummer Night's Dream* the magic and the freedom that magic encourages, not to say the glittering dream, also initiated by a lord, are even more complete. The moon, the season, and youth see to it. But then this 'dream' is a brief interlude before marriage and the resumption of the chores and cares of the daily world. In *The Merchant of Venice* the freedom and the magic sponsoring it, the freedom then adorning the magic, also derive from the means and the dispositions of the play's more lordly ones. But the light of common day—here really a darkest night in that it threatens to eclipse their amiable moonlight—via Shylock sets out to show them that they are not nearly so superior or free as they think.

Now in Richard II we have a principal figure who is almost eloquence itself, and who loves, more than anyone else (who, unless it be an Armado, is as smitten with or as convinced by his speech as Richard?), to linger in its ripplings; and surely more than others he has the means to indulge that eloquence's uninterrupted flow. What other point is there in being King? In fact he seems to think he should do little beyond declaiming. From his tenth year on he has been King, in an age which officially believes in the divine right of kings, in kings as 'God's substitute' on earth. No one believes this more categorically and as the first article of his faith than Richard. It is one thing, and a comic thing at that, to transform a Christopher Sly from a tinker to a waking lord, with some difficulty however for his sturdy common sense; quite another to have a lord virtually born to the kingship. Having filled the role as long as he can remember, Richard has confused himself with it altogether; not only is he a king, he is King. Accordingly, he is confident–if he thinks of it at all–that he can do no wrong; however arbitrary the act may seem to others, the fact of his doing it makes it automatically right. He self-obligingly forgets that, though kings have rights, they also have responsibilities. He forgets too, that God long ago ceased to be arbitrary; Christ, the figure Richard will compare himself with, come down to earth as a man, had to suffer the trials of a man, thereby suffering with and for all men. Rather, Richard takes it for granted that, being King, he has in his sacredness thrown off the limitations of men, and that they must suffer and sacrifice for him.

For a while his assumption works. For just as the divine right of kings still obtained in his day (by Shakespeare's time it was being subjected to sharp scrutiny and challenge), so the people of that day, the Middle Ages, believed and delighted in ceremony, pomp, ritual, and in the extent to which through them a man participated in a world other and larger than his own. For Shakespeare's age, like the ages before it, festivity and holiday were a principal source of pleasure and freedom; ceremony and ritual, sponsoring solemnity or festivity, guaranteed the individual a respite from his daily life, even as it exalted him into a realm of the spiritual or what we today, since church and state have shrunk so much for most of us, might call the poetical. Richard by his office assumed that he could live in, indeed must perform, such ceremony all the time. Some good measure of his attractiveness in his play resides in the intensity and skill he lavishes on the great 'art-forms' of ritual, in the power of his faith in his execution of that ceremonialist's role.

Unfortunately he is so certain of his perfection, and of the sufficiency of ceremony as reality, that it never occurs to him that he might occasionally need to curb his will or to recognize a world beyond. For some twenty years he has been able to sustain such a view. But by the very capriciousness that view has fostered he has been chiefly responsible for the difficulties brewing, the collecting of forces that will, breaking through ceremony, which is little more after all than an agreement among men, destroy its inviolability and so him. His imagination, in short, roomy and volatile though it is, is opaque, an end in itself when it is not busy justifying itself to itself or glossing over unsavory truths. This imagination pleases him in being expressive and not, alas, since unrooted in reality, perceptive of things as they are; thus he is by his very powers cut off from the world, unavailable to it for its warnings, its essential nourishment and support.

Yet, late as it is, and little though most of us acquiesce to ceremony, in his superb performance, what one might call his consummate uselessness, Richard is extremely winsome; he touches many of us with a certain strong wistfulness. Most men have surely yearned to live in a single world or, better, one compact entirely of their dreams against the coldness of the outside world and the maraudings of time. In *The Merchant of Venice* Lorenzo urges that fundamental, everlasting music, the music of the spheres which the body in its limitations and self-preoccupations shuts us off from. Richard thinks himself wholly attuned to that music; in fact he is its chief musician, ordained to shower it through his golden tongue on his less fortunate, muddy subjects. He resents anything that might interrupt the course of that music. And lovely as his voice is, if we allowed it to drown all else, we might be tempted to agree.

Yeats in his essay 'At Stratford-on-Avon', dated May 1901, writing of Richard II and other Shakespearean characters, insists that their deeds 'had no obvious use, were, indeed, no more than the expression of their personalities', and that 'a man's business may at times be revelation, and not reformation'.

> *Fortinbras was, it is likely enough, a better king than Hamlet would have been, Aufidius was a more reasonable man than Coriolanus, Henry V was a better man-at-arms than Richard II, but, after all, were not those others who changed nothing for the better and many things for the worse greater in the Divine Hierarchies?*

Few, I suspect, would quarrel with Yeats' preference of Hamlet to Fortinbras. But I do feel that he gives Henry V, certainly Hal, too short shrift. Interestingly enough, almost thirty years later T. S. Eliot, in his introduction to G. Wilson Knight's *The Wheel of Fire*, seemed to see eye to eye with Yeats on Shakespeare as concerned with 'revelation, and not reformation'. In Eliot's words:

> *It is a little irony that when a poet, like Dante, sets out with a definite philosophy and a sincere determination to guide conduct, his philosophical and ethical pattern is discounted, and our interpreters insist upon the pure poetry which is to be dissociated from this*

reprehensible effort to do us good. And that when a poet like Shake-
speare, who has no 'philosophy' and apparently no design upon the
amelioration of our behaviour, sets forth his experience and reading
of life, he is forthwith saddled with a 'philosophy' of his own and
some esoteric hints toward conduct. So we kick against those who
wish to guide us, and insist on being guided by those who only aim to
show us a vision, a dream if you like, which is beyond good and evil
in the common sense.

But then Eliot goes on to admit:

. . . the very Catholic philosophy of Dante, with its stern judgement
of morals, leads us to the same point beyond good and evil as the
pattern of Shakespeare. Morality, we need to be told again and again,
is not itself to be judged by moral standards: its laws are as 'natural'
as any discovered by Einstein or Planck. . . .

Apparently revelation and reformation are not so far apart after all.

But most of us, according to Yeats, have sunk to the status of 'a
vulgar worshipper of success', have forgotten that 'England, as Gordon
has said, was made by her adventurers, by her people of wildness and
imagination and eccentricity. . . .' In recoil, and erring, I should say,
on the other side – I shall not try to add up the number of us now who
are fairly vulgar worshippers of failure – Yeats concludes:

I cannot believe that Shakespeare looked on his Richard II with any
but sympathetic eyes, understanding indeed how ill-fitted he was to
be a king, at a certain moment of history, but understanding that he
was lovable and full of capricious fancy, 'a wild creature' as Pater
has called him.

The 'capricious fancy' we can readily assent to, and some part of
Richard's lovableness also. But I am not sure that I recognize the
'wild creature' in him. On the contrary, might one not say that he is,
as he is spoiled, a thoroughly cultivated, sophisticated, wilful man?
Rather than 'wild', Richard seems magnificently hot-houseish to me,
a rose indeed, but a rose the result of most careful breeding. Only very
late on will he find some of the wildness and imagination of the
adventurer in him. Yeats admits that he was ill-fitted to be king, but
suggests that he might have been better fitted at some other moment
of history. As if any moment of history is utopian enough to be able
to support a 'useless' king – unless, that is, it be a time that requires a

king to be but little more than decoration. But how many all-shielded lulls of this sort are we likely to find in history?

Obviously Shakespeare could and did enjoy, in the way of great art, both awarenesses. With one considerable part of him, it seems clear, the profoundly reasonable part (but one must not minimize the gusto and enthusiasm in it also), he respected plainness and its able, practical, daylit men; yet moonlight with its dewy, flickering ambiguities, its imaginative potentiality, persisted in attracting him also. But the least we expect of a genius like Shakespeare is that he not take sides or, if he take, take all. In the laboratory-perfect, special circumstances of his art he could enable one side and/or the other to realize itself completely. Richard III, it is not far from the truth to say, in his villainy is the ideal, the consummation, of villainy; Richard II, the very flower of his kind of kinghood. Nonetheless, is there not in life as in letters an ideal possible superior to such one-sided realizations, that of a man capable of combining or unifying in himself both daylight and moonshine, order and wildness, practicality and imagination? Are these two realms irreconcilably divorced? Yeats himself, developing from an interesting minor versifier in his early years to the mature major poet, increasingly appreciated such an ideal. For all his early insistence on dreams and words alone as 'certain good', capable, exultant men attracted him more and more.

Unfortunately for Richard and England, and for any art-for-art's sake position, in his office Richard has forgotten not only that under his splendid robes and words exists a mortal body, but that the world at large is urgently mortal and bedeviled by outrageous noises to the point of confounding the heavenly music altogether. Furthermore, he refuses to recognize how much his own deeds, supposedly attuned to that divine harmony, should be a spreading of it beyond words and ceremonies. Were he a rose and only a rose, set upon by the greedy weeds of the commonwealth, we might indeed sigh for him, his out-of-joint time, and for ourselves gone over to the enemy. But though he may be a rose, he is an overblown one, with thorns often more evident than anything else. Too plainly, under the self-deceiving guise of beauty and royalty, his own deeds partake of violence and outrageousness, and are primarily responsible for their dissemination. Not only, living rapaciously, ruthlessly, on others, does he fail to exercise that heavenly harmony, fail to be the careful gardener his office expects, but he fails to see the predatory weed in himself.

Is it therefore quite enough to say with Yeats of Shakespeare that

He saw that such a man through sheer bewilderment and impatience
can become unjust or as violent as any common man, any Bolingbroke
or Prince John, and yet remain 'that sweet lovely rose.'

We recognize some of the force of this statement. For we recognize the force of Richard's charm. Yet isn't Yeats ignoring not only Richard's selfishness and cruelty but his many moments of callous worldliness, that make him little better—and he God's deputy on earth—than the poorest 'common man'? These moments, rather than 'sheer bewilderment and impatience', prove him unjust and violent. Smitten with himself, he does not know that, without means and stripped of his signs of office, he is a naked man like any other. This the play sets out to teach him by breaking through the fold on fold of his notion of kinghood, and the self-engrossment, the selfish music, that clogs his ears. And what a mighty, almost hopeless, play-long effort it will require. Nevertheless both aspects of his character, the lovely and the ruthless, rose and weed entwined, must be preserved, and in the impressive unity of his person. As the early Yeats himself attests, at least for a time the performing of one's nature can suffice. In his words one must choose between the life and the art. Richard seemed for a protracted period able to make them one, able to live his art. But, his play will show, at tremendous cost to all concerned. And, finally, I think, we can attribute much of the cost to the inadequacy of his art.

Accordingly, the uses and abuses of language with which Shakespeare had been occupied from the start reached a climax in this play. Here—one of the recurrent benefits of his genius—Shakespeare again turns what might be regarded as his own problem, since it did absorb him, into the problem, the grist, of *Richard II*; its drama depends on and, I am inclined to say, grows out of that problem. What better way to try language, to uncover poetry's innate capacities, than by embodying them in a king, that supreme human figure, normally satisfying his will through words? So great was Shakespeare's mastery of words that he might well have been enchanted by his own music. But this mastery resulted in equally great understanding. Thus he could see beyond words and poetry, see that they, however rich, subtle, alluring they may be, come from the world and must never be allowed to become self-devoted or overpowering, to lose sight of that world. There is always that ultimate poet, Orpheus, to remind us that, though his music seemed all-puissant, tumultuous dissatisfactions, gathering head against it, could by sheer volume overwhelm it. In Richard II Shake-

speare presents a character apparently in a position to give a free rein
to words. And what a poet he is, with one of the likeliest captive
audiences imaginable, the whole populace of England in supposedly
permanent attendance! It is not hard to imagine that Shakespeare,
bent on moving people with words, would be taken with a king all
consummate language, one who relied on it far beyond the fearfully
articulate but action-loving Richard III.

In fact *Richard II* constitutes a swan-song for words as things or
occupations in themselves, just as Richard sings a long swan-song for
a dying order of which he is the climax and the lovely seal; for his is
the will responsible perhaps more than anyone else's for finishing that
order. The old style, now and then obtrusive in its artificiality in
Shakespeare's earliest plays, is here deliberately employed, often at its
most complicated. Shakespeare, rehearsing the greatest flowering of
that style, makes it the material and the dramatic resource of the play.
At the same time this style, incarnated in one person, amounts to lyric
poetry and what happens to it in that person. More, it constitutes
through him this play's—or Shakespeare's—movement to larger drama,
more urgent, more telling dramatic poetry. In short, *Richard II* works
its way through medieval grandeur, for all its loveliness verging in its
extremity on grandiloquence if not fulsomeness, to its succeeding
Elizabethan vigor and immediacy.

Three plays roughly contemporaneous, *A Midsummer Night's
Dream*, *Romeo and Juliet*, and *Richard II*, contain, it is worth observing, more rimes and more of the overtly poetic—except of course for
Love's Labour's Lost – than previous plays. This fact might seem surprising till we remember that during that period Shakespeare had also
been writing his two narrative poems and his sonnets. This occupation
reflects itself in the lyrical nature of the three plays. The reflection is,
I suggest, far more than a matter of external form or mechanics. The
plays are lyrical everywhere, in situation, in characters, in language.
Romeo and Juliet is replete with an assortment of short poems, from the
sonnet on. *A Midsummer Night's Dream*, the most rimed of the three,
is checkered with moonlit arias, poems virtually complete in their
sovereign loveliness. These poems help to set the atmosphere, the
mood, of their plays. The young lovers in *A Midsummer Night's
Dream* and *Romeo and Juliet* are at that time of life closest to lyrical
poetry. Love possessing them, their situations evoke the maximally
lyrical out of them. At the same time the benign, comic atmosphere of
A Midsummer Night's Dream shields the two pairs of young lovers;

its lyricism proves resilient enough to see them through. In *Romeo and Juliet*, however, tragedy that it is, we have two lovers circumscribed by hostility, two against the world. Only internally do they, via their lyricism, survive.

How does Richard II fit into this lyrical ambience? No love, of the romantic variety, occurs in this play; none, that is, beyond self-love. Richard's anointing long ago blinded him, like the juice of love-in-idleness in *A Midsummer Night's Dream*; but, unlike the juice, that anointing blinded him almost irreparably; or rather it made him love the first one he saw and by the nature of his anointing it was himself, the lovely, hard, bright exterior that lets him see no one else. Unlike Navarre, say, or Romeo, Richard, priding himself on his uniqueness, cannot have a young woman (who beyond himself is worthy or able enough to love him enough?) shake him loose from his pretensions or his Berownesque affectations, his 'three-piled hyperboles'; he cannot know a love that would shatter his hard-shelled arrogance and complacency. Only reality in the shape of his own fate, which he brings down upon himself, gradually, belatedly, penetrates him. But nearly to the end, in this new brisk world, he tries to maintain his old poetic manner. After so many years how is he—like Richard III, also the victim of his own self-realization – to resist or change it? It is, so Berowne said, a sickness not easily cured.

Richard II, we soon see, is one against the world or rather one and his language, a lyricism in its imagery and extravagant eloquence like that of the lovers in the other two plays. Books, and images out of books, for instance, are common to both *Romeo and Juliet* and *Richard II*. And fitting, if not inevitable, they are for work so literary. In fact, a bookish world of romance prevails in the three plays. Richard is a romantic bookish figure to himself. Rimes, imagery, high-flown language are entirely apposite to him. And to the world surrounding him. The rimes, stilted though they may sound to us, too consciously artificial, are what we might expect of such an ornate world and of a royal speaker utterly proud of his art. Since it is primarily Richard's world, comedy is eschewed and so is prose. The unity he imposes must not be interrupted; nor must his lofty, lyrical tone be deflated.

The play's first scene shows him capable enough, for he is firmly enthroned here in his official role of ceremonialist. We are at a high point, with King Richard sitting above two nobles on trial, a trial involving blood-ties and proclamations of love for the King. But formal and therefore presumably lofty and objective though the occasion is, in speaking to Gaunt of Bolingbroke as his 'bold' son with his 'bois'trous' appeal which 'our leisure would not let us hear', Richard's attitude and partiality are clear. Thus he questions if Bolingbroke accuses the Duke 'on ancient malice/Or worthily, as a good subject should,/On some known ground of treachery. . . .' He concludes:

> . . . face to face,
> And frowning brow to brow, ourselves will hear
> The accuser and the accuséd freely speak.
> High stomached are they both, and full of ire,
> In rage deaf as the sea, hasty as fire.

He does not seem to realize the applicability of the last two verses to himself. But unwittingly he here anticipates his own confrontation with Bolingbroke. How accurate his last words are he has yet to learn, and what little power his words will have to reach that sea or to quench that fire. But we can feel his resentment at the deafness of the two, their impassioned disobedience before him.

The passion of their charges bursts forth in full fire. Mowbray begins with restraint and an apparent contempt for words,

> Let not my cold words here accuse my zeal.
> 'Tis not the trial of a woman's war,
> The bitter clamour of two eager tongues,
> Can arbitrate this cause betwixt us twain.

(nor patently can a king's words so arbitrate), and at least an acknowledgement of Richard,

> First, the fair reverence of your Highness curbs me
> From giving reins and spurs to my free speech,
> Which else would post until it had returned
> These terms of treason doubled down his throat.

(words, though Mowbray may think them womanish, swiftly become that image of power and passion common in Shakespeare, here—at least potentially—in action: a headlong horse). But he soon moves on to something like Bolingbroke's pitch. Richard asks Bolingbroke for his specific accusation, the climax of which is the claim that Mowbray killed the Duke of Gloucester, Bolingbroke's and Richard's uncle:

> Sluiced out his innocent soul through streams of blood,
> Which blood, like sacrificing Abel's, cries,

Even from the tongueless caverns of the earth,
To me for justice and rough chastisement.

These words, bringing together blood, tongue, and the earth, three recurrent, crucial images in the play, suggest that man in his blood is the tongue of the earth (Bolingbroke cannot anticipate how resonant and haunting the cries of the eloquent Richard's blood will be from the 'caverns of the earth'). More directly, they set off Bolingbroke at once with his arrogant stress (especially before his king, the proper judge and executor of justice) on 'To me' and 'by the glorious worth of my descent' and 'This arm shall do it'. Richard sees this proud ambition plainly enough, fears and resents it, in his 'How high a pitch his resolution soars!' This reaction, added to Richard's already visible irritation with Bolingbroke, well prepares us for the latter's banishment.

Both accusers grow extravagant. Mowbray boasts that he will meet Bolingbroke

. . . were I tied to run afoot
Even to the frozen ridges of the Alps,
Or any other ground inhabitable,
Wherever Englishman durst set his foot.

And Bolingbroke insists on battle with him 'Or here or elsewhere to the furthest verge/That ever was surveyed by English eye'. (It is pertinent to notice that both bound their extravagance with 'English', and that in its vehemence Bolingbroke's

Ere my tongue
Shall wound my honour with such feeble wrong,
Or sound so base a parle, my teeth shall tear
The slavish motive of recanting fear,
And spit it bleeding in his high disgrace,
Where shame doth harbour, even in Mowbray's face.

relates to what will be said of the loss of speech.) Their extravagance almost suggests banishment. Richard urges them to be ruled by him and to be reconciled. At their refusing he ends the scene ominously:

We were not born to sue, but to command,
Which since we cannot do, to make you friends,
Be ready, as your lives shall answer it, . . .

Scene II provides a feeling of lapsed time and expresses the abiding sense of loyalty to the throne in some. It presents John of Gaunt, being entreated by the Duchess of Gloucester to revenge her murdered husband and his brother, for whom, we have just heard, Bolingbroke is eager to venture his life. Unlike his son, Gaunt puts the King of England before his own personal interests, his own blood, even justice. A good man as well as an old one, he is committed to the legitimate order, about to be challenged and destroyed by his son. So Gaunt concludes:

> *God's is the quarrel. For God's substitute,*
> *His deputy anointed in His sight,*
> *Hath caused his death. The which if wrongfully,*
> *Let heaven revenge, for I may never lift*
> *An angry arm against His minister.*

With all the pomp of the medieval, courtly lists the next scene begins. Elizabethans, still involved in a goodly remnant of such rites, must have responded enthusiastically. Both combatants approach the fight with high, formal zeal as 'This feast of battle'. After his stiff words to Bolingbroke, Richard's partiality in his last ones to Mowbray is plain: 'Farewell, my lord. Securely I espy/Virtue with valour couchéd in thine eye.' Then, even as a charge is sounded, Richard (with his pleasure in such ceremonies, and with his intention till now hidden, he has allowed all the formality to unfold) throws down his warder and stops the fight. As always he frustrates action and others, here to draw the limelight of all eyes from the combatants to himself and his power. Next, to exhibit himself and that power the more, and to punish the protagonists for refusing to obey him in the first place, he arbitrarily banishes both. He sacrifices Mowbray to get at Bolingbroke who, a relative and scion of the royal blood, cannot be dealt with too harshly, at least not in public. The pride and ambition he accuses them of principally applies in his mind to Bolingbroke. So does the threat to peace he sees in them and in the 'boist'rous untuned drums', 'harsh-resounding trumpets' dreadful bray', and 'grating shock of wrathful iron arms'. He has already called Bolingbroke 'bold' and his claims 'boist'rous' and a threat to his 'leisure'. Certainly he knows that Bolingbroke in his energetic practicality would imperil the conditions that Richard's nature, words, and ceremony require: peace and quiet so that his lyrical music can be heard.

At his sentencing of Bolingbroke, Richard's subtle cruelty insinuates itself further in his wording of that sentence:

> *You cousin Hereford, upon pain of life,*
> *Till twice five summers have enriched our fields,*

Shall not regreet our fair dominions,
But tread the stranger paths of banishment.

Tauntingly he underscores good things lost: not simply ten years away, but twice five summers, and so on. Bolingbroke accepts the sentence with the seemingly small comfort:

That sun that warms you here shall shine on me,
And those his golden beams to you here lent
Shall point on me and gild my banishment.

These words, if we look ahead to his sharp retort to his father's attempt at consoling him, can be thought of as intended for public consumption only. But since the king is generally—especially in this play—identified with the sun, are we wrong to find Bolingbroke's words more ambiguous, richer and more promising for him, than they seem? Even for Richard those beams are merely 'lent'; soon enough they shall be pointing on Bolingbroke.

Now not Bolingbroke but Mowbray, who earlier had belittled 'the bitter clamour of two eager tongues', banished for life, though in Richard's words 'with some unwillingness', sings the praises of his native tongue, a moving elegy. Fitting it is to a play with a central figure made up almost entirely of words and a play in itself an elegy to a lovely, departed time, a lovely if failed mode of life. Surprised, Mowbray broadly hints at his complicity with Richard:

A heavy sentence, my most sovereign liege,
And all unlooked for from your Highness' mouth.
A dearer merit, not so deep a maim
As to be cast forth in the common air,
Have I deservéd at your Highness' hands.

He laments this being 'cast forth in the common air'. Not only does he think English air something very special but an air indeed, quintessential and unique, a kind of music made daily, almost that of Eden if not of the heavenly spheres; for England's little island is an earthly star for him.

The language I have learned these forty years,
My native English, now I must forgo.
And now my tongue's use is to me no more
Than an unstringéd viol or a harp;
Or like a cunning instrument cased up

Or, being open, put into his hands
That knows no touch to tune the harmony.

Anyone who has visited a country whose language is strange to him and whose people know nothing of his tongue can appreciate Mowbray's sentiments. Such a foreigner soon learns how much he lives in and through the words he has taken for granted, how different they are from 'the common air,' and how much he and his tongue belong to the language of his origins. Inevitably Mowbray compares his tongue to a delicate musical instrument. Then, having pondered its misuse, he turns to an image fairly jarring in its difference:

Within my mouth you have engaoled my tongue,
Doubly portcullised with my teeth and lips;
And dull, unfeeling, barren ignorance
Is made my gaoler to attend on me.

An extraordinary, not to say excessive, conceit until one admits that a delicate instrument in the wrong hands is indeed locked up or at least its music is imprisoned, and until one thinks to look ahead to the play's end where, in a sense, this metaphor will be enacted.

Mowbray concludes most powerfully of all:

I am too old to fawn upon a nurse,
Too far in years to be a pupil now.
What is thy sentence then, but speechless death,
Which robs my tongue from breathing native breath?

Language, Mowbray infers, is truly the air we breathe. A man's language like his land—here almost identifiable, for a man's name and title were identical with his land—is what he first learns things and people by; so too his feelings and thoughts discover and develop their natures, their shapes, in his language's words; the name and the thing, the human and the natural, are virtually one. More than that, one of the few semblances of immortality a man enjoys resides in his language. Sharing breath in his words with his own ancestors and with men of the remotest past, he draws breath and nourishment from the very roots of his language and from what earlier men have imbued it with, and he also gives those men a kind of resurrection in his speaking breath. At the same time he already shares breath with the farthest future, the men who will memorialize him by employing his words. Richard now abruptly rejecting him, Mowbray, the reverse of Bolingbroke, says: 'Then thus I turn me from my country's light,/To dwell

in solemn shades of endless night.' In their last exchange, to Bolingbroke's urging that he at least confess his treasons and so unburden his
'guilty soul', Mowbray makes his strongest statement, again in terms
of sacred words:

> *No, Bolingbroke. If ever I were traitor*
> *My name be blotted from the book of life,*
> *And I from heaven banished as from hence!*

We see to what extent, for these men, their very beings, not their
earthly lives alone, depended on words, their names. Ominously
Mowbray concludes: 'But what thou art, God, thou, and I, do know,/
And all too soon, I fear, the King shall rue.'

Then, as arbitrarily as ever, seeing his Uncle Gaunt weep, Richard
reduces Bolingbroke's banishment to six years. Once more, however,
with adroit maliciousness he stresses hardship and loss: 'Six frozen
winters spent, . . .' Bolingbroke, though little possessed of Richard's
inclination to the self-involved delights of language, exclaims in full
appreciation of the power of a king's words:

> *How long a time lies in one little word!*
> *Four lagging winters and four wanton springs*
> *End in a word; such is the breath of kings.*

Small wonder that he will soon be wanting to draw such breath. It is
his father again who, for all his much greater reverence for God's
deputy, disagrees with him and accurately modifies his—and Richard's
—notion of kings, their power, and the power of language. To Gaunt's
insisting that before the six years are over he will be dead, Richard says,
'Why, uncle, thou hast many years to live' and Gaunt replies:

> *But not a minute, King, that thou canst give.*
> *Shorten my days thou canst with sullen sorrow,*
> *And pluck nights from me, but not lend a morrow.*
> *Thou canst help time to furrow me with age,*
> *But stop no wrinkle in his pilgrimage.*
> *Thy word is current with him for my death,*
> *But dead, thy kingdom cannot buy my breath.*

Whatever his respect for kinghood, Gaunt knows too well that, in
matters of life and death, the power of a king is chiefly negative: men,
the noblest, after all, are only men, not gods. This truth, to their great
grief, both Richard and Bolingbroke will have to learn. Again one

might look ahead to the play's last scene. Yet, as always, it is Gaunt's sense of justice and order and his fear of being thought partial that has obliged him to be, against his own wishes, a party to his son's banishment. He had hoped and assumed that some of the lords would call him too strict and reverse his judgement.

Unmoved, Richard leaves. And Gaunt tries, like Friar Lawrence with Romeo—and similarly in vain—to teach his son patience by pointing out to him that time can best be dealt with mentally:

> *The sullen passage of thy weary steps*
> *Esteem as foil wherein thou art to set*
> *The precious jewel of thy home return.*

But Bolingbroke already anticipates his return as a time when he will 'boast of nothing else/But that I was a journeyman to grief.' To this Gaunt replies, much like Bolingbroke earlier on the sun:

> *All places that the eye of heaven visits*
> *Are to a wise man ports and happy havens.*
> *Teach thy necessity to reason thus:*
> *There is not virtue like necessity.*
> *Think not the King did banish thee,*
> *But thou the King.*

How well he is tutoring his son, how much more literally than he intends, we shall see. Finally, in this long speech Gaunt spins out a charming little tapestried scene, most apposite to this court and time:

> *Suppose the singing birds musicians,*
> *The grass whereon thou tread'st the presence strewed,*
> *The flowers fair ladies, and thy steps no more*
> *Than a delightful measure or a dance.*
> *For gnarling sorrow hath less power to bite*
> *The man that mocks at it, and sets it light.*

A similar lesson, we may recall, Petruchio afforded Katherine. Eden garden that this is, we are with Richard who must regard his steps as no less 'Than a delightful measure or a dance'. Such are the powers of the imagination brought to bear upon reality. In short, all of life, down to its commonest daily functions, should be, and can be through imagining, turned into festivity, gaiety. But the young, impetuous Bolingbroke, realist entirely, flouts such philosophic, impractical

advice. Of the line of Theseus he has even less patience for such absurd
imaginings:

> *O who can hold a fire in his hand*
> *By thinking on the frosty Caucasus?*
> *Or cloy the hungry edge of appetite*
> *By bare imagination of a feast?*
> *Or wallow naked in December snow*
> *By thinking on fantastic summer's heat?*
> *O no! the apprehension of the good*
> *Gives but the greater feeling of the worse.*

Anticipating the Richard-to-be, we might be tempted to answer these
would-be rhetorical questions with his name. Yet his ecstasies of
imagining will embody his loss and anguish rather than his memories
of joy, let alone his capacity, past fugitive moments, to establish joy in
the midst of woe. Richard to his chagrin will discover that the saint and
the madman, not to say the total poet, alone can know such triumph
over his world. So, bidding a last farewell not to language but to the
much more tangible 'England's ground' and echoing the word
'English', off Bolingbroke goes.

Next we encounter Richard and his favorites in a moment of
informality. The first part of their talk has mostly to do with words.
Aumerle, describing Bolingbroke's departure to Richard at his
questioning, says:

> *Marry, would the word 'farewell' have lengthened hours*
> *And added years to his short banishment,*
> *He should have had a volume of farewells.*
> *But since it would not, he had none of me.*

Aumerle, knowing and sharing Richard's dislike for Bolingbroke,
harbors no illusions about the power of words. With irony Richard
replies:

> *He is our cousin, cousin; but 'tis doubt,*
> *When time shall call him home from banishment,*
> *Whether our kinsman come to see his friends.*

Richard's aversion for Bolingbroke now openly asserts itself, as does
his contempt for the people:

> *Ourself and Bushy, Bagot here, and Green*
> *Observed his courtship to the common people,*

How he did seem to dive into their hearts
With humble and familiar courtesy,
What reverence he did throw away on slaves,
Wooing poor craftsmen with the craft of smiles
And patient underbearing of his fortune,
As 'twere to banish their affects with him.
Off goes his bonnet to an oyster-wench;
A brace of draymen bid God speed him well
And had the tribute of his supple knee,
With 'Thanks, my countrymen, my loving friends,'
As were our England in reversion his,
And he our subjects' next degree in hope.

These words, brilliant and attractive in themselves, no less visual and vigorous than Richard III's, with the eloquence we expect of Richard, reflect a shrewdness rare to him. They do not mean to say that he objects to performance and play-acting but to their being, ridiculously enough, 'thrown away' on slaves, an audience hardly deserving of such skill. Yet, willingly or not, Richard is acknowledging Bolingbroke's talents for such show, his capacity for diving into the people's hearts. Looking ahead to a not too dissimilar scene, we know how much Richard will suffer for this contempt. His last lines in all their mocking amusement, in all that they tell us of what he has seen and yet not seen, reverberate with irony.

At once then we turn to war in Ireland, which Richard plans to manage in person. But here, caught out of his customary world of ceremony, he must acknowledge a reality the full import of which he continues to ignore. As with any war, to fight this one he needs money. Words, his most glittering ones, will neither summon and pay an army, let alone a belligerent heavenly host, nor mow down the enemy. Thus, since 'our coffers, with too great a Court/And liberal largess, are grown somewhat light', he is 'enforced to farm our royal realm'; that is, for his easy prodigality he is willing to lease out his beloved England. He is not—we hear no doubts or remorse from him—beyond such abuse of his own land nor, since he cannot realize his own costly contradictoriness, of his own person as that land's king and protector. Nor is that all. If money should prove short:

Our substitutes at home shall have blank charters,
Whereto, when they shall know what men are rich,

They shall subscribe them for large sums of gold
And send them after to supply our wants.

This injustice is patently not, as Yeats would have it, a product of 'sheer bewilderment and impatience'. Rather Richard is indifferent, if not insensible, to the effect of such highhanded dealings on his subjects. Aptly also for this moment, Richard's banishment of Bolingbroke doing what Gaunt had said it would, Richard learns of Gaunt's grave illness. With the cynical lack of feeling (at least for others) that betrays him, Richard hopes:

> *Now put it, God, in the physician's mind*
> *To help him to his grave immediately!*
> *The lining of his coffers shall make coats*
> *To deck our soldiers for these Irish wars.*
> *Come gentlemen, let's all go visit him.*
> *Pray God we may make haste, and come too late!*

Such words Shakespeare surely intended to shock the audience and at the same time, more shockingly, to make clear Richard's outrageous intentions toward Bolingbroke. In any case, the need for money Richard sees realistically enough. It is the price of it that he, to his great expense, is blithely oblivious of.

Turning to Gaunt, we learn that with his last breath, for Richard's and so England's sake, he means to try to shake Richard. Gaunt's brother, York, assures him it is futile. But Gaunt counts on the potency of a dying man's tongue. And in Gaunt's mind words and breath, emphasized again, at their best approach the authority of music.

> *O but they say the tongues of dying men*
> *Enforce attention like deep harmony.*
> *When words are scarce, they are seldom spent in vain,*
> *For they breathe truth that breathe their words in pain.*
> *He that no more must say is listened more*
> *Than they whom youth and ease have taught to glose;*
> *More are men's ends marked than their lives before.*
> *The setting sun, and music at the close,*
> *As the last taste of sweets, is sweetest last,*
> *Writ in remembrance more than things long past.*

Whatever one may say of this play, whatever pleasure one may legitimately find in it, the last thing one would dare say is that in it words are 'scarce'. Yet with pain eventually overtaking the words of the play's most beworded character, his end will indeed be more marked than his life before. In the meantime, however, we need not be surprised that, much as youth and ease have taught him to glose, Richard will soon be little listened to. York assures his brother that Richard's ears are already 'stopped with other flattering sounds' and with a music altogether different, 'lascivious metres', 'Reports of fashions in proud Italy'.

But Gaunt, no less set on his course than on death, is not to be dissuaded; he delivers himself, even before Richard arrives, of a mighty, extended paean to England, again like Mowbray about to leave it, at his best at the moment of loss. Gaunt in the very moments of expiring thinks he is a prophet 'new-inspired'. Listening to this famous, prolonged speech, we may feel some deeper understanding for Richard; declamation, full-blown arias are much in the blood of his line, not to say in Englishmen of the time or at least as Shakespeare imagined them. But Shakespeare's time or Richard's, the nationalistic fervor that this play serves achieves its sovereign expression in this speech, which esteems England not only as a garden, a central image of *Richard II* and of the histories generally, but as another Eden. The leisureliness of this paean, banked in a single mighty breath and spent on a highly visible rhetoric of most deliberate balancings, may seem strange coming from a man nearly dead. But it fits splendidly the formal, self-conscious, old world to which it and its speaker belong. Not surprisingly he almost equates his own dying with England's because of what is being done to her, and he sings his swan-song as hers; for the very earth, 'this dear dear land' (and suddenly 'dear' turns into 'expensive'), best contained in its own name, 'this England', that should be receiving him is about to be sold away. Gaunt, it can also be said, belongs to the company of Shakespeare's garrulous old men who, no longer able to act, translate all action into words. But action this language is; we watch 'this England'–the 'this' is repeated seventeen resounding times–a precious jewel set in a 'silver sea', turn into a paltry farm, bound and suffocated with shame. It is hemmed in with a sea of 'inky blots and rotten parchment bonds', or with words, in their writing more indelible in a negative sense than 'watery Neptune' for all his 'envious siege'. Gaunt by no means underestimates the substantiality of words. Thus in his speech 'this England', already lost in its being leased out, becomes 'that England', having 'made a shameful conquest of itself'; only England, it seems, is able to conquer England (thus only Richard will be able to unseat Richard).

To Richard's entering with 'How is't with agéd Gaunt?' Gaunt takes off, as though the pun on his name had struck him only now: 'Old Gaunt indeed, and gaunt in being old,' etc. Breath, apparently, is not breath unless, the last breath notwithstanding, it be molded into words. Is not logomania all in this world? To Richard's 'Can sick men play so nicely with their names?' Gaunt, knowing how much men live, including dead ones, in their names, replies:

> No, misery makes sport to mock itself.
> Since thou dost seek to kill my name in me,
> I mock my name, great King, to flatter thee.
> Richard Should dying men flatter with those that live?
> Gaunt   No, no, men living flatter those that die.
> Richard Thou, now a-dying, say'st thou flatterest me.

This line provides Gaunt with the opening he desires: 'O no! thou diest, though I the sicker be.' And in most rhetorical and, it would seem, nonstop accents he rebukes Richard:

> Now He that made me knows I see thee ill,
> Ill in myself to see, and in thee seeing ill.
> Thy deathbed is no lesser than thy land,
> Wherein thou liest in reputation sick.
> And thou, too careless patient as thou art,
> Commit'st thy anointed body to the cure
> Of those physicians that first wounded thee.
> A thousand flatterers sit within thy crown
> Whose compass is no bigger than thy head,
> And yet encagéd in so small a verge,
> The waste is no whit lesser than thy land.

In his faithfulness Gaunt inevitably equates the crown or the king with the land; Richard sick and dying amounts to England sick and dying.

> O had thy grandsire with a prophet's eye
> Seen how his son's son would destroy his sons,
> From forth thy reach he would have laid thy shame,
> Deposing thee before thou wert possessed,
> Which art possessed now to depose thyself.
> Why cousin, wert thou regent of the world,
> It were a shame to let this land by lease.

Even loyal Gaunt admits that Richard should have been deposed before assuming the crown, and he predicts what will in a sense happen: Richard will be possessed to depose himself. Such speaking, one is tempted to say, for all its eloquence and elegance, is much too good and leisurely and long for any living world.

> *But for thy world enjoying but this land,*
> *Is it not more than shame to shame it so?*
> *Landlord of England art thou now, not King;*
> *Thy state of law is bondslave to the law,*
> *And thou—*

Richard, in all his vanity, cruel as he can be when compelled a moment to see himself as he is, with rage understandably interrupts Gaunt:

> *A lunatic lean-witted fool,*
> *Presuming on an ague's privilege,*
> *Darest with thy frozen admonition*
> *Make pale our cheek, chasing the royal blood*
> *With fury from his native residence.*
> *Now by my seat's right royal majesty,*
> *Wert thou not brother to great Edward's son,*
> *This tongue that runs so roundly in thy head*
> *Should run thy head from thy unreverent shoulders.*

Poor Richard cannot realize that, admonition and all, Gaunt is his last entirely faithful kin and follower.

With Gaunt borne off to die, York assures the King that Gaunt 'loves you, on my life, and holds you dear/As Harry Duke of Hereford, were he here.' Richard curtly if ironically replies, 'Right, you say true; as Hereford's love, so his;/As theirs, so mine, and all be as it is.' In short, little love is lost between them. And thorns in his side that both are, Gaunt in his concerned, courageous honesty, Bolingbroke in his ambition, Richard is happy to be rid of both of them. Announcing Gaunt's death, Northumberland, the eminently practical one, says: 'His tongue is now a stringless instrument./Words, life, and all, old Lancaster hath spent.' Aside from his statement's pertinency to garrulous Gaunt, Northumberland is still of the court and complying with its manner. Despite York's remonstrances and warnings on legal rights and process, on which even Richard's kingship depends, Richard, shrugging with a 'So much for that', at once brazenly seizes Gaunt's possessions. York also, old and of the old order, is a full, not to say fulsome speaker (to sample several instances of his conventional verbosity: 'His hands [Richard's father] were guilty of no kindred blood,/But bloody with the enemies of his kin' and 'O my liege,/ Pardon me, if you please; if not, I, pleased/Not to be pardoned, am content withal.'). Both uncles have now done their noble, super-abundant best to admonish Richard. In vain.

At once the murmurings of the dissident lords, thick with complaints against Richard and his abuses, grow into a raging wind; its vigor, its forthrightness, contrasting with Gaunt's and York's speeches, fits the deep-rankling discontent of the new order, the changed world about to burst forth. In Northumberland's words:

> *But, lords, we hear this fearful tempest sing,*
> *Yet seek no shelter to avoid the storm.*
> *We see the wind sit sore upon our sails,*
> *And yet we strike not, but securely perish.*

This is speech consciously capable enough, but poetry supple indeed beside the orotundities we have just heard. Then, with our sympathies for Bolingbroke—for England also and its abused or neglected subjects—at their highest, we learn from Northumberland, who has been skil-fully molding the lords into a plot against Richard, that Bolingbroke, who cannot yet have news of his latest deprivation, is already well on his way home and with an army. In his account Holinshed presents no such coincidence. According to him Bolingbroke returned only after he had learned of this outrage. Clearly Shakespeare set out to complicate our feelings about both Richard and Bolingbroke; he refused to relieve either of 'commission', of the guilt of acting past justification or justice. His sense of the nature of things as of drama, of the complexity of men's characters and motives, would have hardly let him do so. Northumberland concludes:

> *If then we shall shake off our slavish yoke,*
> *Imp out our drooping country's broken wing,*
> *Redeem from broking pawn the blemished crown,*
> *Wipe off the dust that hides our sceptre's gilt,*
> *And make high majesty look like itself,*
> *Away with me in post to Ravenspurgh.*

Rounded speech certainly, proud and sure of its powers, but bent on moving its listeners to action and not on self-sufficiency.

Then immediately, in sharp contrast to this forceful utterance, we hear the Queen, a perfect speech-mate to Richard, exchanging laborious, courtly conceits with her husband's favorites, relative to her sorrow. And an utterly static affair it is. Like Antonio she knows 'no cause/Why I should welcome such a guest as grief' except that, like Antonio with Bassanio, she regrets bidding farewell to her 'sweet Richard'. But she has a premonition of some great sorrow, now still 'unborn' and 'nothing', but speeding to be born, 'ripe in fortune's womb'; as with Antonio's melancholy, 'At something it [her 'inward soul'] grieves/More than with parting from my lord the King'. The courtiers try to console her with wit-racked, word-tortured stuff; then her premonition's truth in the shape of the news of Bolingbroke's returning in arms breaks in on them. Yet even this, disturbing though it is, cannot shake them loose from their verbal habits.

Promptly we see Bolingbroke on his way. Already hard-headed Northumberland is playing the flatterer to him with 'And yet your fair discourse hath been as sugar,/Making the hard way sweet and delectable.' But we can assume that Bolingbroke has been at least as flattering to Northumberland. Speaking of those wanting Bolingbroke's company, Northumberland lapses altogether into the old, sugary style:

> But theirs [tediousness] is sweetened with the hope to have
> The present benefit which I possess,
> And hope to joy is little less in joy
> Than hope enjoyed.

Perhaps he is not yet sure what style Bolingbroke will assume. The latter, responsive, flatters his flatterer: 'Of much less value is my company/Than your good words.' Something of the courtly style, it seems, must continue. But at this point Percy, Hotspur no less, breaks in on this verbiage with the hearty abruptness of the man of action. Already quite himself, to his father's 'Have you forgot the Duke of Hereford, boy?' he testily retorts, 'No, my good lord, for that is not forgot/Which ne'er I did remember. To my knowledge,/I never in my life did look on him.'

Greeted by others, Bolingbroke is then confronted by his uncle York, in charge while Richard is away. At Bolingbroke's kneeling York says, 'Show me thy humble heart, and not thy knee,/Whose duty is deceivable and false.' And at Bolingbroke's 'My gracious uncle!' York, fine testy old boy that he is, is off on one of his word-twisting, if here pretty pertinent, sallies:

> Tut, tut!
> Grace me no grace, nor uncle me no uncle.

I am no traitor's uncle, and that word 'grace'
In an ungracious mouth is but profane.
Why have those banished and forbidden legs
Dared once to touch a dust of England's ground?

And so on. But Bolingbroke, in his wiliness, appeals to him on grounds
of closest kinship:

You are my father, for methinks in you
I see old Gaunt alive. O, then, my father,
Will you permit that I shall stand condemned
A wandering vagabond, my rights and royalties
Plucked from my arms perforce and given away
To upstart unthrifts?

Then the cleverest thrust of all:

You have a son, Aumerle, my noble cousin.
Had you first died, and he been thus trod down,
He should have found his uncle Gaunt a father
To rouse his wrongs and chase them to the bay.

York recognizes that Bolingbroke has been wronged. Yet like Gaunt
before him he protests against Bolingbroke's and his followers' tactics:
'And you that do abet him in this kind/Cherish rebellion and are rebels
all.' However, since he cannot make them stoop, York, remaining
neutral, invites them to spend the night in the castle. Thereupon
Bolingbroke reveals that he means to do more than merely reclaim his
legitimate own; he urges York

to go with us
To Bristol Castle, which they say is held
By Bushy, Bagot, and their complices,
The caterpillars of the commonwealth,
Which I have sworn to weed and pluck away.

Such weeding if it is to occur, we should realize, is the prerogative and
the prerogative only of the chief gardener, the King.

Next we hear the Welsh in formal vein refusing to wait longer on
King Richard.

'Tis thought the King is dead. We will not stay.
The bay trees in our country all are withered,
And meteors fright the fixéd stars of heaven;

The pale-faced moon looks bloody on the earth,
And lean-looked prophets whisper fearful change;
Rich men look sad and ruffians dance and leap,
The one in fear to lose what they enjoy,
The other to enjoy by rage and war.
These signs forerun the death or fall of kings.

Here the signs of a world everywhere disordered because of the oncoming death of a king are vividly described; they are not, however, as they will later be in some of the major tragedies, enacted: a living, important part of the savage drama. Salisbury, a faithful retainer of Richard, neatly applying the above omens, predicts the doom of his King, who should be the one human 'fixéd star':

Ah, Richard, with the eyes of heavy mind
I see thy glory like a shooting star
Fall to the base earth from the firmament.
Thy sun sets weeping in the lowly west,
Witnessing storms to come, woe and unrest.

This anticipation, humanized through the mind's eye of a devoted follower, has its element of pathos.

Instantly, so efficient, not to say meteor-like, is Bolingbroke, we have him confronting the flatterers. The climaxing drama of the play now begins: Bolingbroke, in all his capable directness moving in on the throne, first addresses himself brilliantly and pertinently to the pressing business at hand – dealing with the King's parasites, bringing charges against them for their deaths:

You have misled a prince, a royal King,
A happy gentleman in blood and lineaments,
By you unhappied and disfigured clean.

This disfiguring, in the next fairly surprising lines – at least surprising before the rest of the play and at home only, it would seem, in Holinshed, but useful certainly for powerful accusations – becomes plain as it grows:

You have in manner with your sinful hours
Made a divorce betwixt his Queen and him,
Broke the possession of a royal bed
And stained the beauty of a fair Queen's cheeks
With tears drawn from her eyes by your foul wrongs.

Nowhere in the play itself is this charge borne out. On the contrary, we see the Queen in most amicable relations with the accused. But how, against such a potent adversary, shall their innocence be proved? Then, more relevantly, Bolingbroke charges them with what they have done to him:

> *Myself, a prince by fortune of my birth,*
> *Near to the King in blood, and near in love*
> *Till you did make him misinterpret me,*
> *Have stooped my neck under your injuries*
> *And sighed my English breath in foreign clouds,*
> *Eating the bitter bread of banishment,*
> *Whilst you have fed upon my signories,*
> *Disparked my parks and felled my forest woods,*
> *From my own windows torn my household coat,*
> *Razed out my imprese, leaving me no sign*
> *Save men's opinions and my living blood*
> *To show the world I am a gentleman.*

Two basic realities they have thrust him back upon: men's opinions and his living blood. Freed in a sense of the customary law by the parasites' outrage upon him, he will take advantage of that freedom and proceed via these two realities. They, he suggests, not Richard, are responsible for his banishment and his losses; they, caterpillars that they are, not Richard, have devoured his domain and his title and name as well. In short, they sought to erase Bolingbroke irrevocably from the world of the living, as though he had never lived. How much, quite apart from his flatterers' encouragement, Richard gladly gave himself to this razing neither we nor Bolingbroke need speculate. But at this juncture, for Bolingbroke's speedy purpose, Bushy, Green, and the rest, name and all, must be plucked out of the garden.

This place may be as good as any to ponder Bolingbroke and his motives. Has he plotted to usurp Richard from the start or, man of the moment, not to say superb opportunist that he is, as against Richard's would-be timelessness, is it that he simply has the talent to recognize and to seize opportunities when they occur? Aside from his judicious guardedness, he is never allowed to soliloquize. We never hear his private heart. In fact, active man that he is, we might easily doubt that he does live much internally. In any event, it serves his function in this play to have us think so. After all, this is Richard's play; it is Richard's life and nature we are principally occupied with. Bolingbroke is here, in large part, to enable that life and nature to display themselves to the full. Only in the next play, by its title his, will Bolingbroke as King deepen in his nature and expose a large portion of its complexity; following what he has done and been through, his nature will have had ample occasion to develop.

At the same time, in the sincerity of his present emotion, a tenor common to this play of 'sighed my English breath in foreign clouds', and in a Dantesque line like 'Eating the bitter bread of banishment', his speech compares most strikingly with Richard's first extravagant words in the following scene, on his return to his land, the land he so casually leased. Richard says:

> *I weep for joy*
> *To stand upon my kingdom once again.*
> *Dear earth, I do salute thee with my hand,*
> *Though rebels wound thee with their horses' hoofs.*
> *As a long-parted mother with her child*
> *Plays fondly with her tears and smiles in meeting,*
> *So weeping, smiling, greet I thee, my earth,*
> *And do thee favours with my royal hands.*
> *Feed not thy sovereign's foe, my gentle earth,*
> *Nor with thy sweets comfort his ravenous sense;*
> *But let thy spiders, that suck up thy venom,*
> *And heavy-gaited toads lie in their way,*
> *Doing annoyance to the treacherous feet*
> *Which with usurping steps do trample thee.*

King and all, the image of himself as a mother is a curious one; so is the lingering 'fond' playing with his tears. Both surely encourage us to remark the feminine aspect of his nature, that and—despite his stress throughout this passage on feeling—his playfulness with feelings, little more than toys. But the coupling of weeping and smiling, common to major Shakespearean figures in moments of extremity, especially suits his temperament with its excesses, its easy, fluid shiftings. Garden this England may be, a gentle earth. Yet, admitting its venom, for his purpose Richard accents its spiders, toads, stinging nettles, adders. Expecting his land, summoned by him, to use these against his enemies, he expects, he says, the earth itself, feeling for him, risen in its stones, to fight for him. Like Orpheus no doubt, his eloquence—also his being its king—will move it. Here already we see the fluctuations he is made of. A kind of manic-expressive, manic-exultant! When Aumerle says

that Richard and his supporters are 'too remiss' and Bolingbroke grows
strong through their neglect, Richard cries out:

> *Discomfortable cousin! Know'st thou not*
> *That when the searching eye of heaven is hid*
> *Behind the globe, that lights the lower world,*
> *Then thieves and robbers range abroad unseen*
> *In murthers and in outrage, boldly here;*
> *But when from under this terrestrial ball*
> *He fires the proud tops of the eastern pines*
> *And darts his light through every guilty hole,*
> *Then murthers, treasons, and detested sins,*
> *The cloak of night being plucked from off their backs,*
> *Stand bare and naked, trembling at themselves?*

This eye (patently it is by assimilation Richard's) by the light of its
look alone is puissant enough to strip—that is, expose to their criminal-
ity and weakness, and so disarm—the boldest traitors and villainies
themselves.

All this is a grand, if grandiose, winding up for

> *So when this thief, this traitor, Bolingbroke,*
> *Who all this while hath revelled in the night*
> *Whilst we were wandering with the Antipodes,*
> *Shall see us rising in our throne, the east,*
> *His treasons will sit blushing in his face,*
> *Not able to endure the sight of day,*
> *But self-affrighted tremble at his sin.*

Richard, by his title and his self-esteem easily identifying himself with
the sun, thinks Bolingbroke, that thief and traitor gathering up his
forces in the night, a revelling moon-man. But actually is not the reverse
true? The great difference in their respective returns to their beloved
England would plainly indicate it. One of course is concerned with
what he has lost and is now set on recovering; the other assumes that all
is his and in no way to be taken from him. Yet Richard, for all his fond
talk of the earth, lives little in it, no more than in common day.
Rather, with his thought, swift as the stars, wandering in remotest,
lofty regions, he is full of far-off, fabulous places and the ecstasies of
his imagining, not particular English parks, forest woods and windows.
Both emphasize thievery, but Bolingbroke in very direct, tangible
terms; Richard in generalized images at large. If Richard has too little

of earth and daytime in him, Bolingbroke might be regarded as inadequately poetic through his preoccupation with the earth and his indifference to the heavens. Compare the imagination which enjoys itself most in cosmic lines like 'Whilst we were wandering with the Antipodes' with one that finds itself in 'existential' lines like 'Eating the bitter bread of banishment', and you have at once the fundamental difference between these two men.

Bolingbroke, we might say, is a man of Theseus' practical, capable stamp. Richard, on the other hand, fits in very well among the company Theseus slurs. Do not Theseus' words, 'The lunatic, the lover, and the poet/Are of imagination all compact', accurately describe Richard, subject as he is to the potent moon of his own imagination? His words on the Antipodes superbly illustrate Theseus' 'The poet's eye, in a fine frenzy rolling,/Doth glance from heaven to earth, from earth to heaven.' And Richard deserves both the contempt Theseus intends and the praise implicit in his words that Theseus himself hardly appreciates. Richard, we shall soon see, fulfills perfectly Theseus' analysis:

> And as imagination bodies forth
> The forms of things unknown, the poet's pen
> Turns them to shapes, and gives to airy nothing
> A local habitation and a name.

Beyond Richard's poetic 'writing' on dust with his tears, 'airy nothing' will crop up again most significantly in his thoughts.

Richard now reaches his resounding climax:

> Not all the water in the rough rude sea
> Can wash the balm off from an anointed king.
> The breath of worldly men cannot depose
> The deputy elected by the Lord.

For Gaunt, we may recall, that sea could not wash away Richard's inky-blotting shame. (Blood, we know, will have a similar indelibility later.) Storms, Richard assures himself, or the sea aroused like villains and villains acting like a tempest, cannot prevail against a king with the steadfast breath of heaven in him and its balm upon him. So confident is Richard of his election and his balm that he can insist:

> For every man that Bolingbroke hath pressed
> To lift shrewd steel against our golden crown,
> God for His Richard hath in heavenly pay
> A glorious angel.

Not earth alone, and his own sun-like look, will fight for Richard. If omens occur at the fall or death of a king, why not expect some special exertion on earth and heaven's part when one of heaven's chosen kings is threatened? Richard conveniently forgets how much he needed cruder 'angels', golden coins, other men's at that, to make his campaign in Ireland possible.

But high as he is here, when he learns from Salisbury that the Welsh have fled to Bolingbroke, he plummets to the other extreme. Salisbury's earlier anticipatory image of Richard's glory, and of him as a shooting star, is not amiss. To a degree that is almost comic in its excess, Richard is no less variable than Shylock, no more master of himself or the occasion. To Richard's 'how far off lies your power?' Salisbury, reminiscent of Gaunt on the negative power of kings over time, says:

> One day too late I fear me, noble lord,
> Hath clouded all thy happy days on earth.
> O call back yesterday, bid time return,
> And thou shalt have twelve thousand fighting men!

Richard's sun is permanently eclipsed. Heaven may serve him, but time relentlessly obeys its own laws, laws no one can countermand. At this Richard, with the kind of royal exaggeration normal to him, cries out:

> But now the blood of twenty thousand men
> Did triumph in my face, and they are fled;
> And till so much blood thither come again,
> Have I not reason to look pale and dead?
> All souls that will be safe, fly from my side,
> For time hath set a blot upon my pride.

Nothing, elegiac as he is meant to be, pleases him more, apparently, than to dwell on and exaggerate the enormity of his losses. Thus his leap from twelve thousand to twenty thousand men. But to Aumerle's 'Comfort, my liege. Remember who you are', Richard promptly takes wing again:

> I had forgot myself. Am I not King?
> Awake, thou coward Majesty! Thou sleepest.
> Is not the King's name twenty thousand names?
> Arm, arm, my name!

But when Scroop on entering says: 'More health and happiness betide

my liege/Than can my care-tuned tongue deliver him', Richard leaps
to the worst:

Mine ear is open and my heart prepared.
The worst is wordly loss thou canst unfold.
Say is my kingdom lost? Why, 'twas my care;
And what loss is it to be rid of care?

He seems impressively philosophical, given over indeed to the heavenly
not the worldly part of his role, and reconciled to his deposition.
Thus he sings away, 'Cry woe, destruction, ruin, and decay./The
worst is death, and death will have his day.' To Scroop's description
of the forces flooding to Bolingbroke, Richard, unable to resist his
word-playing, says: 'Too well, too well thou tell'st a tale so ill.' But
who if not he is capable of appreciating a tale well told? Later, when he
embraces his fate, this line may be perfectly applied to him.

Then he asks about his favorites. 'If we prevail, their heads shall
pay for it./I warrant they have made peace with Bolingbroke.' At
Scroop's ambiguous 'Peace have they made with him indeed, my lord,'
Richard achieves his most thunderous style:

O villains, vipers, damned with redemption!
Dogs, easily won to fawn on any man!
Snakes, in my heart-blood warmed, that sting my heart!
Three Judases, each one thrice worse than Judas!

(At last he draws on the most powerful comparison he can find, and at
that much magnifies it, for Christ had to be satisfied with only one
Judas and one only a third as bad as each of Richard.) But instantly,
when he learns that his favorites are dead, he modulates into his new
elegiac strain. Like the poet in search of a subject, he has finally been
supplied with a first-rate one.

Of comfort no man speak!
Let's talk of graves, of worms, and epitaphs,
Make dust our paper, and with rainy eyes
Write sorrow on the bosom of the earth.

His speech, however, for all its would-be pathos, seems more literary
and artificial than ever, with its dusty paper and its writing, curiously
enough, on the 'bosom' of the earth. And there is something comfort-
able about it too, and indoor, with its 'talk' of graves, worms, epitaphs,
wills, the long-established properties of grave poetry. Not satisfied, in
a rapture of fancy he sums up all the possibilities of royal ending. And

well ahead of time he absorbs himself into the catalogue of tragic plots. Here in his way he is doing for himself what Lorenzo and Jessica at the beginning of Act V of *The Merchant of Venice* did for themselves: imaginatively joining others of their kind. Richard's image of death as a jester is magnificent. Yet a supreme king this jester is, in the very center of kingship, the crown, which Richard now realizes is hollow. And death allows each king his little scene of conceit, folly, foolhardiness so that each one becomes death's fool. But when Richard does confront death in action, it is death wielding 'a little pin'. Though this diminutive emphasizes Richard's new awareness of all men's frailty, kings, alas, being no exceptions, and of death's deftness and ease, it is also most consonant with Richard's literary style, his preciosity, and this medieval illumination or storied world he is eager to slip into.

In any case, at last Richard seems to recognize that he, like everyone else, is only a man.

> *Cover your heads and mock not flesh and blood*
> *With solemn reverence. Throw away respect,*
> *Tradition, form, and ceremonious duty;*
> *For you have but mistook me all this while.*
> *I live with breath like you, feel want,*
> *Taste grief, need friends. Subjected thus,*
> *How can you say to me I am a king?*

We may think of Shylock here. But Shylock's insistence on his human attributes is not much more than a reduction of man to his mechanics. This speech, however, whatever its ironic bitterness in 'Throw away respect,/Tradition, form, and ceremonious duty', does rise to grief and friends. Beside Shylock's descendental view this one, for all its despair, is humanizing. Yet even here Richard cannot resist (being Richard, why should he?) the perfect pun: 'Subjected thus'. And, we see, he still retains his old, lofty notion of a king: 'How can you say to me I am a king?' For surely a king is one who does not live with breath like you and me, does not feel want, taste grief, need friends. Or at least his breath is of a far purer element. In Bolingbroke's earlier awed words: 'Such is the breath of kings.' Aumerle tries to rouse Richard to sensible action, in words, it is true, most self-consciously mannered:

> *My lord, wise men ne'er sit and wail their woes,*
> *But presently prevent the ways to wail.*
> *To fear the foe, since fear oppresseth strength,*
> *Gives in your weakness strength unto your foe,*

And so your follies fight against yourself.
Fear, and be slain. No worse can come to fight;
And fight and die is death destroying death,
Where fearing dying pays death servile breath.

But learning that York has joined Bolingbroke, Richard turns on
Aumerle:

Beshrew thee, cousin, which didst lead me forth
Of that sweet way I was in to despair!
What say you now? What comfort have we now?
By heaven, I'll hate him everlastingly
That bids me be of comfort any more.

Comfort, that much repeated word here, or despair are the only two
courses open to Richard. But the telltale word in his speech is 'sweet'.

Finally, the play's climax occurs. Just before it, however, we must
have a repetition of the style identified with Richard and his world,
manifested in Aumerle's speech and in Richard's line 'A King, woe's
slave, shall kingly woe obey.' It was, it seems, harder for Shakespeare
to depose this old, belabored style than to depose Richard. York
laments that Northumberland has failed to say 'King Richard'. At
Northumberland's 'Your Grace mistakes. Only to be brief/Left I his
title out,' York retorts:

The time hath been,
Would you have been so brief with him, he would
Have been so brief with you, to shorten you,
For taking so the head, your whole head's length.

Bolingbroke intercedes, 'Mistake not, uncle, further than you should.'
York carries on, 'Take not, good cousin, further than you should,/Lest
you mistake. The heavens are over our heads.' The words 'take/mistake'
and 'head' have been wrung enough to satisfy the most hungrily
associative mind. Richard appearing in all his majesty, York is moved
to 'Alack, alack, for woe,/That any harm should stain so fair a show!'
The word 'show' does more serious duty than merely rime with 'woe'.
Richard, rising to his new role and to the show, accurately, however
grandiosely, predicts to Northumberland:

. . . know, my master, God Omnipotent,
Is mustering in His clouds on our behalf
Armies of pestilence; and they shall strike
Your children yet unborn and unbegot,

> *That lift your vassal hands against my head*
> *And threat the glory of my precious crown.*

Eagerly anticipating, almost proposing and insisting on, his deposition, he asks and as quickly answers:

> *What must the King do now? Must he submit?*
> *The King shall do it. Must he be deposed?*
> *The King shall be contented. Must he lose*
> *The name of King? A God's name, let it go!*

He looks to a new sanctity:

> *I'll give my jewels for a set of beads,*
> *My gorgeous palace for a hermitage,*
> *My gay apparel for an almsman's gown,*
> *My figured goblets for a dish of wood,*
> *My sceptre for a palmer's walking staff,*
> *My subjects for a pair of carvéd saints.*

Such handsome, leisurely parallels, especially at such a moment and in their concentrating on objects and, by their being figured and carved, on art, might make us suspect the actual sanctity of the feeling behind the parallels. And like his elaborating on death some speeches ago, he now toys with his own grave:

> *And my large kingdom for a little grave,*
> *A little, little grave, an obscure grave.*

Preciousness, so dwelt on (we may recall the 'little pin' he armed death with) that bitter reality is obscured by if not lost in language, makes it easy to believe that, rather than realizing the gravity of his situation, Richard is simply enjoying himself and his new-found role.

> *Or I'll be buried in the King's highway,*
> *Some way of common trade, where subjects' feet*
> *May hourly trample on their sovereign's head;*
> *For on my heart they tread now whilst I live,*
> *And buried once, why not upon my head?*

So confident, so exultant, and at the same time so contrived is his expression that one cannot even trust his self-pity. Surely there is a touch of bathos in his moving from the living heart down to the dead head, 'head' already overused by York; but such speakers are nothing if not excessive. Seeing Aumerle weep, Richard, with his great improvisatory powers, rapturously inflates their weeping into a mighty storm:

> *Aumerle, thou weep'st, my tender-hearted cousin!*
> *We'll make foul weather with despisèd tears;*
> *Our sighs and they shall lodge the summer corn*
> *And make a dearth in this revolting land.*

(This disturbance might be compared in its seriousness with the upset of the elements attributed by Titania to Oberon's 'brawls'.)

Wantonly Richard embellishes:

> *Or shall we play the wantons with our woes*
> *And make some pretty match with shedding tears?*
> *As thus, to drop them still upon one place*
> *Till they have fretted us a pair of graves*
> *Within the earth; and, therein laid—there lies*
> *Two kinsmen digged their graves with weeping eyes.*

The 'pretty match' is not wanton enough; nor are those tears, their action ably scored in the pun 'fretted', sufficiently milked; he must linger and repeat them in 'Two kinsmen digged their graves with weeping eyes.' Over-ripeness is all!

> *Would not this ill do well? Well, well, I see*
> *I talk but idly, and you laugh at me.*

Any word, no matter how small, how trivial, is subject to taxing by him. To Northumberland's 'My lord, in the base court he [Bolingbroke] doth attend/To speak with you. May it please you to come down,' Richard, beside himself with the suggestiveness he finds in each word, falls into a veritable verbal transport:

> *Down, down I come, like glistering Phaeton,*
> *Wanting the manage of unruly jades.*
> *In the base court? Base court, where kings grow base,*
> *To come at traitors' calls and do them grace!*
> *In the base court? Come down? Down, court! Down, King!*
> *For night owls shriek where mounting larks should sing.*

Such extravagant play-acting is, of course, common at certain moments to many of Shakespeare's leading characters. But this instance of it, I suggest, belongs in its excess to Shakespeare's earlier period and to the style that he was exercising. Thus it can remind us of Juliet's Nurse and parents in their wailing woe, and even of Bottom and his company during their playlet's extremest passion. Certainly if Bottom, also hyper-responsive to cues and potential roles, cannot tell play and reality apart, Richard assumes that his play-acting is reality. In such style comedy, not to say burlesque, and high historical tragedy—here verging on melodrama—meet! But Shakespeare, like any artist, had his basic colors to work with and to explore. To quote Picasso again: 'Actually, you work with a few colors. But they seem like a lot more when each one is in the right place.' Inevitably, striking, if not startling, correspondences crop up, especially in the work of one so aware of the close relationship of the passions, not least those seemingly most antithetical.

Small wonder that to Bolingbroke's 'What says his Majesty?' Northumberland replies: 'Sorrow and grief of heart /Makes him speak fondly, like a frantic man.' Richard who had assumed that he was permanent, if not timeless, is, we see, mercurial, changeable as the clouds, a very Ovidian creature indeed. His genius for vacillation now matured, having made the most of 'down', with Bolingbroke on his 'supple knee' before him, he exploits 'up': 'Up, cousin, up! Your heart is up, I know,/This high at least [touches his head], although your knee be low.' And in an ecstasy of surrending, at Bolingbroke's 'My gracious lord, I come but for mine own,' Richard exclaims, 'Your own is yours, and I am yours, and all.' No woman could capitulate more willingly to a virile lover! Thus, as though still in charge, he eagerly accelerates the course of events:

> *What you will have, I'll give, and willing too;*
> *For do we must what force will have us do.*
> *Set on towards London, cousin, is it so?*

At this point an interesting scene, unlike those around it, interrupts the play's main momentum and its major ceremony. Following all the play's garden imagery, an actual garden is presented; most aptly in view of the emphasis on the reverse – kings and political figures as gardeners in the garden politics – and most aptly also for its gardeners' comment on kings. In its own terms the scene's poetry is impressive, but the language tends to exceed the event. Beyond its observations on Richard, the situation seems mainly an opportunity for verbal display of the medieval variety; this garden of language is a tapestried, hanging one. But at least everyone enjoys his role. And of course, since this is a sequestered corner of York's estate, with the Queen presiding, the old courtly style prevails. The Queen, who has been spurning every effort to lighten her spirits, says of the gardeners: 'They'll talk of state, for every one doth so/Against a change; woe is forerun with woe.' And when the chief gardener in most courtly, formal strains bids his assistants order the garden, one asks:

> *Why should we, in the compass of a pale,*
> *Keep law and form and due proportion,*
> *Showing, as in a model, our firm estate,*
> *When our sea-wallèd garden, the whole land,*
> *Is full of weeds, her fairest flowers choked up.* . . .

The head-gardener answers:

> *Hold thy peace.*
> *He that hath suffered this disordered spring*
> *Hath now himself met with the fall of leaf.*

And he laments over Richard's failures:

> *O, what pity it is*
> *That he had not so trimmed and dressed his land*
> *As we this garden!*

All their talk is too much for the Queen. Indeed, in its simplified, laborious moralizing it may be so for us if we fail to recognize its quaint, deliberately reversed and 'inserted' nature: a garden that should be natural, yet in being old-fashioned and a comment on the play, a kind of a tableau or painting, more 'artificial' than the rest of the play's world. The Queen, in words suggestive of many of the play's characters, certainly Richard: 'O, I am pressed to death through want of speaking!' expresses her resentment:

> *Thou old Adam's likeness, set to dress this garden,*
> *How dare thy harsh rude tongue sound this unpleasing news?*
> *What Eve, what serpent, hath suggested thee*
> *To make a second fall of cursèd man?*
> *Why dost thou say King Richard is deposed?*
> *Darest thou, thou little better thing than earth,*
> *Divine his downfall?*

Richard for her is perfect man all over again. But she forgets the first perfect man's origins and therefore cannot appreciate that one a 'little better thing than earth' might indeed 'divine' Richard's downfall.

In any case, this 'earth' does have a 'feeling' for him far past that of men supposedly much superior. And the truth of his speech apart, it is amusing to hear her call his a 'harsh rude tongue', for it is anything but that. The gardener, unwilling though he is to tell the news, informs her:

> *Their fortunes both are weighed.*
> *In your lord's scale is nothing but himself,*
> *And some few vanities that make him light; . . .*

Appropriately enough, 'nothing' has been the Queen's vexed word; it will be Richard's. The Queen, weeping and cursing, leaves for London to join Richard, and the scene ends with a gentle if poignant touch, one in which this garden symbolizes the memorializing effect of the whole play. One which also proves how little 'a little better than earth' applies to the gardener. He says:

> *Poor Queen! so that thy state might be no worse,*
> *I would my skill were subject to thy curse.*
> *Here did she fall a tear; here in this place*
> *I'll set a bank of rue, sour herb of grace.*
> *Rue, even for ruth, here shortly shall be seen,*
> *In the remembrance of a weeping queen.*

As though to signalize the emerging new order, the opening talk of the next scene is generally more straightforward and swifter moving. At the same time, perhaps to remind us of the play's beginning and to indicate that this moment is the true beginning of Bolingbroke's reign, and therefore of basic change, before him several lords, fiercely accusing each other, resume the play's first issue, the murder of Gloucester. Bolingbroke, still occupied with it, patently means to lop away 'superfluous branches'. Then York tells Bolingbroke that Richard is willing to yield the sceptre; and Bolingbroke, seemingly reluctant, merely swept along by the tide of events, but opportunist that he is, promptly accepts. At this the Bishop of Carlisle cries out:

> *And if you crown him, let me prophesy,*
> *The blood of England shall manure the ground*
> *And future ages groan for this foul act;*
> *Peace shall go sleep with Turks and infidels,*
> *And in the seat of peace tumultuous wars*
> *Shall kin with kin and kind with kind confound;*
> *Disorder, horror, fear, and mutiny*

Shall here inhabit, and this land be called
The field of Golgotha and dead men's skulls.

We have all the earlier history plays to bear out the Bishop's prophecy. As tears in the scene before will blossom banks of rue, so blood will speed disorder, horror, mutiny throughout the land. England, Eden once, will become Golgotha. Here, at least by implication, for the first time by someone other than himself, Richard is identified with Christ.

At last we are ready for the deposition itself. Richard, entering, loses no time; here is a part to be played for all it is worth:

Alack, why am I sent for to a king
Before I have shook off the regal thoughts
Wherewith I reigned? I hardly yet have learned
To insinuate, flatter, bow, and bend my limbs.

But even as he asks 'leave' he turns on those present:

Yet I well remember
The favours of these men. Were they not mine?
Did they not sometime cry 'All hail!' to me?
So Judas did to Christ; but he, in twelve,
Found truth in all but one; I, in twelve thousand, none.

Not only is Richard, at least in his own mind, Christ-like, but in his suffering a thousand times more abandoned and betrayed. In this, his last great public performance, at the point of losing his crown he finds his role. (Richard III, on the contrary, at the point of gaining the crown loses his.) Whatever his luxuriating in self-pity, Richard is at his most kingly, entirely in charge of the ceremony: 'Give me the crown. Here, cousin, seize the crown.' His loaded 'seize' indicates that the stage directions are his to give.

Here, cousin,
On this side my hand, and on that side yours.
Now is this golden crown like a deep well
That owes two buckets, filling one another,
The emptier ever dancing in the air,
The other down, unseen and full of water.
That bucket down and full of tears am I,
Drinking my griefs whilst you mount up on high.

Before Richard's spate of words Bolingbroke can say no more than 'I thought you had been willing to resign.' Richard replies: 'My crown

I am, but still my griefs are mine. . . . Still am I king of those.' At Bolingbroke's would-be consoling remark 'Part of your cares you give me with your crown', Richard takes word-twisting to new lengths of torturousness:

> *Your cares set up do not pluck my cares down.*
> *My care is loss of care, by old care done;*
> *Your care is gain of care, by new care won.*
> *The cares I give I have, though given away;*
> *They tend the crown, yet still with me they stay.*

To Bolingbroke's simple 'Are you contented to resign the crown?' Richard, in a shower of negatives, illustrates his vacillation at its most triumphant: 'Ay, no; no, ay; for I must nothing be;/Therefore no no, for I resign to thee.' 'Ay' and 'I' as they come to 'nothing', or a most positive 'no no' or 'ay', involve a multiple pun and a pun in process.

Then, wanting everyone to appreciate his performance, Richard commands: 'Now mark me how I will undo myself.' Only he, a true king, can do it, do it properly. His language draped about him like his most regal robes, in total formality and ritual, he proceeds to his own deposing:

> *I give this heavy weight from off my head*
> *And this unwieldy sceptre from my hand,*
> *The pride of kingly sway from out my heart.*
> *With mine own tears I wash away my balm,*
> *With mine own hands I give away my crown,*
> *With mine own tongue deny my sacred state,*
> *With mine own breath release all duty's rites.*

Only his tears are strong enough, his words and breath divinely potent enough, to deny themselves as they deny him king. But though his tears may wash away the balm, no water can wash away the sin from his audience's hands:

> *Nay, all of you that stand and look upon*
> *Whilst that my wretchedness doth bait myself,*
> *Though some of you with Pilate wash your hands,*
> *Showing an outward pity, yet you Pilates*
> *Have here delivered me to my sour cross,*
> *And water cannot wash away your sin.*

Again he surpasses Christ in the number of Pilates he suffers. Still not satisfied, he turns upon himself:

Mine eyes are full of tears; I cannot see.
And yet salt water blinds them not so much
But they can see a sort of traitors here.
Nay, if I turn mine eyes upon myself,
I find myself a traitor with the rest; . . .

Perhaps, we begin to think, he has at last understood how in his
weakness and selfishness he has betrayed himself. But no.

For I have given my soul's consent
To undeck the pompous body of a king;
Made glory base, and sovereignty a slave,
Proud majesty a subject, state a peasant.

It is his submission he contemns. But at least it has taken his kingly
soul to betray his regal body. To Northumberland's 'My lord—'
Richard, with every word a fillip now to his excited, feverish imagination, retorts:

No lord of thine, thou haught insulting man,
Nor no man's lord. I have no name, no title,
No, not that name was given me at the font,
But 'tis usurped.

Names, so much is there to them, can be usurped. At this the vanity of
existence itself strikes him:

Alack the heavy day,
That I have worn so many winters out
And know not now what name to call myself!
O that I were a mockery king of snow,
Standing before the sun of Bolingbroke
To melt myself away in water drops!

His title and his identity therefore gone, Richard, reduced to mere
anonymous body, understandably wishes himself relieved of that dead
weight, all melted away in tears.

Then with all his talk of eyes, seeing, weeping, melting, he inspires
himself to his last great act, one that he himself may see and enjoy:

Good King, great King, and yet not greatly good,
An if my word be sterling yet in England,
Let it command a mirror hither straight,
That it may show me what a face I have,
Since it is bankrupt of his majesty.

Irresistible as words are for him, of course he cannot avoid his 'and yet not greatly good'. Bolingbroke, a kind of property man to Richard's show, orders a mirror. And with himself what in a sense he has always been, his own best subject and performance and, in the glass, his perfect audience as well, Richard delivers his most opulent aria:

> *Give me the glass, and therein will I read.*
> *No deeper wrinkles yet? Hath sorrow struck*
> *So many blows upon this face of mine*
> *And made no deeper wounds? O flattering glass,*
> *Like to my followers in prosperity,*
> *Thou dost beguile me!*

Appearances, evidently, cannot be trusted, not even one's own appearance. For this—his beauty, and he here admits he is as beautiful as ever—had seduced him. Next he uses words reminiscent of Marlowe's Helen:

> *Was this face the face*
> *That every day under his household roof*
> *Did keep ten thousand men? Was this the face*
> *That, like the sun, did make beholders wink?*
> *Was this the face that faced so many follies*
> *And was at last outfaced by Bolingbroke?*

Finally, word-twisting and all, the occasion and his language brilliantly blend; his extravagance has arrived at a situation that deserves it.

> *A brittle glory shineth in this face,*
> *As brittle as the glory is the face.*

And to prove it, most dramatically, no less than theatrically, he dashes the mirror to the ground.

> *For there it is, cracked in a hundred shivers.*
> *Mark, silent King, the moral of this sport,*
> *How soon my sorrow hath destroyed my face.*

Bolingbroke, trying to be assuaging, says:

> *The shadow of your face hath destroyed*
> *The shadow of your face.*

Richard, open to every possibility, turning Bolingbroke's thought over in his hyper-responsive mind, reflects:

> *Say that again.*
> *The shadow of my sorrow! Ha! Let's see.*
> *'Tis very true, my grief lies all within;*
> *And these external manners of laments*
> *Are merely shadows to the unseen grief*
> *That swells with silence in the tortured soul.*

May we not be forgiven if we are a little sceptical, especially before his deliberative 'Ha! Let's see,' of the total inwardness of Richard's grief, the 'silence' in his soul? Concluding, he thanks Bolingbroke

> *For thy great bounty that not only givest*
> *Me cause to wail, but teachest me the way*
> *How to lament the cause.*

Richard's sardonics apart, he has ample reason for feeling gratitude to Bolingbroke. With all the world a stage to Richard, the problem has been to turn up an occasion adequate to his histrionic powers. Bolingbroke has made it possible for Richard to fill his most regal role. As a king he was not too convincing an actor; only as an actor, we may say, has he become a king.

The last act opens with Richard's parting from the Queen, in its language completely formal and artificial. The Queen, whatever her grief, speaks in her customary manner:

> *But soft, but see, or rather do not see,*
> *My fair rose wither. Yet look up, behold,*
> *That you in pity may dissolve to dew*
> *And wash him fresh again with true-love tears.*

Is it that she is training for a part in Bottom's *Pyramus and Thisby?* She does pursue her images to their fulsome end. Grotesquely enough, addressing Richard 'thou King Richard's tomb,/And not King Richard!' she, most rhetorically, asks:

> *Thou most beauteous inn,*
> *Why should hard-favoured grief be lodged in thee*
> *When triumph is become an alehouse guest?*

Apparently, the occasion notwithstanding, a King and a Queen of their variety must converse with each other this way; in such deliberately overextended language, feeling and the personal are kept at a proper distance. Richard, stressing reality, is verbally not far behind her. But at least he admits that till now they have lived in a dream:

> *Join not with grief, fair woman, do not so,*
> *To make my end too sudden. Learn, good soul,*
> *To think our former state a happy dream,*
> *From which awaked, the truth of what we are*
> *Shows us but this. I am sworn brother, sweet,*
> *To grim Necessity, and he and I*
> *Will keep a league till death.*

Christopher Sly's 'waking' from his momentary put-on dream is one thing; a man's who has worn 'dream's' robes from birth, quite another. Yet both share a common mistake in that they allowed themselves to be persuaded to take the dream-situation in which they found themselves seriously, as reality. Bidding his Queen enter a cloister, Richard seems reconciled to his fate: 'Our holy lives must win a new world's crown,/Which our profane hours here have stricken down.' But she, rebuking him for being so mild, urges him to be the lion, the King of beasts, that he is. Instead of responding to her animus as she expects, Richard uses her image in his own way: 'A king of beasts indeed. If aught but beasts,/I had been still a happy king of men.'

Plainly, his next words demonstrate, it is too late, if it has not always been.

> *Think I am dead, and that even here thou takest*
> *As from my deathbed, thy last living leave.*
> *In winter's tedious nights sit by the fire*
> *With good old folks, and let them tell thee tales*
> *Of woeful ages long ago betid;*
> *And ere thou bid good-night, to quit their griefs,*
> *Tell thou the lamentable tale of me,*
> *And send the hearers weeping to their beds.*

Chiefly concerned with himself, he has in his own mind already turned into story and art, and he cosily anticipates the telling of his lamentable tale. Telling it, he is already enjoying—living in—his future, his immortality. Since being a king is not the pure poetry and the timelessness that he had thought, he proceeds to the transformation of himself into timelessness: that of folk story and ballad or art. So indeed the heavy flesh, translated, will be disposed of. Despite his present experience, he persists in the notion that his story, especially once it becomes a tale, will, its failures with those around him notwithstanding, not only move 'good old folks' but nature as well. If nature cannot be belligerent on his behalf at least it can be compassionate, elegiac like himself. Thus at his sad story, his funeral many times rehearsed, and appropriately at that season when wintry tales are most enjoyed, the brands, so stirring is his tale, Dantesquely by their sympathetically sputtering sap will douse ('weep . . . out') their fire. Then, they, in ashes some, some coal-black, will form a likely part of the belated funeral cortege. Though this is a very considerable diminution from the incensed stones he expected to hurl themselves in his defense, his talent for conceits continues unabated as ever. So does his proclivity for Swinburnian alliteration. We can hear 'last living leave' lisping on his lips, made especially delectable for him in sounding against 'death' in 'deathbed' just before.

Northumberland speeding their departure, Richard and his Queen now do touchingly take leave of each other, if still in self-conscious terms. For the first time one feels that Richard, gradually awakening to the truth of what he is, may be concerned for someone beyond himself. Words and fancy had till now cushioned him against reality, filled his ears consolingly against all other sounds with his own skill. At last these words and fancy are being overtaken—slowly it is true—by reality and feeling. He says to his Queen: 'So two, together weeping, make one woe./Weep thou for me in France, I for thee here.' And 'One kiss shall stop our mouths, and dumbly part./Thus give I mine, and thus take I thy heart.' Finally and truly, in what threatens, prim couplets and all, to become something like a Romeo and Juliet parting, he says: 'We make woe wanton with this fond delay.' Earlier, he admitted, he relished such making.

The next scene, rather than show it to us, describes the abuse of Richard coming into London. The pathos of it and, at the same time, the preserving of Richard's dignity are better served by such aesthetic distancing; also some portion of the 'lamentable tale' that Richard looked forward to already here begins. And with two 'good old folks' indeed. York, reporting the scene to his wife, for weeping asks her 'Where did I leave?' She answers in an image again suggestive of Christ: 'At that sad stop, my lord,/Where rude misgoverned hands from windows' tops/Threw dust and rubbish on King Richard's head.' The completely contrasting, triumphal procession of Bolingbroke, as King, follows:

> *Then, as I said, the Duke, great Bolingbroke,*
> *Mounted upon a hot and fiery steed*

Which his aspiring rider seemed to know,
With slow but stately pace kept on his course,
Whilst all tongues cried 'God save thee, Bolingbroke!'

Bolingbroke in his energy invokes the kind of enthusiastic response from men that Richard has, as legitimate king, mistakenly assumed. Richard would turn all to art and its ambience, with himself that art's central figure as well as its maker; Bolingbroke, York's speaking painted imagery suggests, turns all, even art, to ardent life. In addition, York points out, Bolingbroke treated the crowd with the political art which Richard, remarking earlier, had scoffed at, an art that clearly prevails:

Whilst he, from the one side to the other turning,
Bareheaded, lower than his proud steed's neck,
Bespake them thus, 'I thank you, countrymen.'
And thus still doing, thus he passed along.

And for 'poor Richard'? Almost inevitably York recounts the crowd's conduct toward Richard in theatrical terms:

As in a theatre the eyes of men,
After a well-graced actor leaves the stage,
Are idly bent on him that enters next,
Thinking his prattle to be tedious,
Even so, or with much more contempt, men's eyes
Did scowl on gentle Richard. No man cried 'God save him!'
No joyful tongue gave him his welcome home;
But dust was thrown upon his sacred head,
Which with such gentle sorrow he shook off,
His face still combating with tears and smiles,
The badges of his grief and patience,
That, had not God for some strong purpose steeled
The hearts of men, they must perforce have melted,
And barbarism itself have pitied him.

For all his failure Richard's nobility, in his 'tears and smiles', previously indulged in, but now genuine enough, shows forth; in fact, it is his grief that has found out his nobility. Ironically, the God and heaven that Richard had counted on to protect him York now believes responsible for the opposite. He knows an old retainer's pity and regrets. But, unlike his brother Gaunt, York is quickly adaptable. He is obviously impressed and converted by the scene he has described,

by Richard's failure to move the crowd. And faithful for order's sake
to whatever power there is, he swears allegiance to Bolingbroke. Here
quite dramatically – for he so swears while his son Aumerle is entering – York, through the effective device of a letter, apprehends him for
treason. Despite all his wife's pleading, York rushes off to appeach
Aumerle to Bolingbroke. Again we are reminded of Gaunt's very
different attitude toward his son in his supposed treason and banishment. Yet in his own way York is altogether faithful to what he is
faithful.

The next scene aptly opens with the first mention of Hal when
Bolingbroke, now King Henry the Fourth, wistfully asks: 'Can no man
tell me of my unthrifty son?' Such concern prepares him–and us–for
his reponse to York's fierce accusations of his own son, Aumerle, and
to Aumerle and his mother's begging for pardon. With the Duchess'
entrance, in deference perhaps to the old couple, the scene changes to
prettiness and worse in its speeches, a formal antiphony belonging to
the former dispensation. York, as if responsive to his wife's approach,
in his last verses lapses into old-fashioned couplets that thereafter
prevail throughout the scene except for one late moment when, grown
serious and himself again, dealing not with courtesy and the past but
with most pressing business at hand, the King returns to brisk blank
verse; in such vigor and resolution, contrasting finely with the em-
broidery of this scene, he meets the threat of the conspirators.

At the Duchess' door-pounding, her 'A beggar begs that never
begged before', Bolingbroke comments amusingly and accurately on
this scene's absurdity: 'Our scene is altered from a serious thing,/And
now changed to "The Beggar and the King." ' We should remember
this bit of melodrama and his comment on it, this awareness of its
becoming mere staginess, for Richard's last speech but a few moments
away. Most relevantly also, for all the staginess and mannered excess,
we are, late though it is, back again at the importance of words.
'Pardon' is hammered at. The Duchess, urging it, says: 'I never longed
to hear a word till now.' When York, sarcastically and no doubt
seriously too, retorts: 'Speak it in French, King. Say "Pardonne moi," '
his wife turns on him:

> Dost thou teach pardon pardon to destroy?
> Ah, my sour husband, my hard-hearted lord,
> That sets the word itself against the word!

Bolingbroke, moved as a father with a recreant son of his own might well be, and respecting York, does pardon Aumerle. After all, hovering over this scene is the fact of Bolingbroke's own 'treason', something his father could also not condone. And something the wilful Richard did not pardon.

At length, we are ready for Richard's last scene, his great curtain speech. In this performance he is, as in a sense he has always been but has never realized before, all alone. The richly figured arras he has lived by, an arras once concealing the palace's and the world's clammy, stony walls, is now ripped away. Down in the basest part of Pomfret Castle, he sets himself to see what he, a past master of them, can do with naked words.

> *I have been studying how I may compare*
> *This prison where I live unto the world;*
> *And for because the world is populous,*
> *And here is not a creature but myself,*
> *I cannot do it.*

At last he realizes that, however valiantly he may try, he must fail; words without other men and the world they make, the breathable air their speech and listening supply, are stillborn. Nonetheless, for his veteran practice in making worlds of his own, now really up against it, stripped of his kinghood, England, the world, he has come to a kind of supreme challenge and final form: his tongue in a bare prison. (Mowbray's desolate image of his jailed tongue in banishment readily comes to mind here.) Never have Richard and his imagination been more called upon. In fact, we might say that before, in the very abundance, seemingly illimitable, of his royal office, despite all his rousing rhetoric he was petulant, often trifling. Now in his imprisonment his imagination, struggling against rock reality, knows a new purity and freedom. Perhaps since he is entirely on his own we feel a basic difference in his words. A maturity, a deep-searching sobriety and detachment, pervades them. He is, for a change, concerned with the content and the aim of his thinking rather than with its high-sounding effect. One recalls Berowne adjured to pit his verbal gifts against the agonized groans of a hospital; Richard's eloquence is framed by a similar unlistening, a completely stony world.

He persists:

> *Yet I'll hammer it out.*
> *My brain I'll prove the female to my soul,*
> *My soul the father; and these two beget*

A generation of still-breeding thoughts;
And these same thoughts people this little world,
In humours like the people of this world,
For no thought is contented.

Far-fetched though the comparison may be, for a moment I am reminded of the lyric poet at work, especially the modern lyric poet in his isolation, a Mallarmé say, in the wintry nighttime solitude of his little room, confronting his blank page, caught in the framing circle of his lamp. In his desperate pride he too would reduce himself to the barest essentials: nothing more than words and his imagination or his life and place in language while he seeks to produce an ideal world. And what eventuates is wonderful; Richard's powers, concentrating, do 'beget/A generation of still-breeding thoughts', much like God's creation, the first making of the world with its self-bearing seeds. Thus these thoughts in their generation become Richard's people. But, alas, as with the world itself, this making is not—not perhaps beyond the making itself—satisfying; for like the world's people no one thought is contented.

                              The better sort,
As thoughts of things divine are intermixed
With scruples, and do set the word itself
Against the word:
As thus, 'Come, little ones,' and then again,
'It is as hard to come as for a camel
To thread the postern of a small needle's eye.'

The loftiest thoughts are riddled, knotted, frustrated by basic contradictions. Richard, arguing with himself, proceeds—and in the only way that he can—by contradictions. A new word is possible through its denying the old or the one just before it, there to be denied. A generation of words and images indeed, but for destroying themselves and each other rather than for breeding. Richard who had loved and lived in words, who had set words to words, loving their cohabitation and their breeding till the words seemed enamored of themselves, now does, repeating the Duchess' very words, 'set the word itself/Against the word' and does 'teach pardon pardon to destroy'. That is, he refuses— since he finds no kingly way—to pardon himself. What action can loftiest thoughts therefore resolve themselves into; or, for that matter, into what action, thoughts most compatible with Bolingbroke in their worldliness?

> *Thoughts tending to ambition, they do plot*
> *Unlikely wonders—how these vain weak nails*
> *May tear a passage through the flinty ribs*
> *Of this hard world, my ragged prison walls;*
> *And, for they cannot, die in their own pride.*

What thoughts indeed, as Bolingbroke will also eventually to his great sorrow learn, can break through this hard world? Too late Richard understands that, king or not, he is no less weak and, finally, immured than all his subjects.

> *Thoughts tending to content flatter themselves*
> *That they are not the first of fortune's slaves,*
> *Nor shall not be the last; like silly beggars*
> *Who, sitting in the stocks, refuge their shame,*
> *That many have, and others must, sit there.*
> *And in this thought they find a kind of ease,*
> *Bearing their own misfortune on the back*
> *Of such as have before endured the like.*

Earlier he found some comfort in joining the company of ruined kings. Now he is able to identify himself with the lowliest, and to know via the thought of their miserable presence a degree of consolation. Amusingly and touchingly enough, only in losing all people does he begin to find them; in being 'subjected' does he feel for and commune with other 'subjects'. But even this content is tinctured with the ironical and is only momentary:

> *Thus play I in one person many people,*
> *And none contented. Sometimes am I King,*
> *Then treasons make me wish myself a beggar,*
> *And so I am.*

Is not Bolingbroke's recent 'The Beggar and the King' with its ironic comment on play-acting still ringing in the air? But full seriousness also attends Richard's musings. Now he is hardly play-acting. In his thoughts Richard finds he is no different from what he was in his life. Odysseus comes to mind who, having to pass through all trials, is not spared the last indignity before he can fully return home and resume his role as king: he must be, and be sorely treated as, a wretched old beggar in his own home. Perhaps that is the last advantage of the great imagination: that it can play in one person many people and, playing them, can thoroughly experience the quality of each one's life. Nor by the very cogency of that experience is such imagination able to settle with any one of them.

> *Then crushing penury*
> *Persuades me I was better when a king;*
> *Then am I kinged again; and by-and-by*
> *Think that I am unkinged by Bolingbroke,*
> *And straight am nothing.*

This word 'nothing', we remember, was set reverberantly going in this play long ago; now it comes into its own. But then what role is there in this life that a man can identify himself with? And shifting from one to another, where and what, beyond these makeshifts, is he? What part of all this is his true basic self, he and only he? The hard, not to say terrible, conclusion follows:

> *But whate'er I be,*
> *Nor I nor any man that but man is*
> *With nothing shall be pleased till he be eased*
> *With being nothing.*

The rich ambiguity of 'nothing' rings out here. Nothing can content him; yet nothing alone can when in death he, released, will become nothing. No longer haunted by the need to know, to be, to be somebody and somebody better than all the rest, he will be all content, one with the all. Alone then becomes all one. For him it has always been a matter of 'all'—a favorite word with him in his expansiveness—or 'nothing'.

At this point of at least imaginative 'melting', music, a matter of time (in its very struggling, like poetry, to become out of its makings of time something above and beyond time, it is a melter also), plays but—it is no more satisfactory than words—out of key.

> *Music do I hear?*
> *Ha, ha! keep time. How sour sweet music is*
> *When time is broke and no proportion kept!*
> *So is it in the music of men's lives.*
> *And here have I the daintiness of ear*
> *To check time broke in a disordered string,*
> *But for the concord of my state and time*
> *Had not an ear to hear my true time broke.*
> *I wasted time, and now doth time waste me.*

Only in true harmony, that being one with the music of the spheres, can one redeem, rather than waste, time. In his easy assumption of immortality, his opaque dream which thought to suppress or to be superior to time, Richard failed to 'keep time'. In their plays both Richards live in and by time, or history; but by their commitments to themselves, the one to the powers of darkness embodied in him, the other to the heaven he thinks realized in him, they believe they are wholly beyond history and time. For their notion of their superiority to time and its claims, of living in timelessness or 'comedy', they are tragic and destroyed. Of course, having been a king so long, Richard II appeared to cultivate a fervor for failure as though his instincts bade him know that only so would he exceed his normal kinghood and be posthumously and forever famous; certainly, we saw earlier, he seemed to live already, and with immense relish, in the aura of his afterlife. But now he realizes too well his costly deafness to his own time, to 'concord', a happy pun that combines 'chord' and 'heart' in the ful-filling of one's own 'state' (also the state of England) and 'time' or life (also one's epoch). Accurately the gardener observed that had this 'wasteful King' 'trimmed and dressed his land/As we this garden', 'himself had borne the crown,/Which waste of idle hours hath quite thrown down.'

Developing a mighty conceit, himself as time's 'numbering clock', and so at last come full circle, become the very thing he thought he was least, Richard concludes:

> *Now, sir, the sound that tells what hour it is*
> *Are clamorous groans, which strike upon my heart,*
> *Which is the bell.*

He understands:

> *But my time*
> *Runs posting on in Bolingbroke's proud joy*
> *While I stand fooling here, his Jack-o'-the-clock.*

Richard, unbeknown of course to himself, has occupied two of man's chief roles as Shakespeare sees them: a slave of fortune, then when his fortune seemed the highest, and, then when he seemed beyond time's reach, time's fool. For his conceit and consequent opacity, the true condition of a certain variety of fool (see Armado, Holofernes or, for that matter, Hotspur and Navarre until he is jarred loose), Richard's play has had no need or room for a clown. In fitfulness he breaks out:

This music mads me. Let it sound no more;
For though it have holp madmen to their wits,
In me it seems it will make wise men mad.

Even that most self-sufficient and often restorative art, music, reminding him of his terrible mistakes, has failed him. Again he shifts, this time to the sweet pathos he can on occasion know, especially now that his fortunes are at their nadir:

Yet blessing on his heart that gives it me!
For 'tis a sign of love, and love to Richard
Is a strange brooch in this all-hating world.

At his speaking of love a groom enters, a realistic character altogether out of sorts with the others in the play, even the gardeners with their florid speech and different purpose. He is one of Shakespeare's wonderful company of low-lifes, vulgars, peasants, rustics, who often save the day when their superiors seem to have irrevocably lost it. Now that we are near the bitter, 'real' end, his appearance, like his speech, is entirely right. Of Richard's stable when he was King, he, traveling towards York, has 'With much ado, at length, . . . gotten leave'

To look upon my sometimes royal master's face.
O, how it yearned my heart when I beheld
In London streets, that coronation day,
When Bolingbroke rode on roan Barbary,
That horse that thou so often hast bestrid,
That horse that I so carefully have dressed!

In their homely vividness these simple details play strongly on the feelings. Richard asks 'How went he under him?', and at the groom's 'So proudly as if he had disdained the ground' (we recall York's description of Bolingbroke's being 'Mounted upon a hot and fiery steed/Which his aspiring rider seemed to know'), Richard fulminates:

That jade hath eat bread from my royal hand;
This hand hath made him proud with clapping him.
Would he not stumble? Would he not fall down,
Since pride must have a fall, and break the neck
Of that proud man that did usurp his back?

He cannot give over his feeling that nature should care for him. But then his almost inevitable turning on himself supplants that feeling:

> *Forgiveness, horse! Why do I rail on thee,*
> *Since thou, created to be awed by man,*
> *Wast born to bear? I was not made a horse,*
> *And yet I bear a burthen like an ass,*
> *Spurred, galled, and tired by jauncing Bolingbroke.*

Richard is not done with his excessiveness yet, nor with the bathos of his too glib analogies. Richard's keeper, entering with his food, bids the groom leave. To Richard's 'If thou love me, 'tis time thou wert away', the groom says movingly: 'What my tongue dares not, that my heart shall say', almost too touching in a play made up of countless loud words rather than heart-felt silences. It is worth noting that the play's lowliest characters, this groom and the head-gardener, are among the few feelingful persons in it, are among the few certainly solicitous about Richard. Contrary to York's belief, there were people present in the crowd who cared for Richard, so much so that in shame and grief they could not speak. The plays to come will often underscore that care.

Now, as though sensing what is about to happen, the hour ripe, and nearly calling it into being, in a fit of rage at the keeper's refusal to taste his food, Richard beats him; and Exton and his murderers rush in to fulfill Bolingbroke's wishes. Richard, recognizing them for what they are and fighting mad, is at last a lion indeed. Crying out, 'How now! What means death in this rude assault?/Villain, thy own hand yields thy death's instrument', he snatches one's sword, kills him and another: 'Go thou, and fill another room in hell.' Exton then strikes him, and Richard says: 'That hand shall burn in never-quenching fire/ That staggers thus my person.' In his dying he is every inch a king, far surpassing in action and magnificence what he has been. Thus at the end lyricism, struggling with itself and having arrived at its extremity, has, if only for a moment, broken into its seeming opposite, the heroically dramatic. As in ancient Greek lyrical tragedy, words fully called upon can become action. Yeat's verses from 'Under Ben Bulben' here come to mind:

> *Know that when all words are said*
> *And a man is fighting mad,*
> *Something drops from eyes long blind,*
> *He completes his partial mind, . . .*

With his last breath, in fierce, brief words unlike his usual pace or Gaunt's dying speech, Richard, completely King again, exclaims:

> *Exton, thy fierce hand*
> *Hath with the King's blood stained the King's own land.*
> *Mount, mount, my soul! Thy seat is up on high,*
> *Whilst my gross flesh sinks downward, here to die.*

Mere mortal flesh that his body has become, he is at last rid of it.

Exton, at Richard's valorous conduct and words, knows instant remorse. Presenting the coffined Richard to Bolingbroke, he reminds him: 'From your own mouth, my lord, did I this deed.' But Bolingbroke has little thanks for him:

> *They love not poison that do poison need,*
> *Nor do I thee. Though I did wish him dead,*
> *I hate the murtherer, love him murtheréd.*
> *The guilt of conscience take thee for thy labour,*
> *But neither my good word nor princely favour.*
> *With Cain go wander thorough shades of night,*
> *And never show thy head by day nor light.*

His love for Richard, though he protested it earlier, does indeed seem late and questionable, as his hate for Exton a little strong. But no doubt this statement is meant for the listening lords (and himself) more than for Exton. We might also wonder at Bolingbroke's failing to realize what a Cain he has made of himself in requesting the murder. His next words to his lords, however, make it clear that he has some good inkling of his involvement: 'Lords, I protest, my soul is full of woe/That blood should sprinkle me to make me grow.' These powerful, ominous words prepare us for the play to follow. And that play will show that though he says:

> *Come, mourn with me for what I do lament,*
> *And put on sullen black incontinent.*
> *I'll make a voyage to the Holy Land*
> *To wash this blood off from my guilty hand.*

he will not be able to mollify himself by fully repenting; nor will he ever find an opportunity to wash this blood off by a crusade to the Holy Land; his sin has let loose too many chaotic, all-time-consuming forces.

His last words, closing the play: 'March sadly after. Grace my mournings here/In weeping after this untimely bier', might be taken to summarize our general feeling about the play, one the play set out to generate. The old order that Richard consummately represented deserved or at least had to die, but its appeal, like his, cannot be gainsaid. Through the elegy that this play delivers, with Richard his own best elegist (elegiac and prophecy-laden as he becomes, he resembles, at least in function, the women in *Richard III*; on leaving the center of the stage he assumes a new, darker role, almost becomes part of destiny), Shakespeare, we can say, brilliantly solved a major problem. He created a character he could visit his own word-play on. This way, detaching and using it, Shakespeare mastered it and simultaneously enjoyed all its qualities. He gave Richard—so himself—free rein as a verbalist. Richard's day seemed to justify him, in some ways its most impressive flowering. And he justifies the presence in the play of all the richest, most complicated, most self-conscious and at times, it is true, most frigidly ingenious poetry, practiced by the courtiers no less than by their King.

Thus we can plot the play in terms of words alone. It moves from its early encomium to language delivered by Mowbray and others, fitting while Richard is still in charge; to Richard's regime of words; to Richard's final admission of language's inadequacy in itself. Those exiled from their language 'die'; those living only in language, no less exiled from experience and reality or their 'mother earth' from which like them that language has derived, also 'die'. Yet, having driven language as far as it can go and turning from it to that only pure utterance, music, finding both insufficient, Richard breaks through. Paradoxically enough, the word in its extremity becomes deed, his last heroic action, or the bridge to tragedy. When poetry or language, become self-infatuated, brings catastrophe down upon itself, it shows itself able, if only in the last moment, to rise to the splendidly dramatic and heroic. Perhaps under stress it has recovered some of the magnificent energy long dammed at its source. Man as actor versus man as poet and thinker, the extent to which dream and action often part company, the way in which absorption in the subjective correlative can eclipse the world at large, *Richard II* is a triumphant enactment of this dilemma, to be surpassed only by Hamlet, Richard's greatest heir. And triumphant to a considerable degree in the way that Yeats proposed in an early poem:

> *Words alone are certain good.*
> *Where are now the warring kings,*
> *Word be-mockers? By the Rood,*

Where are now the warring kings?
An idle word is now their glory,
By the stammering schoolboy said,
Reading some entangled story;
The kings of the old time are dead; . . .

King though Richard was, he was not a word be-mocker. On the contrary, he was a king altogether enamored of words; and with them, idle though they may have been in a troubled world, he helped to compose the tangled story that is this play. His dream in its very destructiveness produced the tale he looked forward to most ardently when his kingship ended. In fact, his idle words, and the dream that sponsored them (in Yeats' words, 'Dream, dream for this is also sooth'), cast in this play, are now his lasting glory.

Now of All Humours

Henry IV, Parts I and II

RICHARD II, my reading of it has proposed, is Shakespeare's most thoroughgoing study of the absorption in words and of the perils such absorption invites. On the other hand, *Henry IV*, written probably some years after *Richard II* but directly following it in historical time, constitutes the triumph of words properly understood, of words immediately, felicitously conjoined with–a very part of–action. From Richard II by way of Bolingbroke to Hal this circle is completed. *Richard II* is, through Richard's doting on words, a forced unity and simplicity. Eschewing subplot and the aeration of comic comment, it establishes a community of expression that, out of rigorous insularity and growing remoteness from reality, must collapse. *Henry IV*, to the contrary, is as free a play, as expansive, complex, and buoyantly inclusive, as any Shakespeare ever wrote. Here he gives his time, now of all humours, full voice. In *Richard II*, celebrating the climax and death of English Medievalism, Shakespeare, like Richard himself, compressed his powers in one splendid if narrow channel. But moving from that almost unaccompanied solo to the full-bodied symphony of *Henry IV*, Shakespeare celebrates the 'modern' Renaissance, the Elizabethan spirit at its most bounteous and exuberant. In *Henry IV* the whole man, exemplified by gallants like Raleigh and Sidney, lives his multiple life; in Hal that life is being lived, as in the play's vast range all of Elizabethan England seems to be living.

Thus one feels called upon to say that nothing in *Henry IV* is inert or unrealized. Rather, everything leaps to instant, teeming life. Like this moment of England itself, Shakespeare's medium is assured enough to encourage his characters and their actions to be genius-like themselves. There is, consequently, something in the individual personae and in their engagements of the rhythm of the dance, movement altogether itself. But of course it is modern dance one thinks of, not a court dance. The movement of earlier plays in their stately, artificial symmetry contrasts sharply with the naturalness, the crackling immediacy, of *Henry IV*'s development. In fact, so crammed and bustling is the play in its use of a language adaptive to all occasions—those of the court, the tavern, the street, the battlefield, lovers—each occasion seemingly wrapped up in its own skin and breath, that not until quite recently have critics been able to see it for the amazing whole it is. The richness, the brio, of *Henry IV* has been ascribed to its nationalistic and patriotic, not to say epical, concerns. Certainly, the play most cogently testifies, this is a young nation breaking loose, joyous in the mere rehearsal of its newly released powers. The work's greatness resides in its very impurity, its gallimaufry-like nature, its bursting of normal bounds.

And critics have gradually become apprised of this freedom, but no less of the extraordinary form responsible for this freedom. Thus so much in modern criticism has been made of the play's multiple structure, of the way in which scenes, one after another, collaborate and comment on each other, a balancing so daring that one scene seems to be, not merely the counterpart of the other, but its subplot, that little more need be said about it here. But the critical vehemence produced by the tavern scenes and their master, Falstaff, must be dealt with. This vehemence has continued for some centuries. Ironically enough, however, perhaps even more than with Shylock, it has been almost equally spent on opposite positions: on the one hand, those who consider Falstaff not only the play's central figure but heroic and, for the abuse he sustains at the end of Part II, tragic as well; on the other, those who excoriate him as a ruffian, a vice, a Satan, to say the least a seducer of the young. But a creation of such magnitude and, simultaneously, of such intimately existential impact yields to no single view, no summary or generalizing. When we try to talk about him apart from his play we are bound to reduce him and so lose him. Whatever his moral worth, he rises, at least until Part II, fat singing dolphin that he is, above the element he lives in; and brimming it to flooding, he intoxicates us with that vintage sack. The intoxicating sack that his wit alone can make of it. Once a lord, he is now the chief lord of delight in a wakening in some sort the reverse of Sly's; he too enjoys a gallery of lusty pictures—impromptus and tableaux—but usually of his own devising. So, generation after generation, because of the sacred, earthy life in him, we, according to the bias of our own temperaments, passionately join or passionately disavow his company. Capable of every eventuality, he enables us to reflect another—maybe, if we are lucky and lively ourselves, even a new—iridescent side of his cornucopious nature. And therefore of our own. If he can animate creatures like Shallow and Slender it is not excessive to expect him to do the same for us.

Much like the contrary views of him is the extreme to which many modern critics have been led by their admiration for the Falstaff scenes. Considering him betrayed, they take his remarks and scenes to be, not only a puncturing of courtly hypocrisy parading as patriotism, but the play's essential meaning. For modern men with their belief mainly in the 'natural', carried to the point where only self-interest and submission to the appetites seem honest, such interpretation is pretty inevitable. Of course, the most faithful reading of the play attests that Falstaff and his scenes do have a fundamental, if low and therefore limited, seriousness that must be reckoned with; and of course, they expose the frivolity and the selfishness hidden away in the high scenes under thick brocades of words no less than of dress. The play's comics, like the zany, intricate carvings in cathedral doors and pews and like those cathedrals' gargoyles, do their part in exorcising evil and in draining off excess by expressing it. But necessary though this exposure may be, rather than fatally damaging those high scenes, it brings us to the reality inside them and, by throwing it into low relief, helps us to realize it.

If it is a fact that by the end of Part II freedom as embodied in these gargoyles is in danger, if order finds itself so threatened or at least so bent on morality that it must outlaw these creatures, then we are indeed involved in a grave matter. Eccentrics and independents, increasingly assertive while the world thrives, are likely more and more to irritate the others, especially the authorities. The State, often in its growing success, which would tend to promote freedom and even extravagance, may become, by its fears on behalf of that success, too rigid to accommodate, let alone benefit from, such dissident elements. Then always more uniformity is exacted. This drying up of geniality, of capacity, may, as I suggested, be at the root of Antonio's sadness, his awareness, not only of the fundamental materialism of life, but of its expanding insistence everywhere, its profound hatred of music, merriment, freedom, and the carefree. So too in *Twelfth Night* Sir Toby Belch's urging of cakes and ale, before the kind of world emerging, may well be tinged with wistfulness if not melancholy.

In any case, challenges and dangers notwithstanding, English history is here having one of its great days, that of the newborn modern world. So great is it, as enacted in this work, that it seems much more than history, in its very reality as fabulous as the Homeric, say. Yet it is painfully clear everywhere that, though this play via its language breathes health and delight, disease and corruption are also loose, on a scale that jeopardizes all the rest. The reasons, beyond abundance itself, are not hard to find. The sickness' principal source can be traced to the society's center, that which should be the source of strength and stability, the King and his deeds in becoming king; the rotting corpse of Richard II refuses to stay buried, and its stench penetrates the world of *Henry IV*. Unfortunately as with virtually all societies, since none can be started out of nothing, this brave new world is founded on old corruption. Henry IV's abilities are most impressive; so are his intentions and his yearning for a unified kingdom, one of peace. Yet his example, his responsibility for the murder of a legitimate king, has brought the reverse of stability to England; and he must exert all his very considerable powers merely to keep his place. By the oneness of king and society, his dis-ease has been spreading throughout England even while it intensifies in his own person. Carrying on robberies and loose living generally, Falstaff and his crew are one manifestation of that dis-ease (however little we may want to stress their 'riot and dishonour') as are, much more urgently, the King's enemy lords. An even more poignant reminder of it, especially since the reminder seems to promise the dis-ease's prosperity after the King's death, is the conduct of his own son Hal.

The play opens with the King's delivering himself of a measured speech, similar to other such curtain raisers. It is a model of stately order, reminiscent in some degree of Richard II's oratory, a touch ironical, perhaps, coming from the eminently practical Bolingbroke, now immensely conscious of his role: the need to maintain a lofty distance from his audience. His oration is neatly divided between peace and war.

> So shaken as we are, so wan with care,
> Find we a time for frighted peace to pant,
> And breathe short-winded accents of new broils
> To be commenced in stronds afar remote.
> No more the thirsty entrance of this soil
> Shall daub her lips with her own children's blood.
> No more shall trenching war channel her fields,
> Nor bruise her flowerets with the arméd hoofs
> Of hostile paces: those opposéd eyes,
> Which like the meteors of a troubled heaven,

> *All of one nature, of one substance bred,*
> *Did lately meet in the intestine shock*
> *And furious close of civil butchery,*
> *Shall now, in mutual well-beseeming ranks,*
> *March all one way, and be no more opposed*
> *Against acquaintance, kindred, and allies.*
> *The edge of war, like an ill-sheathéd knife,*
> *No more shall cut his master.*

That knife, once let loose, is indeed hard to sheathe again or, for that matter, to hold so that it will not cut the hand that loosed it. But recalling the war just ended, he strives to settle it completely by putting his hope for abiding peace in the accents of something like a royal command. Most conspicuous in this attempt at order by way of rhetoric is the would-be bracing, repeated phrase 'no more', artfully, since somewhat unpredictably, placed. The many genitive phrases, occupied for the most part with violence, are also skilfully deployed, and exert themselves to contain or fix that violence, and so give a substance and stability to his words.

Then, with the immediate past taken care of, the King turns to the present and its occupation-to-be.

> *Therefore, friends,*
> *As far as to the sepulchre of Christ,*
> *Whose soldier now, under whose blesséd cross*
> *We are impresséd and engaged to fight,*
> *Forthwith a power of English shall we levy,*
> *Whose arms were moulded in their mothers' womb*
> *To chase these pagans in those holy fields*
> *Over whose acres walked those blesséd feet*
> *Which fourteen hundred years ago were nailed*
> *For our advantage on the bitter cross.*
> *But this our purpose now is twelve months old,*
> *And bootless 'tis to tell you we will go;*
> *Therefore we meet not now.*

Compared with the stiff, opening verses of Richard in his play, this speech at this point enjoys a most appealing fluidity, especially as its lines, keyed to the chasing of the pagans over the vast fields, vaster for the time Christ must span, sweep through the nonstopped five verses beginning 'Whose arms were moulded in their mothers' womb'. Beyond this fluidity our pleasure in the art of these lines is heightened by the way in which they, covering space and time, first by chasing then by walking, are braked by 'nailed' and finally weighed in 'advantage' as against 'bitter'. It is interesting to move from the 'blesséd cross' via those 'blesséd feet' to the advantaging 'bitter cross'. Not to recognize Henry's verbal powers, his suppleness of mind, especially sensitive to his times, is to miss some good part of him. Just to listen to Richard's initial blank verse in its official nature, shaped definite line by line, is to hear the difference.

> *Old John of Gaunt, time-honoured Lancaster,*
> *Hast thou, according to thy oath and band,*
> *Brought hither Henry Hereford, thy bold son,*
> *Here to make good the boist'rous late appeal,*
> *Which then our leisure would not let us hear,*
> *Against the Duke of Norfolk, Thomas Mowbray?*

It is also to appreciate the basic difference between the worlds these men represent. Henry IV's oppression at his own grave difficulties, most of them, he assumes, out of his dedicated effort to serve England and his people, helps to intensify his sympathy for, if not his feeling of identification with, Christ. Distressed by the civil war and the killing of Richard that provoked it, Henry would pay the penance he has been denied for a whole year and thereby, in one great common cause far afield from England itself, would heal his sorely bruised kingdom. In short, his repentance is a complex mixture of policy and feeling, and his present policy an attempt to serve both. Briskly he turns to the business at hand.

However, instead of his council's decree 'In forwarding this dear expedience' he learns that civil war has broken out again. Hotspur's valor and success against the Scotch naturally move Henry, especially at Westmoreland's statement that Hotspur's prize 'is a conquest for a prince to boast of', to thoughts of his own son. Henry admits:

> *Yea, there thou mak'st me sad and mak'st me sin*
> *In envy that my Lord Northumberland*
> *Should be the father to so blest a son,*

and proceeds to describe the difference between the two chief contenders in the play, a description bound to be fairly convincing coming from the father of one of them. For such strong words, and for much of the next scene that seems to fulfill them, who shall not believe this grieving father. Then when he weighs further evidence of Hotspur's nature, his pride in refusing to surrender most of his prisoners, we see what trouble is brewing between Henry and his supporters, the original conspirators against Richard II. It is one thing for Henry to admire Hotspur; quite another for Hotspur to oppose his will. Hotspur's character has been set out before us: the quality that makes him appealing also makes him a problem.

The second scene at once establishes the world Henry has just decried for his own son. Falstaff and Hal, in richly spiced prose, regale each other with a royal buffoonery that would indeed alarm and outrage Henry. (He is, we notice, a king with no time or mind for a jester or courtly clown.) It is amusing and most relevant that the first words of that mocker and enemy of time, Falstaff, should have to do with time. (Henry's first words also had to do with time and as mistakenly: 'So shaken as we are, so wan with care,/Find we a time for frighted Peace to pant. . . .' With consideration of time so quickly pressed upon us here, it does not seem excessive to suggest that it is a major matter in this play.) Falstaff yawningly asks, 'Now, Hal, what time of day is it, lad?' And Hal without a moment's pause laces into him:

> *Thou art so fat-witted, with drinking of old sack, and unbuttoning thee after supper, and sleeping upon benches after noon, that thou hast forgotten to demand that truly which thou wouldst truly know. What a devil hast thou to do with the time of the day? Unless hours were cups of sack, and minutes capons, and clocks the tongues of bawds, and dials the signs of leaping-houses, and the blessed sun himself a fair hot wench in flame-coloured taffeta, I see no reason why thou shouldst be so superfluous to demand the time of the day.*

Humor apart, from his first word Hal's opinion of Falstaff is never in doubt. But hours *are* cups of sack and minutes capons for Falstaff, or at least they are in prompting witty, gusty talk about them. Sly, plucked from his drunken bench in the tavern, found a momentary Eden of sorts in the practical joke of the hunting lord: an Eden, that is, till the actual play began; Falstaff, plucking himself out of the rigors of the court, has found his own Eden in a Slyesque tavern, one that will happily serve him till the 'play' or reality itself breaks in. Falstaff, rising to this raillery (we hear at once, in Hal's words and accents, what a robust boy he is), pretends it is praise:

> *Indeed, you come near me now, Hal; for we that take purses go by the moon and the seven stars and not by Phoebus, he, 'that wandering knight so fair.'*

He admits that he and his ways are not for the day, with its busy, prying nature. Falstaff and his cronies are moon-men. And if they cannot enjoy *A Midsummer Night's Dream's* balmy, lunar wood, they can at least steal by the moon in a world asleep under its influence.

Quickly then Falstaff, as is his wont, shifts subjects. And he proceeds to urge Hal:

> . . . *when thou art King, let not us that are squires of the night's body be called thieves of the day's beauty. Let us be Diana's foresters, gentlemen of the shade, minions of the moon; and let men say, we be men of good government, being governed, as the sea is, by our noble and chaste mistress the moon, under whose countenance we steal.*

It is 'natural' law, its government, that he and his obey. Hal rounds on him, and what might be thought mere wit-chaffing we soon recognize for the much greater mordancy it is. Never does Hal conceal his real sentiments from Falstaff, but Falstaff—also Hal's sharpest critics who accuse him of deceit—fails or refuses to attend to them; no doubt he assumes it pays him to pass them off lightly as banter. And so they go, Hal an obviously fitting mate in wit to Falstaff, an apprentice who already bids fair to surpass his master, and a critic whose acerb remarks Falstaff deftly dodges or turns to momentary advantage. Yet who, listening, can deny the serious tenor, bravura and all, of Hal's rejoinder?

> *Thou sayest well, and it holds well too; for the fortune of us that are the moon's men doth ebb and flow like the sea, being governed, as the sea is, by the moon. As for proof now: a purse of gold most resolutely snatched on Monday night and most dissolutely spent on Tuesday morning; got with swearing 'Lay by' and spent with crying 'Bring in:' now in as low an ebb as the foot of the ladder, and by and by in as high a flow as the ridge of the gallows.*

Falstaff, whatever his persiflage, has heard. For some half dozen speeches later he suddenly asks:

> *But, I prithee, sweet wag, shall there be gallows standing in England when thou art King? And resolution thus fobbed as it is with the rusty curb of old father antic the law? Do not thou, when thou art King, hang a thief.*

Falstaff's would-be topsy-turvying of law and order is plain enough here. Equally plain is Hal's blunt answer: 'No; thou shalt.' However generously Falstaff chooses to understand it, we need not be surprised by his confessing a moment later, in what may be his lurking suspicion of the truth: " 'Sblood, I am as melancholy as a gib cat or a lugged bear.' That Shakespeare's prime comic should come to this!

Drollery it is no doubt. Yet were one to know where to have Falstaff, and fortunately one does not, one might be tempted to propose that, for a comic who is all vitality and mercuriality, he is astonishingly much preoccupied with aging, frailties, dying and death. But if there is one thing we are accustomed to in Shakespeare by now it is his infusing his comedy with sadness, ranging all the way to anguish. Gratiano, we recall, trying to jolly Antonio early in *The Merchant of Venice*, said:

> *Let me play the fool!*
> *With mirth and laughter let old wrinkles come.*
> *And let my liver rather heat with wine*
> *Than my heart cool with mortifying groans.*
> *Why should a man, whose blood is warm within,*
> *Sit like his grandsire cut in alabaster,*
> *Sleep when he wakes, and creep into the jaundice*
> *By being peevish?*

Why indeed? Yet in a world like ours who, even with the best, stouthearted will, can be impervious to its blows inside and out? But Falstaff, old though he may be, is even victorious with this, and makes it by his audacious wit his own. For spirit of play that he is, and age and dying be damned, he insists on making gaiety of winter itself and, at least until late in Part II, of melancholy. Also, we must remember, melancholy was very fashionable at this time. Both Hal and Falstaff, by their droll reeling off of varieties of melancholy, underscore that fact.

After the laying out of plans for that night's robbery Hal, alone, reveals, now properly in poetry, the truth of his feelings, his intentions, no less deliberate and calculated than the best of his father's:

> *I know you all, and will awhile uphold*
> *The unyoked humour of your idleness.*
> *Yet herein will I imitate the sun,*
> *Who doth permit the base contagious clouds*
> *To smother up his beauty from the world,*
> *That, when he please again to be himself,*
> *Being wanted, he may be more wondered at*
> *By breaking through the foul and ugly mists*
> *Of vapours that did seem to strangle him.*

Strong, even fierce, renunciatory language this is; but Shakespeare, it appears, wants to make it clear from the start that Hal is already himself and the man he will be. Whatever his lingerings in, and his returns to, the world of Falstaff, Hal's mind was long ago made up, and he is biding his time, waiting for the proper moment to emerge. He has a happy sense of the dramatic, the need for change and the unpredictable.

> *So, when this loose behaviour I throw off*
> *And pay the debt I never promiséd,*
> *By how much better than my word I am,*
> *By so much shall I falsify men's hopes;*
> *And like bright metal on a sullen ground,*
> *My reformation, glitt'ring o'er my fault,*
> *Shall show more goodly and attract more eyes*
> *Than that which hath no foil to set it off.*
> *I'll so offend to make offence a skill,*
> *Redeeming time when men think least I will.*

In all his hobnobbing with the vulgar then, Hal wisely (unlike Richard II, say) keeps his beauty, his nobility, a little like a fairytale prince, concealed and to himself. And time, given his rich sense of its meaning and its diverse usefulness, his talent for timing, is the element he works in. In fact, time is the element of all the main characters. Henry IV at the play's outset, we saw, wished to redeem the time, but local or immediate time burst in to prevent it. Time for him has thus become a mere wearying, endless sequence. For Falstaff, time is little other than the occasion for amusement, and he strives to make a kind of essence of existence itself, low existence at that. But we must recognize that this low existence is, on the whole, an excuse for high, effervescent wit and hilarious humor. Hal, on the other hand, realizes full well that there is, as the Bible has it, a time for this and a time for that.

Hal's soliloquy, it is true, makes nothing of his enjoyment of Falstaff's company, an enjoyment, however, that his other lively speeches, despite their barbs for Falstaff, plainly betray. In examining earlier plays I have said a good deal about the unemployed, often bored, young lord, who attempts to distract himself or to make a new role for himself. In *Love's Labour's Lost* the King of Navarre sought to establish a School of Night and a different world for himself and his friends. Theseus, impatiently awaiting his marriage, set up a brief regime of merriment. Hal is such a young lord. With an able father in charge of state affairs, and with his sense of the troubled, stifling tedium prevalent in the court, his being elsewhere should not surprise us. He has found such an elsewhere in Falstaff and his cronies. For Hal in the tavern, Falstaff can be the jester that he cannot be in the long-faced court. And here we are in the midst of two vying worlds again, the court versus the tavern, day-men versus moon-men; in the midst of the churning, plot-ridden, daily 'real' world we discover a charmed and charming world of revelry. For a spell Hal is able to retire into it. One remembers Creon's response when Oedipus accuses him of plotting to seize his throne: 'Who would be king if he can, as I do, enjoy his privileges and rights without his duties and responsibilities?' Richard II assumed that only a king could so enjoy himself. A prince would be a likelier candidate.

At this point I recall Auden's surprise in his essay 'The Prince's Dog' at the company Hal keeps. 'Surely one could expect to see him surrounded by daring, rather sinister juvenile delinquents and beautiful gold-digging whores.' Till now, it is true, Shakespeare's young lords tended to travel in like-minded, carefree, devil-may-care packs. But they usually found part of their amusement in comic, if not ludicrous, retainers. For his purposes, serious and secret from the start, Hal can ill afford confidants on his own level; Falstaff is lord enough. Furthermore, the young lords of earlier plays are chummily together only till seriousness strikes either their principal member or all of them. Certainly Falstaff and his crew are nothing like La Dolce Vita. Nor are they sinister juvenile delinquents. Senior delinquents who have kept the child's sense of gaiety and play would be more like it. Enchanted wood or not, the tavern in its snug, familiar atmosphere—like a hearth whose fire counterpoints a most amiable winter's tale, more cosy for the winds just outside, the gathering storms of rebellion and violence—exudes a fairyworld quality while the moon, peeping in, reflects most intoxicatingly on the flames, the wine, and the bubbling wit. And the tavern's charm is all the more potent for being so obviously fragile and evanescent. For a brief, suspended time at least, these fat crickets and proud grasshoppers will not submit, not for all the diligent ants in the world. Of course Hal, like other good, young, noble Englishmen, might have gone off on the Grand Tour to Venice or Rome or Paris or possibly—like Hamlet—to some university. Instead, his plans being what they are, and by the interwovenness of *Henry IV*, he prefers to stay at home with Falstaff's homely, native glamor, his irreverent, often most relevant wit.

Auden continues:

As the play proceeds, our surprise is replaced by another kind of puzzle, for the better we come to know Falstaff, the clearer it becomes that the world of historical reality which a chronicle play claims to imitate is not a world which he can inhabit.

Henry IV's realistic, local detail, its bustle and revel of a swarm of personages straight out of Shakespeare's own day, can hardly be tucked into the dimensions of a chronicle play. Yet there is some truth in Auden's observation. However, one could say that, for most purposes, Falstaff, tavern-becalmed, does not inhabit the world of historical reality until well on in Part I and then—and especially in Part II—with increasingly disastrous results to himself. At that time he proves that he cannot—should not—inhabit it, but for reasons, I shall try to show, other than Auden's. According to him, 'Falstaff has not and could not have found his true home because Shakespeare was only a poet. For that he was to wait nearly two hundred years till Verdi wrote his last opera.' The heightened, timeless world of music is Auden's notion of Falstaff's native element. He does 'not belong to the temporal world of change'. In his dedication to merriment and in his resentment at growing old, Falstaff would surely be happy to agree with this version of him.

But the facts are, I believe, rather different. For whatever our yearning for an existence beyond time with its ravages, Shakespeare knows better: no one is 'an unkillable, self-sufficient immortal'. The world at large—things as they are—comes first. And even though it is the destructive element, it is also the one we depend on for living and, now and then, for living jubilantly. Only this world supplies the resources whereby a few of us realize a style so brilliant that we appear to be invulnerable in the aura of our own personalities. Falstaff is a magician if only through words, almost able, he makes us feel, to bid time loiter and gawk like a yokel. Yet for all his guises and disguises Falstaff too requires a line, life-giving if tenuous, to the world at large. Like Richard II he too needs money, food, shelter, and friends (an audience?). Thus he takes it for granted that, when his own wits fail him, Hal will bail him out of debt and mischief. Shakespeare's earlier, almost enclosed garden comedies lived in the brief time of grace afforded them by some enchanted wood or a spell of moonlight. At the same time these enclosures, no less than the most abstracted college, Navarre's for instance, not to say the dingy little Night-School of Falstaff, are dependent on the outside world. It is only by the grace, or at least the indifference, of that world and by the means derived from it that such communities can be established and go on in the first place. To think of such schools, at least of the Falstaffian kidney, emerging at all and surviving, if only for a time, in a beleagured and beleaguring world, always threatening to flood and muddy our sack, is heartening. However, in maintaining that Falstaff should be spared the world of *Henry IV*, isn't Auden missing the point and splendor of the play entirely? It is, I firmly believe, precisely the brilliant amalgamation of Falstaff and his comedy, comedy which Shakespeare had by now thoroughly explored, with history, the public world he had mastered in earlier plays, that makes *Henry IV* so magnificent. Kept out of the histories till now, comedy is back with a vengeance.

But what kind of school or court is Falstaff's? It is of course that of wit and of rollicksome fun, supervised by one who has awakened from the dream of reality, 'the nightmare of history'. With the nonsense of the court and the world at large bade slip, the good sense of the senses in all their naturalness, employed by living for its own dear sake, is made the law. And Falstaff, usually called a Lord of Misrule, sees to it that his gamesome court's laws are to the letter observed. A ruler he is, capable as any king in his unique way of getting into scrapes and getting out of them. Fat, old and full of infirmities, Falstaff would seem to be little more than a perfect butt, farce's very favorite. And he is a butt, of bottomless, spicy ale, easily broached and tapped by all—not least of all by himself. All his weaknesses, through the happy exercise, the inspiring challenge, that they give his tireless wit, are devoutly to be wished. Nothing, we begin to think, is strong or able enough to capsize him. In fact, his time seems mainly spent in collaborating with his followers to get him into always tighter corners, apparently inescapable ones; these provide him with opportunities to exhibit his skills and by their authority to extricate himself with delight for every-one, thereby newly affirming his right to 'rule'. For kings, especially of such uncertain courts, must constantly prove themselves. In his fashion Falstaff is no less masterly than Henry IV. And his joy in his role, we can safely say, far exceeds Henry's in his.

To make a comparison in some ways ludicrous enough to impress even Falstaff, I suggest that he has established a court of the kind Richard II desired, believed he deserved and in truth had—a court in which words, Falstaff's words, are, for the time being, law. By the amiable glow of his personality Falstaff has persuaded the things around him, basking in that glow, to do his magical bidding. And human beings gladly bask in it as well. Sly, asleep, was spirited away by a hunting lord from a tavern to a mansion. Here, so able is Falstaff to convert the dinginess of his tavern into glamor, a lord, a prince at that, has for a time been captivated and led from the royal palace to that tavern. Yet the fragility of that ambience is clear enough. Meant to live only in the moon's tenuous realm, Falstaff's is indeed an exiguous kingdom, one, like the fairy and lover's world of *A Midsummer Night's Dream*, in danger of being swept away by the first intruding beams of daylight.

But why, aside from the reasons already specified, should a lively young man, a king's son, find such a meager, not to say basically tawdry, environment attractive? Hal understands how much is to be learned from a rare, opulent character like Falstaff, this 'cause that wit is in other men'. For if Falstaff seems out of the world, to the degree that he is rooted in his senses he is the master of common-sense, committed to the senses' meaning—they act as his touchstone—no less than to their pleasures. Thus he is a happy antidote to the court which more times than not, in its professed ideals and confused desires, wanders far from reality and common-sense. 'Wit' in this play, beyond its more obvious meanings, has to do with the exercise and fulfilment of one's mental faculties. Hal, appreciating the variety of men he meets in the tavern world, his subjects-to-be, as well as the variety Falstaff sparklingly bubbles forth, appreciates also what self-realization he can come to in their midst and what lessons he can learn towards understanding other men.

At the same time we must not blink the other side of it. Hal must also find out what is going on in the world outside the court, the dangers, the crimes, the outrages. How else, once he is king, will he be able to recognize them quickly and to deal with them? As late as the Fourth Act of Part II King Henry still fails to understand Hal and his appetite for Falstaff. Warwick tries to reassure King Henry:

> *My gracious lord, you look beyond him quite.*
> *The Prince but studies his companions*
> *Like a strange tongue, wherein, to gain the language,*
> *'Tis needful that the most immodest word*
> *Be looked upon and learned, which once attained,*
> *Your Highness knows, comes to no further use*
> *But to be known and hated. So, like gross terms,*

> *The Prince will in the perfectness of time*
> *Cast off his followers.*

Stern and incomplete though Warwick's interpretation of Hal's conduct may be, as far as it goes it is accurate, not far in fact from Hal's own austerity in his first soliloquy in Part I. Thus Warwick's 'in the perfectness of time' is perfect in echoing Hal's concern with and sense of time and timing. And perhaps, in all their aptness, a measure of resonance beyond what Warwick intends or knows stirs in his next words:

> *And their memory*
> *Shall as a pattern or a measure live,*
> *By which his Grace must mete the lives of others,*
> *Turning past evils to advantage.*

If Falstaff can turn diseases to commodities, Hal will be able to turn evils to advantage.

No doubt all this sounds too deliberate and too ponderous, and no doubt it is. Nonetheless, apart from Hal's amusement in Falstaff and in the play of the imagination Falstaff releases from him before his arduous labors begin, he does have a profound sense of the magnitude of the role he will soon have to fill; of the training, the seasoning, it requires. Who can deny the element of truth in Falstaff's praise of sherry:

> *Hereof comes it that Prince Hal is valiant; for the cold blood he did*
> *naturally inherit of his father, he hath, like lean, sterile, and bare*
> *land, manured, husbanded, and tilled with excellent endeavour of*
> *drinking good and good store of fertile sherris, that he is become very*
> *hot and valiant.*

More exactly, Hal has drunk deeply of that brimming bombard, that overflowing cask, Falstaff. For Hal is fortunately little like his cold and incomplete younger brother, Prince John of Lancaster, all policy and state. As Falstaff says of John, 'Good faith, this same young soberblooded boy doth not love me, nor a man cannot make him laugh; but that's no marvel, he drinks no wine.' The geniality of the spirits ripened out of the good earth must loosen, not to say enlarge, the spirits in a man. (City habitué though he is, a naturalist of the indoors, it is not surprising that at the end Falstaff babbles of green fields.) Most relevantly Falstaff later observes, 'It is certain fact that, either wise bearing or ignorant carriage is caught, as men take diseases, one of another; therefore let men take heed of their company.' Hal takes such heed, takes courses, one might say, when and as he needs them, in timely, graduating sequence.

The early comedies often concentrated on education, the need of young men to be instructed, in books certainly, but perhaps even more in the senses and the feelings, in the ways of life itself. Usually, especially for the feelings, a young woman was required to instruct via those most efficient agents, beauty and love. But in the histories till now education was negligible, and what lessons were learned were learned too late. Furthermore, these histories, with their atmosphere of physical violence and war, did not favor women whose realm is mainly the domestic. Thus they usually were fairly passive (if in their very passivity, as in *Richard III*, often most potent). Now in *Henry IV*, with comedy resumed and some touch, we might say, of the domestic introduced in the tavern, education again becomes all-important, even crucial, and happily successful. But it derives not from a lovely young woman but from an old fat man, a disreputable one at that.

And it is not hard to understand, disreputableness and all, how Falstaff functions, how – more than any Audenesque glittering whore and with a mercuriality Cleopatra might have appreciated – effective and educative he is. He is a kind of low, earthly Socrates (who himself was well compared with Silenus), a latterday satyr who, like Silenus the moon-man, can educate a young man in home truths, strengthen his earth sense, introduce him to the wisdom that inheres in mirth, the comic sense. Without this wisdom a man is incomplete since unaware of mankind's duality, unawakened to that objectivity which enables him to regard himself at a reasonable distance and to laugh at himself no less than at others. Dionysus, tutored and companioned by Silenus, identified with goats and satyrs and the emancipating of the spirits by the kindness of wine, became the presiding deity of theater, of comedy and tragedy alike, its origin and its life-blood. For he taught holiday, self-forgetting revelries by way of the senses away from the drab routine normal to daily life. Falstaff is of this line, a spirit of spirits, of the intoxicating mystery of earth. And he must be understood and used accordingly, must be given his ample due. But he must also – lest this intoxication override all else and tragedy, chaos and dismembering follow – be coped with. The Apollonian must be remembered at least as much. At the same time, however, though Falstaff seems a devotee of the senses and of their offspring, play and gaiety, by his buoyancy – for in Part I at least we never see him drunk or engrossed in the senses and for themselves alone—we understand that he lives by and with them, for their rich bouquet.

Having lived long with observation and a most retentive memory, he possesses boundless provisions of experience. Thus for a time he makes—and is—a god's plenty in a little room, that of the tavern and his commodious being. And for a time how shall that plenty, distilled with his wit and served up piping-hot, not seem sweeter than all the rest of the world? Especially since the rest of the world at its quintessential best seems to be swarming around him. For he is the actor consummate. He lives for the myriad parts he can, spontaneously or deliberately, play. This is his freedom. Of course, because of his bulk he can scarcely be expected to move much, let alone act. He must rely chiefly on his wits and his words, his ability to 'leap about' on the bare boards of the tavern by assuming other men's roles. And for the joy with which he does assume them we can judge that no other taste delights or fulfils him like the taste of being someone else.

In Bottom, Mercutio, and others we have already met effervescent, spontaneous actors. But Falstaff differs from these early actors—at least Bottom—fundamentally. However much he shares their gusto, he is not, until well on in Part I and in Part II, self-involved. Bottom, we recall, desires all the parts but primarily to be himself and more himself; like the puffed-up frog he would fill the world, have it be nothing but Bottom. Earlier characters, the Armadoes and Holofernes, winsome though they were, remain superb, wholly realized, strutting, opaque parodies. And we do have a new member of their company here in Pistol. But, aside from his resolution to avoid being caught and held to anything, Falstaff is a parodist supreme. Mercutio, it is true, has brief moments of this; but brief he and these moments have to be for the purposes of a tragedy like *Romeo and Juliet*. That is, like Richard III only till now, does Falstaff play many parts. However, Richard III, remarkable though he may also be for his immense enjoyment in performing, has his reason for playing parts, a great end, and a desperate one at that. Falstaff, though he can hardly be absolved of self-interest—his play-acting, like Hamlet's, is often a mode of evasion—is, at least for most of Part I, mainly taken up by the roles themselves, the relish of their performance.

We need not wonder, therefore, that so many are smitten with him. Here at last seems to be a man able, like his creator himself, to circumvent the limitations of being a man, the prison of a particular time and place. Already in *The Taming of the Shrew* Petruchio had set himself to instructing Kate in such play, the one way we have of escaping our respective prisons. By learning this freedom Kate could accept and be herself. Furthermore, Falstaff's being a superfluous man–like Richard II with his uselessness, one who will not yield to society and its requirements–has an almost irresistible appeal for many. Malcontent that Falstaff essentially is, in his chameleon-like changing of roles he becomes Shakespeare's most telling comic 'belcontent'. And his most convincing comic individual. Here at last I draw on Keats' valuable obiter scriptum, his notion of the negative capability. For him, quite rightly, Shakespeare was its supreme instance: the genius so enamored of the multifarious world around him that he absorbs himself entirely, finding himself insignificant beside them, in the variety of beings that world pours forth or, in his case, in the beings his genius pours forth. Falstaff, as much as any other Shakespearean character, partakes of his maker's genius: he is a character who exists by being–by creating– other characters, by being the parodist sublime.

It is this rare gift that Hal as a man and an eventual king is drawn to. In fact, from the play's start, we saw, he is Falstaffianly other than he seems, playing a part that has taken everyone in. In a sense, he is like most of those in the court, pretending to be different from what they are. But Hal's pretense is quite the reverse of theirs, and unique. They pretend–see Henry IV–to be better than they are and convince no one. Hal pretends to be far worse than he is, a full-time playboy, and convinces everyone. In a topsy-turvy, bad time one often must, to protect oneself and one's purpose, conceal one's true identity. Thus he is the ablest 'actor' of them all; for he deceives all, is truly a royal counterfeit, on behalf of truth, honor, justice, order. It is Falstaff who can best help Hal carry on and carry out his disguise.

With Hal's gift for learning, and learning at once, from others– apart from Falstaff, his father serves him, and the Lord Chief Justice– and with the importance of that gift in his career, we should consider his other major 'teacher', Hotspur. For many critics Hotspur and Falstaff, the two real conspirators, threaten to tear the kingdom and the play in half. Hotspur's appeal is, aside from Henry IV's endorsement, patent from the start. His wife tells us in Part II, a play full, unlike Part I, of definitions and character observations (for Part II has a past, a 'reality', that of Part I, to draw on):

> *. . . by his light*
> *Did all the chivalry of England move*

To do brave acts: he was indeed the glass
Wherein the noble youth did dress themselves.
He had no legs that practised not his gait;
And speaking thick, which nature made his blemish,
Became the accents of the valiant;
For those that could speak low and tardily
Would turn their own perfection to abuse,
To seem like him; so that in speech, in gait,
In diet, in affections of delight,
In military rules, humours of blood,
He was the mark and glass, copy and book,
That fashioned others.

Thus, because of Hotspur's virtues so gallantly on display, if the company of Falstaff seems to besmirch Hal, by comparison, the comparison that the King himself first proposes, the conduct of Hotspur does so all the more positively. And yet, we should notice, if he is a glass, he is a confining one; in fact, altogether in harmony with his self-crammed nature, he is no glass at all; he is too opaque for that. Rather he supplies others with an image they must imitate; he obliges all, even to the abuse of their perfection, to change to – that is, ape – him. Falstaff, on the other hand, inspires them to be themselves at their lustiest.

For all Hotspur's crusty humor – a volcano with wit! – and occasional insight into others – Glendower and his magic, for example, or the young lovers – he is of such divine peremptoriness, so fixed on the expression and imposition of his own fiery personality, he can hardly pause to know himself, let alone others. Noble and honourable he is, but it is a nobility and an honor altogether out of and for himself. In his own words:

By heaven, methinks it were an easy leap
To pluck bright honour from the pale-faced moon,
Or dive into the bottom of the deep,
Where fathom-line could never touch the ground,
And pluck up drownéd honour by the locks;
So he that doth redeem her thence might wear
Without corrival all her dignities:
But out upon this half-faced fellowship!

Several times, like Hal, he speaks of 'redeeming'. Thus a little earlier he urged his father and his uncle,

> *. . . yet time serves wherein you may redeem*
> *Your banished honours, and restore yourselves*
> *Into the good thoughts of the world again; . . .*

For Hal the redeeming is also personal, but aware of responsibilities larger than himself, he would not merely employ time to serve his own purposes but to 'redeem the time' itself. However, as Hotspur's father says of him just before his speech on honour, 'Imagination of some great exploit/Drives him beyond the bounds of patience.' He is bitten as by swarms of stinging flies, is, when not employed, a blade that cuts itself in a thousand places. The opacity his impatience produces in him, the mistakes it inevitably results in regarding others and events, mistakes he seems to leap to to prove his defiance, his pride, his superiority over circumstances and their consequences, these are what Hal quickly sees and learns to avoid. He will not be one to indulge himself with sentiments like 'I will ease my heart,/Albeit I make a hazard of my head.' or 'O! I could divide myself and go to buffets, . . .'

It is amusing to review Hal's and Hotspur's version of each other as well as to compare their stances. Scornfully Hotspur says of Hal:

> *And that same sword-and-buckler Prince of Wales,*
> *But that I think his father loves him not*
> *And would be glad he met with some mischance,*
> *I would have him poisoned with a pot of ale.*

Later, when the battle-forces gather, Hotspur asks:

> *Where is his son,*
> *The nimble-footed madcap Prince of Wales,*
> *And his comrades, that daffed the world aside,*
> *And bid it pass?*

On the other hand, Hal can say:

> *I am not yet of Percy's mind, the Hotspur of the North, he that kills me some six or seven dozen of Scots at a breakfast, washes his hands, and says to his wife, 'Fie upon this quiet life! I want work.' 'O my sweet Harry,' says she, 'how many hast thou killed today?' 'Give my roan horse a drench,' says he, and answers, 'Some fourteen,' an hour after, 'a trifle, a trifle.'*

How accurate a description this is, even to the interruption of 'an hour after', the scene just before deliciously attests. Hotspur, ignoring his wife's question on what he is up to by ordering his roan, collects himself to say to her:

> *Away, you trifler! Love! I love thee not,*
> *I care not for thee, Kate; this is no world*
> *To play with mammets and to tilt with lips:*
> *We must have bloody noses and cracked crowns,*
> *And pass them current too. God's me, my horse!*

Hal's caricature has brilliantly caught the absurdity of Hotspur's unmitigated blood-and-thunder. But their difference is plain. Hal is 'not yet of Percy's mind', but he will be when the occasion requires. For Hotspur, on the other hand, 'this is no world/To play at mammets and to tilt with lips: . . .' For a temperament like his it rarely is.

But as Hotspur's words on honor suggest, he does not know himself even as a speaker. Nor, for that matter, does he seem to have any idea of how much, tied as he is to his own tongue, he talks. In a sense, like Falstaff, Hotspur is one of Shakespeare's 'plain' speakers and plain-dealers. At least he plumes himself on being direct, curt, down to earth. Tangy words and all, he never for a moment recognizes what a poet he is, especially since his contempt for poetry is based on a most limited notion of it. Thus he says to Glendower's

> *I can speak English, lord, as well as you,*
> *For I was trained up in the English court;*
> *Where, being but young, I franéd to the harp*
> *Many an English ditty lovely well,*
> *And gave the tongue an helpful ornament;*
> *A virtue that was never seen in you.*

with a brusqueness and would-be harshness that amounts to superb poetry:

> *Marry, and I'm glad of it with all my heart.*
> *I had rather be a kitten and cry mew*
> *Than one of these same metre ballad-mongers;*
> *I had rather hear a brazen canstick turned,*
> *Or a dry wheel grate on the axle-tree;*
> *And that would set my teeth nothing on edge,*
> *Nothing so much as mincing poetry:*
> *'Tis like the forced gait of a shuffling nag.*

Understandably for such a headlong stallion, who would be ever immersed in action and nothing but action, the lyrical in its dallying,

the self-conscious preening of courtiers, is bound to be repellent. As
for heroic verse, why that when there are deeds to be done? We need
only remember his first words in the play when he explains his conduct
to Henry IV, ascribing it mainly to 'a certain lord' 'perfumed like a
milliner', who questioned him, just from battle, 'With many holiday
and lady terms.' After his exchange with Glendower, a little later in
self-justification he even betters his words on the Welsh magician:

> *O! he's as tedious*
> *As a tired horse, a railing wife;*
> *Worse than a smoky house. I had rather live*
> *With cheese and garlic in a windmill, far,*
> *Than feed on cates and have him talk to me*
> *In any summer-house in Christendom.*

(We know how important horses are to him, and we have seen one
next to a railing wife in Hotspur's scene with Lady Percy. For one
who would be spending his life mettlesomely enthroned on a horse, a
tired horse like 'a shuffling nag' must be even worse than a railing
wife.) All this of an ally he dearly needs! His uncle rightly rebukes him
for his lack of patience, his 'pride, haughtiness, opinion, and disdain.'

Hotspur, who despite his temper is generosity itself, quickly
acknowledges these words, then passes on to his most charming,
exceptionally mellow scene, one involving ballad-mongering. Mortimer
is about to part with Glendower's daughter, who knows only Welsh.
As she speaks, Mortimer says:

> *I understand thy looks: that pretty Welsh*
> *Which thou pourest down from these swelling heavens*
> *I am too perfect in; and, but for shame,*
> *In such a parley would I answer thee.*
> *I understand thy kisses and thou mine,*
> *And that's a feeling disputation;*
> *But I will never be a truant, love,*
> *Till I have learned thy language; for thy tongue*
> *Makes Welsh as sweet as ditties highly penned,*
> *Sung by a fair queen in a summer's bower,*
> *With ravishing division, to her lute.*

This tribute to ditties in a summer's bower echoes most amusingly
Hotspur's words, his scoffing at 'mincing poetry' and his aversion to
hearing Glendower carry on about his magic 'In any summer-house in

Christendom'. Then, with Mortimer's head in her lap, his wife sings him such a ditty while Glendower bids musicians, that like Ariel 'Hang in the air a thousand leagues from hence', be here and at work. Thereupon Hotspur's realistic wit, pricked by this idyllic scene and momentarily relaxed, finds some of its happiest expression. He bids his wife:

> *Come, Kate, thou art perfect in lying down. Come, quick, quick, that I may lay my head in thy lap.*

The music plays; Hotspur, moved to poetry, observes:

> *Now I perceive the devil understands Welsh;*
> *And 'tis no marvel he is so humorous.*
> *By'r lady, he's a good musician.*

His wife most pointedly rejoins:

> *Then should you be nothing but musical, for you are altogether governed by humours. Lie still, ye thief, and hear the lady sing in Welsh.*

But Hotspur is off to his habitual and characteristic 'I had rather': 'I had rather hear Lady, my brach, howl in Irish.' Appropriately enough for him, his dog's name is Lady. Then he asks his wife for a song too. And at her 'Not mine, in good sooth' he once more vents his feeling about 'holiday and lady terms':

> *Not yours, 'in good sooth!' Heart! you swear like a comfit-maker's wife. Not you 'in good sooth,' and, 'as true as I live,' and 'as God shall mend me,' and 'as sure as day,'*

And, stirred up now, he takes to mouth-filling poetry:

> *And giv'st such sarcenet surety for thy oaths*
> *As if thou never walk'st further than Finsbury.*
> *Swear me, Kate, like a lady as thou art,*
> *A good mouth-filling oath, and leave 'in sooth,'*
> *And such protest of pepper-gingerbread,*
> *To velvet-guards and Sunday citizens.*

We have here his version of a 'lady'.

We might expect such impatience with magic and with poetic language, let alone verbal frills and euphemisms, from a world all activity, one overwhelmed by the pressing encounters of history. Nonetheless, it is striking that magic and bewitchment, prominent in the early comedies at least atmospherically, tend to play little part in the histories. Of course history itself by its nature is contrary to magic and might be expected to be dismissive of it. Yet much of the magical seems to inhere in Richard III. Superstitions and all, when he needs magic to improve his cause he readily assumes its presence and its effects. However, this magic is more announced than seen; and in the historical plays, apart from the mysterious workings out of fate, we recognize chiefly men's own faculties, their violent or crafty acts and the 'witchcraft of wit': that of Richard III, of Richard II, which works only on himself, and of Falstaff, a bewitching or charm that moves others not so much to action or to change as to delight in his wayward skill and then, often to their surprise, in their own. Glendower, for all his assumption of extraordinary powers, plays a very minor role in *Henry IV*, one altogether aborted by the would-be hard-headed, irascible Hotspur. From his own words in their magical quality, '. . . it were an easy leap/To pluck bright honour from the pale-faced moon' and so on, and from his father's comment on him here, 'Imagination of some great exploit/Drives him beyond the bounds of patience,' we might expect some sympathy in Hotspur for the magic that Glendower claims, his 'I can call spirits from the vasty deep." But, no, Hotspur's respect for the 'imagination' lies exclusively in thinking of, then executing, some great deed, as 'magic' for him resides entirely in his own mind, in his expectation of what his own strength and courage can do.

Yet despite this amiable 'Welsh' interlude, and though both Hotspur and Falstaff are first-rate poets, similar in their proclivity to pungent terms and images and to plain-dealing, they are finally and fundamentally as opposite as their names suggest. Falstaff is committed to living itself and to a host-like welcoming of it. But he knows the relevancy of language to living: as a comic, often exposing comment on it (much, it is true, like Hotspur's use of it above); as a comic relief; and as a mirth-making delight in itself. He never suffers from Hotspur's testy, often flyaway, sky-storming impatience. Yet he can resemble Hotspur in a longwindedness claiming to be its opposite. As Falstaff says to Hal in one of their name-calling contests (in a language also reminiscent of Petruchio at his best): 'O! for breath to utter what is like thee! you tailor's yard, you sheath, you bow-case, you vile standing-tuck,—' this after having delivered himself of ' 'Sblood, you starveling, you elf-skin, you dried neat's-tongue, you bull's pizzle, you stock-fish!'

And here, no less than elsewhere with Falstaff and in his parody of Hotspur, Hal proves how quickly he has mastered their expression. Pungency aside, however, one of the most notable instances of Hal's capacity for learning occurs in Act II, Scene IV (and, tellingly, directly after Percy's impatience with his wife). Poins asks 'Where hast been, Hal?' and Hal replies:

> *With three or four loggerheads amongst three or four score hogs-heads. I have sounded the very base string of humility. Sirrah, I am sworn brother to a leash of drawers, and can call them all by their christen names, as Tom, Dick, and Francis.*

The pertinence of such knowledge to a king-to-be is obvious.

> *They take it already upon their salvation, that though I be but Prince of Wales, yet I am the king of courtesy; ...*

Already in *Richard II* we met references to Bolingbroke's 'humble and familiar courtesy' to poor artisans. Early in the First Act of *Henry IV*, Hotspur, spitting out his contempt for Bolingbroke, 'this king of smiles', bridles when he recalls Bolingbroke's conduct to him at their first meeting: 'Why, what a candy deal of courtesy/This fawning greyhound then did proffer me!' And in the Third Act, even while Henry IV rebukes Hal for being so 'lavish' of his presence, 'So common-hackneyed in the eyes of men,/So stale and cheap to vulgar company,' and for not being like him: 'By being seldom seen, I could not stir,/But like a comet I was wondered at,' Henry himself admits to Hal:

> *And then I stole all courtesy from heaven,*
> *And dressed myself in such humility*
> *That I did pluck allegiance from men's hearts,*
> *Loud shouts and salutations from their mouths,*
> *Even in the presence of the crownèd King.*

Now, almost an act earlier, Hal tell us that it is exactly by his growing 'a companion to the common streets', by his 'vile participation', that the drawers think him 'the king of courtesy'. They assure him 'when I am King of England, I shall command all the good lads in Eastcheap.' Finally, repeating some of their lingo, he boasts: 'I am so good a proficient in one quarter of an hour, that I can drink with any tinker in his own language during my life.'

Next, 'to drive away the time till Falstaff come' and to prove his proficiency, he plays his little trick on the dimwitted drawer, Francis.

And on Falstaff's arriving, at Poins' 'But hark ye, what cunning match have you made with this jest of the drawer? Come, what's the issue?' Hal confesses:

I am now of all humours that have showed themselves humours since the old days of goodman Adam to the pupil age of this present twelve o'clock at midnight.

That is, 'it was just a whim of mine: I am in the mood to indulge any fancy any man has ever been possessed by since the creation itself.' Compare this in its gaiety with Lady Percy's charge, affectionate it is true, against Hotspur: '. . . you are altogether governed by humours.' One plays at them; the other is driven by them. We might consider which of these men—the one capable of multiple moods, those of the world he is soon to command, or the one possessed by his own moods, usually with a single, most passionate intensity—is likely to make a better king. There are those no doubt who would plump for the passionate intensity. Yet when the crucial moment is upon him, in battle for instance, Hal rises to an intensity no less impressive, one reinforced by large intelligence as well.

In any case, much though Hotspur has publicly shamed him, Hal is pleased to have one such formidable opponent. For, as he says, by defeating Hotspur he will at one blow crop his glories and instantly become the champion. I have indicated from the start that in my view Hal is the protagonist, the hero, of *Henry IV*; for he is the one character who can learn from all, who can grow, who knows how to use himself, and time, occasions, words. Gone to school to Falstaff and Hotspur, he masters the absorbed detachment, the awareness by way of words, of the one and the directness, when necessary the fiery action, of the other. Thus, like an ideal Homeric hero, he is first in words and deeds, knows when one or the other should be used and how much one should be the complement of the other. At the same time he is the living link, the unifying element, between all the scenes and the play's various worlds. His simultaneous command of word and gesture, thought and act, makes it altogether clear that he alone, the most accomplished, realized man in England, deserves to be king.

Neither figure, not Hotspur, not Falstaff, whatever his fascination, is enough. Nor, for that matter, are both together, except when absorbed, filtered through, by the time-redeeming Prince. The play proceeding, as they merge more and more in Hal, these two principals also come, figuratively and literally, closer and closer together. But not till near the end of Part I, and the end of at least one of them (an end likewise, in a fundamental sense, of the other), dare they meet. Two such, so different yet so similar, cannot exist in orbit. A roaring boy, all actor and common sense, can ill afford to encounter a roaring boy all act and personal idealism. When they finally do meet it is in stances perfect and inevitable to their natures: Hotspur at last truly engrossed by total earnestness—that is death; and Falstaff playing his greatest, most audacious role, the liveliest that vitality can attain— 'counterfeiting' death. Side by side they lie, one completely dead, the consequence and requirement of his passionate nature, and one completely alive in playing dead, the consequence and requirement of his imitative (and his all-prudent, not to say all-sane) nature.

Many have been offended by Falstaff's stabbing of Hotspur's corpse a little later, his callousness, his meaning to reap profit out of a dead man's body. This act has been cited to demonstrate Falstaff's basic evil. From Falstaff's point of view or, we might say, a modern one, if it is all right for Hotspur to be killed in the madness and folly of war, stabbing him after his life is gone (or, as Hal felicitously, understandingly, eulogizes over him:

> *Fare thee well, great heart!*
> *Ill-weaved ambition, how much art thou shrunk!*
> *When that this body did contain a spirit,*
> *A kingdom for it was too small a bound;*
> *But now two paces of the vilest earth*
> *Is room enough. This earth, that bears thee dead,*
> *Bears not alive so stout a gentleman.*)

is not very much of an act, fairly anticlimactic, and even sentimental to make something of. But this is to lose sight of the fact that Hotspur is, his great heart notwithstanding, a rebel, a threat to the peace of England, and so a criminal deserving of death. Yet Hotspur's death, however we interpret it, hardly condones Falstaff's act in all its cold-blooded calculation. Thus Hal's elegy on the other 'corpse', 'stout' indeed, lying near by, an elegy the opposite of that for Hotspur, is most revealing:

> *What, old acquaintance! Could not all this flesh*
> *Keep in a little life? Poor Jack, farewell!*
> *I could have better spared a better man.*
> *O, I should have a heavy miss of thee*
> *If I were much in love with vanity!*

Hal's feelings about Falstaff are clear enough. He had said earlier on the raging battle-field, when Falstaff had given him a bottle of sack for a pistol with, 'Ay, Hal; 'tis hot, 'tis hot, there's that will sack a city.' 'What! is't time to jest and dally now?' In its way Falstaff's fixedness of character is no better than Hotspur's. (In this moment of climax I am reminded of the injunction put upon Berowne to try his wit in a hospital; here it is the hospital of the world. Of course one might observe that Shakespeare's stage is the one place that can put on war, outrage, the worst disaster, and still be a 'time' to jest and dally. For in art the worst that is 'played' is a jest, even if a serious, many-sided one, and a dallying. At least while the play lasts. At the same time Hal's rebuke to Falstaff in midplay makes the play and the jest all the more convincing.) Hal, standing over Hotspur and Falstaff, out of their finished lives begins his life as a royal being and soon king-to-be. And here the negative capability becomes the positive one. Words or thoughts and deeds in Hal will be virtually one; he, in the way of a great king, will once more heal the breach between them, the breach Richard II and Bolingbroke, coming at it from opposite sides, could only continue if not widen. Hal's will be the active imagination able to make out of reality a new kind of magic or at least to restore some of the potency of the old.

Here we should consider one of the major problems of the plays, a problem that has developed for modern readers: the dissatisfaction with the conclusion and, consequently, with Hal. The word that seems to have, like pitch, attached itself to him for his treatment of Falstaff is 'prig'. Hal's failure to be as personal, as self-involved and self-concerned, as Hotspur and Falstaff makes him much less attractive than those two to many of us with our suspicion of large-sounding idealism. Shakespeare was at least as aware as we of the yawning chasm between idealism proclaimed and its practice. Apart from the conduct of many characters in *Henry IV*, we have the grimmer testimony of plays like *Troilus and Cressida* and *All's Well That Ends Well* to prove it.

But *Henry IV*, Parts I and II, are, I maintain, of a very different order. In Part II, Shakespeare is at especial pains to show what happens when a view like Falstaff's, introduced into society, threatens to run wild. Already in Part I, with the outbreak of the rebellion, Falstaff begins to change; or at least, once a larger field of operation is available to him, he exerts himself toward satisfying his interests and appetites far beyond his actions in the tavern. His wit and cutting realism are now in the open, and we find him engaged, at the start it is true on a fairly modest scale, in an opportunism and dishonesty similar to that which the lords are executing on a larger. In fact, lord that he increasingly becomes once more, he is of their faction. He already says in Act III, Scene III: 'Well, God be thanked for these rebels, they offend none but the virtuous. I laud them, I praise them.' A little later we hear him admit that he misuses 'the king's press damnably' and all for money. In a sense, since he is a friend, if not a confidant, of Hal, he is worse than the rebels. But as he says most mordantly to Hal's comment on his poor little substitute company: 'I never did see such pitiful rascals', 'Tut, tut; food for powder, food for powder; they'll fill a pit as well as better. Tush, man, mortal men, mortal men.' An observation no less apt, given his viewpoint, than his stabbing of the dead Hotspur. If you do not mind sacrificing good men, not to say the nation's best, why spare, why be sentimental about, the worst, not to say the semi-dead?

But in Part II, re-established in the court with a name he is proud of and with credit that he means to push to the limit, we watch him truly dwindle. More and more he becomes engrossed and trammeled by use and advantage. Already in our first meeting with him we observe a fundamental change: he is concerned about his health to the point of having consulted a doctor and, even more remarkable, he is at once occupied with examining and defining himself in terms of his best ability:

> *Men of all sorts take a pride to gird at me. The brain of this foolish-compounded clay, man, is not able to invent anything that intends to laughter, more than I invent or is invented on me. I am not only witty in myself, but the cause that wit is in other men.*

Such proud and simple self-consciousness we have rarely encountered in him before. After his following roisterous exchange with the Lord Chief Justice, Falstaff grumbles over his poverty and acknowledges:

> *A man can no more separate age and covetousness than a can part young limbs and lechery; but the gout galls the one, and the pox pinches the other, and so both the degrees prevent my curses.*

But though he cries out against 'this consumption of the purse' and also the pox and the gout, he concludes with something like his old spirit: 'A good wit will make use of anything; I will turn diseases to commodity.' Calculation, however, has overtaken that spirit.

Later, when he drives the roaring Pistol out, thereby winning the admiration and the affection of Doll Tearsheet so that she addresses concerned, sober words to him:

Thou whoreson little tidy Bartholomew boar-pig, when wilt thou leave fighting o' days and foining o' nights, and begin to patch up thine old body for heaven?

Falstaff's answer is unusually simple and sober in turn: 'Peace, good Doll! Do not speak like a death's-head: do not bid me remember mine end.' And even while Doll is kissing him, the pathos of mortality overtakes him again: 'I am old, I am old.' Who would have expected such unmodified dumps from him? His earlier 'melancholy' with Hal now begins to look like the real thing. Evidently in the very middle of lovemaking he has now no trouble telling, in his big toe or elsewhere, the difference between the gout of age and the pox of youth. Thus, rising to Doll's 'I love thee better than I love e'er a scurvy boy of them all', with 'What stuff wilt have a kirtle of? . . . A merry song, come! It grows late; we'll to bed', he relapses into 'Thou't forget me when I am gone', a tone surely more wistful, whatever the simple truth of his sentiments, more one-dimensional, and more self-concerned than we are accustomed to in him. Doll's touching reply handsomely bears out the pathos of this moment.

But when Falstaff recognizes the Prince and Poins, who have overheard Falstaff's abuse of Hal (Poins warns Hal: 'My lord, he will drive you out of your revenge and turn all to a merriment, if you take not the heat.' Perhaps we can understand one reason at least for Hal's necessary sternness at the end), Falstaff, adequately challenged and rejuvenated by Hal's presence, recovers a good portion of himself and does indeed drive Hal out of his revenge with his excuse: 'I dispraised him before the wicked, that the wicked might not fall in love with him.' Then, with news of affairs of state gathering head, Hal is all contrition 'So idly to profane the precious time'. In addition to these words' own strength, their almost religious emphasis, they ring especially strongly against what Falstaff and Doll have just been saying and against what the King is about to say.

In Westminster Palace the sleepless King, full of the terrible burdens of his office and of remorse, expresses a dreadful sense of the times:

> *Then you perceive the body of our kingdom*
> *How foul it is, what rank diseases grow,*
> *And with what danger, near the heart of it.*

and an overpowering sense of what pawns the best of us are. England at this juncture, manifested in this aging, wearied King, his aging, wearied opponents, and the aging yet still renewable—if chiefly by greed and occasional sparks of his former wit—Falstaff, seems centuries away from the England of the opening of Part I. Then, with age and corruption accumulating, we are out in the country in Gloucestershire with that ultimate of loose mouths, that babbler who makes all the voluble old men before him sound like reticence itself, Justice Shallow. That justice should come to this! And Falstaff also. Of course the Lord Chief Justice is an old man too, but for him age would appear to have brought increased wisdom and dignity as well as probity. This local scene, country manners and all, echoing the large one, makes us realize the extent to which easygoing corruption, impotence and oncoming dissolution, via old age, have spread throughout England. The cousins' talk consists principally of remembering and death. But Shallow, admitting: 'Certain, 't is certain; very sure, very sure: death, as the Psalmist saith, is certain to all; all shall die', shifts without pause to life habitual and inevitable, its routine negotiations: 'How a good yoke of bullocks at Stamford fair?' There is a bit of life, if only a flicker, in the old, old boy yet. So withered is he, however, that, though death and a remnant of life are living lean cheek by jowl in him, he sees nothing discordant in their keeping such casual, close company. And no doubt, in view of the nature of the world he is habituated to, he is right not to.

Now Falstaff, expected to recruit some soldiers, arrives. And at Shallow's roll-call, a parade of piping, thistledown monosyllables, with barely a track of thought to hold them floating on the air, as though we were once more in the middle of preliminaries for rehearsal of *Pyramus and Thisby*, the grim comedy of recruiting begins. Falstaff claps himself together a paltry troop, fit indeed for death-watches, of characters tellingly named Mouldy, Shadow, and Feeble. The work done, reminiscence of the good old days, especially on Shallow's part, occurs. When Shallow turns in pride to Silence, 'Ha, cousin Silence, that thou hadst seen that that this knight and I have seen! Ha, Sir John, said I well?' Falstaff gives éclat to the occasion with one of his most resonant statements: 'We have heard the chimes at midnight, Master Shallow.' A statement as laconic as it is resonant. Merry the statement obviously is. Yet, in addition to its implied undertone of delighted nostalgia, in view of the scene's context—the age, if not decrepitude, of these men and the perilous condition of England—it is hard to resist overhearing further undertones of the sad and the ominous. Church bells, measuring time (recall Hal's early promise of 'redeeming the time' and his very recent apprehensiveness that he can 'so idly . . . profane the precious time'), ambiguously signify grave events no less than gay ones. And by now we well know Shakespeare's genius for mingling the merry and the grim.

Learning that Mouldy and Bullcalf are ready to buy their freedom, Falstaff releases them and takes instead the previously rejected Wart and 'this same half-faced fellow, Shadow; give me this man. He presents no mark to the enemy; the foeman may with as great aim level at the edge of a penknife.' We seem to be returned, names, overtones, and all, to the world of the morality play, but of course with none of Falstaff's—or Shakespeare's—juicy, realistic detail forsaken. Off Falstaff goes, and he explains in a lengthy soliloquy why, aside from humoring Shallow, he has been so unusually terse with him:

> *Lord, lord, how subject we old men are to this vice of lying! This same starved justice hath done nothing but prate to me of the wildness of his youth, and the feats he hath done about Turnbull Street; and every third word a lie, duer paid to the hearer than the Turk's tribute.*

Since on parting Shallow bade 'let our old acquaintance be renewed', Falstaff, now altogether committed to the ruthless 'law of nature', concludes:

> *Well, I'll be acquainted with him if I return, and it shall go hard but I will make him a philosopher's two stones to me. If the young dace be a bait for the old pike, I see no reason in the law of nature but I may snap at him.*

Cold advantage and the purely predatory would seem to be all.

In the next scene the weary rebels, foolishly persuaded to yield by the cold, calculating, young Lancaster, a minister indeed of 'the law of nature', are summarily sentenced to death. With the army discharged, Falstaff decides to revisit Shallow. And the Fifth Act gives us Shallow at his shallow best insisting that Falstaff stay the night. Here we have Shakespeare's most extreme case of echolalia, the last husk and wisp of a man; a likely companion for Falstaff approaching his own end. Yet robustiously Falstaff stores him away, cheese-paring though he may be, for future use.

> *I will devise matter enough out of this Shallow to keep Prince Harry in continual laughter for wearing out of six fashions, which is four terms or two actions, and a shall laugh without intervallums.*

Having just heard Davy, one of Shallow's servants, persuade Shallow to favor one of Davy's friends at trial, another casual instance of the times' pervasive corruption, it is natural that Falstaff should resort to legal terms. At the same time we notice that the laughter Falstaff intends to provoke in Hal will interrupt a whole year's round of law. Or justice carried no better than by Shallow. And having observed how much Shallow and his men are affected (infected) by each other's company: 'Therefore let men take heed of their company', with anticipated relish and mistaken contempt for Hal, no doubt in Falstaff's mind much infected by his company, he concludes:

> *O, it is much that a lie with a slight oath and a jest with a sad brow will do with a fellow that never had the ache in his shoulders! O, you shall see him laugh till his face be like a wet cloak ill laid up!*

Falstaff cannot know, ironically enough, what ache and what promise of even more formidable aches Hal has just been experiencing with his dying father. Later, with dinner over and the wine and wit flowing, even Silence feels, *mirabile dictu*, moved to sing. Having made music on that straw Shallow, Falstaff has wakened Silence no less into a chirping little cricket. Thus Silence admits, 'I have been merry twice and once ere now.' Falstaff has met his most arduous challenge: he has found—better, inspired—life, gaiety, even song in two as close to death as men can be and still be alive. But who if not Falstaff is able to stir laughter in death's throat?

Now learning that Hal is King, Falstaff reveals his intentions and expectations nakedly enough: 'Master Robert Shallow, choose what office thou wilt in the land, 'tis thine. Pistol, I will double-charge thee with dignities.' And preparing for the all-night ride, he continues: 'I know the young King is sick for me. Let us take any man's horses; the laws of England are at my commandment. Blessed are they that have been my friends, and woe to my Lord Chief Justice!' Arriving at a public place near Westminster Abbey, they await the King and his coronation train. Since he is about to put on his last, best, certainly most important performance, Falstaff is glad they have had no time to change clothes: '. . . this poor show doth better; this doth infer the zeal I had to see him.' But Hal is hardly to be taken in. To Falstaff's loving entreaties Hal retorts:

> *I know thee not, old man. Fall to thy prayers.*
> *How ill white hairs become a fool and jester!*

I have long dreamed of such a kind of man,
So surfeit-swelled, so old, and so profane;
But, being awaked, I do despise my dream.

Awakened from the 'dream' he idled in as a youth, he, the opposite of a Richard II, knows his true role. However, in the very act of banishing Falsatff, Hal shows him charity, more surely than he needs to. If Hal's words seem harsh, aside from the official and crucial nature of this moment, with questioning eyes hard upon him, Hal must be categorically strong lest, like the past, Falstaff fail to believe him.

But the play has ended, as all plays must, with the reassertion of reality. For much of Part I Falstaff sloughs off almost all concern with the past and its consequences, and with the future. In the Boar's Head he enjoys, we and Hal with him, his moment of 'the immortal'. His sporadic bouts of remorse, like his sudden accesses of desire for reformation, we take to be additional garnishings of merriment. It is Hotspur who is a Puritan of time, set on employing it most exacerbatedly for betterment, a personal ideal of perfection, ever about to be achieved. Only in his moment of dying does he recognize how much life is 'time's fool'. In the latter portion of Part I, and certainly in Part II, when the court and the world at large claim Hal and Falstaff, Falstaff with patent pleasure and good will slips more and more into fairly commonplace attitudes towards time. As with Christopher Sly, suddenly metamorphosed from a bar fly to an important lord, time for Falstaff becomes something to attain material ends in; his tavern pleasures in their immediacy, time in its immensity of now, no longer suffice. Overtaken by the future, he has become not much more than advantage-seeking. Hal alone is able to enjoy all times; he fully participates in the present moment, but not to the oblivion of other things, including the past and the future. He understands too well their interdependence.

Some critics have gone so far as to call Part II the tragedy of Falstaff. If aging and succumbing to greed are tragic, then Falstaff is tragic; and he is, if succumbing at last to the world he seemed free of is tragic. One might be tempted to conclude that he abandoned the court in the first place, not so much because he was superior to or disdainful of it, but because he was not equal to it and, impoverished, had to flee it. At the same time, for all his penetration, we must appreciate one significant fact about him in Part II. Unlike us, he can have no sense of what has been happening to Hal, his grave confrontations with his father and his coming from his father's painful death, as well as his important meeting and reconciliation with the Chief Justice.

It must be admitted that already in Part I, Act III, when in Hal's first 'private conference' with his father the King berates him and identifies Hotspur with himself and Hal with Richard, Hal conducts himself most nobly. And a little later in the rebel camp Vernon, at Hotspur's inquiry after Hal's whereabouts just before battle, praises him unreservedly:

> *All furnished, all in arms;*
> *All plumed like estridges that wing the wind*
> *Baited like eagles having lately bathed;*
> *Glittering in golden coats, like images;*
> *As full of spirit as the month of May,*
> *And gorgeous as the sun at midsummer;*
> *Wanton as youthful goats, wild as young bulls.*
> *I saw young Harry with his beaver on,*
> *His cuisses on his thighs, gallantly armed,*
> *Rise from the ground like feathered Mercury,*
> *And vault with such ease into his seat*
> *As if an angel dropped down from the clouds*
> *To turn and wind a fiery Pegasus*
> *And witch the world with noble horsemanship.*

This spate of glittering images eagerly mounts from estridges to eagles to the sun itself. Then with a moment's back-to-earth digression to sweep up goats and bulls, it mounts again, arms and all, but now far above mere earthling birds; for it seems to reach its climax in 'feathered' Mercury only to top it with that loftiest of winged creatures, an angel, but now one not rising but dropping as from heaven. Such praise, to say the least, is especially impressive coming from an enemy and delivered to Hal's chief opponent. Shortly after we have Hal's altogether magnanimous public praise of Hotspur in the very moment of challenging him. And then again Vernon, reporting that praise, so praises the praiser,

> *But let me tell the world,*
> *If he outlive the envy of this day,*
> *England did never owe so sweet a hope,*
> *So much misconstrued in his wantonness.*

that Hotspur understandably says: 'Cousin, I think thou art enamoured /On his follies.' The battle follows, and Hal's acquittal of himself puts the final seal of approval on him. He has proved himself as a fighter, first against the kingdom's second most successful warrior, Douglas, and then against Hotspur himself. He has also established his filiality, and so become King, and his nobility out of his relations with the Lord Chief Justice. Falstaff, in the other hand, has steadily deteriorated. Here at last, in a way not present in the history plays before, we see character in the making, in Hal's case, and in the unmaking, in Falstaff's; or perhaps it would be more accurate to say character emerging. For both are, in a basic sense, what they are throughout; it is the change of circumstances that provides them with the stage and scene for their fullest unfolding.

Despite Hal's constantly harsh, bald words about the future, Falstaff loved Hal or, perhaps more to the point, assumed that Hal loved him. At the end he may still love Hal, but apparently above all in his illusion that Hal will be his bottomless royal exchequer. It is a capping irony that Falstaff, able seemingly to see through all, should not have recognized Hal's real feeling. Ironically too, at this moment of denial, in spite of the strength of its utterance, Falstaff is naive enough to persist in his misinterpreting Hal's meaning:

> *I shall be sent for in private to him. Look you, he must seem thus to the world. Fear not your advancements; I will be the man yet that shall make you great.*

In a marvelous reversal, Shallow for once is more aware and witty than Falstaff. He says: 'I cannot well perceive how, unless you should give me your doublet and stuff me out with straw.'

From the beginning then, in Hal's ideal of what his true conduct should be no less than in his playing a part for it, the pupil has surpassed his teacher. And Hal surpasses him to the triumph that is *Henry IV*, clearly the climax in Shakespeare's treatment of English history. Moreover, in it we have at last a magnificent confluence of the historical and the comic. Now the old spirit of comedy, no less than the supposedly noble life of the court, is being directly challenged while it is being used; it is no longer merely one portion of a play or the elegant pause of imaginative and timeless time that is the play. Furthermore, though what moonlit gaiety and charm *Henry IV* has is mainly identified with Falstaff and his tavern, the spirit of comedy in the largest sense, the sense this play intends, resides elsewhere – in Hal. (If we are willing to recognize tragi-comedy as a genre, because of Hal we might, at risk of pleasing Polonius, adopt for this play the term histori-comedy; certainly both comedy and history are proved to their uttermost here, one fulfilling the other.)

For Hal, by his character and through his experience in these plays, is the only one able to move with most notable sprightliness from one world to another and able to be equally at home in all of them. Most of all, with Falstaff's having coached and paced him, Hal not only has learned to know other men through observing and playing them, but in doing so has also prepared for his most ambitious role, the most taxing short of sainthood that a man can play – king. Because of his intelligence and the amplitude of his experience, he will not, like Richard II confuse himself with his office. Rather, like the great actor that he must be, he will set aside his personal life or, better, put it and its diverse ingredients altogether at the service of his royal role. The theater then, whether Shakespeare's or Falstaff's in the Boar's Head with his kaleidoscopic improvisations, is one of the principal academies for all of us, not least a prince.

Hal, we might say, like Theseus, has his play, his Midsummer Night's Dream, before action; but, unlike Theseus, he through his Master of the Revels performs in it and cultivates the moon-man side of him enough to be a fully matured daytime leader. It is quite appropriate and natural that Shakespeare's genius, bearing its ripest comic fruit in Falstaff, should also achieve its greatest historical drama by way of Hal. But this is more than a mere quantitative growth in comedy and history. *Henry IV* happily tops even Shakespeare's major comic moments in Falstaff with this larger, overarching accomplishment in comedy that is Hal and the whole play. For a time, if only a time – no longer than Hal's reign or the two parts of *Henry IV* and *Henry V* – England and its people, now of all humours, attain an almost perfect equipoise.

Hal, I have suggested, does not confuse worlds and times. But he does marry them again, as Richard II could never do, in ceremony, the state's solemnity renewed; for he has the power, the wit, the glamor out of reality to do so. Through him, holiday and the daily come together again. His is the true, synthesizing Elizabethan genius, able to unite the time's most diverse elements into one victorious state. In this genius Hal is like his maker who, with the incredible hodgepodge of materials, classical and romantic, popular and courtly, fabulous and historical, remote and local that he inherited, found out of their jostling fecundity the language of an air brisk and fresh enough to accommodate and harmonize them all. In *Henry IV* the merry part of pomp, of spectacle, through its rootedness in the people and reality, has been restored, just as daily life has been transformed into something of the mellowness of holiday. And England, whatever the threats to it, the diseases struggling to overwhelm it, for a spell is as endearing and fundamentally benign as the life-giving, life-enhancing *polis* of Athens was to its grateful, greatest sons. England is, corruption and all, once more 'this scept'red isle/This earth of majesty, this seat of Mars,/This other Eden, demi-paradise' that dying Gaunt extolled.

One might be reminded of another series of magnificent plays, a trilogy that was also a kind of national epic, singing the praises of a country even while exploring that country's birth pangs, the terror and the anguish that racked it, and the chaos that threatened to engulf it before it could attain its full greatness. That is the *Oresteia*, a paean to Athens as the tetralogy of *Richard II*, *Henry IV*, Parts I and II, and *Henry V* is to England. With Apollo's help Orestes, the King's son, a King guilty and killed by guilty ones, breaks the blood curse, which has sullied all his family and therefore the kingdom as well; law is at last established, the furies are halted, appeased, transformed and included, and justice is enthroned as against bloodshed and revenge, the arbitrary, the irrational, the personal. Such establishment is an ideal the fitfulness of whose realization Aeschylus appreciated no less than Shakespeare, Shakespeare no less than Aeschylus. The plays would not have been written, and in times perilously close to civil war, had this awareness not been most alive in both and had they not been concerned with showing how easily such an ideal can be lost or destroyed, and what the terrible consequences must be. Hal, unlike Orestes, has no heavenly advice and guidance, none beyond his own intelligence and experience, what he learns from a satyr-wise figure like Falstaff. And he kills no one surreptitiously; but he does kill Hotspur and curb Falstaff. A considerable price to pay no doubt in their immense attractiveness, it is nonetheless a necessary one and to be expected of a noble youth undertaking a role more important, and in a basic sense far larger, than himself.

A Dying Fall

Twelfth Night

COMING from the Henry trilogy to *Twelfth Night*, though probably only a few years separate them, we seem to have travelled a vast distance; but for plot, material, and themes, mainly backwards in time. What, against the crackling, kaleidoscopic activity of the histories, are we to make of *Twelfth Night's* mellow, musical atmosphere? What of our having to leap from a world very much at large to one redoubtably indoors? Except for a brief whiff of the Illyrian seacoast, several turns in an Illyrian street and in Olivia's garden, we are ensconced in two houses, actually only two spacious chambers at that: one in the Duke's palace, the other in Olivia's manor. (We must not forget, however, what worlds transpire in two places in *Henry IV*, Part I: Henry IV's palace chamber and the Boar's Head Tavern.) But this shrinkage is hardly to be construed as a lapse or a temporary retreat on Shakespeare's part into lesser work. His interest in and his genius for English history having been well satisfied, he turned to comedy once more, to the conventions of romantic comedy that he had already enhanced as he had accepted them. In short order, having turned out *Much Ado About Nothing* and *As You Like It*, out of his apparent fondness for working in braces of plays, he rounded them off with *Twelfth Night*. Filtered through them and the earlier comedies and through the history plays, *Twelfth Night* is a marvel of most delicate balances.

Perhaps the greatest praise we can accord it—and it deserves the most intelligent praise we can muster—is to remark the pains we must be at to realize what diversity of materials it interfuses, and how much in those materials and their emphases it is a recapitulation of previous comedies. The Shakespearean company's trunk of props, and of occasions, was ample yet limited; but Shakespeare had learned to combine them in such an assortment of effects that they seem endless. At the same time here is harmony so confident, so zestful, that it attunes whatever seemingly contradictory elements occur; the more various, the more discordant and cacaphonous even, the more harmonious. And it is all the more extraordinary in its grace when we recall that *Hamlet* and *Troilus and Cressida* are not, whether before or after, far off. But then the exuberant balancing act of *Henry IV* is not far off either. Since I have often enumerated the elements Shakespeare felt called upon to employ to see how many amiable, surprising changes he could ring, it would be tedious to elaborate on them again: dead fathers and brothers, a shipwreck, identical twins and their separation through shipwreck, their being tossed and lost and tossed onto a strange shore, the assumption of disguises, the confusion of loves, the mistaken identities, the steady outcry of madness (that, rather than madness cum witchcraft or magic) and so on.

One feels obliged, however, to probe a little into the source, beyond practice itself, of this new harmoniousness. *Twelfth Night*, the last of three plays which it is customary and right, apart from mere chronology, to think of together as joyous, romantic comedies, is also the most mellow. The first two open fairly vigorously: *Much Ado About Nothing* with the end of a victorious battle and the expectation, momentarily, of the conquering heroes, and with a most disagreeable confusion soon to be launched; *As You Like It* with the just disgruntlement of its young hero Orlando at the niggardly treatment of, his disinheritance by, his older brother; a treatment that threatens to become downright villainy. *Twelfth Night*, on the other hand, opening, and also keynoting its overall tone, with music—music to counterpoint the melodic, languorous speeches of Duke Orsino—and in a room filled almost to swooning with mixed fragrances, is altogether remote from any disturbances from a bustling outside world. Thus, consonantly, Shakespeare holds off the seacoast, talk of storm, shipwreck, and fortunes till the second scene; in fact these, set off by the perfumed music of Scene I, virtually become, we might say, the matter of the romantic ditty that Orsino, an auditor pure, bids play.

Twelfth Night is then, in tone and in setting, the most contained, the most gentle, domestic play Shakespeare wrote. There is no magical wood nearby because it is not needed; Illyria is as close to the idyllic, the artfully pastoral, as an orderly, relaxed, congenial little country can be. But, as I have said, it is remarkable how little Illyria itself figures in the play. Though we are at moments on the seacoast and 'a street', and taverns are referred to, and though officers and a priest appear, a sense of Illyria beyond Orsino's chamber and Olivia's lively household and garden is in no way established. Actually Illyria is a little, drifting island, a recess like Orsino's bank of flowers. Antonio, the sea captain, does, it is true, late in the play introduce threats, reality, the sea. And the sea itself is often laid under contribution, but chiefly as an image, a salt to flavor the idleness or at least the dallying of the play.

And such airy containment is appropriate since, whatever the play's occasion, this is *Twelfth Night* or *What You Will*; January Sixth, the last night of a long holiday that brought Christmas festivities to an end, it was the climax of the sweetest season of the year. On this night not only did all sorts of sports and revelry occur, but in its congeniality and relaxedness all sorts of antics as well. Servants could mock their masters and even, as we see in this play, poorer moments of the church. Thus the church is present a good deal, but usually in jocular phrases like Sir Toby Belch's 'go to church in a galliard' and Feste's 'I live by the church'—or the church, like that in *The Merchant of Venice*, nowise in its more rigorous, moral character—and of course most importantly in Feste's merry assumption of the role of Sir Topas, the curate, or in his words when he dons the gown and beard: 'I will dissemble myself in't; and I would I were the first that ever dissembled in such a gown.' But prevailingly the play's atmosphere is one of gentle goodwill and well being, usually luxuriantly so.

An Elizabethan closed household, teeming with luscious-stuffed crannies, ventilated by songs, images, witty exchanges, recollection, sweet airs of earlier times, the play, to borrow Orsino's words, comes over the ear—the other senses too—'like the sweet sound/That breathes upon a bank of violets,/Stealing and giving odour.' With wit, music, love, and sparkling high spirits as well as lowjinks, the play swaddles itself most ingratiatingly against winter and the outside world. Though almost nothing is made of winter (or, for that matter, of the sea in violence) till the conclusion of *Twelfth Night* (certainly winter is not exploited for rollicksome comedy in the way of *The Taming of the Shrew* or even taxed for lively images as with the cosy Poland winter of *The Comedy of Errors*), the audience must have enjoyed the increased intimacy and snug pleasure of a world, beseiged by winter, turned in upon itself. Since the season is winter and since the play was probably played in winter, let winter not once be mentioned, admitted, allowed.

Of course, like its season, the play has some aspect of Janus, forward looking to spring but backward looking to winter or, rather, to the winter of the tragedies immediately ahead. For, marking the end of the Christmas festivities, this play also marks the end, with the exception of *The Tempest*, of Shakespeare's happy comedies. Indeed, the worst of winter is soon to be. Thus for maximal, accurate pleasure one should probably view the play bifocally: near for its gaiety, its gentle, warm amusement, and for the place it occupies in the whole of Shakespeare; and far as it is wistful, already aware of the winds waiting to do their worst. For the play's loveliness is deepened by its sense of the elegiac and loss. It is its own and its world's swan song; that world's loveliest breath is virtually its last. How little *Twelfth Night* has, for instance, of the youthful, carefree lyricism of *A Midsummer Night's Dream*. Less than six months separate these two days of the year, but some six or seven years of playwriting have intervened and that world of difference between summer and winter.

Here Shakespeare is singing a song that celebrates and preserves a dying order. Malvolio, the one ill-will among all the congenials, though rejected and exposed for the self-loving fool that he is, will, in the growing, busy winter of the world, soon blow down the sweet defenses of merry England and, in the person of others cut of his whole, drab cloth, indeed become steward or major-domo of the land. We have already met a lovely elegy in the tragedy of *Richard II*. In *Twelfth Night* once again we encounter hints of the growing conflict between the old world of merry England, in all its flower, and the new world of the upstart, the 'useful' man, the rampant opportunist. Now, however, he is not much more than one fairly scant, silly invader, serving chiefly to add to the amusement and jollity of the members of the play's still prevailing world, a snowman for their japes and warm-breathed songs to melt while they dance around him, a world that hardly knows that its days are numbered. But though this threat is never overtly focused on, is as muted as the outside world, with its dangers that this threat belongs to, it does introduce a somber note into the play. And the principals, being unemployed creatures of refinement and hyper-sensitivity, are most available to it. However, Sir Toby's memorable cry also shows some deep awareness of it: 'Dost thou think, because thou art virtuous there shall be no more cakes and ale?' The question is clearly rhetorical, with no answer expected. Yet the answer is, as far as daily cakes and free-flowing ale are concerned, more 'yes' than 'no'. Still, since this is a comedy, for a time the ale will flow, the clink of the cups mingling with the songs and the laughter.

The opening scene, with Orsino's mellifluous if heavy, love-lorn speech, sets the prevailing tone. He is revealed at once as a man of intense refinement, an exquisite if not a decadent, burning with a softly flickering flame rather than a hard, gemlike one. The end product of his civilization, it is not war, not arguments and inheritances, not ruling or order he is after, not even hunting as normally pursued, but music and his own poetry as it mirrors and intensifies his own more delicate, poignant feelings. Sybaritically, like Richard II in his way and Falstaff in his, he would do little more than luxuriate in his own reveries. He is not even for putting on a play; rather, he would be played upon, drowned by music as by his brimming senses. Surely it is illuminating to compare his lounging, his elegant passivity, with Theseus' mood at the opening of his play, Theseus who also orders entertainment. Like him, Orsino claims that he would be at love and loving, but it is obvious that he much prefers to be occupied with love's musings.

Meet to his temperament, his first word – one very common to this play – is 'if'. At once we have a strong image, recurrent in Shakespeare, of food and eating to excess (later Orsino will admit men's easily sated appetites). But how mild that eating and that excess are when they become no more than 'a dying fall' and a 'sweet sound/That breathes upon a bank of violets'. At the same time we cannot deny a wistfulness here, something of the hothouse in the luscious blooms of this speech, not alone in the words and images with their excess, sickening and dying, but in the settled languor of this gentleman who should be ruler of his world. He is truly a kind of Richard II gone to seed, living, it would seem, for superfine titillations that will inspire him to finer and finer, semi-swooning speeches. It is as though we had a moment in the career of Richard II, a moment completely recessed, free of the outside world and its threats, a Richard imagining himself into a transport of fantasy. It is almost surprising that Shakespeare did not borrow, as he did 'sweet wood' burned 'to make the lodgings sweet' and music procured 'to make a dulcet and a heavenly sound', some of the pictures used upon Christopher Sly, 'wanton pictures' hung round the lord's 'fairest chamber'. However, perhaps the whole play, like *The Taming of the Shrew* for Sly, is such a picture come alive for the Duke's delectation and, though it is the opposite he is after, edification or 'awaking'.

But something of Orsino's flower-bedded condition (and a little Lethe weed-like too) hangs over the world of this play. Thus he immediately proves the sad validity of his first words. For while the music plays, in his moodiness and indulgence he quickly wearies and the sweet sound is 'not so sweet now as it was before'. Only the 'spirit of love' is 'quick and fresh' for him. Accordingly, a woman who will

spurn him, keep him unsatisfied, not to say unsurfeited, is alone
perfect for his condition. For he would not have love and his manifold
images of it interrupted by a flesh-and-blood, problem-making, single
lover. And he can take delight out of his sad proof. Rather than seeing
what sorry stuff his kind of love is, he exults in the fact that it is like
the bottomless sea, and that consequently whatever enters it, no matter
its quality or worth, in a mere minute loses its savor. A destructive
element indeed, this love! (However, let us remember that element as
we move on; for both Viola and her brother *rise* from the sea almost
like Aphrodite, and 'resurrected' as they are, they are the sea's products
not its victims.) Orsino concludes that this love of his is alone self-
sufficient: only it, identified with the imaginative faculty, is able to
discover within itself shapes enough and changing enough to satisfy it.
Hardly a Theseus-like or Slyesque conclusion!

With such a supine hero, and such a complex opening, one might
well wonder how either the hero or the play will ever stand erect, let
alone act. What can possibly stir them? Surely this beginning might
seem less promising, much more suffocating and benumbed, than even
that of *The Comedy of Errors*, with its first lugubrious scene. And yet
what more Turkish bath-like atmosphere against the winter? In any
case, Orsino is to the letter Theseus' version of the lover. Much like the
lunatic and the poet, if of the lesser, romantic type, he is in love with
his own figures, not the world's: a mental Narcissus, an egotist sublime.
Unheard music may not be sweetest to him, but beyond doubt an
unseen or at least unavailable love is.

Orsino's attendant, Curio, perhaps to jolt his master out of his
bemusement, breaks in with 'Will you go hunt, my lord?' We remember the vividness and delight hunting released in earlier plays. But when
to Orsino's 'What, Curio?' the reply is 'The hart', this prompts not only
the inevitable pun but what Orsino has been all along immersed in.
Everything, we see, feeds his voracious fancy. He is, he assures Curio,
already well on into the hunt. He is busy hunting the hart, 'the noblest
that I have'. At first one naturally assumes it is some lovely lady. Thus
he does now name Olivia with very high-toned praise: 'O, when mine
eyes did see Olivia first,/Methought she purged the air of pestilence!'
His thinking – 'methought' – does all. Beauty, love, and music may be so
efficacious, but it will take a Viola to purge the air of such a mooncalf
(moonbull would be more accurate were there such a word). A proper
preliminary, Olivia is to purge the air so that the violets, music-sweet,
can do their work. Actually one not altogether sympathetic might

suggest that she has helped, along with the violets, to fill the air with the pestilence of his paralyzing love. Anyone can see, however, that Olivia has merely been an innocent bystander. He thinks her the cause of his condition; rather his condition has sought her out and now battens on her refusals as on his dreamy notions of her. But now the truth is out: the noblest hart he hunts, even as it is love after love, is his own heart, himself. In his words, seeing her 'That instant was I turned into a hart.' He embroiders this notion further by calling on a classical allusion, Acteon and his hounds: 'And my desires, like fell and cruel hounds,/E'er since pursue me.' We see little cruelty, little rending here. These velleities of his are more like fawning lap dogs! Compare them with Theseus' leash or, for that matter, those of the lord of *The Taming of the Shrew*, the crisp, outdoor music of real dogs. But Orsino's hounds are no more real, no more urgent, no less literary than the sea he earlier drew on. In short, Illyria itself, a most civil, bosky garden, altogether man-made, has no animals in it other than those created out of man's mind or feelings.

Having heard of Olivia, we now learn more through Orsino's servant, Valentine. Aside from the etiquette proper to a duke (unless he be a man like Theseus), Orsino knows his imagination has more to feed on through report than through direct action of his own. Olivia's handmaid (not Olivia: both she and Orsino live and act through their servants) has told Valentine that Olivia, in memory of her recently dead brother, will not show herself even to the sky for seven summers (summer is stressed, not winter, in this balmy winter's tale). She is, we appreciate at once, a fitting female counterpart to Orsino's notion of himself; one equally given to extravagance and self-deception, she is able like him by her station and her means, and prompted by her leisure and consequent boredom, to indulge herself in such fancifulness, and likely therefore without fail to attract Orsino. Free these two are, but free to the point of being unrooted, without a world. Their acts, if one can call what they do acts, are not action at all; mostly theirs is the stir of footless musings, reveries that overwhelm thoughts of living itself.

Commentators have pointed out how much talk, not action, characterizes *Twelfth Night*. But talk, not action, is precisely the condition of its inmates and most of Illyria. It requires outsiders and those from the sea, Feste, Viola, Sebastian, Antonio and, alas, Malvolio, to prod it to action. It is Olivia's plan to keep her grief, her memory of her brother, also a 'flower' of the fancy, alive by watering it 'once a day her chamber round' with her tears. Little 'freshness' or real 'seasoning'

can one expect of such slight briny water. But then no doubt it is of
the same freshness and source as Orsino's sea. Her so delicate yet
strong melancholy, her lopsided piety, must appeal perfectly to
Orsino's. How else out of wealth, wellbeing, and tedium shall two
unemployed, refined beings entertain themselves but with such excessive roles? They are cater-cousins of the Prince of Navarre and his
gentlemen embarked on similarly unrealistic, absurd seven-year vows
of chastity. Though this is Twelfth Night, a time for revelry and
freedom, and though theirs is an attitude which for all its folly Shakespeare appreciated the appeal of, we can understand why curt reality and
the bustle of life itself must soon burst in on them with the antidote of
'plainness'. Their melancholy and their aimless boredom, related if at
some considerable removes to Antonio's and Portia's in *The Merchant
of Venice*, require it. But that reality will end their charm, their graci-
ousness, as well. (Melancholy apparently enjoyed a vogue in Shakespeare's time, something like alienation in ours, and one could with
profit examine Shakespeare's thoroughgoing exploration of it in its
variations, all the way from the frivolous variety of Orsino and Olivia
to the savage and corrosive brand of Hamlet and Timon of Athens.)

Orsino, more enamored of Olivia than ever, responds most nobly
to her vow:

> *O, she that hath a heart of that fine frame*
> *To pay this debt of love but to a brother,*
> *How will she love when the rich golden shaft*
> *Hath killed the flock of all affections else*
> *That live in her; when liver, brain, and heart,*
> *Those sovereign thrones, are all supplied, and filled*
> *Her sweet perfections with one self king!*

But, though he uses a vigorous hunting image, apt to his earlier talk,
and thinks of a king for her, instead of stalking the game himself at
last or, as we might expect, rousing himself to be that king, he prefers
to 'think' on it some more. 'Away before me to sweet beds of flowers!/
Love-thoughts lie rich when canopied with bowers.' A very robustious
lover and hero this! One might be reminded of the flower-tickled
Bottom, but ass and all, there was little long supine or indolent about
him. Obviously Orsino has no intention of interrupting Olivia's so-
winning orisons.

Moreover, the new image of Olivia moves him to literalize his
earlier bank of violets, a veritable bed of loves-in-idleness or Titania's

bower. And his own metaphor becomes a place to go to—this in winter—
or more deeply into the dream idyl that this play is for much of its
duration. But if Hamlet is 'slothful' what shall we call Orsino? From
the first in their passivity, as in their images—the sea in which, deadly
enough, nothing endures; his desire, a love that finds nothing but itself
sufficient; and the pointless tears of Olivia in her abnegation of life, a
kind of death-in-life—are not both Orsino and Olivia flirting dangerously with death, easeful, absolving death? By their similarity in no
way meant for each other, they need their lively opposites, treasures
out of the fecund—as well as destructive—sea.

Accordingly, to open this suffocatingly florid atmosphere and to
blow some fresh air into it, in Scene II Shakespeare carries us to
Illyria's seacoast to meet the play's principal character, the one mainly
responsible for educating both Orsino and Olivia. Like the sleeping
beauty, they require her to shake them from their long slumber. Viola
alone, through the vitality of the sea in her, and perhaps because of the
sea-change she has experienced through her immersion in it, has something of the 'quick and fresh' that only 'the spirit of love' can know;
she alone does not, fair as her mind is, fall 'into abatement and low
price/Even in a minute'. And for her changing shapes she partakes of
the imaginativeness of love itself.

It may not be too fantastical to recall at this point one of the rare
moments of lyricism in a play also full of shapes, *The Comedy of Errors*.
My chapter on it dwelt on the visiting Antipholus' sudden enchantment
with Luciana. Speaking uncertainly of who he is, he delivers himself of
a burst of lyricism which in using a sea image suggests something of
the atmosphere suffusing Orsino's first speech, and his inclination
throughout much of the play: a yearning to drown in loveliness,
especially in its shapes or images, not so much as they are the sea or
Olivia, but his mind's girl. How much Orsino is a victim, a most
willing one at that, of the sirens singing through him we need hardly
say. And how much he lies in a bed of such imagery, on Antipholus'
'golden hairs' 'spread o'er the silver waves', we know. Antipholus'
simile, as Shakespeare activates it here, becomes Orsino's reality. At
the same time one thinks of Prufrock and his last verses, his singing
sea-girls and the chambers of the sea, and his fear lest human voices
wake him and he drown. Viola, sea and all, will have to 'transform'
Orsino back to living and reality. But is it far-fetched to be reminded
here also of Oberon's dolphined mermaid with her sea-civilizing song?
Such mermaids, sirens that they are, are doubtless too much for

mortals—that is, unless the mermaids are embodied in human beings as gentle and sane, as sensitive to and considerate of others, as Viola.

It is of course important to realize how deliberate the placing of scenes here is. In earlier plays, whether *The Comedy of Errors* or *A Midsummer Night's Dream*, the cross-grained matter that the play must digest is presented at the outset: a shipwreck, its woes, and the immediate danger of its survivors; or an angry father demanding his will of his daughter, that or her dire punishment. But in *Twelfth Night* no old father threatens the young with his crusty will; it is as *they* will. So too, by its placement and emphasis, or lack of it, Shakespeare makes it clear that the shipwreck we now learn about is a minor note, much subordinated to the Duke's swelling, floribund melody. And though we are given details of the shipwreck, a real sea with a real storm, the painful separation the shipwreck caused, Viola's predicament, and the uncertain fate of her brother, all this grimness is assuaged by an image much of the order of Orsino's imaginings, truly of the realm of fancy as it mollifies and gilds reality. The sea itself would seem to have been re-channeled into Orsino's mental one. The Captain tells Viola:

> *I saw your brother,*
> *Most provident in peril, bind himself,*
> *Courage and hope both teaching him the practice,*
> *To a strong mast that lived upon the sea;*
> *Where, like Arion on the dolphin's back,*
> *I saw him hold acquaintance with the waves*
> *So long as I could see.*

A good deal is made, very relevantly, of Sebastian's practicality, his capacity for living; he is quite the opposite, it would seem, of Orsino. Nonetheless, we see what swaddling a classical allusion can be. Thus we gracefully leap from Acteon to Arion, with Orpheus inferred between them. Whatever strains out of *A Midsummer Night's Dream* the Captain's last verses may echo, in their distancing and elegance ('hold acquaintance with the waves') they further underline the tapestry-like effect, the sea-change into art the Duke's first speech has established. For behind the music of the Captain's lines sounds the music Arion, an Orphic poet, struck from his lyre which charmed the dolphins and the waves to bear him safely to shore. Similarly music is intended to soothe and sweep all before it here.

Quickly now without self-pity, capable like her brother and unlike Orsino and Olivia, Viola, learning where she is and who the governors are, for protection's sake hits on the scheme of a disguise. She wittingly will be, as Orsino and Olivia are unwittingly, other than she is, but of necessity and vitality and not of too much freedom or leisure and malaise. After observing, most pointedly for this play with its enclosing walls, '. . . nature with a beauteous wall/Doth oft close in pollution,' Viola, about to enclose herself, decides:

> *I'll serve this Duke.*
> *Thou shalt present me as an eunuch to him.*
> *It may be worth thy pains, for I can sing*
> *And speak to him in many sorts of music*
> *That will allow me very worth his service.*

Though she never sings, she, true to her name, whether it be taken to mean the musical instrument or the violet or both, does 'speak to him in many sorts of music', for his nature a decision most felicitous. Out of his passion for such 'speech', she will promptly win his complete confidence and admiration; and then—disguise, saltant, penetrating wit and all—his love.

For the next major ingredient of the play we turn to the third scene which, as it presents the inmates of Olivia's household, also gives the core of the holiday's festivities and most obviously relates to and justifies the play's title; these are among revelry's most accomplished and most ardent servitors. A household of mourning that intends to be convent-like has a leaping tavern at its heart! We may not care to designate Sir Toby Belch the Lord of Misrule; for, rollicksome though he is, with shrewd energy enough to produce scenes, if not playlets, and to cast people into ludicrous roles, beside Falstaff, say, he is a poor cousin at many removes, with much water—if not drunkenness—mixed into the original, pure sack. Clearly whereas Falstaff is of and above his element, Sir Toby is too much in his. Yet his first words assure us that he too is on the side of life, a champion of summer everlasting. By his status as an uncle of a rich countess he is able, unlike Falstaff who had to live chiefly on his wits, to loll, though his allowance be fairly modest, in such carefree summer all his days. So with this fat cricket and his fellow-stridulates we are in the most intimate, most domestic part of the play, at the glowing hearth of the holiday. In comic sentiments redolent of Falstaff, *The Merchant of Venice*'s Gratiano, and others dedicated to the here and now, Sir Toby says: 'What a plague means my niece to take the death of her brother thus? I am sure care's an enemy to life'. There seems to be precious little feeling of an uncle for a nephew here. But the nephew is dead and he, praises be, older and poorer, is alive, with urgent obligations to life and pleasure that he must satisfy. Certainly the local realism, the smack of this scene and its characters, and of all the scenes they occupy, helps to ballast the romantics we have so far met. At the same time we must recognize that Sir Toby and his, in their resolution for pleasure, obvious and immediate and earthy as that pleasure is, are not so far from the dispositions of the much loftier Orsino and Olivia, more refined and spiritualized though their pleasure may be.

Maria, diminutive in body only and almost as important in affecting her world as Viola hers, trying to curb Sir Toby, at once proves herself a perfect mate for him. But to her urging, for fear of Olivia: 'Ay, but you must confine yourself within the modest limits of order', he replies:

> Confine! I'll confine myself no finer than I am. These clothes are good enough to drink in, and so be these boots too; an they be not, let them hang themselves in their own straps.

Falstaffian the idiom and emphasis, if not the wit. Come what may, he'll not affect any disguises, not be any other than what he is, his unbuttoned, brawling self; and he makes it plain what he is by what he is for, one categorically given over to his appetites. Of course he does not realize how 'disguised' he actually—and like the others—is. His frequent drunkenness elicits the best definition of his state from Feste, when Olivia asks him 'What's a drunken man like, fool?':

> Like a drowned man, a fool, and a madman. One draught above heat makes him a fool, the second mads him, and a third drowns him.

Olivia responds:

> Go thou and seek the crowner and let him sit o' my coz; for he's in the third degree of drink, he's drowned. Go look after him.

But Feste assures her:

> He is but mad yet, madonna, and the fool shall look to the madman.

(We gather from *Hamlet* and, more oppressively, from the later *Othello*, what Shakespeare would seem to think of drunkenness, the pathetic state it reduces a man to, as much as to say that in its befuddlement of his senses it makes him mad.) Olivia, drunk on her own imaginings, is more kin to Sir Toby and his 'madness' than she realizes.

Only much later will she recognize 'A most extracting frenzy of mine own.' But already in the Third Act, hearing of Malvolio the smiler, she admits, 'I am as mad as he,/If sad and merry madness equal be.' In this play, if sad and merry are not the same at least they depend on and borrow from one another; certainly they provide a similar amusement.

In the talk that follows, Sir Toby and Maria introduce and, for their amusement and ours, describe Sir Andrew Aguecheek. A gull who thinks he is a gallant or at least yearns to be one, he is most gullible in his would-be gallantry. His likes we have not met since *Henry IV*'s equally piping straws, Shallow and Slender. Sir Toby makes no bones about his interest in Sir Andrew. It is purely fun, games, finances. Belch, lusty parasite that he is, has fastened on to a leaner one that he can milk. Of course, aside from admiring Sir Toby, Sir Andrew has also latched on to him out of hopes of winning Olivia. In a twist of wit, quite Falstaffian, Sir Toby says to Maria's 'They that add, moreover, he's drunk nightly in your company,'

> *With drinking healths to my niece. I'll drink to her as long as there is a passage in my throat and drink in Illyria. He's a coward and a coystrill that will not drink to my niece till his brains turn o' the toe like a parish-top.*

A fulltime, sobering, high-minded profession his! Sir Andrew, now entering, fulfils all that has been said of him. The 'business' here savors of comic scenes in earlier plays, cross-examining, word-filliping, and all the rest; but now with a lightsome touch that makes the wit and amusement immediate, effervescent, on the whole free of the crotchets and quodlibets Shakespeare's earlier low comedy tended to fall into. Through Falstaff and the last two comedies before *Twelfth Night* the necessary refining has taken place. And the touching occurs here too, Sir Andrew's simple, wistful 'I would I had bestowed that time in the tongues that I have in fencing, dancing, and bear-baiting. O had I but followed the arts!' Who better than Shakespeare has blended the ludicrous and the touching?

Sir Toby keeps putting Sir Andrew through his paces, just as earlier he had urged him to 'accost' Maria. At poor Sir Andrew's confusing of the word with her name, Sir Toby sets him straight: 'You mistake, knight. "Accost" is front her, board her, woo her, assail her.' Though such conduct be an affront to Sir Andrew's notion of a gallant's behavior, it suggests the attitude and vigor that Orsino should be using on Olivia who, whether she knows it or not, wants least of all a behavior like her own. Sir Toby sweeps Sir Andrew past his reservations and his remorse at his failure to follow the arts. As he does past his doubts about Olivia, her availability to his courting, by reminding him of his native talents into which, giddy top to Sir Toby that he is, Sir Toby whips him:

> *Wherefore are these things hid? Wherefore have these gifts a curtain*
> *before 'em? Are they like to take dust, like Mistress Mall's picture?*
> *Why dost thou not go to church in a galliard and come home in a*
> *coranto? My very walk should be a jig. I would not so much as make*
> *water but in a sink-a-pace. What dost thou mean? Is it a world to*
> *hide virtues in? I did think, by the excellent constitution of thy leg, it*
> *was formed under the star of a galliard.*

Such god-given, godly talents it is death to hide! Thus to the music of such spheres, this being the right season for it, Sir Toby sets Sir Andrew going. Who would not want every step, wherever it may need to take us, turned into the freedom, delight, and self-fulfilment of the dance. We are back with Orsino who would live, if not melt, altogether in song. With song and dance, as against prose, especially the prose of utility, among the few releases we have from the daily, workaday world, to turn everything we do into dance would be to heal the breach between the daily and holiday, work and play, necessity and desire, reality and fancy. So Adam and Eve must have comported themselves in Paradise.

In the next scene we learn how far Viola, through her many-sorted musical speaking, has advanced in Orsino's affection. One cannot be sure whether it is her vitality alone, shining through her disguise, that wins him or, since he himself is much for disguise at this point, the fact of disguise itself. But after a mere three days she is the first he calls for on entering. She to whom he has 'unclasped . . . the book even of my secret soul' has become his messenger to Olivia. And, directing her to the very conduct he ought to be following himself with Olivia, he exhorts her to greater insistence: '. . . stand at her doors,/And tell them, there thy fixéd foot shall grow/Till thou have audience' and 'Be clamorous and leap all civil bounds/Rather than make unprofited return.' He does indeed provide Viola with the tactic that will win Olivia. But Viola must do all the accosting, must becomingly 'act' his woes:

> *Surprise her with discourse of my dear faith.*
> *It shall become thee well to act my woes.*

> *She will attend it better in thy youth*
> *Than in a nuncio's of more grave aspect.*

How accurate he is he fortunately does not know. Then he expresses full confidence in Viola's youth, her delicacy, and their powers, especially the power of her voice:

> *Diana's lip*
> *Is not more smooth and rubious; thy small pipe*
> *Is as the maiden's organ, shrill and sound;*
> *And all is semblative a woman's part.*
> *I know thy constellation is right apt*
> *For this affair.*

She too must have been formed under the star of a galliard. But even as he recommends clamor, odd perhaps for a 'small pipe', and forcefulness, he himself withdraws: 'I myself am best/When least in company.' Love-thoughts, particularly love of one's own thoughts, a company in themselves, must be given uninterrupted attention; company, clamor, urgency are certainly not for them.

The next scene is mainly concerned with introducing the play's last two principals, and most complete opposites, Feste and Malvolio. Their names make their polarity clear and their place in the play: 'Feste' is the very nature of this play as 'Malvolio' is its enemy. Both, it is true, need and want money and, unlike most of the others around them (with the exception of disguised, needy Viola), are 'workers', but one out of wit and foolery or entertainment, the other out of sober-sided service, one for amusement and wisdom, the other for status and power. Feste, it seems, has been unexcusably absent, out in the world somewhere till needed. With Viola, also a creature from the outside world and also dependent unlike the rest on her wits, he brings an awareness into the play, and an enlivening, a leavening. He proves at once what a matured, experienced, sensible wit he is. Thus when Maria merrily vies with him, he shows his insight and reaches her shrewdly enough with 'If Sir Toby would leave drinking, thou wert as witty a piece of Eve's flesh as any in Illyria.' Now on Olivia's entrance, appropriately accompanied by Malvolio, that side of her at present in ascendancy, Feste girds himself for the contest with:

> *Wit, an't be thy will, put me into good fooling! Those wits, that think they have thee, do very oft prove fools; and I, that am sure I lack thee, may pass for a wise man; for what says Quinapalus? 'Better a witty fool than a foolish wit.'*

Again he exhibits his excellence (for as he accurately says to Olivia, unlike others in the play, 'I wear not motley in my brain': he is not a natural or a born fool, but a professional who must always have his wits about him, and well honed, in the difficult, risky business of earning his keep) in a series of exchanges which, successfully sharp, serve to expose the folly of Olivia's mourning. Feste is, by profession but also by choice, a sidekick of Sir Toby. Malvolio, and in his first words, now gives himself away. To Olivia's 'What think you of this fool, Malvolio? Doth he not mend?' Malvolio wryly, long-facedly, if with some pointed irony, replies: 'Yes, and shall do till the pangs of death shake him. Infirmity, that decays the wise, doth ever make the better fool.' Feste promptly focuses on Malvolio's inadequacy:

> God send you, sir, a speedy infirmity, for the better increasing your folly! Sir Toby will be sworn that I am no fox, but he will not pass his word for twopence that you are no fool.

And to Malvolio's acerbity at this:

> Unless you laugh and minister occasion to him he is gagged. I protest, I take these wise men, that crow so at these set kinds of fools, no better than the fools' zanies.

in Olivia's criticism of him, Shakespeare speedily lets us know what manner of man Malvolio is, and what we are to make of him:

> O, you are sick of self-love, Malvolio, and taste with a distempered appetite. To be generous, guiltless, and of free disposition, is to take those things for bird-bolts that you deem cannon-bullets. There is no slander in an allowed fool, though he do nothing but rail; nor no railing in a known discreet man, though he do nothing but reprove.

What Malvolio eminently lacks is 'To be generous, guiltless, and of free disposition.' And the capacity for fooling, play. He is not one, owing to the fierce, tight-gript seriousness with which he takes himself, ever to know or to learn any detachment from himself. Were he in charge there would be no 'allowed fools' (in due time, for the growing likes of him, no fools will be allowed, and no plays either). Here Olivia, on the other hand, whatever touch of self-love she may herself be suffering from, displays her generosity and good sense, the promise in her, her capacity to extricate herself from the deception of her present foolish role.

Aptly then, Feste having given her her first push out of it, the one who will give her the next, major push (though it will have to take time and involve considerable new deception) appears—Viola. But first we learn a bit more about Malvolio. Smugly shut up in himself—self-miser that he is, like a coffer, flourishing his chained key—he is much more lost in self-love than Orsino or Olivia; his is indurated and most industrious beside theirs, which is chiefly idle, a phase of those not yet called on sufficiently to break out of their cosy cocoons. Holiday apparently, in all its folly of being carried too far, becoming daily, is easier to cure than everyday's overrunning holiday. Holiday, that is, in such gracious beings if not in Falstaff or Sir Toby. So Malvolio's condition is stressed by his indifferent reply to Olivia's asking about Viola, 'What kind o' man is he?' 'Why, of mankind.' His following speech however, far-fetched though it may be, in its earthiness, with something like a touch of the all-knowing Bottom in it, reflects Shakespeare's inability to treat anyone altogether narrowly or niggardly:

> *Not yet old enough for a man, nor young enough for a boy; as a squash is before 'tis a peascod, or a codling when 'tis almost an apple. 'Tis with him in standing water, between boy and man. He is very well-favoured and he speaks very shrewishly. One would think his mother's milk were scarce out of him.*

Viola by her very tartness, the extravagance and curtness of her utterance, hopes to offend Olivia. But youthful and lively as her manner is, and the opposite of Orsino's, instead she intrigues Olivia. Of course Orsino's and Olivia's self-deception naturally blurs their perception. They see only what they want to. Their mind's eye has completely eclipsed the physical one, or allows it surfaces only. Thus they accept Viola at 'face value'. Adding to Feste's criticism of Olivia, Viola pricks her further with 'what is yours to bestow is not yours to reserve', a sentiment suggestive of more flower talk, 'stealing and giving odour'. Later too, Viola says to Olivia 'Most excellent accomplished lady, the heavens rain odours on you!' (Both their names, whatever the spelling, are redolent of violets and good will as against 'Malvolio', all bad odor and ill will.) And in being twitted by her, Olivia is drawn to Viola. For all Olivia's beauty, which Viola readily acknowledges, and for Olivia's ' 'Tis in grain, sir; 'twill endure wind and weather' (the ditty at the play's end might question such confidence), Viola with full feminine awareness reaches her again with 'I see you what you are, you are too proud.' But this understanding, by its truth, seems only to attract Olivia the more. It is amusing to see what sturdy stuff Olivia's vow is made of.

And when Viola tells her how she would act if she loved her, with an ardor altogether absent in Orsino:

> *Make me a willow cabin at your gate,*
> *And call upon my soul within the house;*
> *Write loyal cantons of contemnéd love*
> *And sing them loud even in the dead of night;*
> *Halloo your name to the reverberate hills*
> *And make the babbling gossip of the air*
> *Cry out 'Olivia!' O, you should not rest*
> *Between the elements of air and earth,*
> *But you should pity me!*

Olivia replies 'You might do much.' In this speech about what she would do, Viola has already done much! If she cannot curb or control the wind, and her own sighing as well, she can at least shape it, and to the shape of her desire. How much she has done is evident in Olivia's next question, which promptly gets down to business: 'What is your parentage?' She is patently ready to agree with Viola's 'what is yours to bestow is not yours to reserve.' We recognize this in Olivia's own words to herself, 'How now! Even so quickly may one catch the plague?' Orsino, we recall, thought that Olivia's beauty 'purged the air of pestilence'. Now we learn that love itself is that plague. In any case, aware though Olivia is of her headlong nature, she cannot restrain it. But she realizes that her own will is not all, and may have its will most by yielding to another, stronger will.

> *I do I know not what, and fear to find*
> *Mine eye too great a flatterer for my mind.*
> *Fate, show thy force; ourselves we do not owe;*
> *What is decreed must be, and be this so.*

Here she admits to the common 'infection' of the comedies: love taken in through the eye, rather than through the mind, or love at sight. In her submission to fate, a rather different position from that of the first, vow-stiff Olivia, she is already clearly under Viola's spell: we 'steal' best by 'giving', like the flower with every breath freely spending its fragrance. Of course in her mistake, her falling in love with a disguise however engaging, in her myopic, loose hold on reality and in her rashness, Olivia is still her imperious, not to be denied self.

Having unwound this much, Shakespeare must now produce Viola's identical twin Sebastian, also saved to complicate the plot, and so save the day by relieving Viola of Olivia's hand. He too, as though Olivia's words were still lingering in 'the babbling gossip of the air', speaks of fate which, even as he calls it malignant, is about to become the reverse and to join them. He, informing us further about his and his sister's past, assures us that Viola is beautiful and, more important, 'she bore a mind that envy could not but call fair'. Like her fellow spirit in good sense, Feste, she, also playing a part, wears 'not motley in my brain'. At this late date Shakespeare uses a plot device first met in *The Comedy of Errors*: Antonio, the sea captain, out of love for Sebastian would follow him to Orsino's court; but Antonio is an enemy to this country, and his being discovered would be most dangerous. Nonetheless, his love prevails. At last the outside world begins to assert itself; even battle is admitted, if in the past and remotely.

A favorite property of Shakespeare, a ring, especially as it symbolizes love and in its circularity unity if not marriage, is employed in the next scene to forward the plot and to fill Viola with distress when she sees that Olivia has fallen in love with her. With a sigh almost Hamlet-like and in a submission resembling Olivia's she concludes: 'O Time! thou must untangle this, not I./It is too hard a knot for me to untie!' Following her sense of the frailty of women before love, Scene II, bringing the play's main revelers together, presents one of its loveliest songs, sung by Feste, a *carpe diem* ditty, filled with his kind of awareness and a deepening touch of wistfulness. For even as it proposes that 'journeys end in lovers meeting', it recognizes life's uncertainty and urges immediacy:

> *What's to come is still unsure.*
> *In delay there lies no plenty;*
> *Then come kiss me, sweet and twenty,*
> *Youth's a stuff will not endure.*

Again Olivia's pride in her beauty, ' 'Tis in grain, sir; 'twill endure wind and weather', is called into question.

With Sir Toby and Sir Andrew's praise of Feste:

> Sir And.   *A mellifluous voice as I am true knight.*
> Sir To.   *A contagious breath.*
> Sir And.   *Very sweet and contagious, i' faith.*
> Sir To.   *To hear by the nose, it is dulcet in contagion.*

we are ludicrously reminded of Orsino's romantic bank of violets and at the same time of the pleached, not to say confused, senses of Bottom with his 'flowers of odious savours sweet'. It is surely important to realize that with Feste singing and providing the music that the world of *Twelfth Night* requires, his songs are especially appealing because, while they are gay and timeless, of the mood of holiday itself, they are also, like the play, tinged with sadness, pathos, home truths about the world as it is.

Then the revelers move into a rowdy catch. And Maria rebuking them, the main confrontation with their opposite, Malvolio, occurs. In a speech that superbly catches up his prissiness, he declares his hatred of music and all that it entails:

> *My masters, are you mad? Or what are you? Have you no wit, manners, nor honesty, but to gabble like tinkers at this time of night? Do ye make an alehouse of my lady's house, that ye squeak out your coziers' catches without any mitigation or remorse of voice? Is there no respect of place, persons, nor time in you?*

His affected, not to say pursed, speech, he being one who most calculatingly counts and only most stingily lets loose his small change, betrays his rigor of mind, his frigid deliberateness. His phrasing, in the methodical way in which it is paid out, his love of noun compounds in negative triplets, and of the preposition 'of' or the possessive case, in that they make of most things he utters an object to be kept and controlled, reveal the man most transparently.

When he asks, 'Is there no respect of place, persons, nor time in you?' Sir Toby—answering 'We did keep time, sir, in our catches. Sneck up!' while he and Feste sing their mockery round Malvolio to prove their 'timeliness'—seems to be deeply stung by the charge; for he, lines and subjects later, returns to it:

> *Out o' tune, sir! Ye lie. Art any more than a steward? Dost thou think, because thou art virtuous, there shall be no more cakes and ale?*

We have here the play's two basic, antipodal versions of time: that of Malvolio, who believes it something to be 'watched', to be hoarded, to be regularized, never to be squandered, thus his aversion and contempt for song, a mere waste of time and the ruin of law and order; and that of Sir Toby, who thinks time the medium of or the opportunity for play, amusement, joy, most consummately employed when turned into music. For music is time in time against time; it is a time when we are free and flowing, when all knots are cut. Accordingly it may, as in Feste's recent song, draw on the wistful, the melancholy, even the tragic, and in triumph: the triumph of singing it, the tragic's being contained forever more in a mouthful of air, Sir Andrew's 'so sweet a breath to sing', translated into the very stuff of warm, human life—our breathing. A Shylock and a Malvolio, however, by their dark, secretive natures must hate the ease of music, the open geniality of song, breath spent exclusively in the enjoyment of being spent. But those like Sir Toby gladly surrender to it, and as they do so, exultant, free, they also see its temporariness, its being lost or consumed in its very loveliness, in the very moment of its illumination. Malvolio, like Shylock, is a clangorous grating against song that, challenging, evokes all the song's strength.

Smarting from this killjoy, Sir Toby and the others eagerly turn to Maria with her scheme for making Malvolio a source of entertainment for them all. She understands him perhaps best of all:

> The devil a Puritan that he is, or anything constantly, but a time-pleaser; an affectioned ass, that cons state without book and utters it by great swarths; the best persuaded of himself, so crammed, as he thinks, with excellencies, that it is his grounds of faith that all that look on him love him; and on that vice in him will my revenge find notable cause to work.

Malvolio's sycophancy on behalf of self-betterment, his narcissism, his asinine imperviousness to himself and to others, she rousingly scores. And most shrewdly she rears her ruse on his own pathetic assumption of his universal irresistibility. When she leaves, praise of her results in Sir Toby's 'She's a beagle, true-bred, and one that adores me.' And in Sir Andrew's most touching-amusing 'I was adored once too.'

Turning to the Duke and his company, we find him at the same old standstill. It's more music he is after, this time a repetition of 'That old and antique song we heard last night.' Nostalgic that he is,

> Methought it did relieve my passion much,
> More than light airs and recollected terms
> Of these most brisk and giddy-pacéd times.

Of course he is deceiving himself; he wants this music to feed his passion, not to relieve it; whatever his protestations, relief is the last thing he desires. But the whole play addresses itself to affection for the past; brisk and giddy-paced though the times may be, apart from

Malvolio we scarcely see and hear that modern tune. While he sends
for Feste to sing the song, Orsino is again at pains to describe his love
for Olivia, this time a little differently:

> *For such as I am all true lovers are,*
> *Unstaid and skittish in all motions else,*
> *Save in the constant image of the creature*
> *That is beloved.*

Viola's masterly reply makes Orsino conclude that her eye, young
though she is, must have been snared by some 'favour' or face. Viola
admits it in a sweet pun: 'A little, by your favour'. When Orsino learns
that the 'woman' involving Viola is of his 'complexion' and 'years', he
warns her that such a woman is too old. Again, one with his changeability, he shifts his position on love by insisting that a woman should
marry a man older than herself so that she can instinctively adapt herself to him. For despite his talk of 'the constant image' and his devotion
to it, he now confesses that men's 'fancies are more giddy and unfirm,/
More longing, wavering, sooner lost and worn,/Than women's are.'
And a melancholy truth, like Feste's song with its conclusion 'Youth's
a stuff will not endure', emerges: women must be younger than men,
'For women are as roses, whose fair flower/Being once displayed, doth
fall that very hour.' 'Constant image' indeed! A sorry, shallow observation this, especially coming from a flower-fancier, we might say, with
little interest apparently in minds and natures 'that envy could not but
call fair.'

On Feste's entering, Orsino felicitously gives the provenance of the
song we are about to hear:

> *Mark it, Cesario, it is old and plain.*
> *The spinsters and the knitters in the sun*
> *And the free maids that weave their thread with bones*
> *Do use to chant it. It is silly sooth,*
> *And dallies with the innocence of love,*
> *Like the old age.*

A song out of the good old days, or the sort that Orsino likes, it was
sung by carefree girls, who, we notice, however much simpler their
lives may have been, were working not idling while they sang; thus
their song was and is 'plain' in itself, 'silly sooth' or simple truth since,
at least in Orsino's eyes, it belonged to a much less complicated time.
And it enjoys a sense of wellbeing and lightheartedness through the

very pangs it expresses, the old 'innocence of love' that Orsino in all his sophistication yearns for. Death is the song's burden. But it is its desolation and poignancy, strewn as it is with fragrant absences, 'Not a flower, not a flower sweet,/On my black coffin let there be strown,' that makes the song especially sweet. As Feste says, when Orsino pays him for his 'pains', for him no less than for the spinners, though he appreciates and needs money, the song and its singing come to 'No pains, sir; I take pleasure in singing, sir,' especially if it be so deliciously sad a song, all dying fall.

When Orsino bids him leave, Feste, understanding his client very well, says mockingly:

Now the melancholy god protect thee, and the tailor make thy doublet of changeable taffeta, for thy mind is a very opal. I would have men of such constancy put to sea, that their business might be everything and their intent everywhere; for that's it that always makes a good voyage of nothing.

He accurately diagnoses Orsino's 'melancholy' and the changeability that supports and characterizes that melancholy, the 'giddy' fancies Orsino a short time ago acknowledged. Though the moon is not mentioned it surely lies most potently behind such 'constancy', and Orsino is a fulltime moon-man. Thus the sea in its restlessness is right for such men whose business occupies them altogether and whose destination is everywhere and so nowhere. In the previous song Feste had told us that 'Every wise man's son doth know' that 'Journeys end in lovers meeting.' But for opalescent wits like Orsino, constant travel or change—and no end—is all. (When we first met Sebastian he said sadly to Antonio that 'My determinate voyage is mere extravagancy.' But encountering the determined Olivia will put him, lost and shipwrecked though he has been, on his true course and provide his journey's end, and Viola will do the same for the errant Orsino.)

Alone, Orsino orders Viola to try Olivia for him again. Having asked 'But if she cannot love you, sir?' to his spoilt 'I cannot be so answered', she wisely and prudently (for she must bring him into line with reality) replies, 'Sooth, but you must'—that is, you must, like it or not, acknowledge and accept things as they are. This play may be 'What You Will' and Orsino since he is the Duke may seem to be in a position to have what he wills. But life, alas, is not that fully or easily at our disposal. Thinking of her own feeling for him, and hoping to shake him loose from his sense of his uniqueness by being made aware of others and their suffering, she now tells him of the possibility of some woman's being in his situation with unrequited love for him. He, having earlier confessed man's greater fickleness, once more reveals his 'opalescence' by insisting,

> *There is no woman's sides*
> *Can bide the beating of so strong a passion*
> *As love doth give my heart; no woman's heart*
> *So big, to hold so much. They lack retention.*
> *Alas, their love may be called appetite—*
> *No motion of the liver, but the palate—*
> *That suffer surfeit, cloyment, and revolt;*
> *But mine is all as hungry as the sea*
> *And can digest as much. Make no compare*
> *Between that love a woman can bear me*
> *And that I owe Olivia.*

Again he calls on a sea image to describe his love, and again he stresses its bottomless hunger and digestive power. For, whatever his romanticism, love for him from the start is an appetite—if, as here, much more profound than any woman's—that would be ravenously feeding. But now he uses the sea to impress Viola with—not, as Feste rightly put it, his restlessness, his fickleness, his speedy satiety—the vastness of his capacity as a lover.

Viola, disagreeing, poses a case of feminine constancy and 'poses' as her own sister (we might at this point beguile ourselves with thinking on the pleasures—and to the audience—of disguises: a girl playing a boy, now proposing that she be regarded as a girl—with a boy playing Viola in the first place!):

> *My father had a daughter loved a man,*
> *As it might be, perhaps, were I a woman,*
> *I should your lordship.*

To Orsino's 'And what's her history?' she most poetically replies:

> *A blank, my lord. She never told her love,*
> *But let concealment, like a worm i' the bud,*
> *Feed on her damask cheek. She pined in thought,*
> *And with a green and yellow melancholy*
> *She sat, like patience on a monument,*
> *Smiling at grief.*

Here Viola is indeed speaking to Orsino the 'sort of music', a sad, sad song, that he most enjoys, singing him silence, her love which she tells she cannot tell! And what a touching, fragrant melancholy it is, with its image of the woman's cheek a flower and a worm at it. But Viola's words might also be construed as a warning, to herself no less than to him, against the dangers of 'concealment', disguise, will-lessness, inactivity. Think of Gratiano in *The Merchant of Venice* chiding Antonio for his melancholy:

> *Why should a man, whose blood is warm within,*
> *Sit like his grandsire cut in alabaster,*
> *Sleep when he wakes, and creep into the jaundice*
> *By being peevish!*

Vitality it is versus passivity. Even more striking in juxtaposition would be Oberon's mermaid on a dolphin, uttering her 'dulcet and harmonious breath', certainly, for her being all alive, all influential, the opposite of Viola's image. Nevertheless, in presenting this patience Viola is having a musical effect somewhat like the mermaid's: she is moving, and slowly changing, Orsino. And who's to say the mermaid did not sing a song of such pathos? In any case, this patience on a monument, or on her own tomb, lovely if wistful image of acceptance that she is, in her smiling at her grief experiences some superiority over it. But smiling tears, we know, is a favorite image of Shakespeare, here particularly in its reflecting something of the fundamental nature and attitude of *Twelfth Night*. Honoring his own sentimentality, the Duke asks, 'But died thy sister of her love, my boy?' Viola neatly sidesteps this question with the truth that we, not Orsino, can appreciate: 'I am all the daughters of my father's house,/And all the brothers too;—and yet I know not.' She, of 'a green and yellow melancholy', yellow for jealousy, but green for hope, can predict her own end no more than she can be absolutely sure she has no brother.

With the next scene the trap is sprung for Malvolio, the bait a telling device that Shakespeare often employs, a letter. How super-ripe for catching and plucking Malvolio is, his musing words on his entering make all too clear:

> *'Tis but fortune. All is fortune. Maria once told me she did affect me; and I have heard herself come thus near, that, should she fancy, it should be one of my complexion. Besides, she uses me with a more exalted respect than any one else that follows her. What should I think on't?*

He is blissfully indulging himself–such is his pastime–in daydreams of himself as 'Count Malvolio'. He obviously desires Olivia herself no more than Orsino does. Malvolio also has his far-fetched reveries. His strutting, absurd performance, even as it infuriates Sir Toby, makes his being duped all the more just and timely. We, hidden with Sir Toby and the others, watch him–with outraged interpolations from Sir Toby–acting out the role he longs for:

> *Having been three months married to her, sitting in my state,–. . . Calling my officers about me, in my branched velvet gown, having come from a day-bed, where I have left Olivia sleeping,–. . . And then to have the humour of state: and after a demure travel of regard, telling them I know my place as I would they should do theirs, to ask for my kinsman Toby,–. . . Seven of my people, with an obedient start, make out for him. I frown the while, and perchance wind up my watch, or play with my–some rich jewel. Toby approaches, curtsies there to me,–. . . I extend my hand to him thus, quenching my familiar smile with an austere regard of control,–. . . Saying, 'Cousin Toby, my fortunes, having cast me on your niece, give me this prerogative of speech,'–. . . 'You must amend your drunkenness.' . . . 'Besides, you waste the treasure of your time with a foolish knight,'–. . . 'One Sir Andrew,'–.*

Having play-acted himself into a rapture of fulfilment, he almost inevitably stumbles on the letter, as though his wish were strong enough to create its object. So his will, already well primed, sugars and gladly gulps the bait. Maria cleverly wrote 'M,O,A,I, doth sway my life.' These letters, obliging his mind to grapple with them for the enjoyment of those of us watching, are bound to ensnarl him much more thoroughly than a simple whole spelling out of his name. The prose that follows, psychologically brilliant, must have its desired effect:

> '*In my stars I am above thee, but be not afraid of greatness. Some are born great, some achieve greatness, and some have greatness thrust upon 'em. Thy Fates open their hands, let thy blood and spirit embrace them; and to inure thyself to what thou art like to be, cast thy humble slough and appear fresh. Be opposite with a kinsman, surly with servants; let thy tongue tang arguments of state; put thyself into the trick of singularity. She thus advises thee that sighs for thee. Remember who commended thy yellow stockings, and wished to see thee ever cross-gartered. I say, remember. Go to, thou art made, if*

thou desir'st to be so; if not, let me see thee a steward still, the fellow
of servants, and not worthy to touch Fortune's fingers. Farewell. She
that would alter services with thee,

'THE FORTUNATE-UNHAPPY'

Apart from being a perfect mirror of his daydreams, his fervent sense
of his 'fortunes', the letter in its artful phrasing, by guying him with
his own idiosyncratic expression, his vocabulary and syntax: 'tang
arguments of state', 'the trick of singularity', and so on, overwhelms
him.

So at last *Twelfth Night's* consummation is arrived at. Malvolio, a
kind of spirit of winter with its restraints, its rigors, like winter
intensifies the pleasures of indoors; now for joy's and summer's sake
he is tricked into turning into a snowman, much against his grain
absurdly decorating himself—like a scarecrow that birds enjoy sitting
on—with yellow stockings, smiles and all, or the paraphernalia of
summer. This is indeed winter become the motley fool of summer's
minions. Like Shylock before him, Malvolio in his stewardship, as in
his nature, is a dour father-figure or curb; but ironically a curb out of
the new 'law' of opportunism, materialism, practicality. Thus this new
father law must be duped into entertaining those he abhors, into
increasing the very fun he despises and would destroy.

But Malvolio, one to inspire laughter by his opaque, one-dimensional pomposity, is incapable of laughter, and therefore he must be
abused or in a basic sense rejected. To be as deprived as he is and as
self-righteous and overweening in his deprivation is to be pathetic;
but also, since, secure in his own notions of his perfection, he wishes
to impose his deprivation on others, he is depraved. Like Armado,
Holofernes and their ilk he is quite sealed into his own condition.
But they were amiable, windy, harmless butterflies; he, on the contrary, grim creature that he is, yearns to put his seal on all. If Falstaff
is too purely laughter and play for itself alone and at the expense of all,
so finally to be dealt with, Malvolio, pure aspiration and self-aggrandiz-
ing and therefore a threat to large, sane, open living, must also be dealt
with. The former would, like Sir Toby, have it always late summer and
brimming harvest-time, great beeves flying slowly through the air,
to be had for the mere reaching of the hand, and all the rivers cascading
sack; the latter would turn all time into frozen, and so controllable, yet
busy winter. Unlike the changeable Orsino and Olivia, there would
seem to be, beyond 'melting' or rejecting, no way of moving Malvolio.

His nature is among the few that Shakespeare presents apparently past nurture.

Act III, roughly the play's center, is the appropriate moment for the two guiding if not presiding spirits of the play, Viola and Feste, to meet. After a bit of word play and Feste's denial that he is a 'churchman' (later he will play the part well enough), he, master of words that he is, remarks a common failing of the times, one that Shakespeare's plays, especially since they are steeped in it themselves, are fond of rebuking, the playing with words to the deliberate twisting or the oblivion of their meaning: 'To see this age! A sentence is but a cheveril glove to a good wit. How quickly the wrong side may be turned outward!' Viola agrees, 'Nay, that's certain. They that dally nicely with words may quickly make them wanton.' And he quickly does so by selecting out a sexual overtone from what Viola has said. Then to Viola's 'Thy reason, man?' he answers: 'Troth, sir, I can yield you none without words; and words are grown so false, I am loath to prove reason with them.' In view of the dallying that words have been just put to in tricking Malvolio, this little exchange is most apt. Yet for all Feste's demurring, a moment later he says that he is not Olivia's fool but her 'corrupter of words'. At Viola's 'I saw thee late at the Count Orsino's', Feste declares 'Foolery, sir, does walk about the orb like the sun; it shines everywhere.' Though this can be gayly understood to mean 'amusement shines everywhere', foolery for foolishness is also obviously intended. At Feste's departure Viola accurately observes:

> *This fellow is wise enough to play the fool,*
> *And to do that well craves a kind of wit.*
> *He must observe their mood on whom he jests,*
> *The quality of persons, and the time,*
> *And, like the haggard, check at every feather*
> *That comes before his eye. This is a practice*
> *As full of labour as a wise man's art.*
> *For folly that he wisely shows is fit;*
> *But wise men, folly-fall'n, quite taint their wit.*

Much as Viola has had to 'observe their mood' on whom she waits if not jests, she can appreciate the sharp eye and intelligence needed for such successful service. It is indeed not motley in the brain; rather, Shakespeare's own art knows, the opposite.

Sir Andrew, aroused at seeing Olivia's kindness to Viola, once more resolves to leave. But Sir Toby continues to detain him by persuading him to improve his suit with Olivia by challenging Viola. Thus another plot, with another letter to catch another gull, and to produce further Twelfth Night entertainment, is wound up: 'Let there be gall enough in thy ink. Though thou write with a goose pen, no matter.' Sir Toby understands his victims very well:

> *I think oxen and wainropes cannot hale them together. For Andrew, if he were opened, and you find so much blood in his liver as will clog the foot of a flea, I'll eat the rest of the anatomy.*

Instantly, with one gaiety on the heels of the other, Maria enters to tell us—and so prepare us for the sight—that Malvolio has right heartily taken to his disguise. Set on advantage as he is, there is little he will not do, even to the flouting of his own character, to gain it: 'He does smile his face into more lines than is in the new map with the augmentation of the Indies.' Brave new world this! Interestingly enough, Maria's image is the one sudden admission in this play of that far-off world's existence. But we need hardly indicate how relevant it is to Malvolio and his concerns.

Now at last Antonio and Sebastian appear, Antonio refusing out of love to leave him despite the danger. Back we are at the beginning of *The Comedy of Errors*, and in it further with the giving of the purse that will abet the confusion to follow. Promptly with Malvolio's ludicrous entrance before Olivia, the 'official' Twelfth Night's frolics begin. He assures her that he is 'not black in my mind, though yellow in my legs'. How right he is! For who better bears motley in his brain? Yet motley notwithstanding, black is surely the one true color of his nature. Olivia, cleverly prepared for his appearance by Maria's 'He is, sure, possessed, madam', and 'Your ladyship were best to have some guard about you, if he come; for, sure, the man is tainted in 's wits', and convinced by his ridiculous behavior, concludes, amusingly enough for January, yet most appropriately for this play: 'Why, this is very midsummer madness.' Viola arriving, with Olivia eager to greet her, Olivia entrusts Malvolio to the tender mercies of Sir Toby and his crew, who bind him and lock him in a dark room, customary treatment for the insane. Since he is by his nature in the dark, let this treasure be properly hidden in actual darkness. For lacking some touch of 'madness', he must have it thrust upon him. Those without it, being incomplete, may be the maddest of all.

And here, with Sir Andrew's challenge and what follows, out

of the kind of economy we have come to expect of Shakespeare, he is once more employing effects that he had first found useful in the play I have proposed his first. Such effects he employs though he is more or less at the midpoint of his playwriting career. At once, with *The Comedy of Errors* – like complications and confusions, the plot proceeds to what appears to be an impossible tangle, but actually – again resembling *The Comedy of Errors* – it is a tangle that serves to unravel all knots. The duel of Viola and Aguecheek, proceeding in its delicious absurdity, engrosses Sebastian and Antonio as well. And through the duel reality at last asserts itself. Yet after an exchange of blows with Aguecheek Sebastian understandably wonders, 'Are all the people mad?' Once more we are reminded of *The Comedy of Errors*, though there witchcraft was the steady cry rather than madness. Olivia intercedes, rebukes Sir Toby, and appeals to Sebastian who is now utterly baffled:

> *What relish is in this? How runs the stream?*
> *Or I am mad, or else this is a dream.*
> *Let fancy still my sense in Lethe steep.*
> *If it be thus to dream, still let me sleep!*

With Sly he knows a good thing, dream or not, when he sees it. And like the good Elizabethan gentlemen we have met in earlier comedies, he is equal to the occasion and seizes fortune's forelock however puzzlingly it is thrust upon him.

And now the last disguise and Twelfth Night license remains to be assumed: Feste, at Maria's urging, with beard and gown plays Sir Topas the curate. The fool looks to the madman. With vast show of esoteric learning, and with hairsplitting where no hair is, Feste splendidly dons the role:

> Bonos dies, *Sir Toby: for, as the old hermit of Prague, that never saw pen and ink, very wittily said to a niece of King Gorboduc, 'That that is is'; so I, being Master Parson, am Master Parson; for, what is 'that' but 'that', and 'is' but 'is'?*

So, for all he's worth, he plays not only two parts with Malvolio, Sir Topas and in quick shift his own, but Malvolio as madman. To Malvolio's insistence, 'Fool, there was never man so notoriously abused. I am as well in my wits, fool, as thou art', Feste wittily answers, an answer sardonically recalling Malvolio's first dismissal of him: 'But as well? Then you are mad indeed, if you be no better in your wits than a fool.' In the brief scene that follows a little more madness must be considered before the play's resolution. Sebastian, pondering what is happening to him, muses:

> *This is the air, that is the glorious sun,*
> *This pearl she gave me, I do feel't and see't;*
> *And though 'tis wonder that enwraps me thus,*
> *Yet 'tis not madness.*

Like Sly he cannot deny the testimony of his senses, the truth of experience. But he goes on:

> *For though my soul disputes well with my sense,*
> *That this may be some error, but no madness,*
> *Yet does this accident and flood of fortune*
> *So far exceed all instance, all discourse,*
> *That I am ready to distrust mine eyes*
> *And wrangle with my reason that persuades me*
> *To any other trust but that I am mad*
> *Or else the lady's mad.*

Thus when Olivia appears with priest in hand Sebastian unhesitatingly follows them.

The final act upon us, Orsino does at last bestir himself and comes to look after his affairs personally. We see him in his first bit of acting as Duke: confrontation of an enemy of the state, the arrested Antonio. And as we hear of a sea-battle, the sea itself for the first time asserts and is itself. Antonio, justifying his presence, says that 'A witchcraft drew me hither', and tells how he saved 'That most ingrateful boy' by Orsino's side: 'From the rude sea's enraged and foamy mouth/Did I redeem. A wreck past hope he was.' Olivia interrupts. She scorns Orsino's suit as that 'old tune' that 'is as fat and fulsome to mine ear/As howling after music.' So much for his kind of music, which is here seen and judged for what it really is. At this Orsino necessarily rises—almost—to action. He says to Viola, a most willing victim:

> *Come, boy, with me; my thoughts are ripe in mischief.*
> *I'll sacrifice the lamb that I do love,*
> *To spite a raven's heart within a dove.*

To this confusion Sir Toby and Sir Andrew, bloodied by Sebastian, lend their assistance. Here, in perhaps his worst moment, Sir Toby reveals his true feelings for Sir Andrew when he turns on him and his gentle offer of help with 'Will you help?–an ass-head and a coxcomb and a knave, a thin-faced knave, a gull!'

Clearly the revelries are over. Old father summer has had his day. Reality with blood and law is upon us. Sebastian entering, the confusions are unconfused, and all is brought to a happy ending; all, that is, but Malvolio, who for the slight done him is rankling, unredeemable anger: 'Madame, you have done me wrong,/Notorious wrong.' And as he hurls out, with 'I'll be revenged on the whole pack of you', in his folly any pity for him is surely wasted. Orsino and Olivia have been awakened, 'educated', restored to sanity; they have the wherewithal in person as in purse to be so. Malvolio, however, for his parsimony, his one-dimensionality, cannot be. No more than Shylock, though music here, as in *The Merchant of Venice*, and winged words have sought to bridge the discontinuity of winter, of icy or absent feeling. And for a time the denizens of this play enjoy a reprieve, but brief it is. Whatever revenge Shakespeare means–Malvolio and his sort will be revenged on the world that this play represents, on Sir Toby and his and their aimless merriment, on Orsino and Olivia, and on the play world itself–*Twelfth Night* ends with an admission in epilogue, a lovely song it is true (so much control the play still has) and sung aptly enough by true-seeing, sweet-voiced Feste, of the world as it is, the world outside, of 'the wind and the rain' waiting their turn once this interlude of a play, this holiday, is done. One might compare with the play's opening music this much deeper, not to say real, melancholy. The rain–anyone who knows England knows this to be reasonably accurate–'it raineth every day'. 'A great while ago the world begun', and whatever we may will, the world will not suspend its laws or change itself for the likes of you and me. Nonetheless, though the rain raineth every day, such is the good will of art and the theater that 'we'll strive to please you every day.' This although more and more of the wind and the rain will be admitted in the plays to come. From now on let winter have its day and yet, most paradoxically, let it please us while it does.

Meantime, we have enjoyed the ripest comedy of the triple cluster. But though the sweetest, it is, in being last, also underlying sad. It has, we have seen, depths, shadows, a poignancy that the earlier comedies could not know. The thunder of a giant storm, sensed if not yet heard, is quickly gathering. Nonetheless, though the new world and the oldest of all, man at his most wintry, stript to tooth and claw, is about to breach these walls and, far more savagely than anything in the previous history plays, from within, from the secret recesses of man himself—'nature with a beauteous wall/Doth oft close in pollution'— the old world, troubled and edged with the grave, is here regnant still and most resonantly. In the play's charmed circle we witness characters as resilient and many-sided as life and we at our best can be. By that resiliency the play maintains itself, no less freshly than on the day that it was produced. There will not be many such moonlit banks of violets hereafter.

INDEX

Page numbers in **bold type** *refer to the main sections devoted to a play in the text.*

THEODORE WEISS

Theodore Weiss was born in Reading, Pennsylvania, and grew up in Allentown, Pennsylvania. He studied at Muhlenberg College and Columbia University. He has taught literature at the University of North Carolina, Yale University, Bard College and the Massachusetts Institute of Technology. After a year as poet-in-residence, he became a Professor of Creative Arts at Princeton University. Over the years he has received various awards and honors for his poetry, including a Ford Foundation Fellowship, a National Foundation of Arts and Letters Grant, and an honorary degree in letters from Muhlenberg College. He is the author of six books of poetry, including the recently published *The World Before Us: Poems, 1950–1970*. His criticism has appeared in various magazines and several books. Since 1943 he has edited and published *The Quarterly Review of Literature* with his wife.